THE EVOLUTION OF HUMAN SOCIETIES

Allen W. Johnson & Timothy Earle

The Evolution
of Human Societies

From Foraging Group
to Agrarian State

Second Edition

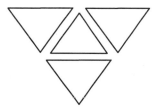

Stanford University Press, Stanford, California 2000

Stanford University Press
Stanford, California
©2000 by the Board of Trustees of the
Leland Stanford Junior University
Printed in the United States of America

Library of Congress Cataloging-in-Publication Data

Johnson, Allen W.
   The evolution of human societies : from foraging group to agrarian state /
Allen W. Johnson & Timothy Earle.
      p.   cm.
   Includes bibliographical references and index.
   ISBN 0-8047-4031-3 (alk. paper) —
   ISBN 0-8047-4032-1 (paper : alk. paper)
   1. Social evolution.   2. Ethnology.   I. Earle, Timothy K.   I. Title.
GN360.J65   2000
303.4—dc21   00-041329

This book is printed on acid-free, archival-quality paper.

Original printing 2000

Last figure below indicates year of this printing:
09   08   07   06   05   04   03   02   01   00

Typeset in 10/12 Palatino

Dedicated to
Marvin Harris and Marshall Sahlins
For their inspiration and disputation

Preface to the Second Edition

In the first edition of this work we attempted to synthesize the current understanding of the processes whereby human societies grew (or did not grow) in scale and complexity under a broad range of environmental circumstances. Our joint experience of teaching courses in economic anthropology and cultural ecology showed us the advantages of combining the perspectives of ethnology and archaeology for a comprehensive theory integrating both subjects. In order to do so, we had instinctively organized the case materials in our course from small-scale mobile foragers to agrarian states, as do many of our colleagues. We decided to make explicit the implicit evolutionary theory in such an ordering from simple to complex, and this work was born.

For this second edition, we have taken advantage of more than a decade teaching with the first edition. Through their bold questioning and insights drawn from their own learning and experience, our students have shown us many ways to improve on the original, and for this we owe them a profound debt of gratitude. As a result of their comments, and those of many of our colleagues, we have completely rewritten the theoretical chapters, to strengthen and improve the flow and clarity of the argument. We have also reviewed all the cases and where possible, in consultation with experts, have corrected errors and brought the cases up to date, often illuminating the ways in which the basic processes of social evolution continue to operate to the present time. We have also added a new ending chapter that links our evolutionary argument to an account of how and why traditional societies like those we discuss transform in our world of today.

In our preface to the first edition we noted a certain turning away from social evolutionism in the anthropology of the time. The situation today is different. A great many excellent works have been published dealing with warfare, leadership, intensification, trust and cooperation, and many other topics in ways that either are frankly evolutionist or at least are framed to be of use to the evolutionist. In addition to this general climate of theoretical debate, we have benefited from careful specific comments on parts or all of this work by Jeanne Arnold, Robert Bettinger, Ben Campbell, Napoleon Chagnon, Myron Cohen, Sam Coleman, Terence D'Altroy, Norma Diamond, Rada Dyson-Hudson, Paul Ehrlich, Walter Goldschmidt, Daniel Gross, Raymond Hames, William Irons, Patrick Kirch, Richard Lee, Sibel Kusimba, Cherry Lowman, Mervin Meggitt, Mark Moberg, Philip Newman, John Olmsted, Wendell Oswalt, Melanie Renfrew, Tawnya Sesi, Nazif Shahrani, Mariko Tamanoi, David Hurst Thomas, Jan Weinpahl, Lynn White, Jr., Johannes Wilbert, and Yun-xiang Yan. Amalie Orme drew the settlement pattern figures and they reflect her creative input. Valued colleagues Roy Rappaport and Annette Weiner, whose works have influenced our own, have died. We mourn their passing and miss their thoughtful advice.

In preparing this revision we rediscovered the stimulation and new thinking that comes with a collaboration across the subdisciplines. Archaeologists and ethnologists, although they work with such different empirical materials, share great areas of common interest when it comes to the evolution of human societies, and each has much to gain from a thorough understanding of the other.

Contents

Part III: The Regional Polity

Tables and Figures

Tables

Figures

THE EVOLUTION OF HUMAN SOCIETIES

ONE

Introduction

OUR PURPOSE IN this book is to describe and explain the evolution of human societies. Some societies are of small scale and flexible; others are large and highly structured; and still others fall in between those extremes. A central question of anthropology is how to understand the variability in human societies across space and time. But can the historical processes of human social evolution be explained? In some sense each society is unique, a product of its own history in a distinct environment, with its own characteristic technologies, economies, and cultural values. Yet this cultural relativism—anthropology's effort to recognize and respect cultural integrity—must coexist in a dynamic tension with the effort to identify and explain cross-cultural patterns in the development and operation of human societies.

Our emphasis here is on the causes, mechanisms, and patterns of social evolution, which, despite taking many divergent paths, is explainable in terms of a coherent theory. As teachers of cross-cultural economics and as field anthropologists—one author being an ethnographer, the other an archaeologist—we have sought a theoretical framework to help make sense both of the long-term prehistoric cultural sequences now available to us and of the diversity of present-day societies.

The Khoisan foragers of southern Africa produce abundant food with a few hours' work per day—are they the "original affluent society"? The Yanomamo of South America fight one another with peculiar ferocity—is this the unrestrained expression of innate human aggressiveness? In the striking North American Potlatch and Melanesian *kula* ring, "men of renown" publicly compete to gain prestige at others' expense—is this the human hunger for fame in a primitive manifestation? These comparative questions are of interest, alike to the anthropologist, economist, geographer, historian, political scientist, and sociologist, for they are ultimately questions about human nature—the common heritage of humankind as a species—and its expression in diverse environments, mediated by diverse cultural traditions. In this book we provide a systematic theoretical approach for answering these and similar questions in a broad, cross-cultural frame of reference.

Our theory pays particular attention to the causes and consequences of population growth. Although we will see that its precise role is hotly contested, population growth is undeniably central to the process of sociocultural evolution, because of its clear consequences for how people meet their basic needs. In any environment, population growth creates problems in technology, the social organization of production, and political regulation that must be solved. We will show how the solutions to these problems bring about the changes we know as sociocultural evolution.

Theorizing Sociocultural Evolution

Whether or not sociocultural evolution has taken place is no longer an issue. Archaeological work from all continents documents changes from early small-scale societies to later complex ones. Although there is no intrinsic necessity for every society to evolve in the way we describe here, the three interlocked evolutionary processes of subsistence intensification, political integration, and social stratification have been observed again and again in historically unrelated cases. Foragers diversify and adopt agriculture; villages form and integrate into regional polities; leaders come to dominate and transform social relations. How does this orderly and widespread pattern come to be?

Progress

Over the years, many answers have been proposed, each raising new questions in a series of debates that continues to the present day. In the nineteenth century, social evolutionists tended toward the optimistic view that human societies were evolving from an inferior to a superior condition. Morgan's scheme of stages (1877), from Savagery to Barbarism to Civilization, described improvements in all aspects of life from technology to morality. Maine (1870) saw new public law ("Contract") liberating the individual from the tyranny of kinship and rank ("Status"). Even Engels (1972 [1884]), who with Marx focused on the exploitation and suffering of the industrial working class, believed that history was driven by an irrepressible burgeoning of human mastery over nature, propelled by improvements in science and technology.

The problem that these social theories posed for anthropologists was their implicit embrace of a culture-bound concept of progress—that history is a sequence of changes leading inevitably in the general direction of the lifestyle and values of the intellectual elites of Europe and Euroamerica. This deeply ethnocentric belief—amounting to a kind of faith—had two components that came under attack separately at widely different periods in the history of evolutionist thought. The first component was a racist assumption that progress in science, technology, law—indeed all knowledge and morality—was intrinsically linked to race: inferior races could not aspire to the higher levels of achievement because they were incapable of it. The second component was the nature of progress itself, the question of who, if anyone, benefits from the changes we call sociocultural evolution.

Relativism

Turning to the first component, the link between race and progress came under devastating criticism from Boas (1949 [1920]), who made the separation of race and culture the centerpiece of his vision for American anthropology: individuals, he said, take on the cultural characteristics of the communities in which they are raised, whatever their racial backgrounds. Committed to a thoroughgoing cultural relativism, Boas and his most famous students, Robert Lowie, Alfred Kroeber, Ruth Benedict, and Margaret Mead, rejected cultural evolutionism. Each culture is unique and equally to be valued; if it changes, it does so in ways unique to itself, and no general upward trajectory can be discerned. The Boasian attack was largely persuasive, in part because it was linked to new, higher standards of ethnographic field research and data collection. As a result, in the first generation of American anthropology, ideas of progress and sociocultural evolution were effectively submerged.

Like many "solutions" to tough theoretical issues, however, the Boasian attack went too far: even as it correctly eliminated race from the equation, it inappropriately denied the existence of any kind of social evolution. The skepticism regarding nineteenth-century bias and data was broadened into an attack on the search for patterns in human social life generally, and a pervasive suspicion of all explanations for such patterns. Like the Boasian particularists, many anthropologists simply do not find any explanation interesting or appealing—but that is not acceptable to those wanting to account for patterned similarities and differences among societies (Carneiro 1982: 418).

Unilinear Evolution

Systemic change toward complexity was clearly evident in the archaeological record and could not simply be denied or wished away. In the second quarter of the twentieth century an influential new generation sought to reinstate the idea of progress but without racist baggage, in the scientific language of "unilinear evolution" (White 1959; cf. Childe 1936, 1942, 1951). In this theory, cultural evolution is potentially the property of all human communities, the cumulative growth in mastery over nature by means of culture (technological knowledge).

For Leslie White, the scientific foundation of his theory lay in the link between cultural evolution and energy capture: whereas small-scale hunter-gatherer economies were based on harvesting of the energy provided by nature (in the form of game, roots, seeds, etc.), more advanced agriculturalists had succeeded in harnessing energy through the domestication of plants and animals. The grand course of human history was one of harnessing increasing amounts of energy—from crops to draft animals to steam engines and on through internal combustion to presumably endless future mastery. White (1959) tried to lay a scientific basis for his arguments in formulas like the following:

$$E \times T \longrightarrow P \tag{1}$$

where E is energy, T is technology, and P is the production that results.

White and Childe were obviously right in many respects. Archaeology, for example, can document hundreds of thousands of years of increasing technological mastery in the manufacture of stone tools, ceramics, metals, and the like. Contemporary ethnographers can document that communities at greater levels of technological and social complexity do indeed control greater—sometimes vastly greater—quantities of energy (Harris and Johnson 2000: 69).

The problems raised by the theory of unilinear evolution, however, are serious, if somewhat subtle. Two emphases in particular required fundamental revision. The first was the theory's high degree of abstraction. Abstraction itself is not a fault; the strongest scientific theories are admired for their abstraction. But White's theory, reducing sociocultural evolution to calculations of energy capture, was too removed from empirical data. It harkened back to older typologies—such as Stone Age/Bronze Age/Iron Age—which worked for describing tool traditions but did not begin to account for the remarkable diversity of societies within each type: for example, that some Stone Age communities were larger and more complex than some Bronze Age communities. White (1959: 241) was also sometimes guilty of overlooking the broader importance of social activities that he could not link directly to energy capture, as when he dismissed the dramatic self-aggrandizing public displays of wealth found in the "prestige economies" (see chapter 7) as "social games" irrelevant to economic process.

Multilinear Evolution

One solution to White's excessive abstraction, and critical for the further development of social evolutionism, was Steward's theory (1955) of "multilinear evolution." Steward did not deny outright the theoretical value of a general scheme of social evolution from small-scale to complex. In fact, his empirical work on native South American cultures made extensive use of a unilinear typology: nomadic hunter-gatherers/village farmers/theocratic-militaristic chiefdoms/civilizations (Steward and Faron 1959: 13). But as Kroeber's student, Steward sought to restore the Boasian grounding of theory in local details: how did real people in their own communities obtain energy, indeed, the whole range of needed goods? Furthermore, how did they organize their labor, their property, their interactions with other individuals and social groups, their knowledge, attitudes, and beliefs, in order to meet their needs? If, as the adage has it, all politics is local, then for Steward all evolution is local, since it is people actively solving the problems of daily life, changing their behavior or refusing to change it, that constitutes the process of social evolution. This local process he termed *adaptation*, and it was through adaptation that Steward forged a connection to a vast body of theory and knowledge in economic anthropology that had hitherto developed on a parallel, largely independent track. We will explore this crucial linkage below in the discussion of economic motivation.

At the same time that Steward was writing, Barth (1956) showed how adaptation to local conditions must also implicate broader regional and interregional relationships of competition and exchange. In the region of Swat, northern Pakistan, three different ethnic groups with separate histories and economies existed together, exploiting different environmental zones and exchanging specialized products with each other: irrigation farmers living in densely populated areas, scattered pastoralists, and mixed herder-farmers. The high-density social groups with the most intensive economy excluded all others from the prime valley lands, while the pastoralists remained only in the uplands, where farming was impracticable. The pastoralists could then exchange their animals for the farmers' cereals. Each society had to adapt not only to local geography but also to the political and economic realities of neighboring societies.

The concept of multilinear evolution offers greater theoretical flexibility than does unilinear evolution. The idea that social evolution can follow different courses depending on local history and ecology readily embraces the possibility that particular communities, having achieved a working solution to the problems posed by population and environment, need not evolve at all if conditions do not significantly change. No intrinsic perfecting tendency drives technology to ever-increasing levels of energy efficiency. Hunter-gatherers can remain hunter-gatherers indefinitely; horticulturalists and pastoralists, though having harnessed energy, can remain small scale and egalitarian.

In a further advance over unilinear evolution, anthropologists after Steward turned away from the technological reductionism of using tools, energy, or mode of production to typologize levels of sociocultural complexity, moving instead toward typologies focusing on broad patterns of social organization. Service (1962) proposed a typology of bands/tribes/chiefdoms/states, and Fried (1967) followed with a three-stage typology focused on political organization: egalitarian society/rank society/stratified society. Both Service's and Fried's terminologies are widely employed in contemporary discussions of sociocultural evolution and are closely reflected in our own choices.

In light of multilinear evolution, such broad organizational typologies recognize that each kind of adaptive solution contains its own possibilities for evolution. The common textbook typology (based largely on Service) that even today begins with hunter-gatherer camps or bands and proceeds through horticultural villagers to agricultural states (with pastoralists somehow appended) can be replaced by evolutionary lines that have hunter-gatherers ranging all the way from camps to chiefdoms (Arnold 1996a), with similar ranges for pastoral peoples and agriculturalists.

Multilinearity is abundantly evident in the cases we have selected for analysis in this book. Although our cases fall into the familiar categories of forager, herder, and farmer, these are crosscut by our unilinear scheme of social scale: family level society, local group, and regional polity. Hence, in multilinear fashion, foragers may be found at the family level (e.g., Shoshone, Case 1), but also in local groups, including quite complex Big Man systems, possibly chiefdoms (e.g., Northwest Coast, Case 9). Farmers are found across the whole range of levels of social complexity, from family level (e.g., Machiguenga, Case 3) to regional polity (e.g., Kali Loro, Case 19). Herders may also be found at quite different social scales. Why one group of herders is barely different from familistic foragers (e.g., Nganasan, Case 4), while other herders live in chiefdoms embedded in agrarian states (e.g.,

Basseri, Case 14) may be understood only by careful analysis of local geography, history, and social environment. We outline our evolutionary typology in greater depth later in this chapter.

Although Service and Fried agreed on a similar typology, their contrasting explanations for the emergence of greater political control and social stratification in the course of social evolution exposed an old theoretical fault line. Fried followed Marx and Engels in seeing the emergence of stratification as essentially political, the result of ambitious and greedy individuals—sometimes called "aggrandizers" (Hayden 1995: 16–21)—who take advantage of abundant production (see the discussion of surplus, Chapter 9) to satisfy their excessive need for dominance. In a multilinear frame of reference, an aggrandizer's success would depend on local opportunities to seize control of surplus production and turn it to his own profit.

Service, on the other hand, took a more ecological perspective. He did not see how leaders could dominate the political process unless they provided real value to their followers and subjects. Uncontrollably greedy and aggressive individuals, after all, are often killed off in egalitarian societies. Leaders organize war parties and defenses, build and maintain irrigation systems, store food as famine relief, and manage intergroup trade. People allow them a greater share of community wealth precisely because they are necessary to the well-being of community members. In this version of multilinear evolutionism, a leader's success would vary depending on local need for the organization of labor and the control and development of resources.

This old debate, which is essentially about whether leaders take power from or are given power by the community, continues to energize theories of the evolution of complexity (see Chapter 9). Our take will be that these are two aspects of the same process, artificially separated in theoretical debates but inextricably linked in practice.

Antiprogress: Population and Diminishing Returns

The second major shortcoming of nineteenth-century evolutionism, after racism/ethnocentrism, was an uncritical belief in the inevitability of progress. In the first half of the twentieth century, neither unilinear nor multilinear evolutionism fully confronted this deficiency. Stripped of racist (and imperialist) biases, the notion that sociocultural evolution represents progress has a powerful appeal, both as description and as explanation. To many theorists it has seemed evident that technological progress is the cause of population growth, and hence of growth in social and political complexity. Why did populations grow? Because new sources of food were discovered and made available by technological improvements. Why did village life replace mobile foraging? Because gardening is more secure and less arduous than constantly moving about. Why did iron tools replace stone? Because iron is more malleable, can hold a sharper edge, and can sustain more rough use. Why did paddy fields replace slash-and-burn cultivation of rice? Because irrigated paddy is more productive. Why did regional governments integrate politically autonomous villages? Because central government provides services (security, infrastructure, coordination) beyond the means of a single village to provide for itself.

The association between economic activities and scale of society has seemed self-evident to many observers and has recently been confirmed in careful studies of how people spend time in different societies:

The time allocation study reassuringly confirms what we thought we already knew: the smallest-scale societies (as revealed by settlement size, population density, isolation from urban centers, and other social and ecological indicators) tend to spend the bulk of their production time foraging for wild plants and animals. As settlements grow and become more complex, foraging is increasingly supplemented by—and then replaced by—agricultural production. With further increases in scale agricultural production tends to be combined with commercial activities like cash cropping and wage laboring. In industrialized societies almost all production time is spent in commercial activities; even food production comes to be an occupational specialization for which workers obtain a wage. (Sackett 1996: 337)

Even in our age, far more skeptical about progress than a half-century ago, we often speak of technological and social change as making life better. Indeed, if the changes were not for the better, why would people accept them? The theory of technological progress has the virtue of providing a direct and plausible explanation for economic change: people invent new techniques, some of which are found acceptable and are therefore copied and shared, remaining in use until yet more desirable inventions displace them. In this quasi-Darwinian logic, people accept changes in the way that they do things because they recognize the benefits of doing so. In Childe's hopeful phrase (1936), "Man makes himself."

Opposing the optimism of the progress theorists, however, have been a series of more pessimistic views. Even before the nineteenth century, Malthus (1798) had proposed the view that population growth leads not to progress but to scarcity and misery. And at least one nineteenth-century evolutionist, Herbert Spencer (Carneiro 1967), saw social evolution as driven not by progress but by war: with the need for increasingly organized defense against enemies, society was becoming more complex on the rebound, so to speak, and people's lives were not necessarily improving as a result. In these views of history, it was not progress but the Four Horsemen of the Apocalypse—War, Famine, Disease, and Death—that held sway.

After Steward, theorists became increasingly skeptical of the assumption that sociocultural evolution improves a people's standard of living. Perhaps most influential was Boserup's use (1965) of the economic Law of Diminishing Returns, arguing that many so-called technological improvements are actually less efficient than what preceded them; they are adopted out of desperation, as growing populations are forced into ever more labor-intensive techniques if starvation is to be avoided. Long workdays in advanced modern economies and a growing sense of "time famine" fed doubts about whether progress is really occurring (Linder 1970; Scitovsky 1976).

In the 1970's, the pessimistic view of human history was part of a growing environmentalism, a widespread political consciousness that environments are not infinitely productive and resilient. Intensive use of the environment comes at a cost, as people exhaust nonrenewable resources and degrade renewable ones. Vivid news media images of forest loss, soil erosion, and desertification drove home the message that intensification can destroy resources. Restoring and sustaining productivity in damaged landscapes require investments of labor and management, and these are practicable only where there is the political will to pay the costs. The "population bomb" (Ehrlich 1968) was seen as a looming threat to the human condition and not an indicator of progress.

The Doomsday Equation. As a way of illuminating a number of relevant theoretical points, we may look at the peculiar history of the mathematical formula that came to be known as *The Doomsday Equation* (Umpleby 1987). About the time that the pessimistic, antiprogress view was emerging in anthropology, Foerster et al. (1960) published an equation that represented a best estimate of the curve of human population growth since the time of Christ:

$$\text{Population} = \frac{1.79 \times 10^{11}}{(2026.87 - \text{time})^{0.99}} \qquad (2)$$

Equation (2) describes an exponentially growing population that theoretically reaches infinity on Friday, November 13, in A.D. 2026. Despite whimsically setting this "interesting singularity" (doomsday) on a Friday the thirteenth, the authors had a serious message: the outcome of

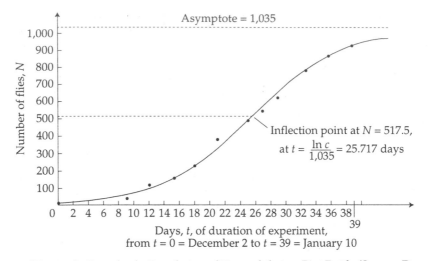

a. "S-curve": Growth of a Population of Drosophila in a Pint Bottle (Source: De Sapio 1978: 447)

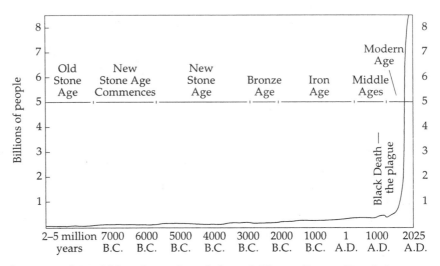

b. "J-curve": World Population Growth through History (Source: Population Reference Bureau 1995: 6)

Fig. 1. Two Kinds of Population Growth: Nature vs. Culture?

two millennia of continuously accelerating human population growth would soon end in disaster, if past trends continue for just a few more decades.

At issue is the uniqueness of the human pattern of population growth. Most biological organisms are capable of rapid population growth when resources are abundant, but their growth must taper off and finally stop as the environmental limit, or carrying capacity, is reached (Pearl 1925). This pattern of population growth, documented in countless laboratory and field studies, conforms to a logistic growth curve with a sigmoid shape, the so-called S-curve (Fig. 1a).

By contrast, the exponential growth pattern, or J-curve, described by the Doomsday Equation is what would be expected in "paradise" (Foerster et al. 1960: 1291)—that is, where resources are so abundant that the four horsemen scarcely make an appearance. The Doomsday Equation confirmed what many had believed, that human population grew slowly in the remote past but has been gathering steam ever since and in the modern age is rising apparently without limit (Fig. 1b). What Foerster et al. argued, in essence, was that humans—through "food technology and the industrial sciences" (Schmeck 1960: 10)—have changed the rules of nature. Instead of being subject to the limits set by carrying capacity, humans are in a contest with nature that they are winning, in the sense that their population continues to rise exponentially. The J-curve of human population growth represents the triumph of culture over nature.

What seemed to capture most attention at the time was the prediction that on that calamitous day, human population would go to a "universe-filling infinity" (*Time* 1960: 90). Of course, that cannot happen. Indeed one contemporary journalist, striving for a metaphorical way of describing the inconceivable, humorously asserted that on that doomsday the mass of human bodies would expand outward from the earth in all directions at the speed of light!

Critics at the time responded that the rate of growth of human population had been slowing and that the Doomsday Equation no longer applied. Yet a reexamination of the Doomsday Equation in 1987 showed that, not only had population growth not slowed, but world population was actually ahead of the prediction (Fig. 2). Indeed, had World War III broken out in that era, as many feared, the expected four hundred million casualties in Europe and America would merely have adjusted actual world population down to the level predicted by the Doomsday Equation (Umpleby 1987: 1556). What was going on?

Throughout history the four horsemen have certainly limited human population growth, just as they have limited growth in nonhuman populations. For tens of thousands of years humans have also had access to culturally mediated means of population control, including pregnancy prevention, abortion, and infanticide, which they have used in some circumstances to keep populations below carrying capacity (Read 1986: 20–21; Read 1998). Yet world population has inexorably risen, and in recent decades vast improvements in public health, new efficiencies of food production, and the expansion of agriculture into forests, deserts, and swamplands have kept pace (to a degree) with at least two of the horsemen—disease and starvation. Culture has enabled people to keep raising the earth's carrying capacity.

The Doomsday Equation, in this sense, supports the optimistic view that human cultural mastery over nature will allow population to grow indefinitely. But this is optimism with a bitter twist:

Thus, we may conclude with considerable confidence that the principle of "adequate technology," which proved to be correct for over 100 generations, will hold for at least three more. Fortunately, there is no need to strain the theory by undue further extrapolation, because—and here the pessimists erred again—our great-great-grandchildren will not starve to death. They will be squeezed to death. (Foerster et al. 1960: 1295)

This "optimistic" view is, of course, as pessimistic as any other. In the final analysis, what the Doomsday Equation most dramatically illustrates is that population cannot continue to grow indefinitely. At some point any real population must grow more slowly than the J-curve. In fact, although world population continued to exceed the predictions of the Doomsday Equation until about 1992, the inevitable finally happened: actual population began to fall short of the predictions of the equation (Fig. 2). By whatever combination of disasters and fertility regulation, the actual growth of world population in recent years looks more like a straight line, as the world adds between eighty and ninety million people each year. Whether it will begin to curve off to the right, taking on the shape of an S-curve, remains to be seen. Intuition tells us that world population growth must slow sometime, and recent signs suggest that the slowdown may already be underway (United Nations 1996). Evidence is mounting that current rates of use are depleting essential resources, even the soils and fresh water on which agriculture depends (Ehrlich et al. 1992: 23). Yet specialists debate whether the carrying capacity of the earth is ten billion people or more, or whether we already greatly exceed carrying capacity and should begin to shrink population toward a sustainable population of about one billion (Ehrlich and Ehrlich 1997; Moffat 1996).

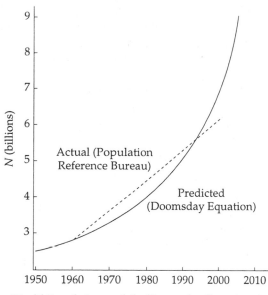

Fig. 2. World Population and the Doomsday Equation since 1960

The lesson of the Doomsday Equation is that human population is capable of growing rapidly and inexorably when resources are available to sustain it. The capacity for culture, which optimists see as mastery of nature, allows humans to increase available resources at an unprecedented rate. Yet this process cannot go on indefinitely. In modern times—and indeed throughout history—resources have barely kept pace with population, which has grown despite the absence of anything like paradise except for an affluent minority. For the vast majority, population growth has posed constant challenges for the provision and management of the resources on which they depend to meet their basic needs. Knowledge of these challenges, and how they have been met, is the key to understanding the processes of sociocultural evolution.

In the intellectual milieu of population bombs and doomsday equations, cultural anthropologists such as Harris (1977) and Carneiro (1970b), and archaeologists such as Cohen (1977; 1994), explored this likelihood that sociocultural evolution is driven by people's struggle to cope with the deterioration in quality of life caused by relentless population growth. Cross-cultural evidence demonstrates a strong positive correlation between socioeconomic complexity and population pressure (Keeley 1988). As competition for resources increases, people must live close together to defend themselves, their stored foods, and their

lands. Leadership becomes a necessity for defense and alliance formation. Complicated and difficult group projects must be undertaken to
make the most of diminishing resources. In this light, population
growth and a chain reaction of economic and social changes underlie
sociocultural evolution.

Population Growth and Social Evolution. Whether or not these changes
represent an improvement in the quality of individual lives (the subsistence economy) depends upon your interpretation of the evidence.
Time allocation data show a consistent pattern of changes from small-
scale to industrial societies (Sackett 1996: 338–42):

1. Daily work time increases dramatically, from an average of a little
less than six hours per adult among foragers and about six and three-
quarters among horticulturalists, to nine hours among intensive agriculturalists and slightly less among industrialized urbanites. The
growth in work time is evenly distributed between men and women.

2. Time spent manufacturing and repairing family possessions decreases by about two-thirds (probably as a result of purchasing such
possessions from specialists via the market).

3. Time spent housekeeping grows from about one-half hour per
day to nearly one-and-three-quarters hours, related to the growing
permanence of houses and the numbers of possessions kept in them. As
the size of the society increases, women's time spent at daily house-
work increases while men's declines.

4. Work increasingly comes to be divided into two domains: a female domestic realm centered on the household and family, and a male
productive sphere focused on commercial activities (cf. Minge-Klevana
1980).

These patterns are strongly supported by quantitative cross-cultural
data. But they do not answer the question of whether technological innovation makes possible an overall increase in production, or whether
population increase forces technological improvements to catch up.

In this book we will focus attention away from the chicken-and-egg
debate over whether population growth or technological advance
drives social evolution. Here we identify the process of feedback between population and technology as the engine of the evolutionary
process. For humans, both population growth and technological creativity are ever-present possibilities. As represented by the S-curve,
populations will grow until they reach environmental limits (carrying
capacity). This process is subject to Leibig's Law of the Minimum,
which states that populations will be limited by critical resources (e.g.,

water) that are in shortest supply (Hardesty 1977: 196–97). Individuals will try new creative solutions to the problems created by overpopulation, consistent with their existing technology and the possibilities presented by the environment. Not all environments permit population growth, and not all technologies provide a base on which to build new productivity that would raise carrying capacity. But where the process of feedback between population growth and technological change is active, changes in socioeconomic complexity are likely to follow according to the model we develop below (p. 31).

The Problem of Warfare. The case studies in this book will illustrate a basic truth: that humans everywhere and at all times have the potential to resort to violence to achieve their goals (Keeley 1996: 26–32). If we take warfare to be "armed conflict and associated activities and relations between independent political units in all types of societies" (Haas 1996: 1357), then certainly, as Herbert Spencer argued, the need to defend one's own group from powerful outside threats is in itself enough to encourage political integration within, in order to resist annihilation and to pose effective counterthreats. To this degree, warfare has been correctly identified as one of the causes of social evolution (Carneiro 1970b). As important a process as warfare is, however, the search for the causes of warfare is actually a diversion that obscures the nature of warfare and its place in the evolution of human societies.

Theories of the causes and reasons for warfare are legion, from popular ones, such as competition over resources, to idiosyncratic ones, such as a king's obsession with revenge (Keeley 1996: 114). The problem is that the attempt to explain warfare assumes that it is an entity that can be described, analyzed, and explained. A more productive approach is to acknowledge that the resort to aggression to achieve one's goals is part of our biological heritage and that what is to be explained is how aggression is expressed under varying circumstances. Then it becomes clear that aggression takes forms appropriate to the social and political systems in which it occurs.

In small, family-level societies, aggression is personal and may or may not lead to a cycle of revenge killing; it is possible that warfare as we define it rarely existed prior to ten thousand years ago (Haas 1996: 1360). In local group villages, warfare pits small groups of warriors against one another in raids; sometimes these groups attack each other within the village, fissioning it. In clan-based local groups, warfare is organized by leaders and at least partly regulated by the intergroup collectivity. In chiefdoms, a chief imposes order within the chiefdom, bringing a highly valued peace to his subjects, but then wages violent and systematic warfare against neighboring chiefdoms and states. In short, warfare is no one phenomenon but the varying expression of aggression in varying institutional settings.

We explain the nature of warfare, then, when we explain the level of sociopolitical integration at which it takes place. War itself explains some integration, but other principles (risk management, capital technology, trade) are required for a full explanation of the evolution of society. This approach to explaining warfare has a further advantage: instead of focusing only on warfare as violence and the breakdown of order, we attend also to the achievement of order by which people have always tried to avoid warfare and control its devastating effects (Sponsel 1996). If resort to violence is part of the human tool kit, so too is resort to cooperation, generosity, and trust. In the evolution of human societies, both potentials are actualized differently as the scale of sociopolitical integration changes.

Theories of Economic Motivation

Working for the most part separately from the evolutionists, economic anthropologists have historically been less interested in explaining long-term patterns of change than in explaining the economic motivation of individuals in culturally diverse communities. Here the tendency in Western scholarly thought at the turn of the century had been to assume (explicitly) that individuals are motivated by their own economic self-interest, and (implicitly) that this self-interest is primarily served by the acquisition of material wealth. Although theoretical economists did not crudely say that people merely want to get rich, their methodological emphasis on how firms maximize profits embedded acquisitiveness and the profit motive at a deep level of implicit theory.

Economic Anthropology

A distinctive anthropological economics emerged in the process of identifying economic theory as rationalist, materialist, and ethnocentric. Westerners are notoriously materialistic in their values, whereas many peoples around the world place other goals above material wealth, particularly social relations and prestige. They encourage the sacrifice of personal wealth to achieve socially and culturally valued ends. Malinowski (1922) helped originate this anthropological critique of standard economics with his classic analysis of the Trobriand *kula* ring (Case 12), setting the stage for a fundamental debate that, with some changes, continues today.

In its original form, the debate was ostensibly about ethnocentrism, and the anthropological solution was a relativism similar to the Boasian program: individual economic behavior is motivated primarily by values that do not originate in the material self-interest of the individual but in a social and cultural matrix of beliefs and commitments. As cultural communities vary, so do the economic motivations of their members.

Substantivism. As developed by Polanyi (1957), the anthropological critique crystallized into "substantive economics," which he saw as the antithesis of standard economics. Rejecting material needs as the basis of economic motivation, Polanyi defined the economy as "instituted process," how economic behavior is structured by social rules. For example, in peasant societies (Chapter 13) people are often required by the community to underwrite lavish ceremonial feasts, and they have little choice but to comply, however much they may resent the expense. In such cases, "the economy is embedded in society," and what individuals may want is of little importance.

In one of his most influential contributions, Polanyi argued that the way in which goods and services are exchanged in society may be instituted in three fundamentally contrasting ways. *Reciprocity,* in which individuals (or groups) of roughly equal standing engage in a customary give-and-take of equivalent value over time, characterizes the pattern of exchange typical of households, lineages, villages, and many other small social groups. *Redistribution,* an intrinsically hierarchical flow of goods into a center where they are controlled and then redistributed by some central authority, typifies the feasts and gift-exchanges of some Big Man systems and the centralization of larger-scale communities like chiefdoms (see Chapters 7 and 9), as well as most modern governments. *Exchange,* the market driven flow of goods and services under the regime of supply and demand, typifies the modern market economy (Chapter 14). One of Polanyi's main purposes was to draw our attention to the limited distribution of the exchange type of economic transaction, to overcome the ethnocentric tendency to assume that our contemporary economic way of life, as described by economic theory, is somehow natural, inevitable, and universal.

A helpful consequence of the elaboration of the substantivist viewpoint was that the ethnocentrism of nineteenth-century economic ideas could now be seen to entail two assumptions that have no necessary connection to each other: first, that economic behavior is rational; and second, that it is motivated by material self-interest.

Formalism. The idea that economic behavior is the result of rational decision-making, which Polanyi called "formal economics" (following Weber 1947: 184–86), simply states the common-sense assumption that a person "so disposes of his total resources as to obtain the maximum satisfaction" (Goodfellow 1968 [1939]: 60). This maximizing (also, "optimizing," or "satisficing") assumption of standard economics is that all people have criteria by which they decide what to do at any given moment (Burling 1962; Homans 1967; LeClair 1962). Polanyi, by contrast, denied that individuals make rational calculations of their own self-interest when confronted with a range of economic options. Like peasants faced with community demands for "generosity," they have no alternative but to conform to social expectations. They do not make choices but follow rules (Dalton 1961): their economic motivation is instituted in society.

The formalist response to the substantivist critique was straightforward. Formalists simply pointed out that they make no assumptions about where self-interest comes from. For one person, self-interest may be served by storing wealth and investing it for profit; for another, it may be served by spending wealth and incurring debt to host a feast. In either case, the behavior is rational if it is reasonably satisfying to the person. In fact, in Chapter 8 we explore examples where individuals serve their own self-interest by doing both: they scrimp and save in order to spend and incur debt hosting a feast, all in hope of a profit. To say that economic behavior is rational is not to say that it conforms to our ethnocentric notions of reasonableness. If we agree that economic behavior is the result of decisions, formalism and substantivism need not conflict: people's behavior can be both rational (optimally satisfying) and instituted (conform to cultural values).

Formalist economics, therefore, draws our attention to the importance of choice in economic behavior, but deliberately refrains from trying to explain the motivation behind economic behavior. In essence, formalist economics does not care where the motivation comes from. People may be motivated by anything: they may even seek pain rather than pleasure, prefer evil to good, esteem poverty above wealth. Why one rather than the other? To answer that people will do whatever maximizes satisfaction does not touch upon what motivates economic behavior—why *this* satisfies rather than *that*—a huge question that must be settled prior to, or apart from, the formal analysis of rational decision-making.

The substantivist answer—that values motivate economic behavior—was an appropriate anthropological perspective. But it shared the weakness of Boasian relativism, an anything-goes possibilism in which economic behavior of whatever sort—food taboos, the savagery of primitive warfare, destruction of wealth during feasting, sacred cows—

did not have to make any sense. They were just "riddles of culture" that we had to accept as products of spontaneous cultural creativity (see Harris 1974). But many observers wondered why some values (e.g., endemic raiding and trophy-taking) predominated in certain kinds of societies (e.g., tribes) but not others (e.g., among peasants). Their search for answers beyond historical accident led them back to a nineteenth-century economic assumption that had been attacked by substantivism, the idea that economic behavior is motivated by a desire for material well-being.

Materialism. Although they were on firm ground in denying that people are universally motivated to seek profit in the manner of a capitalist firm, the substantivists tended in fact to have a broader, implicit, and less easily defended agenda: to deny the importance of human biology as a source of economic motivation. Substantivists evidently felt that referring to the clamor of bodily needs for explanations of economic behavior was incompatible with the axiom that economy is embedded in society (Sahlins 1976). In a revival of substantivism, "structural Marxists" have labeled reference to biological motivation "vulgar Marxism" (Friedman 1974). With their focus on how social structure determines economic process (Godelier 1977; Legros 1977; Meillassoux 1972), these substantivists divert attention from biology and toward culture, rather than exploring links between the two.

Yet of course people must be fed, sheltered, and protected if they are to live to reproduce the species (and the culture). Human biologists, ecologists, and psychologists have provided us with abundant and sophisticated knowledge of motivation that is consistent with biological evolution and adaptation. It is here that Steward's use of the concept of adaptation built a bridge between social evolutionism and economic anthropology. The theories of social evolution that followed Steward increasingly attempted to be consistent with the findings of biology and ecology. Such material sources of economic motivation may be approached from two directions that—though sometimes seen as competing explanations—are better understood as alternate sides of a coin.

Evolutionary Biology. One approach is to focus on what many consider the primary source of motivation in living organisms, the urge to reproduce. Evolutionary biology and psychology have compiled and systematized quantities of findings on this subject that go far beyond the scope of this book (Boyd and Richerson 1985; Ridley 1997; Tooby and Cosmides 1992; Wright 1994). We must briefly mention several key findings, however, if the specific arguments that appear in the discussion of cases below are to be fully understood.

1. Men and women have different goals in mating and marriage, similar to male-female differences found in many other species. Men seek mating opportunities with many women and seek mates who are young, with long fertile futures ahead of them. Women prefer to mate with a man who controls resources, who will be a stable provider as husband and father. Such men are often senior in age and high-ranking politically.

2. Humans are jealous of their mates, and men are especially prone to be aggressive in defending their exclusive right to mate with their spouses.

3. Both men and women are strongly attracted to territories where resources are abundant, and are liable to become aggressive in defending their exclusive rights to territories from outside encroachment. Defense of territory by men is a means of attracting and holding women as mates.

4. People know who their close kin are and nurture, defend, and support them (kin selection). Loyalty, trust, and altruistic behavior are highest between close kin and tend to decline among distant kin and to disappear with strangers.

5. The large primate brain, especially the extraordinary human brain, evolved at least partly to store and maintain the extensive social knowledge necessary for making the complex interpersonal judgments upon which trust and cooperation are based, and to communicate about them (Dunbar 1996). Constant talking within a group can act like grooming among apes to establish intimacy and coordination, and the symbolizing power associated with human speech becomes available for building social relationships beyond the biological boundaries of kin selection.

6. In any community some individuals, especially men, seek dominance over all others. Such aggrandizers generally are willing to take substantial risks of physical harm in aggressively establishing and defending their dominance (Hayden 1995). Differences among individuals in this regard may explain why some individuals appear to have greater hierarchical strivings than others.

7. In social interactions, deception and cheating undermine efforts to cooperate for mutual advantage. Cheaters, or "free-riders," must be controlled by cooperative members of the community, or the advantages of cooperation disappear.

8. Nonetheless, human beings "come into the world equipped with predispositions to learn how to cooperate, to discriminate the trustworthy from the treacherous, to commit themselves to be trustworthy,

to earn good reputations, to exchange goods and information, and to divide labour" (Ridley 1997: 249).

9. People acquire much of their new behavior by imitating apparently successful persons, first their parents and later high-ranking members of their community. In these cases, it is not rational choice but modeling the behavior of others that determines economic behavior.

As we shall see, the behavior described in our case studies is seldom in conflict with these basic principles. But because they are basic, and more or less universal, they alone cannot help us understand the patterned differences we find among types of human societies. Human nature is distinguished by its malleability to different necessities. To explain these differences in human behavior, we need a theory encompassing patterns of adaptation characteristic of particular combinations of population, environment, and technology.

Human Ecology

Despite the doubts about the universality of rational choice, many adaptive behaviors clearly reflect calculations of the costs and benefits of alternative strategies. In human ecology the biological perspective shifts from an emphasis on reproduction (the individual as a vessel for the transmission of genes from one generation to the next) to an emphasis on the health and well-being of the vessel itself (i.e., the individual). The two approaches are complementary, since, if individuals are to reproduce, they must survive in reasonable health to reproductive age and remain healthy to be able to nurture their offspring until they can survive on their own.

From the standpoint of human ecology, economic motivation is centered on the quest for health and safety. This begins in ensuring a steady and nutritious diet and protection from hazards (illness, predators, severe weather, enemies). Individuals and their core groups require access to a resource base and a technology for exploiting it. They participate in social groups that make this possible, and agree to certain restrictions on their own behavior in order to reap the benefits of society, including protection from hazards. But these restrictions can, under certain circumstances, include requirements to participate in ritual occasions, share wealth in communal distributions, and take orders from authorities. Thus the materialist focus of an ecological perspective does not remain on nutrients, shelter, and defense, but expands out into the entire social and cultural world, where many adaptive solutions are found to the problems faced by individuals in their efforts to achieve health and safety.

This range of sociocultural means for solving adaptive problems was referred to by Steward (1955: 37) as the "culture core." In this book, we have used a culture-core checklist to guide our choice of topics to cover in our case studies:

> Environment
> Population
> Technology
> Social Organization of Production
> Territoriality/Warfare
> Political Integration
> Stratification
> Sanctity

Each human community exists in an environment of possibilities and constraints, equipped with a technology for meeting the basic needs of its population. Intrinsic to this process is the social organization of production, characterized by a division of labor and practices for obtaining, storing, modifying, and sharing resources. Competition over access to resources must be met and resolved. With increasing scale, all these features—technology, social organization of production, and competition—come under regimes of leadership and inequality. And at all levels, adaptive practices and institutions are sanctified by rituals, taboos, and other means of invoking awe to stabilize patterns of behavior.

The Subsistence Economy and the Political Economy

Consistent with our materialist, ecological approach, we define the economy as the way people meet their basic needs, provisioning the material means of their existence. The economy includes the production and distribution of food, technology, and other material goods necessary for the survival and reproduction of human beings and of the social institutions on which their survival depends. Whether we study the subsistence support of the household or the finance of the larger institution, the problem of material provisioning is basic.

Our definition of the economy is close to the ecologist's notion of niche, or the way a population derives its necessary matter and energy from the surrounding habitat (Odum 1971). It is also similar to the substantivist's notion of the economy as "man's interchange with his natural and social environment, in so far as this results in supplying him with the means of material want satisfaction" (Polanyi 1957: 243). Unlike the substantivist, however, we see the economic motivation that Polanyi calls "material want satisfaction" deriving primarily from basic (biological) needs (although we acknowledge that cultural values are not easily separable and often coincide).

Analytically, the economy can be subdivided in two: the subsistence economy and the political economy. Their basic dynamics differ, and they contribute quite differently to social evolution.

The Subsistence Economy. The locus at which basic needs begin to be filled is the subsistence economy, which is at root the household economy. It is organized at the household level to meet needs for food, clothing, housing, defense, and procurement technology. The simplest form of the subsistence economy is the "domestic mode of production" (Sahlins 1972). In this model, each household is taken to be similar and self-sufficient, producing all that it needs, incorporating a division of labor by age and sex.

In a merging of the human ecologist's focus on basic need fulfillment with the formalist emphasis on rational decision-making, our perspective is that the nature of the subsistence economy is determined by the needs of the population and the cost of procuring necessary resources (cf. Earle 1980a). Theoretically no surplus is produced beyond a security margin—what may be needed if things turn bad. The overriding goal is to fulfill the household's needs at the lowest cost that affords security.

To meet this goal, families select from among potential procurement strategies those that seem best suited to obtaining food or other products from the environment. Following the law of diminishing returns, for any given strategy the cost of producing food tends to climb as output from that strategy increases: as hunters kill more deer, fewer deer are left and the difficulty of hunting them increases. When a community first enters virgin territory, the strategies available for obtaining food differ in their initial costs. For example, it may be cheaper to get a good diet by hunting deer than by collecting seeds and insects. But over time, as deer are hunted, they become less abundant and hence more expensive to obtain. Then other strategies, such as collecting seeds or insects, are added as their costs become comparable to the rising cost of deer. Thus, the number of strategies foragers use in obtaining food tends to increase the longer they inhabit a given area.

Population growth has two key consequences for the subsistence economy: as growing numbers of people deplete resources, they must (a) turn to less desirable and more costly alternatives; and (b) improve productivity by developing new technology and modifying the environment (e.g., agricultural development). Local attempts to improve lifestyle by increasing resources open up great potential for growth, but population soon fills all the new opportunities and more changes are needed. The cycle has continued to the present day as an increasingly modified environment sustains a human population pushing toward some unknown maximum.

This logic is derived from formal economics (cf. Earle 1980a) and its application to optimal foraging in animal populations (Pianka 1974; Winterhalder and Smith 1981). In the subsistence economy, the goal is not to maximize production but to minimize the effort expended in meeting household needs. A specific mix of strategies all exploited at the same cost level minimizes procurement costs for the households of a region. Such a mix should remain stable except where upset by changes in population, technology, or the environment. As one example of such change, the diets of the peoples of the prehistoric world gradually broadened to include an increasing range of foods as the landscape was gradually filled in by hunter-gatherers.

Growth in the subsistence economy results from the positive feedback between population growth and technological development (cf. Wilkinson 1973). As seen in the Doomsday Equation, in technologically simple societies population growth was often very slow, but over the centuries the overall growth rate has increased dramatically (Taagapera 1981). As population grows, total needs expand. The availability of resources to support a population is determined by the environment and by the technology used.

Although we tend to think of the environment as a constant, the more we learn of history, the more we come to see the environment as an artifact of human activity. Forests are cleared, fields and irrigation ditches built, resources transformed. Humans become increasingly involved in managing the processes of nature, and that takes much work. The feedback between population growth and technological development increasingly modifies the environment in ways that limit people's choices. The usual outcome is to bind people to their land and its careful management.

The Political Economy. Within the sphere of the subsistence economy, rooted in small family households and the provisioning of basic needs, the relevance of a biological theory of economic motivation is abundantly clear. But human beings routinely exceed these narrow subsistence boundaries in their economic behavior. As substantivists, the structural Marxists place special emphasis on how ownership of the means of production (land, labor, and capital) acts to channel the flow of goods and to support existing power relationships (Earle 1997). At first glance, their insistence on political control as a key structural feature of society appears to take us far from basic need fulfillment. Indeed, it suggests the possibility, as Fried saw, that the process of material want satisfaction in the subsistence economy is hijacked by the ma-nipulations of a power-wielding, self-serving elite.

Understanding the distinctive nature of the political economy allows us to bridge this apparent gap between the subsistence economy and elite power. In the course of human evolution, the emergence of the ca-pacity for culture provided solutions to fundamental problems in the subsistence economy. As landscapes occupied by humans (or, origi-nally, protohumans) became crowded, a constant potential for aggres-sive competition over the most desired resources led to conflict, dis-placement, and even death, much as is observed among primate groups today (Manson and Wrangham 1991). Within the intimate family group—the subsistence economy—a certain amount of family feeling, based on biological reinforcers (as predicted by kin selection theory), but strengthened by myriad small reciprocities, would minimize such competition and allow for reconciliation after violent episodes (Waal 1996). But with distant kin and strangers, where such family feeling is weak or absent, the difficulties of regulating destructive competition are massive, and we are in the realm of what Thomas Hobbes called "the war of all against all."

The capacity for culture makes possible a powerful and decisive new solution to the dilemma of subsistence competition. Through symbolic means—encoded as rules of proper behavior, embodied in identities such as lineage and clan, fictive kinship and ethnic unity, and emotion-ally grounded in awe (sanctity)—people are able to treat distant kin and strangers with some of the same respect and concern they show close kin. There are rules that require the !Kung (Chapter 3) to request permission to drink at another group's water hole, and rules that re-quire the Eskimos (Chapter 7) to request permission to hunt in the home range of another, even though the host group in both cases is equally rule-bound to give permission.

A highly significant example of the way in which a destructive po-tential of the subsistence economy is resolved in the political economy is what Hardin (1968) called "the tragedy of the commons." Hardin's classic case of the problems that arise when strangers seek to exploit the same resources involves pastoralists exploiting a common pasture. If one herder conscientiously seeks to keep the pasture viable by restrict-ing his herd's grazing time, the next herder may simply seize the op-portunity for extra grazing for his own herd. The "good" herder's re-straint thus operates to his disadvantage, and the "bad" herder's greed to his momentary advantage. Eventually, the pasture is degraded by overgrazing, and all herders lose. An intuitively obvious example of the same phenomenon is evident to freeway drivers who attempt to observe a safe speed and safe distance from other cars, only to have selfish drivers recklessly pass or cut in front, imposing more crowded and dangerous conditions on all drivers.

The only practical solution is for a group's members to observe a code of behavior that regulates all of them and protects the common resources. Violators of the code (free-riders) must be punished. It is only through the political elaboration of institutions and rules to control free-riders that communities larger than small family groups can be maintained in a competitive environment. We shall call any economy exhibiting such institutions and rules a political economy. Although the political economy exists because it solves real economic problems of individual families—that is, problems of the subsistence economy—it creates new forms of social complexity that take on lives of their own.

The political economy involves the exchange of goods and services in an integrated society of interconnected families. All societies have at least a rudimentary political economy, inasmuch as families can never be entirely self-sufficient but are linked by needs for security, mating, and trade. The political economy becomes more elaborate through the process of social evolution. Whereas the subsistence economy, based in the household, is remarkably stable and enduring through time, the dynamics of the political economy make for dramatic changes in its nature. As it evolves, the political economy becomes geared to mobilizing a surplus (or tax) from the subsistence economy. This surplus is used to finance social, political, and religious institutions that in their more elaborated forms are run by those who do not produce food. These institutions in turn are used to support and justify elite ownership of the region's productive resources, especially improved agricultural land.

Perhaps the most important difference between the political and subsistence economies is seen in their different rationalities and dynamics. The subsistence economy is geared to meeting household needs—if key subsistence variables (population, technology, and environment) are held constant, it is inherently stable. By contrast, the political economy is geared to maximizing production destined for use by the ruling elite—it is growth-oriented in a highly competitive political domain, and thus inherently unstable.

Elites maintain their positions and income through power, their ability to resist other aggrandizers' efforts to coopt their spheres of economic control. Power in turn depends on maximizing income by investing in income-producing projects. Indeed, to stay ahead of the game, elites must plow much of the income from new investments back into further investments. The political economy grows by positive feedback between investment and expanding income.

The political economy will grow unless checked by factors that cause declining yields. In most complex societies we find a cyclical pattern in which the political economy expands to its limit, collapses by internal conflict, then begins to expand again. Elites recognize the limits to growth and try to overcome them by instituting major capital improvements. In Hawaii, for example (Chapter 11), where there was competition among chiefs for control of island populations, the chiefs invested in such capital improvements as fish ponds, irrigation systems, and land reclamations in an effort to increase their income and with it their military power. By contrast, in Denmark during the Bronze Age (1700 to 700 B.C), local chieftains expanded cattle-raising to obtain animals for trade, but the intensification degraded the region and brought on a collapse, as unproductive heaths replaced grasslands and destabilized sands drifted inland over agricultural fields (Earle 1997).

Social Evolution as Political Ecology

We have used Steward's adaptivist approach to bridge between social evolutionism and economic anthropology, particularly to draw the structural Marxist's emphasis on power and the control of resources into a larger, more ecological conception of the political economy as a set of solutions to problems arising in the subsistence economy. This is not to say, however, that the integration of subsistence and political economies is itself smoothly adaptive and without contradictions. More than an analytical construct, conflict between subsistence and political economies—between household needs and the demands of the political sphere—is commonplace and near to the experience of householders everywhere. War leaders find it difficult to recruit warriors, feast-givers must cajole and even bully followers into provisioning the feast, governments must track and punish tax evaders. In the privacy of their homes, householders discuss the demands of the political economy and their degree of commitment to fulfilling political obligations. The "solutions" of the political economy, including wars, extraction of surplus to finance the investments of distant elites, and the eradication of outlaws, can be maladaptive for the many households victimized by them.

This potential for contradictions between the subsistence and political economies—as dynamic interaction of ecology and politics—helps explain the limits to growth of the political economy at any point in time. Since the political economy is financed by a surplus taken from the subsistence economy (Chapter 9), the political economy cannot function, let alone grow, unless family participation is ensured. The evolutionary question, What makes the political economy grow? finds its answer in economic motivation: the household will participate in the political economy to the degree that the benefits of participation exceed the costs.

In small-scale societies with scattered populations, the benefits of integrating into larger polities are small and the costs are great. As population grows, landscapes fill in and competition for resources increases. Serious problems arise in the subsistence economy, of which the tragedy of the commons is only one example. Populations become circumscribed by their investments in their own landscapes and by the lack of freedom to move, since neighboring landscapes are also filled with people prepared to defend them (Carneiro 1967: xxxvii; 1970b). Solving subsistence problems increasingly requires group action and leadership, the very conditions that encourage economic control and expansion of the political economy.

As problem solvers, leaders manage the economy to the advantage of constituent families, increasing the benefits of participation in the political economy as population pressure grows. Saying the same thing in other words, the cost to the household of not participating in the political economy becomes unbearable—in arid lands, what farm family can turn its back on the elites who control the irrigation water? We visualize the evolving political economy as expanding like a bubble. For families inside the bubble the benefits of participating in the political economy exceed the costs; for those outside, the costs exceed the benefits.

Since it is extremely costly to control hostile populations that see no benefits to themselves from participating in the political economy, elites will not invest in the military control of outlying populations without compelling reasons to do so. By way of example, the Inka state succeeded in integrating settled agrarian communities over a strip of territory running some two thousand miles north and south in the Andean highlands yet largely failed to bring under its control the scattered hamlets and villages of the adjacent Amazon rain forest a mere fifty miles to the east. As our discussion of the Machiguenga (Case 3) and the Inka (Case 16) will show, the costs and benefits of family participation in the Inka political economy were utterly different in the highlands and the rain forest.

By outliers, however, we really mean those outside the benefit structure of the political economy (the bubble), rather than simply those at a geographical distance from power centers. It is not unusual for segments of a population that do not benefit from participation in the political economy to remain outside the law (outlaws) while within the borders of the polity. In contemporary urban areas—even Washington, D.C., at the apex of world power today—there are outlaw groups whose political and economic behavior more closely approximates that of local groups (Chapter 5): high rates of male death by violence, limited leadership of small groups by valiant males, loose collectivities of leaders (who sometimes coordinate from prison), and endemic, violent competition over territories and resources marked by opportunistic homicides. Although in the state, they are not politically of it. They live for the most part outside the bubble. The state tries to limit their disorganizing effects on the rest of society but is surprisingly powerless to bring their behavior under control.

Most commoners' options are, however, fully circumscribed, with few possibilities for remaining outside the bubble of the political economy. This lack of options is a source of opportunities for control by means of which elites gain power. To this degree—and this is ultimately what Fried and the structural Marxists were getting at—the elites can use their positions of power for self-aggrandizement. The political economy, whose origin lay in solving problems of the subsistence economy, eventually comes into partial opposition to the well-being of households, raising the specter of domination and exploitation. The adaptive ecological process of the subsistence economy confronts the power arrangements of the political economy, with a contradictory and conflictual political ecology as the result.

The Evolutionary Process

The evolution of human societies is an upward spiral. As a consequence of the process of intensification—the positive feedback between population growth and technological development—serious problems arise that must be solved if the intensification is to be sustained. If not, a crisis of overpopulation would precipitate low fertility/high mortality, readjusting population downward to carrying capacity. The solutions to these problems are most often found in the creation or elaboration of institutions of the political economy, bringing about broader political-economic integration and more powerful leaders. As these solutions are tested and refined and become a part of ordinary experience, they set the stage for still further intensification and development of the political economy in an upward spiral.

Figure 3 models this iterative process of social evolution. Although intensification is not an imperative, and we can find examples, such as the inland Eskimo (Case 6), where elegant technological refinements had only a small consequence in population growth for thousands of years, the archaeological and historical record over the long course of human cultural development shows a consistent and eventually dramatic increase in human population worldwide (Coale 1974; Fig. 1b). As a result of population increase, the subsistence economy must be intensified to provision greater numbers of people on the same resource base. Intensification does not come cheaply, but typically creates four kinds of problems, their relative importance varying according to environmental conditions. These are production risk, raiding and warfare, technological needs, and resource deficiencies. The solutions to these problems generally require increasing the economic integration of communities and the power of leaders.

The first problem is production risk. As a landscape fills with people, the most desirable foods are soon depleted, and less desirable foods, those that once served as buffers against starvation in bad years, come to be part of the regular diet. With fewer buffers and less food generally, the risk of starvation increases, and each household faces the need for a margin of security in food production against the possibility of lean seasons or years (cf. Leibig's Law of the Minimum, above). Households can do some of this individually, through overproduction (e.g., Case 3) or private food storage (e.g., Cases 9 and 12). But at some point it becomes more efficient for the community to share the costs of security. A classic form of risk management is community food storage; another is reciprocal arrangements between communities for visiting (and feasting) in lean times. A region with community storage or reciprocal feasting can sustain a larger population; but such arrangements call for leadership and create opportunities for control.

The second problem is resource competition. At all ethnographically known economic levels, competition between families for prized resources occurs. At the family level, characterized by low population densities and dispersed resources, households tend to avoid competition by scattering and staying out of each other's way. With intensification, however, locally rich resources, such as fertile bottomlands, become even more precious, and improvements to the land, such as long-yielding tree crops, become more common. Such developments increase the benefits of the violent seizure of territory relative to the costs of violence. The general level of violence in a region accordingly rises, and small groups form alliances with other small groups for more effective defense of their resources. Effective defense also requires greater social integration and generates opportunities for control.

The third problem, inadequate use of resources, refers to resources that may be used only if costly technologies are developed. As popula-

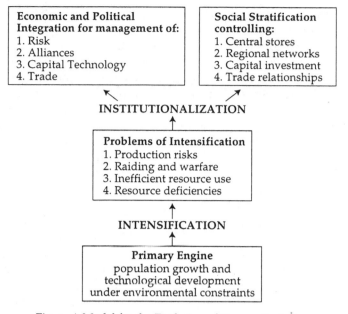

Fig. 3. A Model for the Evolution of Human Societies

tion rises in a resource area, and with it production risks, it becomes advantageous to invest in technologies that utilize resources that were ignored at lower population levels. For example, the efficient use of marine resources may require the construction of huge canoes or whaling boats; the use of arid lands for farming may require an irrigation system; in the far north, the abundance of food in summer may stave off hunger in winter only by means of large-scale technologies for harvesting and storage. These technologies are frequently beyond the capacity of a single family; they require the collaboration of households in a community and in due course come under the control of a manager.

Fourth, the depletion of local resources brought on by population growth may increase the need for goods that cannot be produced locally but can be obtained in exchange for local goods. Trade can even out seasonal or annual shortfalls in production, and it can increase food production by making tools (e.g., axes) available in places poorly supplied with the raw materials for producing them. In both these ways trade in specialized goods increases the overall efficiency with which a population can be provisioned from limited resources, and thus the capacity to sustain a larger population on the same resource base, which is what intensification essentially is. But trade, especially long-distance trade, requires a knowledgeable head trader who can make decisions binding the trading group. And this, too, is an opportunity for control.

Production risk, then, is countered with risk management arrangements; resource competition leads to the formation of alliances to defend resources; inefficient resource use is corrected by group contributions to larger scale technologies; and resource deficiencies are made up by trade. These responses to intensification are open to individual families only in partial and limited ways. They require larger, integrated groups with leaders, and these come into being. The problems of intensification are solved, but population inevitably presses against resources. Technological responses continually present themselves, and the process is iterated up the spiral to the development of the nation-state.

The Evolutionary Typology

Nineteenth-century evolutionists tended to classify their evolutionary stages in technological terms: Stone Age, Bronze Age, Iron Age. As knowledge of the complexity of economic systems grew, these technological labels gave way to more generic terms such as hunter-gatherer, horticulturalist, and pastoralist, which indicate broad economic systems rather than single features of technology. But anthropologists are no longer comfortable with typology that lumps together such divergent groups as the !Kung and the Northwest Coast Indians as hunter-gatherers, the Machiguenga and the Mae Enga as horticulturalists, and the Turkana and the Basseri as pastoralists.

Following Service (1962) and Fried (1967), we have chosen more global designations based on the social and political organization of the economy. We have identified three critical levels of socioeconomic integration as a basis for organizing our discussion in this book: (a) the Family-Level Group, including the family/camp and the family/hamlet; (b) the Local Group, including the acephalous local group and the Big Man collectivity; and (c) the Regional Polity, including the chiefdom and the state.

The Family-Level Group. The family or hearth group is the primary subsistence group. It is capable of great self-sufficiency but moves in and out of extended family camps or hamlets opportunistically as problems or opportunities arise.

The family/camp is characteristic of foraging societies of low density (less than one person per ten square miles). Camp groups of twenty-five to fifty persons typically form when resources are highly localized or when a group larger than the individual family is required for risk management or for a particular subsistence activity. The group can then dissolve into small segments consisting of single families (five to eight persons) that independently exploit low-density, dispersed resources. These societies are characterized by a simple division of labor by sex. Suprafamily leadership is ephemeral and context-specific, relating to immediate organizational requirements such as a hunting expedition requiring the participation of numerous families. Although homicide is fairly common, organized aggression (warfare) is not. Ceremonialism is ad hoc and little developed. A camp characteristically has a home range but does not claim exclusive access to this territory or strictly defend it against outsiders.

The family/hamlet is characteristic of somewhat higher density societies (from one person per ten square miles to two per square mile) in which families cluster into a settlement group or hamlet (twenty-five to thirty-five persons) on a more permanent basis. The subsistence economy continues to rely heavily on wild foods, sometimes in conjunction with the beginnings of horticulture or herding. Storage is more prevalent. During the year individuals or families move out to exploit specific resources; from year to year, the hamlet re-forms and fragments as households change locations to minimize resource procurement costs.

The hamlet does not form a clearly demarcated political group, and leadership continues to be context-specific and minimal. Ceremonialism is little developed. As with the family/camp, the hamlet's territory consists of undefended home ranges, and warfare is uncommon.

The Local Group. Local groups of many families, running to five or ten times the size of family-level groups, form around some common interest such as defense or food storage. They are usually subdivided along kinship lines into corporate lineages or clans. Depending on the extent of their common interests, these groups are either acephalous, village-sized units or larger groups integrated by regional networks of exchange headed by Big Men.

The acephalous local group is typically found in societies with densities greater than one person per square mile. The subsistence economy in most cases focuses on domesticated species, although in some cases wild resources, especially maritime resources, dominate. A frequent settlement pattern is a village of perhaps one hundred to two hundred people subdivided into clan or lineage segments of hamlet size (i.e., twenty-five to thirty-five persons). The local group forms a ritually integrated political group and may have a headman; but it typically fragments into its constituent kin groupings either seasonally or periodically as a result of internal disputes. Because of endemic warfare intercommunity relationships of various sorts are critically important for community security, but such relationships are contracted essentially on an individual, family-by-family basis. Ceremonialism is important for publicly defining groups and their interrelationships. Resources are held exclusively by kin groups, and territorial defense is common.

The Big Man and his managed intergroup collectivity are found at higher but variable population densities in areas in which warfare between territorial groups has traditionally been intense. Subsistence is focused heavily on agriculture, pastoralism, or extremely productive natural resources. The local community of perhaps three hundred to five hundred people is a territorial division, typically containing multiple clan or lineage segments that either live together in a village or are dispersed throughout the well-defined territory of the group. The local group is represented by a Big Man, a strong, charismatic leader who is essential for maintaining internal group cohesion and for negotiating intergroup alliances. The Big Man is also important in risk management, trade, and internal dispute settlement, and represents his group in the major ceremonies that coordinate and formalize intergroup relationships. His power, however, is dependent on his personal initiative; if his followers desert him for a competitor, little may be left of the reputation he has tried to build for himself and his local group, or of the alliances he has contracted.

The Regional Polity. Regional organizations arise out of formerly fragmented local groups under conditions we shall examine in detail. Depending on the scale of integration, these are either chiefdoms or states.

Chiefdoms develop in societies in which warfare between groups is endemic but becomes directed toward conquest and incorporation rather than toward the exclusion of defeated groups from their land. The subsistence economy is similar to that of a Big Man collectivity and requires similar management. Economic strategies, however, notably irrigation agriculture and external trade, provide opportunities for elite investment and control, which are used to extract surplus production from the subsistence economy to finance the chiefdom's operations. As the regional integration of the polity proceeds, clearly defined offices of leadership emerge at the local and regional levels and are occupied by members of a hereditary elite.

Always in search of new sources of revenue, chiefs seek to expand their territorial control by conquest. Here a typical cyclical pattern is found, as local communities and thousands of people incorporate under the control of an effective chief only to fragment at his death into constituent communities. Competition is intense, both within a chiefdom for political office and between chiefdoms for the control of revenue-producing resources. Ceremonies legitimize the leadership and control of the ruling elite.

The development of states and empires involves the extension of political domination, usually by conquest, to a still larger area. States formed by conquest may incorporate vast populations, often in the millions, that are ethnically and economically diverse. As in chiefdoms, elites carefully manage the economy in order to maximize surplus production that may be translated into power and political survival. Elite ownership of resources and technology is typically formalized in a system of legal property. National and regional institutions are developed—an army, a bureaucracy, a law-enforcement system—to handle the state's increasingly complex functions. Ceremonies mark significant phases in the annual economic round and legitimize unequal access to resources.

Quantity into Quality: The Emergence of New Social Forms. So far our emphasis has been on gradual, quantitative change, but in the chapters to follow we will address the difficult problem of qualitative change in the creation of new social institutions. In the evolution of social complexity a critical change occurs when it becomes necessary to integrate formerly autonomous or separate units (cf. Steward 1955). As Service (1962) has argued, larger sociopolitical units cannot be formed unless new integrating mechanisms arise that inhibit their segmentation into their component smaller units.

Mechanically, it appears that new integrative institutions such as the village or chiefdom are formed by "promotion" (Flannery 1972): from among the original autonomous units, one becomes dominant and subordinates the others. For example, in Polynesia a single local lineage may expand by conquest to form a regional chiefdom. The chiefdom is at first organized by the kinship principles formerly governing the local lineage, but its new regional functions inexorably lead to changes in this mode of organization. Kinship-based forms and institutions gradually give way to novel, more bureaucratic institutions designed to solve the problems of integrating society on a much larger scale.

Anthropologists in the past have insufficiently stressed the dynamic nature of evolutionary change, probably because the convenience of "stage" typologies has led them to ask simple questions of origin such as, What caused the evolution of chiefdoms? As this book will demonstrate, chiefdoms are not suddenly created and cannot be explained as direct outcomes of some single condition. Rather, any such complex social form evolves gradually, responding to quantitative change in the variables of intensification, integration, and stratification. A new level of integration may not represent a significant qualitative change if it is not accompanied by changes in these underlying variables; it may be only weakly formed and subject to fragmentation, like the Heian empire of medieval Japan (Chapter 12). In our view, it is more important to understand how a new level of integration is achieved and stabilized than to answer any simple question of origins; and that will be our task in this book.

The Plan of the Book

This book is organized into three parts corresponding to our three critical levels of sociocultural integration: the Family-Level Group, the

TABLE 1

Cases Examined in the Book

Socioeconomic level	Chapter	Case	Area
FAMILY GROUP			
Without domestication	3	1. Shoshone, Great Basin	North America
		2. !Kung, Kalahari Desert	Africa
With domestication	4	3. Machiguenga, Peruvian Amazon	South America
		4. Nganasan, Northern Siberia	Asia
LOCAL GROUP			
Acephalous local group	6	5. Yanomamo, Venezuelan Highlands	South America
	7	6. Eskimos, North Slope of Alaska	North America
		7. Tsembaga Maring, Central New Guinea	Australasia
		8. Turkana, Kenya	Africa
Big Man collectivity	8	9. Indians of the Northwest Coast	North America
		10. Central Enga, Highland New Guinea	Australasia
		11. Kirghiz, Northeastern Afghanistan	Asia
REGIONAL POLITY			
Chiefdom	10	12. Trobriand Islanders	Oceania
	11	13. Hawaiian Islanders	Oceania
		14. Basseri, Iran	Asia
Early state	12	15. Medieval France and Japan	Europe/Asia
		16. Inka Empire	South America
Nation-state (peasant economy)	13	17. Boa Ventura sharecroppers, Northeast Brazil	South America
		18. Taitou villagers, Northeast China	Asia
		19. Kali Loro villagers, Central Java	Asia

Local Group, and the Regional Polity. Table 1 identifies the ethnographic cases we discuss and their level of integration. It is only by the careful examination of these cases, together with such archaeological evidence as we have for prehistoric times, that we can begin to understand the evolution of the political economy. It is here that a unilinear theory of universal stages of development can be fruitfully combined with a multilinear theory of alternative lines of development arising from unique environmental and historical conditions.

Part I

The Family-Level Group

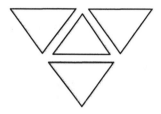

The Family Level

FAMILY-LEVEL ORGANIZATION is an elemental form of human society. A typical group has around twenty-five members coresidential as a
camp or hamlet of perhaps five nuclear or minimally extended families.
The key relationships are biocultural—parent-child, husband-wife, and
siblings. A forager camp is like a grown-up family, including older siblings, their spouses, and their children. Individuals can move between
camps, joining small groups in which they have close relatives.

The biological family of parents and children organizes many basic
complementary activities—eating together, cooperating, and sharing.
Men often assist each other and like to sit apart, engaged in male activities. Women come together for mutual help and company. Children
play and work as friends and competitors. Relationships are personal
and intimate. Each family maintains a broad network of relationships
that loosely binds the small camps or hamlets of a region, allowing easy
movement and flexible association within and between settlements.

Anthropologists have been slow to acknowledge the family level as a
distinct type of human society. We take for granted that families,
households, and kindred groups are fundamental economic units. Yet
we think of families, even in nonstratified societies, as subordinate to
larger social institutions. In the past, anthropological portrayals of the
"primitive" tended to focus on societies with more developed social
structures, such as corporate kin groups, ranked political systems, and
ceremonial associations. This focus has too often caused us to describe
family-level societies in terms of what they "lack," as though they ex-
hibited a regrettable failure to achieve respectable size and institutional
sophistication (e.g., Evans-Pritchard 1940: 262; Holmberg 1969: 124–
60). Even Steward (1955: 120), whose account of the Shoshone (Case 1)
did the most to clarify the concept of the family-level society, considered them to be "typologically unique" and denied their theoretical

significance in prehistory. Service (1962: 64–66) denied the existence of the family level altogether, except in isolated instances of modern contact and social breakdown.

Yet Steward's analysis of the family-level Shoshone remains valid for many foraging societies—some with domestication—that exist today, and for many others known only through the prehistoric record. Steward was right to identify a pattern of scattered populations seeking locally variable resources that consist of wild vegetable foods and a few animals. And he was right that in these situations a family, by which he meant a nuclear family augmented by a few close relatives, could be largely self-sufficient and not permanently subordinate to a stable multifamily group (Steward 1955: 102).

The striking characteristic of family-level societies is their freedom from formal institutions above the family. Rather than mistake this for a deficiency, we should regard the flexible rules of the family level as a natural adaptive consequence of the specific dynamics of low-density foragers. Family-level economies depend on being able to get and use resources opportunistically. Access to the life-sustaining bounty of the land must be but little restricted, and the labor and technology to realize that bounty must be available to all families. In economic terms, the primary factors of production—land, labor, and capital—must be held by the family. As we will see in later chapters, only with the erosion of the family's independent access to the means of production do we see the formation of broader-scale institutions.

We must be sure, however, not to overdraw the unstructured character of the family level. As fully cultural as any human community, family-level societies abound in structures that regulate access to resources, patterns of production, the distribution of food, and economic relationships beyond the family. Typical of these are rules governing the sexual division of labor and interpersonal sharing. These are not so much formal principles as common understandings concerning the proper spheres of activity for women and men and the proper support for one's kin and friends. A violation is not a crime but an embarrassment; the violator is less likely to be physically punished than teased and ridiculed. The structural basis of these rules is so deep and enduring that men and women rarely perform the same task: even in a common pursuit like food-gathering, they tend to divide the tasks into male and female activities rather than blur the gender distinction. And, when an animal is killed, a set pattern of meat distribution is expected to follow. The social organization of the economy, flexible and individualistic though it is, constrains behavior powerfully and pervasively through cultural understandings of what is respectful, proper, and courageous.

Following the culture-core checklist of eight variables (see Chapter 1), we summarize the main characteristics of family-level societies:

1. *The Environment*, for modern cases, is marginal for intensive subsistence strategies. Resources are characteristically scattered, unproductive, and highly variable. In prehistory, and under some situations down to the ethnographic present, foragers existed in much richer environments. As long as human population densities were quite low and the focus of the economy was on plants, a family-level society probably continued; as population densities climbed, more complex institutions became necessary.

2. *Population* density is low, usually well below one person per square mile. Causes of low population density can include recent settlement, low fertility resulting from subsistence activities, or—less commonly—high mortality resulting from disease.

3. *Technology* consists of personal tools, such as the ubiquitous digging stick and bow and arrow, that are used individually to procure and process food and raw materials. By and large the technology of gathering and horticulture is less complicated than that for hunting, and thus more easily procured and used within the family context (Oswalt 1976).

4. *Social organization of production* is familistic and informal. Bilateral, flexible kinship allows small groups to form and disband. The sexual division of labor organizes production within families, and reciprocity between families helps solve problems of daily unpredictability, especially in the hunt. Individual families can be more self-sufficient where and when plant foods predominate. Within camps and hamlets, friendships form between individuals of the same sex and similar age, who are drawn together for cooperation and company.

5. *Warfare and territoriality* are virtually nonexistent. The primary mechanism for exclusion is social; to use a resource, a person must be networked by kin or other ties to members of the local camp. The scarcity and unpredictability of resources favors open reciprocal access such that families can move to more promising areas whenever they need to. Personal hostilities, especially among men, can result in impulsive homicides when aggressions flare over women or other issues, but aggression is discouraged so as to maintain an extensive network of relationships. Since home bases are large relative to population numbers, intergroup confrontations over exclusive access are uncommon. The defense of territory is difficult, if not simply impractical.

6. *Political integration* is minimal and not institutionalized. At most there is some group cultural identity, but flexibility of association—opportunistic coming together and moving apart—pervade relations among families.

7. *Stratification* is absent in any meaningful sense of the word. To possess more in wealth or resources is to be required to share more with others. Leadership occurs for the moments when needed to provide direction, then evaporates, as with the Shoshone rabbit bosses. Differences in skill, while widely known and acknowledged, do not confer power over others, although they may lead to some advantages in procuring food or mates.

8. *Sanctity* is largely confined to shamanistic practices aimed at the health and well-being of the family: curative rituals, hunting magic, and the like. Shamans may acquire some local aura of power that others view ambivalently as both beneficial and threatening, but shamans' reputations rise and fall over time. They tend not to preside over elaborate communal rituals. The occasional ad hoc ceremonies that accompany resource windfalls are not distinctively ritualistic or sacred occasions.

In the family-level society, pragmatic considerations are paramount. People procure food, move, form groups, and perform ceremonies according to perceived benefits and necessities. Particularly striking, as our cases will show, is how households pragmatically divide the world of work into men's and women's spheres. Nearly always, men do the hunting, building, and heavy hauling. Women gather wild plant foods, process food for meals and storage, make clothing, and raise children. This division of tasks makes for a strong interdependency between husbands and wives: each is incomplete alone, and need for the other is so strong and immediate that gender relations tend to be egalitarian, founded on respect for what each brings to the partnership.

At the family level, the first and foremost consideration is the need to minimize risk—this results in an eclectic diet, an extensive network of kin and friendship ties, and the opportunistic aggregation and dispersion of camps and hamlets. This description constitutes a basic model for the economy and social organization of most low-density foragers that rely on gathering and often hunting. And the pattern can continue for groups using domesticated plants and animals. The incorporation of domesticates does not itself result in the settling and domestication of humans: horticulturalists can live independently in small family groups; tending herds of domesticated animals requires such opportunistic mobility that, even in the more complex societies that we will examine later in this book, herders fiercely resist control and revert to small familistic groups whenever possible.

In Search of Undomesticated Humans

The search for the primitive has been a long-lasting concern of anthropologists. We seek to know the depth of our history and to document our extraordinary achievements across time and space. The Cultural Revolution was the first profound change in human history, taking place well before forty thousand years ago. An outcome of natural selection, the evolution of humans came to include a capacity for culture—creating technologies, languages, understandings, and ordered interpersonal relations. While many animals have the ability to make tools (from spider webs to bird nests to the chimpanzee's termite stick), the flexibility in the human capacity to fashion new technologies is remarkable, as are human capacities for perception, decision-making, and sociability.

We have little direct archaeological evidence for the emergence of these first human societies, however, and we cannot find the past in societies that ethnographers study today. These living societies exist in modern worlds and each has a cultural history as deep as our own. Still, although primitive societies of our past cannot be discovered living isolated in some dark forest, remote island, or barren desert, we may accept a universalistic assumption about humans that allows us to understand the past in conjunction with available archaeological evidence, namely that *the processes operating in the present apply also to the past to the degree that conditions were the same then as now.*

For example, geologists know that the Pleistocene is a prehistoric moment long past, but similar conditions of ice formation and movement exist today that may be used to model features of the Ice Age. Many aspects of the modern world, such as industrial technology and international trade, are certainly novel, but, where these features have a limited presence and conditions of environment, technology, and economy are similar to those that held in the past, we can expect to observe similar challenges and similar solutions.

By at least one hundred thousand years ago modern human physiology had evolved from earlier hominid forms, and it is reasonable to assume that human behavioral characteristics were already largely in place. Archaeological evidence certainly suggests that by forty thousand years ago humans were modern in all physiological senses. Human cognitive abilities for language, symbolism, and abstract thought are shared across all human populations, some isolated from each other for tens of thousands of years. These capabilities, which are themselves products of long evolutionary histories, constitute a human nature shared by people modern and ancient. People may have very different cultures, but the bases of their thoughts and emotions are equivalent to our own. The search for the primitive is a tour into ourselves—a search for human nature.

To understand the workings of humans, we can look to the contexts under which we evolved—the one hundred thousand years or so that humans existed as foragers before the domestication of plants, animals, and ourselves. Foragers have complex knowledge of their world and effective and often quite complicated technologies. In a recent review of the ethnography of foraging societies, Kelly (1995) stresses their variability. There is no single foraging mode of production, no foraging means of organization, no forager technology. Yet the variation is anything but haphazard or infinitely variable. Being pragmatic, humans share a certain rationality that allows them to survive and prosper under extraordinarily different situations. It was this pragmatism, consciousness, and creativity that allowed humans to recognize the opportunities in vastly different environments, to develop cultural means to live in them, and to colonize the world.

The "domesticated" humans we will discuss later—tied to narrow locales, surrounded by restrictions on access to mates and resources, subject to domination backed by force—contrast with the organizationally elemental foragers of the family level. The latter differ not in a lack of capacity to develop but in a preference to live without the burdens of institutional elaboration: no large villages, no hierarchies of power. It is under these conditions that humans most likely existed through much of prehistory, and it is on these conditions that all that came later—the possibilities, promises, and problems of human civilization—is grounded. We seek the primitive, or perhaps better, the real human, at the family level, and we see the dynamic of that world, now largely lost, as underlying all later human achievements.

Theorizing the Family-Level Society

Our biological drives for survival and reproduction place humankind firmly in the animal kingdom. The family-level society forces us to recognize this kinship, especially with the great apes. Perhaps that is one reason why some anthropologists have neglected the theoretical importance of this level of sociocultural integration. But from the early

Stone Age humans created tools in formalized and repetitive ways that document an early capacity for culture, a strategic capacity to create a partly manufactured world. Somewhere along the line this was augmented by a capacity for self-reflection and creativity that must go back at least for tens of thousands of years. As Boas insisted, all humans are equal in their capacity for culture, at least in the sense that intelligence and creativity are distributed throughout any human community in roughly equal proportions. Almost certainly, somewhere early in the evolution of culture, a set of immensely powerful and generative cultural practices emerged from the evolving capacities for trust, sharing, and reciprocity that form the basis of social relations at the family level.

Reciprocity

Even at the family level, the human capacity to build social relations through exchange is remarkable and unique compared with that of the great apes and other animals. The nuclear family itself depends on the unparalleled willingness of the human father to share food with his own mate and offspring, and that in turn is made possible by the mother's acceptance of cultural rules requiring her to be sexually faithful to her husband. This simple but profound reciprocity, which increases the food supply for mother and offspring in exchange for the father's (more or less) exclusive reproduction rights in his mate, is a human universal with rare exceptions.

A man's willingness to provision his wife and her offspring—which is costly to himself—depends on his trust that he is the father of her children. As elemental as that trust is, it is evidently beyond the capacity of our closest primate relatives; indeed, it is not an entirely easy achievement for humans. Yet human social life even at the family level is based on relationships of trust that go well beyond the nuclear family, using the combined power of exchange and symbolic reinforcers to construct lasting ties of mutual aid between comparatively large numbers of individuals.

In *The Gift*, Mauss (1967 [1925]) showed how humans use a highly structured set of understandings about reciprocity to build the trust that underpins reliable give-and-take relationships between relatives and friends. Although Mauss believed his analysis to apply primarily to gifts between social groups, he did in fact accurately describe how individuals in family-level societies also build enduring ties through *prestations*—gifts that, although they may be presented as having no strings attached, in fact carry with them implicit obligations.

The three main obligations associated with prestations are to repay, to receive, and to give. The first of these is most obvious and familiar: a gift creates an obligation to repay. A verbal "thank you" is a small effort to repay a gift, but the most common rule is that eventually something of equivalent value will be given back to reciprocate the gift. When this rule is broken, the likelihood of resentment grows (unless the relationship is inherently nurturant, like parent-infant), and a failure to reciprocate is a blow to the relationship. Although the deepest relationships will not necessarily be based on an explicit reckoning of "fair exchange," anyone who values a relationship must be careful to reciprocate gifts over time, or place the relationship at risk (Homans 1958).

Mauss's deeper contribution was to show us how the obligations of the gift go beyond mere repayment. The second obligation in a trusting relationship is to receive a gift when it is offered. Because to receive a gift is to accept the obligation to repay it, in receiving a gift we are in fact accepting a relationship with the donor. We could immediately repay the gift and thereby try to nip the relationship in the bud, but if we value the relationship we will first simply accept the gift that is offered and worry about repaying it at the appropriate time. To refuse to accept a gift, or to repay it immediately, is an insult to the donor, a rejection of the gesture of trust the gift embodies.

Finally, in a relationship of reciprocity, there is an obligation to give. This may be as simple as an obligation to be generous when one has resources—that is why so many friends and relatives show up when they learn of a hunter's good luck. Or it may be highly structured culturally, as with obligations to host a feast or bring ritual gifts. Just as in the case of the obligations to repay and receive, refusal to give when appropriate is a rejection and a blow to a relationship. Strong relationships, founded on many gifts given, received, and repaid, can survive a few such blows. But each rejection sets off ripples of discontent, and people are generally careful to repair the damage unless they have decided that the relationship in question is no longer worth the effort.

Reciprocity itself may be structured differently at different levels of social complexity. In his construction of substantivist economics, Polanyi (1957) described reciprocity as the form of economic relationship particularly characteristic of egalitarian societies. Being equals, people exchange goods and services with trusted friends and relations in the manner that Mauss described. As much as these exchanges may have economic content and functions, they remain social because in these marketless societies the economy is fundamentally social. Individuals may be born into families and preexisting networks of relationships, but as they mature they begin to create and maintain their own social worlds through reciprocity; they choose whom they trust by voting with their gifts. As discussed in Chapter 1, Polanyi saw the nature of

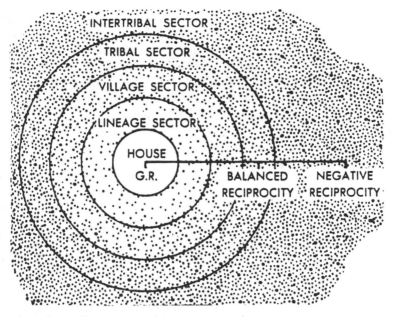

Fig. 4. Reciprocity and Social Distance (Source: Sahlins 1972)

exchange as determined by the social organization of the economy. We will encounter the patterns of exchange he called redistribution and exchange in later chapters dealing with more complex social orders.

Following Polanyi, Sahlins (1972) analyzed reciprocity as itself a complex behavior, differently structured according to the social distance of the individuals involved (Fig. 4). *Generalized reciprocity* tends to characterize the intimate relationships of the close family, reminiscent of the Marxist ethic, "From each according to his ability, to each according to his need." Here there is no strict accounting of payment and repayment. People share with each other to emphasize their sociability, help out in need, and bank against risk and uncertainty. By contrast, at a greater social distance, relationships tend to be structured by *balanced reciprocity*, requiring a greater sense of fair exchange. Those engaging in balanced reciprocity pay attention to the value of the back-and-forth exchanges and will complain of unfairness if they believe that the trades are becoming too one-sided. Among people with no social ties, the goal is likely to be *negative reciprocity*, a frankly exploitative effort to get as much as possible while giving as little as possible in return, even to the extremes of theft and thuggery. Whereas generalized and balanced reciprocity are used to create warm familistic and friendly ties, negative reciprocity characterizes social relations between strangers and enemies.

Mauss, Polanyi, and Sahlins all focused their arguments about reciprocity on more complex social institutions than those found at the family level, especially the corporate kin groups of the local group level. As substantivists, they tended to want to derive patterns of reciprocity from a preexisting social structure, whereas at the family level it makes more sense to turn this argument on its head: reciprocity does not derive from the existing social structure; rather, society is created and renewed by means of reciprocity in the effort to build the highly flexible, individual-centered networks that connect individuals to families, camps, and regional populations.

The family itself, based on a division of labor by age and sex, is organized by the principles of generalized reciprocity. The formal division of duties is a way to materialize that mutual support continuously. Within the camp or hamlet, aspects of economy require cooperation, either because of risk, as in the daily hunt of the !Kung (Case 2), or because of labor demands, as in the Shoshone rabbit drive (Case 1) and the Machiguenga fish poisoning (Case 3). Sharing creates a sense of common purpose; it is a mix of generalized and balanced reciprocity that effectively creates and maintains the camp or hamlet group. Outside the camp or hamlet, each individual establishes a broad personal network of regional ties (balanced reciprocal exchanges), such as the !Kung *hxaro* exchanges, which allow families to move across the land, find mates, trade for locally valued materials, and simply have fun in larger social gatherings.

Competitive and Cooperative Modes

If reciprocity allows us to understand how family-level society is built up, Steward's analysis (1955: 105–7) of the competitive aspect of family-level foraging allows us to understand the limits beyond which family-level society does not grow. Unless an economic basis for continued cooperation exists, two or more families living together simply get in each other's way by depleting locally available resources and competing with one another for the most convenient and desirable foods and raw materials. In that case, their natural tendency is to disperse in order to minimize interference.

The simple rule, with far-reaching implications, is that competitive forms of food procurement favor dispersion and cooperative forms favor aggregation. Steward's description (1938) of the settlement pattern of the Shoshone serves as a model of dispersion and aggregation at the family level. Over the course of the year, individual families move to position themselves close to the best foods of the season. In winter they live in small, multifamily groups close to the pine nuts gathered from highly productive groves and stored near water sources. When spring arrives, the families break out to live independently in the countryside. Larger groups form for short times to conduct such group activities as the rabbit drive. Groups form and dissolve through the year according to the availability of food and the specific requirements for obtaining it.

Steward's insight into Shoshone family-level organization has been reinforced by the research reported in the landmark *Man the Hunter* (Lee and DeVore 1968). That volume, which some have said might as readily have been entitled "Woman the Gatherer," showed that many foraging societies depend on wild plant resources and maintain a highly flexible organization. Seasonal aggregation and dispersion is also seen in the settlement pattern of foragers described archaeologically, with many small camps and a few larger base camps occupied for specific seasons. Binford (1980) sees this as the basic settlement pattern of a "forager strategy."

In family-level society, the nuclear or close-knit extended family is the basic economic unit in which most decisions about daily activities are made. Wolf (1966a) has pointed out that, in a broadly comparative frame of reference, the family economic unit (usually a household) is required to allocate a good portion of its total resources to separate "funds": caloric minimum, replacement, ceremonial, and rent. The caloric minimum fund covers the family's expenditure to meet its basic needs for nourishment, while the replacement fund includes expenditures for shelter, clothing, seed, tools, draft animals, and whatever else is "needed to replace . . . minimum equipment for both production and consumption" (Wolf 1966a: 6). Together, we will refer to these as the "subsistence fund." The ceremonial fund covers those expenditures, especially for food and drink, used to host social gatherings, and valuables used to build and maintain social relations through reciprocity. The fund of rent refers to expenditures to elites (landowners, nobles, priests, and other power-holders) in exchange for rights of access to the means of production.

In the family-level society, the subsistence fund is the most evident. The ceremonial fund involves small and occasional (ad hoc) feasting and gift-giving. The fund of rent can hardly be said to exist at this level, since the freedom and flexibility of the family level ensure all of access to resources, notwithstanding conflicts between individuals over particular resource sites. These emphases reflect the autonomy and self-sufficiency of the household at the family level. The family, as the decision-making clique in consultation with close kin and friends, must figure out how to supply the subsistence fund from day to day, planned through the year and into the future. Householding in this sense runs through all human societies and helps us understand some of the common processes as well as the individual character of human economies (Halperin 1994).

Nonetheless, the production, exchange, and use of primitive valuables plays a significant role in the emergent ceremonial fund at the family level. Our cases show that relationships between families both within and between camps are essential and that the network of these relationships is materialized though the exchange of objects. Primitive valuables like the ostrich-shell beads of the !Kung serve many purposes. Most directly, people decorate themselves with them. But of equal significance, the valuables carry social meaning: they tell of the cultural identity of individuals and their relationships within regional social networks. In some cases, the valuables also serve to store value, obtained by exchanging extra food and held for future need (compare Vayda's discussion [1967] of shell beads among the Pomo).

The Primary Dynamics of the Family-Level Economy and Society

Our challenge is to understand the dynamics of how decision-making among forager groups results in the variability described in the archaeological and ethnographic record. To do this we return to the basic model laid out in Chapter 1 (Fig. 3).

Humans at all levels of social complexity are highly intelligent and continually creative. Ever pragmatic, they will find and evaluate the costs and benefits of the full range of foods within an environment. Of course, some foods may remain unattainable pending development of such specific technology as fishing gear or domesticated seed. But history proves that necessity is the mother of invention where provisioning the family is concerned; in the long run, humans can be expected to develop the technology to get the job done.

Two key variables affect what the job is: the environment and the human population. The first variable, the environment, is created by physical and biological processes. Contrasting environments result from variable climate (especially rainfall and temperature), geology (topography and soils), and the biogeographical processes of animal and plant dispersal. Added to this are diverse anthropogenic changes to the environment. These include many intended changes, such as annual burning to encourage specific plant or animal species (common in many forager societies), the introduction of domesticates, and the modification of the environment to capture game or produce crops. Unintended consequences include potential degradation of the environment, as when easy game, like the flightless birds of New Zealand, are hunted to extinction. Among family-level societies, low population density and small-scale technology tend to minimize, but certainly not eliminate, anthropogenic changes. We will see these changes becoming increasingly significant in the evolution of more complex societies.

In the Pleistocene, human foragers colonized the world and confronted the extraordinary range of environments and potential foods. Human cultural creativity allowed our ancestors to live in vastly different conditions, from the wintry Arctic to lush tropical forests and barren steppes. Much of the economic and social variability found in human foragers is the result of their adaptive flexibility in the face of the full diversity of environmental circumstances they encountered and exploited (Kelly 1995).

As seen in the technodemographic model of Figure 3, intensification is the engine for change in the subsistence economy, as population growth and technological change chase each other. In a sense, given the extraordinary cultural creativity of humans, the surprise is how long it took for populations to grow (Cowgill 1980). We have come to recognize that humans regulate their reproductive capacity. In family-level societies, women determine how many children to have, spacing births to help guarantee the survival of their children and minimize their daily burdens. Such rational choices may well have maximized reproductive success under the conditions experienced by foragers and simple horticulturalists.

The press of population on resources over a long enough time span, however, ultimately called forth intensified exploitation of existing environments. As envisioned by Kelly (1995), intensification takes different lines channeled by the opportunities and constraints of specific environments and technologies. The most general process is the widening of the diet in the "broad spectrum revolution" that took place at the end of the Pleistocene. Across much of the globe human groups exploited a large variety of species, especially plants, to meet the needs of expanding populations (Earle 1980a). These societies probably looked much like the classic family-level foragers described in Chapter 3. Under some conditions, however, intensification could result in adding domesticated plant and animal species to broaden the diet while allowing family-level groups to continue on largely unchanged (e.g., Machiguenga [Case 3] and Nganasan [Case 4]). Eventually, problems posed by the need for further intensification to support still greater populations would require the creation of new institutions that organized people above the family level. These changes follow different lines in hunter-gatherer, farming, and pastoral economies, which can be traced through this volume.

THREE

Family-Level Foragers

STARTING OVER TWO MILLION years ago, human foragers spread throughout the world to occupy a remarkable diversity of environmental zones. The very long growth and dispersion of human hunters and gatherers served as the context for our biological evolution and as the foundation for all later cultural development. Foraging economies have the simplest form of subsistence production: gathering wild plants and hunting wild animals. Although these economies are quite variable, they have in common certain elements of resource use, technology, ownership, and organization. These shared elements define what Lee (1979: 117–19) calls a forager mode of production.

This forager mode of production is predicated on a low population density, characteristically less than one person per square mile. At low population densities foraging is probably the most efficient mode of production; it has typically prevailed until higher population densities made it impractical. As we have seen, the efficiency of a subsistence strategy is inversely related to its intensity; the more people there are out looking for wild yams or wild boars, the harder it is to find one. Where population densities are low, efficiency is high, and the relative attraction of domesticated agriculture or pastoralism is diminished.

At low densities, foragers have been called "the original affluent society" (Sahlins 1968a). Although this characterization downplays the seasonal and periodic hardships encountered by foragers, they do in fact live well in important ways. On the strength of data on the !Kung and on Australian aborigines, Sahlins argued that foragers' limited needs can be satisfied by a few days of work each week, leaving their remaining time free for noneconomic activities. A broad cross-cultural study by Hayden (1981a), which considers time spent processing food in addition to time spent procuring it, concludes that hunter-gatherers need expend only two to five hours per day in these activities.

In short, low-density foragers live a good life of sorts, and we feel that evolutionary change from this simple economy cannot be seen simply as a matter of developing improved technologies. Given that foraging efficiency depends on low-intensity resource use, why did population density remain very low for literally millions of years? Did people of those times not have a potential for rapid population growth and the technological capability to sustain that growth? The low growth rate in human populations during the foraging period must be explained if we are to understand the tempo and the causes of cultural evolution.

At least four biological and cultural factors associated with a foraging way of life combined to keep the population low. First, a chronic caloric deficiency lowers fertility; because of seasonal cycles in food availability and limited storage capabilities, periods of food shortage were common. Second, a long nursing period delays renewed ovulation; since most wild foods are apparently not well suited for weaning young infants, nursing among foragers typically remains a child's main food source for the first two or three years. Third, the intense physical exercise required for mobile foraging may lower female fertility (Frisch et al. 1980). Fourth, because closely spaced children are an economic hardship in a mobile society, infanticide may have been used to space births (Birdsell 1968a). Although these factors no doubt operate differently under different environmental conditions, the fertility of mobile groups is invariably low.

In addition, the law of the minimum, in the form of periodic disasters such as drought, can cause famine in foraging populations, cutting them down to a fraction of their "potential density"; at low growth rates, such a population would be slow to regain its numbers. According to Lee and DeVore (1968), the population densities of foragers are characteristically only 20 to 30 percent of average carrying capacity. Foragers must adapt to the worst conditions available seasonally and periodically, not the average conditions (Bartholomew and Birdsell 1953).

The efficiency of low-density foragers rests also on pragmatic decisions with regard to diet, technology, movement, and group affiliation. They are acutely cost-conscious, using only a portion of the available resources and varying their diet from place to place and from season to season to minimize their procurement costs and risks (cf. Reidhead 1980; Winterhalder and Smith 1981). The diet of many foragers, among them the Shoshone and the !Kung, emphasizes plants over animals because plant foods are more abundant. When game is abundant, by contrast, hunting is more efficient than gathering, and meat sources dominate the diet, as among the Eskimo. In his cross-cultural study of foragers, Kelly (1995: 71) concludes that "diets are clearly variable . . . being systematically related to a few simple environmental variables [such as effective temperature and primary productivity] that measure the gross abundance of terrestrial foods. . . . [H]unter-gatherer diets are the products of a decision-making process that takes the cost of acquiring resources into account, whether this means hunting, gathering, fishing, or exchanging for them."

The technology used in food procurement is characteristically personal. It is small-scale, generally available to all families, multipurpose, and portable. The power of the technology to transform the ecosystem is limited, and the availability of resources is not generally much altered by human exploitation. (Exceptions of course exist, such as the overhunting of some large game species, the overharvesting of sessile shellfish, and various uses of fire.) The technology, however, is certainly not simple in the sense of lacking intelligence. In fact, some of the most complicated traditional technologies were developed by foraging societies for hunting and fishing (Oswalt 1976). They are appropriate and often ingenious solutions to the problem of procuring resources at least cost.

Foragers follow a cyclical pattern of aggregation and dispersion that is responsive to the availability of food. When resources are uniformly distributed, the costs of exploiting them are uniform, and maximum efficiency is gained with a dispersed population that minimizes competition among individual foragers. When resources are concentrated in one or two areas, the costs of exploiting them increase with the exploiter's distance from those areas; in such cases efficiency is gained by groups coming together. Or, as we shall see in the Shoshone and !Kung cases, resource availability may change through the year, with the population coming together at one season to exploit the concentrated resources of that season, such as the pine nuts of the Shoshone, only to break up again when food resources become more generally available.

Anthropologists have offered various explanations of forager social organization (Hayden 1981a; Lee and DeVore 1968; Service 1962; Steward 1936, 1938; Williams 1974). In this book we interpret the family level of low-density foragers as an effective way to live under particular environmental and economic conditions. The key economic conditions required for a family-level economy are often encountered. Technology is personal. The division of labor is elemental (by age and sex), and the labor required in a procurement activity rarely extends beyond the family. With little territoriality and comparatively free movement of population through a region, necessary resources are available more or less directly to all households. This elemental level of organization is, however, always part of a more complex social system that binds families together into camps and regional networks.

As we argue throughout the book, the primary causes of group formation are risk management, technology, warfare, and trade. Among foragers, risk management is of critical importance and results in the formation of informal and flexible social ties between families. As we will see through the course of the book, foraging people are highly variable (Kelly 1995), and the evolutionary dynamics of foragers created a number of lines of evolutionary development reflecting the interrelated variables of environment, technology, warfare, and trade. As among the Eskimo (Case 6) and the Northwest Coast fishers (Case 9), the social responses to these factors are of a different nature from the social response to risk management, reflecting, as we shall argue, higher population densities and more intensive subsistence economies.

The critical problem of risk stems from two somewhat different economic conditions. First, and more general, is the risk associated with plant-gathering. On a daily basis gathering is quite predictable, since plants are sessile (immobile) and once located are available until harvested. On a year-to-year basis, by contrast, plant resources are unpredictable; an area that is good one year may fail utterly the next. To compensate for this variability the population must be mobile, moving from one location to another to exploit the best available opportunities. But in order to do this, families must maintain broad regional networks of relationships, often with exchange and intermarriage, that give them access both to information on where food may be found and to the home ranges of other groups. A flexibility in group composition and a lack of territorial exclusiveness underlie the basic foraging economy and its use of fluctuating wild resources.

Second is the risk associated with hunting. Hunting, unlike gathering, is unpredictable on a daily basis: the game sought by the hunter cannot always be found, and when found cannot always be killed. Any hunter has a good chance of coming home empty-handed, and the camp, consisting of a number of hunters, acts to average these high daily risks by sharing meat. Although the camp functions like the household in this regard, the sharing and cooperation are usually limited to meat and do not diminish the independence of the household, which can move from camp to camp.

By and large, the family level of organization is remarkably unstructured. Temporary social and economic rewards bring groups together only to have escalating procurement costs and social friction push them apart. Ceremonialism and leadership, two elements of group formation that we will track throughout the book, are ad hoc. They exist to resolve particular difficulties of group cohesion that occur only as long as the multifamily group is together. Both ceremonialism and leadership exist among foragers, but both are context-specific and comparatively unelaborated.

Where is the band, of which so much has been made (Service 1962; Williams 1974)? In search of the primitive, some scholars have described the band as the basic form of human social organization that evolved under conditions of foraging. In general, the band—a patrilocal group with exclusive rights to territory—appears often to be a construct of the anthropologist's search for structure in a simple society. The band in the sense of a camp certainly exists among foragers, especially where hunting requires a high degree of sharing. But the band as a territorially defined corporate group regulating marriages and resource use seems inappropriate to foragers, because it would restrict the flexibility of movement on which their survival depends. The Owens Valley Shoshone come close to being a band in this sense, but as we shall see, they depend on relatively rich and dependable resources. Most low-density foragers, however, are not territorial because they cannot afford to be.

In our view, it is unreasonable to identify a primitive form of social organization. Rather, like foraging itself, we expect early human social institutions to have been highly variable (cf. Kelly 1995). What is common to human societies is their malleability, the way in which humans form relationships appropriate to life's conditions. The family level of foragers dramatically illustrates the pragmatic nature of human society from which more complex, institutional forms are fashioned. The Shoshone and !Kung cases illustrate the similarities and differences among low-density foragers who rely on gathering. Then we return to the more general issue of the place of foragers in the evolution of the political economy.

Case 1. The Shoshone of the Great Basin

The Shoshonean groups of the American Great Basin were historically low-density foragers. As we shall see, the Shoshone were in fact organized at different levels of complexity that represent the spectrum of hunter-gatherer "types" as outlined by L. Binford (1980; D. H. Thomas 1983a). But before evaluating this interesting example of evolutionary development, let us examine the family-level foragers as originally described by Steward (1938).

The organization of these foragers was not formalized, with relations above the family being ad hoc, temporary, and minimal. Elemental family units of Shoshone came together and split apart according to the fluctuating availability of wild resources. Their organization of work and patterns of movement and association were adapted to exploiting sparse and unpredictable resources with a simple technology.

The Environment and the Economy

The Great Basin is dry, with rainfall at lower elevations typically less than ten inches a year, falling seasonally in the winter months as snow; the vegetation is sparse and xerophytic. Especially during the hot, dry summers, water is restricted to small springs along the bases of mountains and to the few permanent streams.

The topography of the Great Basin is broken, with elevations varying from valley floors at 3,900 feet up to towering mountains above 12,000 feet. Within the small home ranges of a local Shoshonean group, individuals had access to terrain with elevations varying by as much as 6,000 feet. Both rainfall and temperature are dependent upon elevation; for every 1,000 feet of elevation, mean rainfall increases about two inches and mean annual temperature drops about 3°F (D. H. Thomas 1972: 142).

This locally sharp variation in elevation and microclimate results in a vertical arrangement of microenvironments (Steward 1938: 14–18; Thompson 1983). Most important are the Basin Range Alpine Tundra (over 10,000 feet), the Limber and Bristlecone Pine zone (9,500 to 16,500 feet), the Sagebrush-Grass zone (7,500 to 10,000 feet), the Pinyon-juniper zone (4,900 to 7,500 feet), the Sagebrush zone (4,900 to 5,900 feet), and the Shadscale zone (3,900 to 4,900 feet). Distinct plant and animal resources are to be found within these different microenvironments. In the high forested zones are the economically important pine nut trees, a number of plants producing useful berries, roots, and seeds, and several hunted species, including deer, elk, and mountain sheep. In the drier, lower elevations are seed-producing grasses, edible roots, jackrabbit, and antelope, and fish in the permanent streams.

Seasonality is extreme in the Great Basin. Summers are hot and dry, with diurnal temperatures usually above 90°F (often above 100°F) and without significant rain. Winters are very cold and wet, with temperatures often below freezing all day (not unusually below 0°F) and with snow common, especially at the higher elevations. These dry summers and wet winters make conditions difficult for a technologically simple society.

The Shoshone's home environment is harsh. Resources are scarce, unavailable in the wild for much of the year, and unreliable from year to year. That foragers using a simple technology could survive here is a testament to their ingenuity. The population, subsistence economy, and social organization of the Shoshone are best understood as pragmatic solutions to the severe conditions.

Population density for the aboriginal foragers of the Great Basin was low, perhaps one person per sixteen square miles (Steward 1938: 48), with variations of from less than one person per forty square miles to one person per two square miles (ibid.: fig. 6). D. H. Thomas (1972: 140–41) finds a modest correlation between the population density of the Shoshone and annual rainfall, much as Birdsell (1953) had found for Australian foragers. But the basic factor limiting the population density of foragers such as the Shoshone was not rainfall so much as the availability of food.

The Shoshone were broad-spectrum foragers. The bulk of their diet was provided by plant foods such as nuts, seeds, roots, tubers, and berries. Insects, such as fly larvae and grasshoppers, were also collected, especially when they occurred in abundance, washed up along lake beaches. Most important, when available, were pine nuts, which were harvested in large quantities during a brief period in the fall and stored for consumption during the winter, when they were the main food to be had. Late winter and early spring were times of hardship, as stored foods ran out before new foods became available. Moreover, the pine nut crop is notoriously unreliable; the ripening cones are often damaged by wind, rain, and insect infestations, and harvests can be low. The severe seasonal famines recounted by Steward (1938) should caution us against any simple notion of forager affluence, especially where the availability of food varies seasonally and unpredictably.

Unlike most foragers, indeed perhaps unlike all others, the Shoshone made limited use of irrigation. In the Owens Valley, where population densities were unusually high, Steward (1930) reports that irrigation systems were developed to increase the yield and predictability of the grass seed harvest. As we shall see, the Owens Valley Shoshone illustrate certain aspects of intensification and social evolution in forager societies that foreshadow changes discussed in later chapters.

Hunting was important but secondary to the Shoshonean diet (Steward 1938: 33–44). Included were such large game as deer, mountain sheep, antelope, elk, and bison, and such small game as jackrabbits, rodents, and reptiles, as well as fish and insect larvae. Although the range of animal species appears quite extensive, meat made up a small portion of the total diet, probably less than 20 percent.

The technology included simple, portable items, such as digging sticks, seed beaters, baskets, and bows and arrows, that could be manufactured by each household. Most food procurement, including all gathering of plants and grubs and some hunting of game, required no cooperation beyond the individual household. Men hunted and built the structures needed by the family and camp. Women collected widely, for example often working in groups to beat seed from grasses into their carrying baskets. To collect pine nuts, men pulled down cones from the trees; the women picked them up and carried them to camp for storage and processing.

Warfare was rare or nonexistent, although raiding may have taken place in certain areas of higher population density such as the Owens Valley. Individual acts of violence occurred, but intergroup aggression was rare.

Trade certainly existed among the Shoshone, as among other foragers. Most important was the exchange of food for raw materials, such as obsidian, for which local substitutes were limited or unsatisfactory. The extensive trade in obsidian has been well described for aboriginal California foragers (Ericson 1977).

To summarize, Shoshonean foragers had to solve six major problems of production and reproduction. They had to collect sufficient quantities of low-density plant foods, which they supplemented with game. They had to cope with weather extremes and the serious risk of food failure. They had to develop appropriate mating patterns, and to find reliable ways of obtaining needed raw materials. As we shall argue, family-level organization with ad hoc group formation, leadership, and ceremonialism was the effective way of getting these things done.

Social Organization

By and large, gathering was an individual affair: although gatherers may work together for company, there is nothing inherent to the work that makes cooperation necessary. The daily risk is generally low. To be sure, resources such as the pine nut may vary from year to year, but within a year their availability is reasonably predictable once the status of the local crop has been ascertained.

Individual hunting was common, but group hunting was perhaps more important in terms of its contribution to the food supply. Cooperative hunting of jackrabbit, antelope, and mudhen took place irregularly in the open lower valleys. Rabbit drives were impressive undertakings, requiring the coordination of fairly large groups. Huge nets, similar in height to tennis nets but hundreds of feet long, were placed end to end in a large semicircle. Then men, women, children, and dogs beat the brush over a wide area and drove the animals toward the nets. The jackrabbits caught in the nets were clubbed to death. "Rabbit

bosses" provided the leadership needed for these drives—deciding
when and where to hold a drive, where to place the nets, and what job
to assign each of the participants.

Although much less frequent—perhaps only once every twelve
years—antelope drives were organized in a similar fashion. The animals were driven across a broad area into a funnel made of brush wings
up to a half mile long that led into a circular corral, where the herd was
impounded and slaughtered. An "antelope shaman" thought capable
of attracting the souls of the animals played a central role in coordinating the drive. These large-scale hunts sought to obliterate the local animal population in the interest of maximizing the immediate food supply; no attempt was made to save a breeding stock. A whole population
was destroyed, and antelope were not hunted again until they reached
numbers sufficient to justify another drive.

The most innovative part of Steward's work on the Shoshone (1938,
1955, 1977) was to show how the distribution and organization of
groups were adapted to environmental patterns and corresponding
problems of resource procurement. The annual movement of population responded to the seasonal cycle of resource availability. In the fall
families concentrated in the pine nut groves, where large harvests were
prepared for storage. In the winter, camps of some five to ten families
were established near both a spring and the pine nut groves. In the
springtime, as the temperatures warmed, families departed from the
monotonous life and monotonous diet of the winter camp and dispersed in search of new sources of food. Nuclear families moved to
higher and lower elevations and remained spread out through the
summer. The environmental verticality and seasonality made for a
pronouncedly patterned movement, often called a seasonal round.

Much of the year, then, the Shoshone moved as individual family
units consisting of a father, a mother, children, and often a son-in-law, a
grandparent, or some other closely related person. This unit, called
"kin clique" by Fowler (1966), corresponds to the elemental family of
Steward (1977). Each family was a separate economic and decision-
making unit.

During the fall and winter, camps of several family units formed
around common resources, but these camps of at most fifty people had
neither a sense of communal integration nor a group leader (Steward
1977). The reason for the winter camp was the proximity to water and
pine nuts, and the fact that winter was a time of potential scarcity when
it made sense to pool resources and average risks.

The weak development of the Shoshone camp as a suprafamily organization reflects the relatively minor importance of hunting, with its

pressures for cooperation and sharing between families. The irregular rabbit and antelope drives were a different matter, occasioning a periodic shift toward a considerably more complex social organization. A large group, probably consisting of upward of fifteen families (seventy-five or more people), gathered together for such a hunt, for which ad hoc leaders, the rabbit boss or antelope shaman, directed group activities.

On occasions of abundance, such as rabbit drives and unusually good nut harvests, many Shoshone families gathered for a fandango festival. As Steward (1938: 106–7) described, in reference to the Reese River Shoshone, the men from the assembled families hunted jackrabbits for five days, and at night all danced. The dancing was primarily for pleasure, and the festival was first and foremost a party; families who normally lived an isolated existence came together to enjoy each other's company, to dance, and to court. Although not a dominant element, ceremony was a part of this gathering. The round dance brought rain, and the recent dead were mourned.

The gaiety of the fandango marked a temporary suprafamily group that, in addition to its recreational pleasures, had a number of important economic functions (D. H. Thomas 1983a: 86). First, the gathering pooled labor from many families, without which the cooperative hunting of jackrabbits or antelope would have been impossible. Second, it made for the most effective possible use of the animals killed. Third, it facilitated the sharing of information about where food was to be found; that is, it radically reduced the costs of searching for food. Fourth, it served as an opportunity for trade in raw materials, such as obsidian, and for building a network of friendships through exchange. Fifth, it was an excellent time to find a husband or wife, not always easy given the prevalence of small groups, low population densities, and infrequent encounters.

The ad hoc ceremonialism of the Shoshone illustrates an important characteristic of dispersed forager populations. Although normally spread out as families to make optimal use of dispersed resources, occasionally the population must come together in suprafamily activities that benefit all. The ad hoc ceremonial, involving families from several winter camps, acts as a strong inducement to families to participate. As we shall see, the development of ceremonialism becomes pronounced as territories become more defined and defended. The ceremony is an official invitation to neighbors to enter a group's territory without undue fear of attack.

These infrequent but economically and socially important gatherings highlight three points. First, population aggregation among foragers depends on locally dense resources that are frequently ephemeral and unpredictable. Second, leadership solves specific problems of organizing the activities of such a group, but like the large group itself this leadership is ephemeral and context-specific. Third, festival activities are very much tied to seasonal and irregular patterns of resource availability that encourage larger groups to form for economic reasons.

Among the Shoshone, there was also an apparent absence of strongly demarcated territories. Although families owned pine nut trees and facilities such as irrigation ditches, hunting blinds, and corrals, group territories were in most cases vague (Steward 1977: 375–78). Rather, flexible and nonexclusive rights to use both plant and animal resources appear to have been characteristic. Steward (1933: 241) describes how pine nut territories could be shared, but that trespass was resented and could provoke a camp to stone intruders. Warfare was of minor importance and not organized in precontact times.

Steward's description of the pragmatic and flexible Shoshone forms the basis for our model of a family-level society in which ceremonialism, leadership, warfare, and territoriality are of little importance. Service (1962), by contrast, argued that the family-level Shoshone were simply ethnographic remnants of a society of suprafamily "bands" who had been driven into marginal habitats by groups using horses and guns. Only archaeology can decide which model best fits the prehistoric Shoshone, and it has. In the 1960's and 1970's, D. H. Thomas (1972, 1973) studied the archaeological settlement pattern for the Reese River Basin, a Shoshonean area of relatively sparse and unpredictable resources. Finding that this pattern fits closely the predictions of site location, frequency, and type derived from Steward's model, Thomas (1983b) concluded that the prehistoric Shoshone of the Reese River Basin were a family-level society.

Recent work by D. H. Thomas (1983a) and by Bettinger (1978, 1982) shows that different groups of Shoshone across the Great Basin organized themselves in different ways, ways that can best be seen as local adaptations to specific resource conditions (Thomas 1983a). At one end of the spectrum were the Kawich Mountain Shoshone, living at very low densities (one person per twenty square miles) in a region with restricted water and sparse and unpredictable resources. Storage was uncommon because there was little to store; for the same reason the population was highly mobile, with a flexible family-level organization and no territoriality. Rules about who was eligible to marry whom were also flexible. Groups formed only irregularly for hunting drives and short fandangos. At the other end of the spectrum were the Owens Valley Shoshone, living at much higher population densities (one person per two square miles) in a well-watered environment that produced, with the help of irrigation, a comparatively rich and predictable resource base with a storable pine nut harvest. Populations were fairly sedentary, and some groups stayed in one centrally located camp throughout much of the year. These Shoshone were territorial and organized into local groups. Marriage rules were less flexible and became an important aspect of intergroup relations. The fandangos in Owens Valley provided the important function of permitting access across defended boundaries to food, trade, and mates (Bettinger 1982).

The Shoshonean case thus illustrates two kinds of forager organization. A population of low density, resulting from sparse and unpredictable resources, is organized at the family level, with suprafamily organization largely informal and ad hoc. A population of higher density, resulting from richer and more dependable resources, is organized at a higher level, as a local group with a defined territory. Why? We will provide a more general answer in Chapter 5, but for now it is clear that in the case of the Shoshone, the rich, predictable resource base of the Owens Valley both permitted a suprafamily group to form and may have required that group, if it were to survive, to defend its resources against encroachment by other populations living in less favorable environments.

We now turn to the !Kung of the Kalahari, another family-level society, but one in which camps are more enduring. The importance of hunting and camp organization will be explored.

Case 2. The !Kung of the Kalahari

The !Kung of Southern Africa are our main ethnographic example of a forager society organized at the family level.* Although their lifestyle is a specific adaptation to local environmental and economic conditions, we chose them for detailed analysis because so much has been written about them, especially with regard to the ecological and economic variables of central concern to our approach. Lee's excellent ethnography (1979) is our basic source. Other valuable sources include Howell (1979); Leacock and Lee (1982); Lee and DeVore (1976); L. Marshall (1976); Silberbauer (1981); Wiessner (1977); and Yellen (1977). For the !Kung we have chosen as our ethnographic present the 1950s and early 1960s, when ethnographers recorded a foraging way of life. In a comparative study of the Khoisan people, Bernard (1992) emphasized

---

*The "!" in !Kung is a clicking sound that cannot be represented by a letter. Some other symbols of this sort are used in !Kung names in this chapter.

that they are quite variable and that the !Kung, although most studied, are not typical.

A lively debate (Denbow and Wilmsen 1986; Lee and Guenther 1991, 1995; Solway and Lee 1990; Wilmsen 1989; Wilmsen and Denbow 1990) has engulfed Khoisan studies. The central issue is the degree to which the ethnographic !Kung can be viewed as isolated groups useful for constructing models of forager societies that existed in prehistory. In his original work, Lee emphasized the isolation of the !Kung and believed that they provided the framework for modeling independent foraging economies and societies prior to agricultural expansion and colonial domination. Denbow and Wilmsen attacked this position, arguing that for two millennia the Khoisan had existed as part of a broad regional economy in which they served as client herders. While recognizing that !Kung traded with the outside, Lee argued that such trade was relatively minor and that the trade would not have transformed their society; Wilmsen and Denbow countered that Khoisan were part of Botswana's rural poor, and that their foraging economy was a response to peripheral and unstable ties to the world economy. In a recent review of the archaeological data, Sadr (1997) argues that the !Kung were hunters (not pastoralists) and that until recently they were not encapsulated into regional and world economies.

We consider the !Kung to have been largely independent foragers, whose ethnography can help explain the dynamics of family-level societies as already described for the Shoshone. Without historical ties, the !Kung and Shoshone are nonetheless similar in many elements of their culture cores, and differences between them can often be accounted for by contrasting environmental and economic conditions. Like the Shoshone, the !Kung are foragers dependent primarily on plant resources in a dry environment. Population densities are low, apparently limited by resource availability. Their family level of organization permits maximum flexibility in movement and in marriage, and suprafamily organization is informal and changeable. Territoriality, leadership, and ceremonialism are ad hoc and little developed, and warfare is nonexistent.

As in the Shoshone, we witness in the !Kung the basic pragmatism of a family-level society. Decisions on what to eat, where to move, what group to join, and when to leave it are made by the family on the basis of straightforward evaluations of benefits and costs. As a correlate, the "affluence" of the forager even under severe conditions is evident, with some reservations.

The !Kung, however, do not live as isolated families but are organized into camps of several families and joined by personal networks of exchange that interconnect families and their camps across broad regions. The importance of these suprafamily organizations in handling the daily risks of hunting and the longer-range risks of an unpredictable resource base shows clearly the limits to family independence.

The Environment and the Economy

The !Kung, the northern linguistic group of the Khoisan people, comprise over fifteen thousand people living in what are today the nations of Botswana, Namibia, and Angola (Lee 1979: 34–38). Our information is particularly rich for the Dobe area, which straddles the Botswana and Namibia border, where the traditional foragers have been studied in detail by the Kalahari Research Group (Lee and DeVore 1976).

The Kalahari desert is a large and dry basin thirty-three hundred to four thousand feet above sea level. The impression of this landscape is of an immense flatness (Lee 1979: 87). The underlying rock is covered by sand except for infrequent outcrops and eroded streambeds. The main topographic relief is provided by long, low dunes, separated by broad troughs that run parallel to each other through the region. The dunes, stabilized by vegetation, create an undulating surface from the dune crests to the lower interdune trough, or molapo. Coarser, bleached sands are found along the dune crests, and finer sand and silt are deposited along the molapo.

The seasonal cycle in the Kalahari is characterized by a dry and cool winter and a rainy and hot summer. The !Kung recognize five seasons based on differences in temperature and rainfall (Table 2). Bara is the time of plentiful resources, with rains and warm temperatures, and the abundance continues into ?Tobe as the landscape begins to dry out without rains. In !Gum, days are a comfortable 75 to 81°F and without rains; nights can become quite cool, however, with temperatures dropping close to or below freezing for about six weeks. Then in !Gaa temperatures rise rapidly, with many days above 93°F, and the continued lack of rain parches the landscape. With the first showers in !Huma, the land quickly greens and plant resources again become more available.

TABLE 2

!Kung Seasons

Bara	?Tobe	!Gum	!Gaa	!Huma
(summer)	(autumn)	(winter)	(early spring)	(late spring)
Dec.–Mar.	Apr.–May	June–Aug.	Sept.–Oct.	Oct.–Nov.
hot	cooling	cool	hot	hot
rainy	drying	very dry	dry	showers

A definite seasonality exists in the Kalahari, with times of resource scarcity, hot days, and cool nights. The extremes, however, are relatively mild, especially in comparison to the harshness of the Shoshone's environment. Wet does not combine with cold; and, except for a short period, heat is mitigated by rain.

From year to year, however, rainfall is variable, and dry years with poor plant yields are not infrequent. Lee (1979: 113) estimates mean annual rainfall at eighteen inches, varying from a low of eight inches to a high of almost thirty-six. A drought (less than fifteen inches) occurs two years in five, a severe drought (less than thirteen inches) one year in four. Additionally, rainfall patterns, especially in the spring, are localized and can result in a marked local variation in food supplies.

The environment is fully natural, being but minimally altered by the !Kung. The plant communities in the Kalahari are dominated by small trees, bushes, and grasses. Some regional differences in vegetation covary with rainfall and hydrologic patterns, but most correspond to different soil and water conditions (cf. Lee 1979: 97). In the loose and well-drained dune soils are sparse groves of broad-leaved trees like the mongongo (*Ricinodendron*); in the more compact and moister molapo soils are acacia trees and scrubs, with several important edible species.

Water is limited in the Kalahari. Permanent water sources are quite rare, restricted to rock fissures exposed in the dry streambeds. The Dobe area has nine permanent water holes (Lee 1979: 306); some areas like Nyae Nyae are better supplied (L. Marshall 1976: 64), but others like ?Kade are without permanent sources (Tanaka 1976: 100). Temporary water sources, existing for up to six months during the rainy summer, are found in the dry streambeds and molapo depressions. Additional water comes from small pools that collect in tree crotches following rain (Lee 1979: 94) and from plants (Tanaka 1976: 100–104, 114). For the !Kung, water is a limiting factor.

There are about a hundred edible plant species in the Dobe area, including some forty species producing usable roots and bulbs and thirty producing berries and fruits. Fruits, melons, and berries are found in the summer and fall, and most roots, nuts, and bulbs are found in the winter and spring. Most important in the Dobe area is the productive mongongo tree, valuable for its fruit and nut. The mongongo fruit is seasonal, but its interior nut remains available on the ground throughout the year.

The !Kung rely on plant foods for about 70 percent of their caloric intake. In the diet recorded in Dobe for July and August, plants provided 71 percent of total calories and 64 percent of total protein (Lee

1979: 271). These figures are even higher in ?Kade, where animals are scarcer (Tanaka 1976: 112).*

In Lee's summary description (1979: 98–102, 158), the total range of plant resources eaten by the !Kung is impressive. This broad diet, however, shows considerable selectivity and flexibility to minimize procurement costs and to respond to environmental variability in space and time. The remarkable mongongo stands alone for its superabundance, year-round availability, and high nutritional value. In the July–August diet recorded by Lee (1979: 271), the mongongo tree provided 82 percent of the plant calories.

Both Lee (1979: 167–72) and Tanaka (1976: 105) record a hierarchy of preferred foods. Species are ranked on the basis of procurement costs (overall abundance, spatial distribution, seasonality, and collecting difficulties) and of desirability (taste, perceived nutritional value, and side effects). For example, reflecting procurement costs, individuals preferred fruits to roots, and preferred roots found in soft, shallow soils to roots that are harder to dig out. Interestingly, the ranking in foods varies markedly by region. In Marshall's area, mongongo is rarer than in Dobe and is of secondary importance behind Tsin bean (*Bauhinia esculenta*). In ?Kade, where mongongo trees are absent, the nuts are not eaten (Tanaka 1976). Within the Dobe region the hierarchy of major and minor plants changes noticeably from water hole to water hole according to the availability of local species (Lee 1979: 176–80). In Lee's words (1979: 168), "[P]lant foods are evaluated pragmatically and rationally; few species are restricted by magicoreligious taboos."

Animals are also important in the diet of the !Kung. Over fifty mammalian species are recorded in the Dobe area, with various ungulates (notably kudu, wildebeest, and gemsbok) providing the most available biomass. The broken topography, however, restricts herd size to small groups or individual animals, and the scarcity of water limits animal populations. Animals are ranked by hunters on the basis of abundance and individual biomass (Lee 1979: 226–35); the most abundant ungulates are the most commonly killed. Other edible animals such as lizards, mice, ostriches, African buffalo, and elephant are avoided because of low individual biomass, poor taste, high level of danger, or high procurement cost.

As might be expected, land-use intensity varies inversely with distance from a permanent water source (Yellen and Lee 1976: 44). Lee

*It is important to remember that the /Gwi and //Gana of ?Kade are language groups different from the !Kung. Most of this case's information is drawn from studies of the !Kung.

(1979: 175) describes the process of how a !Kung camp "eats its way out" from the living base:

The !Kung typically occupy a campsite for a period of weeks and eat their way out of it. For instance, at a camp in the mongongo forest the members exhaust the nuts within a 1.5-km radius the first week of occupation, within a 3-km radius the second week, and within a 4.5-km radius the third week. The longer a group lives at a camp, the farther it must travel each day to get food. This feature of daily subsistence characterizes both summer and winter camps. For example, at the Dobe winter camp in June 1964 the gatherers were making daily round trips of nine to fourteen km to reach the mongongo groves. By August the daily round trips had increased to nineteen km.

This progressive increase in walking distance occurs because the !Kung are highly selective in their food habits. They do not eat all the food in a given area. They start by eating out the most desirable species, and when these are exhausted or depleted they turn to the less desirable species. Because plant food resources are both varied and abundant, in any situation where the desirable foods are scarce, the !Kung have two alternatives in food strategy: (1) they may walk further in order to eat the more desirable species or (2) they may remain closer to camp and exploit the less desirable species.

As the preferred mongongo continues to be exploited, it must be exploited at greater distances, which means increasing transport costs. As the costs of mongongo climb, people shift to less preferred but now relatively less costly alternatives.

Throughout the year the use of resources closely reflects seasonal availability and procurement costs. Mongongo, the least seasonal of all resources, is procured all year long, albeit with less frequency near the end of the dry season, when distance from the water hole increases costs. Other resources are used in a more seasonal pattern (Lee 1979: 188–90). During the wet season, when plants are most available, emphasis in the diet is on such easily procured resources as fruits, berries, and melons. Waterfowl and some migratory ungulates are also hunted. Then, during the dry season, when food is less available, the diet is broadened (Yellen and Lee 1976: 44, 45) to include higher-cost foods like roots and bulbs. As indicated in Chapter 1, the broadening of the diet under resource stress is predicted by our model of the subsistence economy.

From year to year changing rainfall and other environmental factors also determine the availability of resources, and by extension affect the dietary pattern of the !Kung. Lee (1979: 174) records a major shift in plant food hierarchies between two years of differing rainfall. Good years for a favored species result in decreasing procurement costs for that species and an increase in its use. Bad years cause significant broadening of the diet.

The annual movement of the !Kung population through the environment, as they gather around limited winter water and then disperse close to plant resources, is designed to minimize procurement costs (Fig. 5). In the Dobe region, for example, water distribution creates a pulsating pattern in population that Lee (1976; 1979: 103–4) has called a "dialectic" of concentration and dispersion. During the winter, the dry season, standing water is limited to a few permanent water holes around which the !Kung cluster. These base camps, such as the one at Dobe, can be quite large (accommodating perhaps thirty-five people in twelve huts) and are occupied for more than half the year. In the Kalahari there are many more camps than permanent water sources, so that several camps (from two to six) cluster around a single water hole (Lee 1976: 79). When the spring rains begin in October and November, the camps quickly disperse to temporary camps in the mongongo groves, where they use the water that collects in hollows in the trees. These camps are smaller (containing perhaps only ten people) and are occupied for only a few days each. As the seasonal pans fill up with summer rains, the population becomes maximally dispersed while remaining close to both water and resources. As autumn comes on, the pans begin to recede; the population falls back on the larger pans, and eventually on the permanent sources.

The goal is to maintain the maximum possible dispersal of camps consistent with the availability of water. This goal corresponds to the strategy of minimizing procurement costs in terms of movement to and from the camp, and is a further example of the settlement principle Steward described as "competitive" among the Shoshone. In addition to this annual pattern of movement, the distribution of the population responds to unpredictable changes in water sources under the drought conditions common to the Kalahari. The "permanent" water holes do not always retain water in dry years, and these sources can be ranked according to the severity of the drought necessary to dry them out. Under drought conditions, camps progressively aggregate around the more amply supplied sources. During one bad drought, for example, J. Marshall (1957: 36) found seven camps at one water hole. During such droughts whole areas in the Kalahari may be abandoned as the !Kung migrate in search of suitable water and food (Hitchcock 1978). This flexibility in movement is essential to the economy, which relies on social ties rather than storage for handling risk (Wiessner 1982).

The !Kung's diet and movement patterns illustrate the importance of cost considerations in deciding what resources to exploit and how to

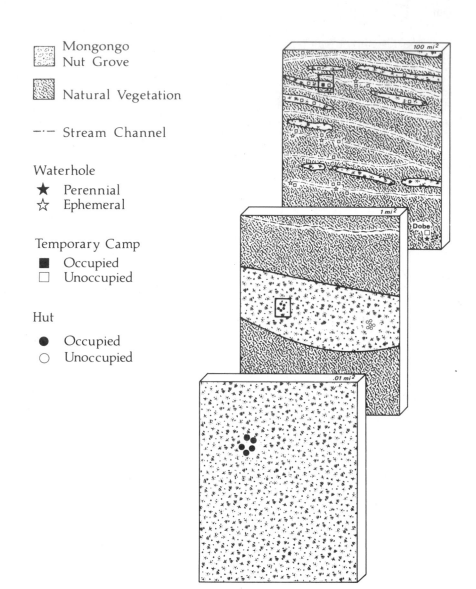

Mongongo
Nut Grove

Natural Vegetation

—·— Stream Channel

Waterhole
★ Perennial
☆ Ephemeral

Temporary Camp
■ Occupied
□ Unoccupied

Hut

● Occupied
○ Unoccupied

100 mi²

1 mi²

Dobe

.01 mi²

Fig. 5. Settlement Pattern of the !Kung. The base camp at Dobe is occupied for much of the dry season, but during the wet season camps scatter and sites are occupied for only a few days at a time.

exploit them. Their high selectivity and flexibility in space and time correspond to changing resource availability and procurement costs. Environmental conditions, because of their direct effect on procurement, determine in large measure the nature of the subsistence economy and related social and cultural characteristics. This close interrelationship between ecology, economy, and society, which is summed up in Steward's notion (1955) of "culture core," is central to our concerns in this book.

The regional population density of the northern Khoisan averages one person per ten square miles, varying from one per thirteen square miles in ?Kade to one per eight square miles in Dobe and one per 1.4 square miles in Nyae Nyae (Lee 1979; L. Marshall 1976: 18–19; Tanaka 1976: 1100).* As might be expected, the population density order roughly corresponds to the availability of permanent water sources for these areas (none in ?Kade, nine in Dobe, sixteen in Nyae Nyae). Population is not evenly distributed in a given area, but is highest within one day's travel of the permanent water sources. In Dobe this "economic density," as Lee calls it, is about one person per square mile (Lee 1979: 306).

What limits population to such low densities in a foraging society like the Khoisan? The obvious explanation is the scarcity of resources, and the correlation of population density with water availability seems to bear this out. Yet Sahlins (1968a) sees the !Kung as affluent, and Lee makes it clear that they rarely have trouble getting enough to eat. In a one-month study, Lee (1979: 271) estimated an individual's average daily intake at 2,355 calories and the average daily expenditure at 1,975. On the strength of those figures, obesity might be a bigger problem than starvation!

Perhaps instead of average scarcity, we should focus on periodic scarcity. The !Kung do not eat that much or expend that little every month of the year; if the year is taken as our unit, Wilmsen (1978) postulates a cycle of weight gain and loss of roughly five to ten pounds.† The diet, generally well balanced, may at times be calorie deficient (Truswell and Hansen 1976), with the result, according to Howell (1979), that fertility rates in !Kung women are low. This argument is based on more general work suggesting that a minimum level of body fat in females is necessary for fertile ovarian cycles (Frisch 1978). In addition, the periodic droughts cut the population back to levels well below average carrying capacity (cf. Hitchcock 1978).

---

*The relative order of these three !Kung regions is probably more accurate than the absolute figures, since there is no standard way of calculating population density.
†Lee (1979: 440–41) disagrees. See also the discussion in Konner 1982: 372–73.

Another factor limiting population growth in foragers such as the !Kung is long spacing between births. Lee (1979: 324) suggests that births were traditionally spaced about four years apart; with a relatively short reproductive period, population growth in these circumstances would thus have approached zero. Why was the spacing so long? Perhaps it was based on the mother's potential productivity as a gatherer. Lee speculates that because a !Kung woman carries her children under four years old with her as she moves about in her gathering tasks, her workload is greatly affected by the number and weight of children that she must carry. With a birth spacing of four years, a woman does not need to carry more than one child at a time. As spacing increases from two to three to four years, the maximum weight of children that must be carried decreases from forty-seven to forty-one to twenty-six pounds. Increasing the spacing of births decreases the workload of the mother; additionally, spacing children may actually increase the overall reproductive success of a woman, meaning that the increased effort of an additional child lowers the survival rates of all children (Blurton Jones and Sibly 1978).

Women may choose to limit births as one way of lowering their food procurement costs. How is this apparently desirable spacing maintained? Birdsell (1968a: 243) has suggested that infanticide may be used by foragers to space births, but !Kung women rarely practice infanticide: Howell (1979) records six cases out of 495 births. A more likely explanation, we think, is nutritional deficiencies, as discussed above. Another is the long nursing required by a lack of suitable weaning food (Konner and Worthman 1980; Lee 1979: 328). Both appear to inhibit ovulation and thus provide a biological mechanism to limit growth rates.

In short, then, we think that some combination of biological and economic factors, along with the occasional disastrous year, acted to keep the !Kung population low, and that this low population density allowed foraging to continue on the margins of pastoralism. However, by the 1920's, Herero pastoralists were already moving into the Dobe area (Soloway and Lee 1990), and by the latter part of the 1960's, expanding pastoralism created a strong demand for !Kung labor herding Herero cattle, whose numbers were degrading the ecosystem and its ability to support subsistence foragers. The !Kung have become settled herders, now certainly part of the broad regional economy of Botswana. But this is getting ahead of the story.

!Kung technology consists of a few multipurpose tools made from locally available materials (Lee 1979: 119). Included are the women's kaross (a treated animal skin used to carry foods and other materials), the digging stick used for procuring roots and bulbs, the man's bow

and arrow used for hunting, the general-purpose knife used for all cutting jobs, and the ostrich eggshell canteen. The tools typically are made
from natural materials that require little modification. For some time
scavenged or traded metal has been cold-hammered to the desired
form for arrowheads and knives, and trade goods such as pottery and
Western metal pans are becoming increasingly important. But the traditional tools of the !Kung were manufactured individually from local
materials for the maker's own use.

Unlike the Shoshone, the !Kung have no storage facilities for vegetable foods, presumably because unstored food is available in adequate
quantities throughout the year. (Although the !Kung also do not store
water for extended periods, the /Gwi are reported to bury several
hundred filled ostrich-eggshell canteens in preparation for the dry season [Lee 1979: 1231].)

For all its simplicity, !Kung technology is effective and often ingenious. For example, the light bow (with twenty-pound pull) is deadly
against even large game, thanks to the use of arrows tipped with a poison derived from the pupal form of chrysomelid beetles (Lee 1979: 133–
34). The arrow itself is an ingenious composite tool made from the stem
of a large perennial grass, a bone linking shaft, and a metal point ham-
mered into shape from a piece of fencing wire. Other effective implements include an iron-tipped hunting spear to finish off wounded animals, a 10-foot-long flexible wooden shaft with metal hook used to
catch sleeping springhares deep in their burrows, and baited rope
snares for smaller mammals and game birds.

E. M. Thomas (1959) titled her book about the /Twi Khoisan *The
Harmless People*. Warfare, in the sense of organized intergroup aggression, is not present among them, and outward signs of violence are discouraged. To be sure, homicide, especially between men in conflicts
over women, is not uncommon: anger swells, and poison arrows fly.
Such conflicts, however, are seen as disruptive, and the aggressors are
not supported. Lee (1984: 96) records the following dramatic scene:

/Twi had killed three other people, when the community, in a rare move of
unanimity, ambushed and fatally wounded him in full daylight. As he lay
dying, all the men fired at him with poisoned arrows until, in the words of
one informant, "he looked like a porcupine." Then, after he was dead, all the
women as well as the men approached his body and stabbed him with spears,
symbolically sharing the responsibility for his death.

Personal violence is not allowed to expand into intergroup conflict because of the overriding importance of intergroup ties; rather, disputes
are settled by separation.

Trade in special craft products, and now especially in Western goods, exists among the Khoisan, and, as in other foraging societies, probably existed on a small scale in prehistory (Lee 1979: 76). As with the Shoshone, frequent trading would not have been necessary because the range of objects used was limited and generally of long life. Nothing like economic specialization existed.

To summarize briefly, the major problems of production and reproduction facing the !Kung were remarkably similar to those facing the Shoshone. Like the Shoshone, they had to collect an adequate supply of low-density plant foods, which they supplemented by hunting dispersed and unpredictable game. Their problems of seasonality and possible food failure, if less extreme than those confronting the Shoshone, were broadly analogous, as were their needs for a reliable system of finding mates and a way of obtaining special craft goods by trade. Not surprisingly, the overall pattern of !Kung organization is very similar to the Shoshone pattern. The different role of hunting and its implication for camp organization is the main difference.

Social Organization

Among the !Kung, as in other simple subsistence economies, the family with its own shelter and hearth is the elemental economic and social unit. The individual or the family makes all basic economic decisions: what to collect, how to collect it, when to move, what group to join (cf. Yellen 1977). Goods are brought into the family by its members, who are involved in different procurement activities according to the sexual division of labor. Within the household, resources are pooled and shared out freely. Most plant foods eaten by the family are gathered by family members.

The organization of work among the !Kung is, like the technology, a simple and direct response to procurement problems. Most subsistence activities can be performed by individuals working separately. Women are the gatherers; they also do some manufacturing (e.g., of canteens), most food preparation, and all child care. Men are the hunters; they also do some gathering and considerable manufacturing, especially of materials used in hunting.

Gathering is usually done individually or in small groups (Lee 1979: 192–93; L. Marshall 1976: 98). Groups engage in parallel work, with no division of labor and no obvious gain in efficiency over lone procurement. In the mongongo nut harvest, for example, individuals go out in a group but each works a separate tree, and the roasting and cracking of nuts are done individually. Tasks are performed together but are not coordinated, except to establish a rhythm for the work.

In hunting, men also work singly or in small groups. Because there are no herds in the Kalahari, large hunting parties are impractical. A hunting party for large game consists of one to four men (Lee 1979: 211; L. Marshall 1976: 132). When an animal is spotted, a single hunter stalks it so as to minimize the chance of alarming it (Lee 1979: 217). The group of three or four is, however, important. As an animal is pursued, its tracks often become obscured and the hunting party fans out to pick up the trail. When the animal is spotted and a single hunter begins to stalk it, others position themselves at likely escape points to get a second shot. Once an animal has been mortally wounded, three to six people butcher it and carry the meat back to camp. This activity requires a co-operative work effort, because a single hunter cannot carry a large kill himself and without assistance would have to abandon edible meat to scavengers.

For the !Kung, even more so than for the Shoshone, an organization above the family level is essential for the family's survival. The two levels of suprafamily organization are the camp and the regional inter-family and intercamp network. Although these levels are highly flexible and informal, they are essential for handling problems of subsistence risk.

The camp is the basic local group, a noncorporate, bilaterally organized set of people who live together for at least part of the year. A camp settlement commonly has five or six small grass huts (about six feet across) that face onto a central space (Fig. 5). A hut houses a nuclear family, and a camp consists of several closely related families (Yellen 1976: fig. 4). In Lee's study (1979: 56–57), camp size ranged from nine to thirty persons. Camp groups, adding and losing members, move through the environment to position themselves close to critical resources. Sometimes, especially in winter, camps are close to each other, and the staccato sound of mongongo nut pounding (called !Gi speech) drifts from camp to camp. At other times the separate camps are spread out across the vast and empty landscape.

The upper limit on camp size is apparently set by internal disputes that fragment the camp, and by the higher subsistence costs associated with larger groups. (Larger groups eat up the resources in the immediate camp area more rapidly, resulting in rising foraging costs and more frequent moves.) The lower limit is established by the desire to maintain a ratio of producers to dependents of about three to two (Lee 1979: 67) and by the requirements of hunting.

Sharing, an important cultural value among the Khoisan seen most clearly in the distribution of meat from a large game kill (L. Marshall

1976), binds the camp together economically. According to Marshall's account, for example, the carcass belongs to the owner of the first arrow to wound the beast. Because of reciprocal exchanges of arrows among camp hunters, however, the owner of the arrow is often not the successful hunter (Lee 1979: 247). Meat from the kill is distributed by the owner to close and more distant relations within camp until everyone in camp has a share.

Broad sharing of meat handles two problems. First, it distributes food that could not possibly be eaten by a single family without storage; second, it averages the risks of unpredictable hunting so that all families get a share regardless of an individual hunter's success. Meat exchange eliminates what might otherwise be moments of intense envy and friction when one hunter's success is contrasted with another's failure. Hunting creates the need for an exchange-based group larger than the nuclear family and socializes it through generalized reciprocity.

Although the group is of great economic importance to the !Kung, its membership is not rigidly defined. People may affiliate with a camp through bilateral descent or marriage, so that a household can join any of several camps. Marriage rules are very flexible and help create a web of kin relations between camps. Visiting, which incurs a reciprocal obligation, is so common that the number of people in a camp varies from day to day. Individuals form broad networks of exchange (hxaro) that bind families and give access to a partner's camp and territory (Wiessner 1977, 1982). These regional networks, which permit a family and its camp to move comparatively freely in space, also permit rapid adjustments to changing economic opportunities across the !Kung landscape. They are central to the !Kung's adaptation to changes in resource availability (Lee 1976).

Regional networks are created when camps cluster together around the permanent water holes during the dry season. This is the time for ceremonies and intercamp activities. The dry season is a social time, and the whole tempo of life changes as population gathers. Lee (1979: 446–47) argues that this concentration of population offers strong social rewards in addition to economic ones, so strong in fact as to override the consideration that such aggregates may not be optimal for resource procurement in the short term. When several camps gather for all-night trance dancing and curing ceremonies, ties within and between camps are created and strengthened by such activities as marriage brokering, socializing, and exchange.

The concentration and dispersion dialectic described by Lee represents a very real and basic human ambivalence toward life in groups.

The self-sufficient individual and his family enjoy independence and an ability to control their own destiny. The group offers social rewards and critical economic assistance, but also limitations, frustrations, and personal conflict. The small social group of the camp has probably been necessary to the individual since earliest hominid times, satisfying as it does what Goldschmidt (1959) calls the "need for positive affect." The tension between family and group persists, but it is secondary to the group's manifest economic and social advantages. The group eventually fragments when resources are broadly distributed and predictable, only to come together again when resources are localized and uncertain.

The regional mobility of the !Kung requires a deemphasis on territoriality. Steward (1936: 334–35) described the !Kung as organized territorially into patrilineal bands, but the reinterpretation presented by Lee and his collaborators emphasizes nonexclusive access. A group's "home range" is simply the area it uses most frequently, an area that is not sharply bounded, is nonexclusive, and is not actively defended. (See DeVore's and Hall's description [1965] of a baboon group's home range.) Territoriality is not based on recognized boundaries but is focused on a key resource, which for the !Kung is the water hole.

The !Kung recognize a locality (*n!ore*) of roughly one hundred to two hundred square miles that is associated with a core group with long residence in the area (Lee 1979: 334):

Within a n!ore, the water hole itself and the area immediately around it is clearly owned by the Kausi group [a camp], and this ownership is passed from one generation to another as long as the descendants continue to live there. But this core area is surrounded by a broad belt of land that is shared with adjacent groups. In walking from one n!ore to another, I would often ask my companions, "Are we still in n!ore X or have we crossed over into n!ore Y?" They usually had a good deal of difficulty specifying which n!ore they were in, and two informants would often disagree.

Access to resources within the n!ore is said to be unrestricted for members of and visitors to the associated camp (Lee 1979: 335–36). A different camp must ask permission of the core group to use a n!ore's resources, especially its permanent water. This right apparently may be refused; if it is granted, the boon imposes a reciprocal obligation on the visiting camp. The general impression, however, is that access to resources is only minimally encumbered, and that individuals may gain access to resources either as visitors or as members of a requesting camp.

Yellen and Harpending (1972) have emphasized the lack of territoriality among the !Kung, which they see as inevitable in an unstable environment in which population must continually distribute itself according to variable resource yields. Although group ownership of land tracts is recognized, as is individual ownership of tools, harvested foods, and perhaps some natural resources, the low population density and minimal capital improvements that characterize !Kung existence appear not to require restricted access to land. In addition, to defend such a low-density resource as a !Kung land tract would almost surely cost more than the tract is worth. The Khoisan do not defend territory per se; rather, access to resources is controlled by reciprocal arrangements that exclude outsiders without social connections to the camp (Cashdan 1983).

To summarize, the !Kung camp has a fluid composition and no clearly demarcated corporate nature. Although the pervasive exchange of meat among camp members may give the camp the appearance of a clearly demarcated group, in many other aspects it is an opportunistic aggregation of independent households.

As this assessment suggests, the camp is largely without established leadership. Leadership is minimal and informal. Lee (1979: 343–44) summarizes the situation as follows:

In egalitarian societies such as the !Kung's, group activities unfold, plans are made, and decisions are arrived at—all apparently without a clear focus of authority or influence. Closer examination, however, reveals that patterns of leadership do exist. When a water hole is mentioned, a group living there is often referred to by the !Kung by a single man's or woman's name: for example, Bon!a's camp at Xangwa or Kxarun!a's camp at Bate. These individuals are often older people who have lived there the longest or who have married into the owner group, and who have some personal qualities worthy of note as a speaker, an arguer, a ritual specialist, or a hunter. In group discussions these people may speak out more than others, may be deferred to by others, and one gets the feeling that their opinions hold a bit more weight than the opinions of other discussants. Whatever their skills, !Kung leaders have no formal authority. They can only persuade, but never enforce their will on others.

To be sure, age and special skill confer respect, and a respected person's opinion carries weight when a decision must be made—for example, a decision to move camp. L. Marshall (1976: 133) notes that in a hunting party a recognized good hunter acts as an informal leader. However, when asking a !Kung elder about local leaders ("headmen"), Lee (1979: 348) was told: "Of course we have headmen! . . . In fact, we are all headmen. . . . Each one of us is headman over himself!" A repeatedly successful hunter is respected but can also be envied, and he will often stop hunting for a while rather than try to assert strong leadership over the group. Leadership appears to be largely specific to a context, such as an individual hunting party, and does not extend generally to camp affairs. Most decisions made by the group are made by consensus; they are largely informal and are reached through long discussion by all concerned (Silberbauer 1981).

The independent !Kung foragers, like the American Shoshone, now live in a world transformed by the encroachment of and incorporation by external societies and economies. For the !Kung, the expansion of Herero pastoralists created opportunities for employment that gave more access to foreign goods such as steel knives and copper pans, tobacco and coffee, glass beads and clothing. Expanding herds and herders also changed the environment by intensifying its use (grazing), making foraging increasingly difficult. The !Kung have settled down to work for the Herero and now depend on food from the herds and the outside. Tragically, their special skills, such as tracking, have made them valuable to the army, and their fame as a result of the successful movie *The Gods Must Be Crazy* made them another tourist attraction in the game park.

For cultures without historical ties and at opposite ends of the earth, the Shoshone and !Kung are remarkably similar. In both cases aridity and environmental variability make their regions marginal for agriculture or pastoralism, and as a result foraging continued as the basic subsistence mode down to the recent past. In both cases population densities are very low and highly dispersed, and both subsistence economies are essentially pragmatic, selecting among possible food resources so as to meet the group's needs. The resulting diets derive the bulk of their calories from plant resources. Game meat, although highly desired, is of secondary importance. (This deemphasis on hunting is very important; as we shall see, it may not apply to all forager groups.)

Certain differences, however, do exist between the Shoshone and !Kung, differences that reflect specific contrasts in their environments. For example, the marked seasonal differences in the Shoshone region require the use of food storage to avert starvation in the late winter. In winter camps the sharing of stored pine nuts is an important element in group cohesion. The !Kung pool their risks in a different way, though one that finds an echo in the Shoshone's occasional rabbit or antelope drive. Hunting contributes daily to the !Kung diet, and reciprocal arrangements within the camp are ideal for distributing the more risky yield of meat in comparison to the more predictable yield of plants. The Shoshone represent a dichotomized society, spread out in nuclear families for gathering plant resources and then briefly concentrated for group hunting. The !Kung represent a more stable intermediary position, with a balanced gathering-hunting economy and less variation in organizational makeup.

Prehistoric Foraging Societies

What do these close looks at the Shoshone and the !Kung tell us in a general way about foraging, especially in prehistoric times, when it was the universal mode of human existence? To review the evolution of foraging societies prior to agriculture, we shall briefly consider three periods that witnessed major changes for early human populations: the Lower and Middle Paleolithic, the Upper Paleolithic, and the post-Pleistocene. These periods saw three progressive "revolutions" in human society, resulting finally in a foraging mode that we believe was analogous to that of the Shoshone and the !Kung.

Can we imagine that living societies will help us understand how human groups were organized in the distant past? What makes modern societies potential analogs for past social forms is not their inherent primitiveness but the flexibility and adaptability of humans to organize for survival and prosperity under divergent conditions. Thus the Khoisan or the Shoshone, like all humans, are not primitive but pragmatic. Their social lives provide analogies of earlier forms, because the economic and demographic conditions under which they existed are similar.

First, by far the longest period was the Lower and Middle Paleolithic (very roughly from 2,000,000 to 35,000 B.P.), the time of human origins both as a biological species and as users of tools. During the Pleistocene, or Ice Age, our erect hominid ancestors developed into modern *Homo sapiens*, and members of that species, with greatly enlarged cranial capacities (increasing from perhaps 650 to 1,450 cc), began using tools as their basic means of adaptation. A slow but consistent population growth resulted in some increase in population density, but more significant was the expansion from an initially restricted distribution in Africa to a very broad distribution throughout Africa, Europe, and Asia. This unprecedented expansion resulted in part from population growth in the core areas, and in part from the opening of unexploited environments with the help of new technologies. Critical technological inventions included fire and clothing for survival in harsh European and Asian winters close to the glacial ice masses, and efficient strategies for hunting large game. Early in this period the diet was apparently quite eclectic, including small and large game either scavenged or clubbed to death at close range. By the Middle Paleolithic hunting appears to have become more important thanks to the development of an effective hunting technology, including well-crafted stone projectile points that must have been hafted to throwing spears.

What archaeological evidence we have suggests that early hominids were organized into small mobile groups. At sites such as the Olduvai Gorge (1,750,000 B.P.) and Olorgesailie (900,000 to 700,000 B.P. [redated with better methods; see Bye et al. 1987]), the concentration of flaked stone tools and remains of butchered animals suggested that early humans may have returned regularly to a base camp where food was shared (Bye et al. 1987; Isaac 1978; Wenke 1980). But a debate raged among researchers: were they inappropriately extending models of modern family-level foragers to a distant past when our ancestors were differently adapted (see summary in Kelly 1995)? Attention has focused on bone taphonomy, how the conditions of the bones from killed animals were the result of different actions, including carnivore predation, human hunting and butchering, scavenging, natural weathering, and the like. Many of the bones were consistent with a pattern expected for carnivore predation, probably by the region's famed felines, and the earlier theories of early human organization fell into disrepute. A recent interpretation by Blumenschine (1995) concludes that (a) the mixture of animal sizes indicates nonhuman predation, but (b) the cultural butchering practices seen on the bones show that humans had scavenged the bones soon after the kill and had broken them up with hammer stones to extract the marrow. These early human ancestors were apparently scavengers, not hunters. However, we can still infer that they were organized into small groups to scare away predators and other scavengers from the kills, and to transport the carcasses to a secure base camp; there they would process the carcasses with rudimentary tools and defend them against competing scavengers such as hyenas. The first convincing evidence for hunting is later in the Early Paleolithic, associated with the time period of Acheulian hand axes; a recent find of wooden spears may date to 400,000 B.P.! Hunting is evidence for organized participation in group efforts that made new sources of food available.

Certainly Middle Paleolithic sites (100,000 to 35,000 B.P.), including the important caves of the Dordogne region in France, were repeatedly occupied base camps suggestive of a family-level organization. Artifact assemblages from the end of the Middle Paleolithic have been grouped into "tool kits" associated with different economic activities (Binford and Binford 1966). For example, Tool Kit I had twelve tool types, including borers, end-scrapers, and knives, that were apparently used to work bone, wood, and skins; Tool Kit V had six tool types, including projectile points, discs, scrapers, and blades, which were apparently used in hunting and butchering. Sites differed systematically in the tool kits found, suggesting to the Binfords that certain sites emphasizing a broad range of activities (including manufacturing) were probably base camps, and that other sites emphasizing food procurement were short-term, special-activity sites. Rolland and Dibble (1990) argue that extensive retouch on stone tools at certain Middle Paleolithic sites indicates a fairly long winter occupation when humans were living off reindeer. Intensive use of the stone was then necessary to conserve available raw material, because sources of stone were distant and stone unavailable at that season. The implied settlement pattern fits the general aggregation-dispersion model outlined in our forager cases. The importance of protection from predation in the Lower Paleolithic and the importance of hunting in the Middle Paleolithic would have necessitated a camp group integrated by generalized reciprocity.

Much has been made of the Upper Paleolithic transition that took place at the end of the Pleistocene between 35,000 and 12,000 B.P., especially in Europe (Conkey 1978; Gilman 1984; Hayden 1981b). The dramatic changes of this time in the economy and in the social organization of humans were apparently impelled by a continued growth in population; the spread into the New World took place during this period, and a sharp increase in the number of recorded sites argues strongly for higher population densities.

Coupled to this population growth must have been a significant intensification in resource use. New technologies included spear throwers (atlatl, said to increase the maximum range of a throw from two hundred feet by hand to five hundred feet by atlatl), barbed harpoons, and fish gorges (Wenke 1980). In many economies the staple food seems to have been large migratory game animals such as reindeer or wild cattle. It is not clear why, since intensification characteristically results in a broadening of the diet (Earle 1980a). Perhaps because intensification is most difficult in the leanest season (winter), when few if any additional food sources are available, people in some areas solved their food problems in the Shoshone manner, not by broadening their diet but by increasing the exploitation of a rich resource available in fall that can be stored for use in the winter. Whatever its origin, this focus on a rich, storable resource appears to have had a profound effect on human society.

The settlement pattern of the Upper Paleolithic probably continued to include base camps and special activity sites. The main change was in the size of settlements at the base camps. Settlements such as Solvieux in southern France could be quite large (over seven acres) and probably represented a group of several hundred people (Sackett 1984). At Dolni Vestonice, a palisaded camp in Czechoslovakia, five huts were occupied. One large hut that was forty-five feet long contained several hearths, suggesting that it housed several nuclear families. In general, the size of some settlements in the Upper Paleolithic implies a local group larger than is found commonly among foragers and closer to our expectations for village communities like the Yanomamo (see Case 5).

As we shall see in Part II, with the formation of more or less long-term groups of a hundred or more people comes considerable institutional elaboration that includes ceremonialism and group leadership. In the Upper Paleolithic, cave art from sites such as Altamira in Spain and Lascaux in France, and carved "venus" figures from eastern Europe, offer unambiguous evidence of ceremonial activities. Various Upper Paleolithic artifacts, such as the large and carefully flaked Solutrean spear points and bone batons with engraved animals, are almost surely status markers of leadership.

Can this be? Can hunters be organized well beyond a family level? As we argue in the Eskimo and Northwest Coast cases, we believe that foragers develop higher levels of integration under particular economic and political conditions. It seems plausible that local groups and even Big Man systems existed for the Upper Paleolithic. Three conditions potentially important for this development were risk management, large-scale hunting, and territorial defense.

The need for risk management in hunter-gatherer populations like the Shoshone and the !Kung is commonly identified as leading to social relationships beyond the nuclear family. Since there is no reason to suppose that the nature of risk has changed significantly from earlier periods, it would seem that the camp arrangements and flexible regional exchange network that characterize foragers like the Khoisan are comparable to what they were thirty thousand years ago.

The problems of hunting large migrating game have been singled out by both S. Binford (1968) and Wobst (1976) as causing the cultural elaboration seen in the Upper Paleolithic. To simplify their arguments, hunting migratory species like reindeer requires far more hunters than a single camp can provide and therefore leads to ceremonial elaboration as a way of integrating normally dispersed camp groups. As the Shoshone case shows, such a tie between aggregation for hunting and ceremonial elaboration is plausible enough, but its importance for the Paleolithic has been questioned. Gilman (1984) notes that dependence on migratory herd animals in the Upper Paleolithic varies considerably and does not determine cultural elaboration. For example, the Upper Paleolithic populations in Spain that produced some of the most sophisticated art were dependent on deer, which were apparently non-migratory and would probably not have been hunted in large group drives.

Territorial defense may have been critical for Upper Paleolithic societies that depended on large game. Gilman (1984) argues cogently that the local-style groups that characterized the Upper Paleolithic can be seen not as mechanisms for including greater numbers of people for cooperative hunting but as mechanisms for excluding people—by defining a bounded social group. In essence, Pleistocene societies, with their high population densities (for hunters), were dependent on exclusive access to favorable locations for hunting. In this context the stylistic differences that differentiated one local group from another in the Upper Paleolithic may in fact represent attempts to limit the extent of social obligations and thus restrict access to critical resources by neighboring groups.

Specifically, it can be argued that linked technological improvements and population growth focused hunting on highly productive and storable animal foods. To hunt such species efficiently, hunters must control their migratory paths, such as mountain passes and river ponds for reindeer (S. Binford 1968), and river bends for salmon fisheries (Jochim 1984); for nonmigratory species like deer and mammoth, it means control of their optimally productive home ranges. An intensified use of animal resources would tend to emphasize differences in the costs of hunting from locale to locale, and would thus increase the benefits to be obtained from group defense of the best hunting areas.

The development of local groups in the Upper Paleolithic is getting ahead of our story and into issues described in Chapters 5 through 8. Let us return to our family-level foragers. During the immediate post-Pleistocene period (12,000 to 7,000 B.P.), referred to as the Mesolithic in Europe and as the early Archaic in the New World, the diet of human populations in many areas changed radically to include a large number of new species (L. Binford 1968; Mark Cohen 1977). Changes in the environment helped to make this necessary, but its main cause was the growth of human populations. In many locations, such as the Desert Cultural areas of western North America, the subsistence economy for the first time incorporated plant resources. This process of intensification, which has been called the "broad-spectrum revolution" (Flannery 1969), appears to have taken place on a worldwide basis (Christenson 1980; Mark Cohen 1977). With the expansion into virgin territory largely complete, further population growth required intensification.

The most common outcome of this broadening diet was a concentration on plant foods that created a subsistence economy generally analogous to that of the Shoshone and the !Kung. It was during this period that the basic family-level society spread throughout the world, and it is from this base that we trace the evolutionary development described in this book. The flexible family form of organization was a pragmatic and effective means to organize a division of labor and sharing of foragers. Groups could fragment and coalesce to exploit diverse and variable resources.

Even within this broadly shared foundation considerable diversity existed. In some areas intensive hunting continued along with a territorially organized society: an example is the camelid hunters and early pastoralists studied by Rick (1978, 1984) in the Central Andean *puna* (see Chapter 12), whose local groups were apparently sedentary and distinguished by stylistically diagnostic stone projectile points. In other areas intensification concentrated on rich resources that could be stored to carry the population over lean periods: for example, the preagricultural Natufian villages of the Levant (Flannery 1972), where sedentary local populations harvested and stored abundant wild grains. But overriding this diversity was a common pressure that was to result gradually in a shift to domesticates and fundamental changes for human society.

Conclusions

To understand the overall evolution of hunter-gatherers, we must consider the three main evolutionary trends—intensification, integration, and stratification—as they relate to the changing economy and society.

The intensification of food procurement activity in a given area is necessitated by an increasing population or a deteriorating environment. In the Pleistocene and immediate post-Pleistocene periods, a slow growth in population spread humans throughout the world and gradually raised population densities in those areas capable of sustaining more people. Intensification in food procurement was the result (Mark Cohen 1977). First came the gradual occupation of new habitats with suboptimal resources such as low-density large game, small game, and plants that require more costly procurement strategies. Next came the diversification of diets as increasingly costly species were added to support a larger population. Both trends increased the amount of labor devoted to procuring food. Logically and historically, the next step was domestication.

Integration, our second trend, occurs only in human groups of a certain size and complexity, but the degree of integration of a society does not correspond in any simple way to the degree of intensification of its economic activity. In some environmental conditions intensification brings integration in its wake; in others it does not.

Three levels of social integration can be seen in all hunter-gatherer societies, but their relative importance varies significantly with resource availability, with the specific form of resource intensification, and with technological development. The *family* as the basic subsistence unit was nearly universal, although its importance was temporarily diminished when the camp took over some of its economic functions. The *camp*, of four to six families, was also nearly universal. As we have seen, however, its importance and its degree of institutionalization varied widely, being least among plant gatherers like the Shoshone and greatest among the hunters of large game. The intensification of hunting, by creating a need for territorial exclusion, may have caused the camp, in some areas, to become a basic defensive group with stronger ceremonial integration. As camps become important economically, social bonds are often strong within gendered groups, women associating with women and men associating with men. The *region*, a collectivity of some ten to twenty camps, was organized to handle problems of security and defense. Regional networks of plant gatherers made it possible for camps or individual families to learn of and obtain food elsewhere when their own home range came up short. With intensive animal hunting, the regional network may have provided the alliance system used in the defense of hunting territories.

The importance of territoriality is undeniable but variable. In the original discussion of patrilocal bands, Steward (1936) and Service (1962) identified a territorial group of camp size as typical of hunter-gatherers. More recent work, however, has tended to refute the corporate and territorial aspects of forager organization, and shown instead that minimal territoriality made possible a flexibility of movement in search of food that was essential to a forager's survival. Without territorial boundaries restricting regional movements, populations could easily concentrate on the most favorable resource available at any moment. Often enough there was no other.

Territoriality in hunter-gatherers should thus be associated with more stable resources, as in the case of the Owens Valley Shoshone. Territoriality also restricts access to critical resources that either are naturally circumscribed, such as water holes or pine nuts, or have been improved by technical means, such as local irrigation in the Owens Valley or fish weirs on the Northwest Coast (see Chapter 8). Where resources are concentrated, access to them can be restricted more easily. With the increasingly widespread and increasingly successful efforts to restrict access to critical resources, we encounter the beginnings of warfare.

Associated with territorialism and warfare is a suggestive change in the importance of ceremonialism. In comparatively low density groups that lack territoriality, ceremonialism is closely tied to periods of aggregation, as when the !Kung aggregate around the winter water hole or the Shoshone come together for an animal drive. The ceremonialism is particular to the larger group rather than to its component families, and it acts to offset tendencies within the group to fragment from internal disputes.

Among territorial hunters and gatherers ad hoc ceremonies may play a different role, both to define a social group with rights of access and then to override such social divisions as part of broader alliance formations. According to Yengoyan (1972), initiation rites in Australia were timed to take advantage of abundant yields of unpredictable wild resources. When such a good yield was noted, a local territorial group would invite neighboring groups to join in its initiation ceremony and at the same time to join in harvesting the bountiful resource. Similarly, among the territorial Pomo of northern California, unusually good yields in seeds and fish were the occasion for a major ceremony (Vayda 1967). Neighbors of the sponsoring group acquired the seeds or fish in exchange for shell money, which was in due course exchanged for food during lean periods. Some such mechanism to compensate for regional differences in the availability of wild foods appears essential. In some cases, such as that of the Northwest Coast fishers (Chapter 8), such mechanisms are one sign of a developing political economy.

Stratification is not seen in the two cases analyzed in this chapter. In general, foragers are characterized by minimal social differentiation and a strong ethos of equality and sharing. Their goal is the subsistence of each and all, not the differential economic advantage of one or some. Stratification depends on differential access to resources, which in turn must be predicated on a strong notion of land tenure not seen among the !Kung and Shoshone. Elsewhere, however, certain economic and ecological conditions tied to intensification have produced hunter-gatherer societies with differential access to resources and thus with stratification. As we have seen, some Upper Paleolithic cultures may have been of this description. And as we shall see in Chapter 8, social elites are a prominent feature of the high-density, territorial hunter-gatherer societies of Northwest Coast fishers.

FOUR

Families with Domestication

WE HAVE ARGUED that the family is a natural unit of human social and economic organization, rooted in biological capacities and tendencies that evolved over the millions of years when hominids lived by foraging. Our prototypes for the family-level economy were the Shoshone and the !Kung, classic forager groups. In this chapter we generalize our argument to show that domesticated food production as such does not necessarily lead to a more complex social and economic system. In the two cases we examine, the Machiguenga and the Nganasan, the technology of domesticated food production is available and contributes significantly to the economy, yet the family remains the dominant unit of economic integration.

To be sure, we now encounter somewhat more stable settlements, which we refer to as hamlets. But these merely reflect the existence of such stable resources as gardens among the Machiguenga and winter fishing spots among the Nganasan, and do not signal the emergence of a significantly more complex integration of the economy. Apart from the formation of hamlets, we find little to distinguish our cases here from those of the previous chapter: the family remains opportunistic, aggregating and dispersing as the availability of resources dictates, maximizing flexibility and minimizing structural constraints such as territoriality and leadership.

Although interpersonal violence and homicide are known in these groups, organized raiding and warfare are rare, except on the part of more highly organized and more powerful neighboring groups. Multifamily groups cooperate in food production or food sharing only on particular occasions, and household autonomy is repeatedly affirmed in the seasonal or permanent dissolution of hamlets into their constituent households.

In both cases domesticates serve as a dietary supplement to wild foods, which remain very important. The Machiguenga of the Peruvian Amazon, who live in semisedentary family or hamlet settlements, grow most of their food, but also prize a diversity of wild foods. Although they have abundant unused land suitable for horticulture, they prefer to scatter in family units for easy access to wild foods. The Nganasan, reindeer hunters of the Siberian tundra, keep small herds of domesticated reindeer not for food but for transportation and for use in hunting. They employ the technology of domestication but remain essentially foragers.

Why did these groups not take advantage of their technology of domestication to complete the expected evolutionary transition to more densely settled, internally differentiated societies? As we shall argue in Chapter 5, this poses the question backward. After all, as we have seen, in the right circumstances settlement in small, scattered groups offers cost-efficient solutions to basic economic problems. The more interesting question is, What leads people to forsake their family autonomy for larger, more concentrated settlements in which food procurement is less efficient and social tensions are greater?

The archaeological evidence is clear that agriculture by itself is not responsible for revolutionary changes in societal organization. So far as the archaeological record shows, sedentary village life first occurred in societies dependent on hunting and gathering; the Northwest Coast fishers (Case 9) illustrate ethnographically how this is possible. In this chapter we shall argue that the family-level organization that characterized most hunter-gatherer societies after the end of the Pleistocene persisted in at least some instances well after the beginnings of agriculture.

In both the Middle East and Mesoamerica, agriculture and pastoralism appear not as economic revolutions permitting a sedentary lifestyle but as long and gradual transitions not directly linked to villages. Indeed, in the Middle East, sedentary villages predate the beginnings of agriculture; the villagers stored wild cereals to be eaten during lean periods (Flannery 1969). The village of Ain Mallaha, occupied between ten and eleven thousand years ago in what is now Israel, contained about fifty circular, semisubterranean houses that suggest the kind of horticultural village described in Chapters 6 and 7. The first evidence of plant and animal domestication, however, is found only at the end of that period, around ten thousand years ago. At the archaeologically important village of Ali Kosh in southwestern Iran, Flannery (1969) documents a slow adoption of domesticates into the diet. For more than a thousand years after the earliest use of domesticated cereals (emmer wheat and two-row barley) and animals (goats and sheep), hunting and

TABLE 3

Developmental Trends in the Tehuacan Valley

Phase	Population	Percent domesticates	Largest settlement
Late Ajuereado (?–7400 B.C.)	25	0%	camp
El Riego (7400–5800 B.C.)	50	4	base camp
Coxcatlan (5800–4150 B.C.)	150	14	base camp
Abejas (4150–2850 B.C.)	300	22	hamlet?
Purron and Ajalpan (2850–1000 B.C.)	insufficient data		hamlet
Santa Maria (1000–150 B.C.)	4,000	58	village

SOURCE: Christenson (1980).

gathering continued to provide the majority of the diet. In the Middle East as elsewhere, the subsistence economy shifted to domesticates over several thousand years as human populations gradually grew.

The best documented long-term sequence for a growing population, a changing subsistence economy, and a changing social organization comes from MacNeish's seminal research in the Tehuacan Valley of Mexico (Byers 1967; Christenson 1980; MacNeish 1964, 1970). Table 3 presents the basic data showing the relationship among these three key variables. As we interpret this sequence, the long-term development was propelled by a growth in human population and an intensification of the subsistence economy. Initially there was a shift from a mixed hunting and gathering economy in Late Ajuereado and El Riego to a broad-spectrum economy, relying on plants for about 65 percent of the diet, by the Coxcatlan period. Domesticated food products (maize, beans, squash, etc.) were picked up starting in El Riego, and gradually provided an ever higher percentage of the diet.

Linked to population growth and subsistence intensification was a slowly changing settlement pattern. The foragers of the El Riego and Coxcatlan periods were organized at a family level, like the Shoshone or the !Kung, with a characteristic pattern of base camps and smaller short-term camps. Probably by the Abejas period, base camps had increased in size to perhaps fifty people and become more sedentary, indicating a transition to hamlets. Not until Santa Maria, some five thousand years after the initial use of domesticated plants, are true sedentary villages found.

In sum, archaeologically we see not a technological revolution but a slow increase in farming in a family-level society much like that now to be described for the Machiguenga and the Nganasan. Evolution beyond the family level to more complex forms cannot be explained by domestication as such.

Case 3. The Machiguenga of the Peruvian Amazon

The Machiguenga are tropical horticulturalists who live at considerably higher population densities than the !Kung or the Shoshone but closely resemble those foragers in social and economic organization. Like classic foragers, the Machiguenga are pragmatic in their search for food, aggregating and dispersing frequently as the situation may dictate. Although their multifamily groups are more permanent than San camps, the Machiguenga eschew village-level integrated groups and clearly value the economic autonomy of the household.

The Machiguenga environment and technology would appear to make a decent life possible for a larger population than now exists. From the air one's first impression is of an endless and empty natural forest. Occasional small gardens and clearings with one to five houses dot the landscape (Fig. 6). For the forager groups discussed in Chapter 3, we found limiting factors—water for the !Kung, water and winter food for the Shoshone—that kept population densities low. For the Machiguenga, however, no obvious single scarcity limits population growth. Food production is ample to meet basic needs and is secure enough to ward off starvation under most environmental conditions.

This raises the theoretically important issue of whether the Machiguenga (and many other indigenous tropical forest peoples) are living below carrying capacity. Certainly it is possible that their numbers were greater in the past, before contact with Euro-Americans exposed them to the destructive tandem of disease and exploitation. But we will show that, even if their environment could theoretically support a larger population, the Machiguenga experience it as a scarce environment that favors competitive over cooperative adaptations. Unlike the Yanomamo (Case 5), their food staples are not sufficiently dense and concentrated to be worth fighting over. In order to maintain their cultural standard of living, they must scatter and move frequently to keep subsistence costs down and to ensure access to a wide array of foods and materials. All aspects of their adaptation reinforce their family-level economy. This means that not only do the Machiguenga have little motivation to form larger communities, but, in addition, outsiders—

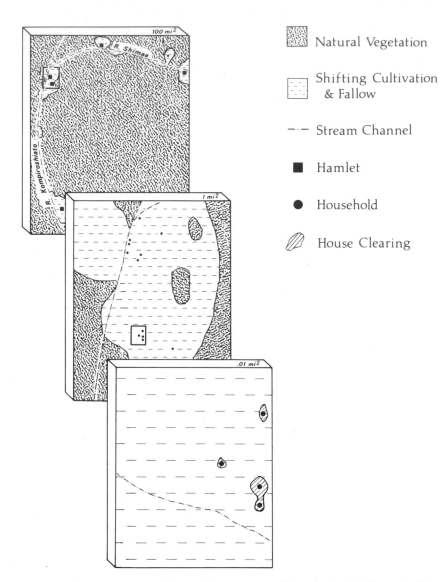

Natural Vegetation

Shifting Cultivation
& Fallow

Stream Channel

Hamlet

Household

House Clearing

Fig. 6. Settlement Pattern of the Machiguenga. People settle in single households or
small hamlets that move every few years when local resources become scarce. Small
gardens, both in production and abandoned, are close to the settlements, forming
islands in a sea of tropical rainforest.

from the Inkas to modern Peruvians—have found it difficult or impossible to control them politically or incorporate them into the surrounding state system.

The Environment and the Economy

The Machiguenga (A. Johnson 1983, 2000; O. Johnson 1978) reside in the western fringe of the Amazon rain forest, along the slopes of the Andes Mountains in southeastern Peru. The high Andean altiplano supported politically complex societies on an intensive agricultural base long before the European conquest of the New World. By the time of the Inkas (ca. 1400 A.D.), an empire state had managed to integrate an area running along the Andean chain more than two thousand miles north and south from the administrative center at Cuzco (Chapter 12). Yet the Inkas, despite numerous incursions into the tropical forest, found it difficult to dominate politically more than a few miles to the east into the *montaña*, a rain forest region of rugged mountains between one thousand and six thousand feet above sea level. The montaña was inhabited by extensive horticulturalists such as the Machiguenga, living in small, scattered hamlets. Fierce as these people could be, they could never have resisted the Inka armies in a direct confrontation; yet the Inkas feared them, calling them *antis*, "savages."

In the Machiguenga environment it is not necessary to band together for defensive purposes or hunting. Machiguenga settlements fluctuate between individual households, isolated from others by expanses of virgin forest, and hamlets of three to five cooperating and related households (Fig. 6). The choice and its timing are determined primarily by the local scarcity or abundance of basic resources.

Machiguenga households are semisedentary. Their main residence is in sturdy houses built to last the three to five years that they will normally reside in a given location. Indeed, an older house at an abandoned site may be left standing to serve as a hunting lodge or a temporary stopover while families visit old gardens, where crops can still be harvested and where small herds of peccary and other game, attracted by the availability of untended root crops, can be hunted.

During certain times of the year, when wild foods are abundant, the Machiguenga leave their houses to live in temporary huts along the rivers or in distant gardens. People value these times as opportunities to get away from their hamlets, where the social costs of sharing and cooperation are high and where wild foods have been locally depleted. Population density is 0.8 person per square mile, high for family-level societies but low enough for overall resources to be adequate for a healthy existence. Although we see the forest of the Machiguenga as unsettled, they often find it crowded. Why this should be is a question to which we will turn shortly.

Of the labor invested by the Machiguenga in food production, nearly two-thirds goes into their highly productive gardens; the other third goes into procuring wild food, notably game, fish, and insects. Although wild food makes up only about 10 percent of what they consume, they consider it essential to their diet. Judging from people's recollections, as recently as 1965 wild foods made up a much larger percentage of the diet. Increased outside contact accounts for the change, partly by making steel tools for gardening easy to obtain, partly by increasing the population density and thus decreasing the availability of wild foods. Later we shall examine some of the implications of these recent changes. For now we note that garden foods provide the bulk of food energy in the diet and are also the main basis of Machiguenga food security, which is achieved by overproducing root crops that can be stored in the ground until needed.

Given the Machiguenga's ability to produce a large surplus of starchy staples above subsistence needs, it is puzzling why their population densities remain low and the family-level organization persists. Early observers assumed that the "limited potential" of tropical soils acts as a brake on population growth in the "green desert" of the tropical forest, just as extremes of drought or cold limit population among foraging groups (Meggers 1954). Tropical soils are often more fragile than soils of the temperate zones. The luxuriant vegetation of a tropical rain forest rests on a delicate balance of nutrients cycling rapidly from forest to soil and back again. A constant rain of detritus—leaves, branches, fruits, animal feces, etc.—falls to the ground, where it is rapidly decomposed into nutrients by insects and bacteria working in the warm and humid topsoil. These nutrients are picked up by the shallow root systems of the forest and quickly used to support new growth. Strip the land of the forest cover and the sun and rain beat down unimpeded, destroying the crumb structure of the thin topsoil. Nutrients percolate down beyond the reach of new roots, occasionally leaving behind laterites (oxides of iron and aluminum) that can solidify into hardpans in which nothing will grow. More commonly, the erosion or depletion of soil nutrients by continuous cropping decreases fertility and in extreme cases destroys it.

Observers disagree on the extent of the poverty of tropical soils. Some Amazonian lands have been continuously farmed for generations without evident loss of fertility, whereas others have been permanently destroyed by intensive cultivation. Typically, soils near the great rivers are replenished annually by silt deposited in the flood stage, and these riverine soils can sustain intensification better than inland (interfluvial) soils (Moran 1993). In other cases, however, we do not yet understand why these differences in fertility and sustainability occur (see Moran 1979: 248–90; Sanchez 1976).

If tropical soils are in fact poor, slash-and-burn, or shifting, agriculture might well be appropriate to the Amazon rain forest. Slash-and-burn agriculture, as practiced among the Machiguenga, requires cutting and clearing small gardens from the forest. After one or two years of farming, the field is allowed to revert to natural vegetation as new plots are cleared. Periods of fallow, during which the fields are unfarmed, are essential to regaining soil fertility. Such agriculture was once assumed to be a backward and inefficient technology. Observers familiar with the tidy, plowed plots of intensive agriculture in temperate zones were dismayed by the sight of fields littered with half-burnt logs and the mingling of diverse crops seemingly without plan or form. Long fallowing was viewed as a wasteful practice because it kept so much land out of production, and yields from these gardens were assumed to be low. However, our growing knowledge of the vulnerability of many tropical soils to degradation has led to a more sympathetic view of slash-and-burn agriculture. What concerns most current critics of the system (e.g., C. Webster and Wilson 1966: 87) is the shortening of the fallow period (to bring more gardens into production) in areas where population is growing. They complain that this practice inhibits the restoration of the soils provided by longer fallowing.

In a common type of slash-and-burn garden often found in less intensive horticultural systems, where wild foods still play an important part in the diet, several distinct species of food plants are intercropped. As Geertz remarks, intercropped gardens "imitate" the tropical forest and go far toward protecting the integrity of the soils. Ground-hugging crops like pumpkin and squash lay down a bottom cover; above these an intercropped matrix of staples such as maize, manioc, and yam fill the middle zone; and above those, tree crops such as banana, cashew, and guava form a canopy.

The diversity of crops is also some protection against pests and disease, which are most devastating when they strike a field all planted to a single crop. The Machiguenga, for example, not only plant from six to ten different crops in the same field but also plant several varieties of each, because, as they say, "We like the differences."* They name fif-

---

*The Machiguenga recognize at least eighty different species of cultigens, but most of them are grown in small quantities in house gardens and serve as condiments, medicines, building materials, etc. In house gardens they also experiment with new crops.

teen varieties of their basic staple, manioc, and ten varieties of maize, their second most important crop. It would take a highly unlikely combination of hazards to prevent all of these varieties from producing.

According to Beckerman, the advantages of intercropped fields for subsistence farmers are generally these:

1. Lower losses due to pests and plant disease.
2. Increased protection from erosion.
3. Lower overall risk of total crop failure, attributable in part to nos. 1 and 2 but also to a spreading of risk over several crops that are unlikely all to fail at once.
4. A more efficient use of light, moisture, and nutrients.
5. The production in a single garden of many commodities needed for household self-sufficiency.
6. The spreading of labor more evenly throughout the year.
7. Fewer storage problems.

Nonetheless, monocrop fields of such staples as manioc or plantain are found in tropical regions under some conditions. Beckerman (1983) explains this practice as a form of intensification, reflecting a community's increased dependence on horticulture for food. Even in these cases, however, many of the advantages of intercropping are retained by planting several varieties of the staple crop.

It is not true that slash-and-burn gardens are relatively unproductive. They typically return one hundred to two hundred times as much seed as planted, compared, for example, with returns of less than 100:1 reported in annual plow cropping in Mesoamerica and the less than 10:1 reported in European grain farming before the modern era. Returns on labor are also high: twenty calories for every calorie of labor invested, making it possible to produce a substantial surplus above ordinary subsistence needs. With less than four hours of combined labor per day, the members of a Machiguenga household produce more than twice the food energy they need to maintain themselves.

Even the long fallows are efficient. Boserup (1965) has shown that the length of a fallow is a fundamental feature of an agricultural system, and that it is closely related to population pressure on resources. In systems with a significant fallow period, she distinguishes three types: forest fallow, in which a year or two of cultivation are followed by a long fallow period, allowing the forest to regrow; bush fallow, in which several years of cultivation are followed by fewer than ten years of fallow, so that only bush, not true forest, regrows; and short fallow, in which a few years of cultivation are followed by an equal number of fallow years, then more cultivation, so that not even bush regrows. Ac-

TABLE 4

Machiguenga Soil Constituents by Age of Garden

Age of garden	Number of observations	Percent organic matter	Percent nitrogen
Primary forest	4	6.8%	0.32%
First-year	12	6.7	0.32
Second-year	2	6.2	0.30
Third-year	3	4.6	0.21
Fourth-year	4	3.6	0.16
Fallow (2 years)	2	3.2	0.14

cording to Boserup, a shorter fallow period requires more labor for the same yield on the land—that is, a loss of labor efficiency.

Two lines of argument support this view. The first argument is that shorter fallows lower the fertility of the soil. Forest growth restores the crumb structure and nutrients to the soil that were lost during cultivation. We do not know exactly how long it takes for the ecosystem to restore itself fully following cultivation. Soil constituents are substantially restored after ten years, but full restoration of the forest complex may take from twenty-five to fifty years.

Boserup could not prove conclusively that shorter fallows lower soil fertility, but evidence from the Machiguenga tends to bear her out. In Table 4 we see that the fertility of Machiguenga soils, as measured by organic matter and nitrogen, declines steadily with the number of years in cultivation. Primary forest and first-year gardens are of virtually identical fertility, with fertility dropping off most sharply after the second year of cultivation. (This, incidentally, is the point at which Machiguengas are likely to begin abandoning their gardens.) The two gardens listed as fallow in Table 4 had been abandoned for only two years, and we see no evidence that their fertility has as yet been significantly restored.

The data in Table 4 support the argument that tropical soils rapidly lose fertility under continuous cultivation and require long fallows to restore fertility. Other soil constituents may be equally important: for example, soil acidity, which rises dramatically with the age of the garden (Baksh 1984). But whatever the chemistry, it is clear that shorter fallows will not fully restore fertility, and this means that yields will be lower. Since labor input will not diminish, lower yields mean a lower return on labor, or a loss in labor efficiency, as Boserup argued.

The second argument against shorter fallows turns on increased weeding costs. Excessive weeds are the main reason that Machiguengas give for abandoning their gardens. In a new garden weeds are a problem, but weeding is needed only every six weeks or so; moreover, it proceeds rapidly, since young weeds are delicate and easy to pull by hand. But as the garden ages, weeds become entrenched until hand pulling becomes impossible and a machete must be used. Ultimately, tough grasses, nettles, and other durable species begin to predominate and the cultivator must give up. With fallowing, which allows the original complex of plants to return, tough weeds diminish to their original small proportion of the whole.

Here again Boserup's evidence is not conclusive. But Bergman (1974: 191) reports that the Shipibo Indians of the Peruvian montaña need invest only 260 hours of labor per hectare in maize gardens cleared on virgin land, whereas they require over 480 hours per hectare in land cleared after short fallows. He attributes the difference almost entirely to the need for extra weeding in the short-fallowed fields.

Boserup's reasoning and the evidence we have just presented support Meggers's contention that there are limits on the potential of tropical rain forests for agricultural intensification. So do the spectacular failures of modern agribusiness technology in such Amazon enterprises as the Ford Motor Company rubber plantations at Fordlandia (Wagley 1976: 89–90) and Daniel Ludwig's paper pulp mill at Jari (Veja 1982). Other subsistence failures are recorded prehistorically for tropical forest environments on Pacific islands (Chapter 9).

The situation, however, is more complicated. In an influential paper, Carneiro (1960) showed that the Kuikuru Indians of the upper Xingu region of Brazil had enough land to support ten times their population and still afford the luxury of twenty-five-year fallow periods. The Machiguenga also have an apparent abundance of cultivable land. Hence land shortage cannot be the only limiting factor in the human ecology of the tropical rain forest.

It is, to be sure, *one* limiting factor, since the Machiguenga distinguish carefully between potential garden sites and regard most land as inferior. They want soils that are soft, free of rocks, fertile, well drained, not too steep, and not too distant. They are constantly on the lookout for good land, and a family may lay claim to an attractive piece more than a year in advance of actual clearing. Good land produces more and requires less labor than inferior land, thereby keeping overall labor costs low. Since increased population density decreases the availability of desired land, it has (and is perceived to have) the effect of increasing production costs.

Finally, even tropical rain forests are unpredictably subject to years of excessively dry or wet weather that can reduce garden productivity drastically. Crop pests, or disabilities to family members from injury or illness, can also interfere with normal garden productivity. Thus the large food surpluses that the Machiguenga produce in normal years have an important security function and cannot be taken simply as proof that their abundant land could support a much larger population.

Given the fundamental importance to any society of producing sufficient food energy, it is understandable that cultural ecologists like Meggers should think first of agricultural potential as the factor limiting population growth among extensive horticulturalists. But of course more than calories is at stake. Especially in tropical regions the most common staple crops (manioc, bananas, sweet potatoes, etc.) are high in calories but low in other essential nutrients. In densely settled regions overreliance on crops like these can result in chronic nutritional deficiencies (Jones 1959). Since protein is second only to calories in nutritional importance, the next stop in the search for limiting factors was protein. Gross (1975) argued that because of the scarcity of protein foods in the Amazon, horticulturalists there need large territories in which to hunt, fish, and collect protein-rich grubs and nuts.

Problems soon developed with this explanation as well (Beckerman 1979, 1980), notably that protein cannot be shown to be scarce in the Amazonian diet. Recent careful studies in native Amazonian communities show people obtaining twice as much protein as nutritionists recommend for good health (Berlin and Markell 1977), and the Machiguenga are no exception. Indeed, the Machiguenga normally exceed the recommended levels of intake of virtually all essential nutrients (Johnson and Behrens 1982).

Yet the protein explanation cannot be simply dismissed. The Machiguenga do not consider themselves to be rich in protein foods. They treasure the nuts, seeds, insects, fish, and game they obtain from their forest and rivers, and they willingly spend far more work energy in procuring such foods than in producing the equivalent weight of garden foods (A. Johnson 1980). Wild foods are sources of high-quality protein, and also of diverse nutrients in addition to protein, such as vitamins and fatty acids.

Horticulture does provide some vegetable protein, but tropical root crops are notoriously poor sources of protein. For example, although it costs the Machiguenga ten times as much effort to produce a kilogram of fish as to produce a kilogram of garden foods, fish have about ten times as much protein per kilo, and so the cost of protein in each case is roughly equal. Hence extensive horticulturalists like the Machiguenga compensate for the deficiencies of their garden foods by foraging for wild foods, and their continued nutritional well-being depends on maintaining the small, scattered settlements and low population density necessary for access to an adequate supply of wild foods.

Although they get enough protein, then, they think of protein-rich foods as scarce and they work hard to obtain them from the wild. Their diet is also low in fats and oils (Baksh 1984: 389–93), of which they consume hardly more than the minimum levels recommended by nutritionists. This may help account for their practice of identifying the quantity of fat (*igeka*) in a food with its good taste (*poshin*). In their terms, poshin foods like meat, fish, and peanuts are delicious because of their igeka.

The Machiguenga frequently complain of other scarcities as well, notably the perennial scarcity of palm leaves for roofing. After living in a fixed location for a few years, even a small hamlet will exhaust the local supply of fish, game, palms, and firewood. A favorite topic of conversation is who went where and saw what palms, fruit trees, fish, game, or spoor. Such matters are recounted and discussed most enthusiastically.

Given this perceived scarcity of good agricultural land and other natural resources, it is perhaps surprising that the Machiguenga have no history of warfare. Tales of homicide are occasionally told, but one hears more often of suicide. Much like the !Kung, the Machiguenga emphasize peaceful relations among themselves, in contrast to their "wild" and violent neighbors living at lower elevations. When disputes flare, families move apart until hostilities cool. Belligerent persons are shunned.

One reason for this peaceable way of life is the marginality of the Machiguenga's forest environment with respect to alluvial land for farming, most game, and especially river fish. Land of this sort is unattractive to populations used to the comparatively rich riverine environments at lower elevations or dependent on intensive agriculture in the highlands. As among the !Kung, the scarcity of resources apparently favored small family sizes and a dispersed population. But why did this scarcity not result in interfamily competition for pockets of good agricultural land and natural resources? Because such resources were not sufficiently dense and dependable to make territorial defense effective. The group aggregation required for defense would soon deplete the resources, and the rapidly escalating cost of procuring food would cause the group to disperse.

To summarize, the fundamental problem faced by the Machiguenga is the scarcity and occasional unpredictability of wild resources in their forest environment. The low population density that results from this scarcity has benefits, especially an absence of warfare. The response to scarcity has been to maintain the flexibility of the family-level society that we will now describe.

Social Organization

The Machiguenga keep production costs low and maintain a healthful and comfortable standard of living by keeping their social groups small and widely scattered. Fully self-sufficient at the household level, they live as isolated households for up to several years at a time, residing at other times in hamlets of several households.

At least 90 percent of the food consumed in a household is produced by its members. In Table 5 we get a glimpse of the degree of complementarity between husbands and wives that allows them to combine into a self-sufficient production unit. Men are out of the house much of the time, hunting, farming, and obtaining raw materials. Women are in and around the house, preparing food, caring for children, and manufacturing cotton cloth. In other areas such as fishing, collecting, and making tools and utensils, both men and women get involved, but even here the specific tasks they undertake differ: men fish in the current with men's nets, women along shore with smaller women's nets; men make bows and arrows, women make plaited sifters and strainers; men make the wooden spindles women use to spin cotton; and so on.

The complementarity of husband and wife encourages mutual respect and affection. Although men take the lead position when walking with their families on forest trails, all family members agree that this is reasonable, because the men—armed with bow and arrow—are best equipped to deal with any dangers that might arise. When they lose a spouse, the Machiguenga feel grief and loneliness keenly, but are most likely to express the loss in practical terms: "Who will hunt for me?" a woman may ask, whereas a man will lament, "Who will weave my *cushma* (gown)?"

Being semisedentary rather than nomadic, the Machiguenga build more elaborate houses and acquire more goods than their nomadic counterparts. Still, because they are seasonally nomadic in search of wild foods, and because they must move their settlements every five years or so, they do not acquire cumbersome stores of goods; at a moment's notice they can travel light and live as foragers off the forest. Goods obtained by trade with outsiders are few, being chiefly confined until very recent times to axes.

The Machiguenga are good craftsmen whose products are typically more serviceable than beautiful. Men build houses, spin fibers for the nets and bags they knit, and fashion bows and arrows from cane and hard palmwood. Women spin cotton thread, weave cloth for their

TABLE 5

Machiguenga Time Allocation

(Hours per day)[a]

Activity	Men		Women	
Food production				
Hunting*	0.7		0.0	
Fishing	0.7		0.3	
Collecting	0.4		0.4	
Agriculture*	2.5		0.8	
Livestock	0.0		0.1	
		4.3		1.6
Food preparation		0.2		2.2
Food consumption		1.1		1.0
Commercial activities		0.0		0.0
Housework				
Housekeeping	0.1		0.4	
Water and fuel	0.1		0.1	
Pet care	0.0		0.1	
		0.2		0.6
Manufacture				
Acquiring materials*	0.7		0.1	
Manufacturing artifacts	1.2		1.3	
Manufacturing clothes*	0.0		0.8	
Manufacturing facilities	0.5		0.1	
		2.4		2.3
Social				
Socializing, visiting	1.2		1.0	
Child care*	0.1		1.0	
Caring for others	0.2		0.1	
Public ceremony	0.1		0.0	
Public recreation	0.2		0.1	
Education	0.1		0.0	
		1.9		2.2
Individual				
Hygiene	0.2		0.1	
Sleeping	0.2		0.1	
"Nothing"	1.6		2.1	
Ill	0.4		0.4	
		2.4		2.7
Other		0.5		0.5
TOTAL		13.0		13.1

SOURCE: Johnson 1975a.
NOTE: Asterisks indicate significant differences between men and women ($p < .05$, t-test).
[a] Daylight hours only (6:00 A.M.–7:00 P.M.)

gownlike *cushmas*, make face paint and other dyes, and weave nets and baskets. A Machiguenga house, made from hardwoods and palms, strikes the Western observer at first as flimsy and crude, but it soon gains respect as a secure, durable, and comfortable structure.

The Machiguenga do not have economic specialists, but as is true everywhere, some people do higher quality work than others. One man is known for making better bows, one woman for her fine weaving. Criticizing and admiring the handiwork of others is a popular pastime. Men may have their bows made by a better craftsman and repay him with favors, though not in a strictly calculated sense. Some young women who do not yet weave are looked down on and considered lazy for their dependence on more experienced women. But these differences are not institutionalized in any sense into occupations or classes.

There is also a division of labor by age. Infants are treated warmly and indulgently, but toddlers are expected to be increasingly self-reliant and useful until the age of five or six, at which time they become responsible contributors to the household economy. Children's tasks include fetching water, carrying seed during planting, relaying messages, and, for girls, the care of younger siblings. After age six, children's work becomes more sex-specific. One finds boys hunting for sparrows and lizards with small bows and arrows, and girls spinning uneven but useful thread on small spindles. By age twelve, boys and girls are able to carry out most of the adult tasks of their sex. At this age they show little initiative and are inclined to avoid work when they can, but their attitude changes as they mature and begin to take on family responsibilities of their own.

In polygynous households there is also a division of labor between wives (O. Johnson 1978). Younger wives are more often involved in work outside the home, in gardens or foraging. Older wives are likely to be found in the home, organizing the productive labor of their children and concentrating on manufacture. Thus younger women are away more often with their husbands, and this evokes the jealousy of older wives. On the other hand, older wives are more productive and earn respect from their husbands and from other women. Older wives also have much larger social networks and increase the flow of exchange with other households.

Each wife in a polygynous household maintains a separate hearth, symbolizing her control over her own food production and the independence of her contribution to the household economy. She prepares her own foods, as well as the staple foods brought in from her husband's garden, and distributes them to household members. Mothers in polygynous households interact primarily with their own children and uncommonly with the children of cowives. Cowives also tend to interact and share food with their husband more than with each other, especially where relations between cowives are tense.

However, most Machiguenga households run smoothly as units of generalized reciprocity. Food is constantly circulated among members. A woman passes an ear of roasted corn to her husband, who breaks it in half and returns half to her. He then breaks his half and gives part to his young daughter, who shares it with other children. Mother's half of the corn is likewise divided, and the children soon pass bits of corn back to their parents. Food is seemingly enjoyed as much in the sharing as in the eating.

Every food item has an "owner" (shintaro): the one who procured it or planted it. In fact, all possessions are owned by individuals, and one must ask to borrow them before using them. If a child should refuse to share a possession, the parent will not force the issue, but teasing and chiding will make the child uncomfortable and generosity becomes instilled over time. The one who shares is made to feel proud for being able to give something of value to others in the household.

For weeks at a time, isolated households may go with little social contact or exchange with other households. Like the Shoshone, they accept isolation because it gives them free access to the natural resources around them. But there are also advantages to living in hamlets of three to five households of related kinsmen, commonly married brothers and sisters. The ties of affection and nurturance established in childhood prepare the way for friendly, cooperative relations as adults.

A Machiguenga hamlet is typically a cluster of houses set well away from the river. Three to five households will live near each other, so that a common clearing can serve them all for work and socializing. Sometimes one or two houses in the hamlet will be built at some distance from the others, with fruit trees or stands of brush between them providing a measure of privacy. The houses remain close enough for easy visiting, food sharing, and mutual aid in child care and food preparation, but each household maintains its own racks and sheds for smoking, drying, or storing food and its own pens for Muscovy ducks or chickens, if any. Nothing is owned communally by the hamlet members. Even when brothers cooperate to clear a garden, they usually divide it into two parts to be cultivated individually. A brother rarely helps himself to products from his brother's garden without asking permission first.

From each garden located fairly close to the hamlet the food is brought home, prepared, and eaten by each household apart, but households often come together for a common meal when wild foods are available. Fish, game, and grubs, being both scarce and greatly desired, are occasions for sharing from a common pot; indeed, such sharing of wild foods is the main economic benefit motivating households to join and remain in hamlets. Women from each household arrive with pots of manioc; they may also bring greens or other foods they have harvested and prepared, and some manioc beer for their husbands. Such meals are unexpectedly complex and structured, and give insight into the balance of individual and group interests that the Machiguenga seek to achieve.

On one occasion anthropologists saw the three households of a hamlet join to share a fish caught by one of the men. The three household heads were related: the first was the older brother of the second, and the third was their sister's husband. The younger brother was married to the older brother's wife's daughter (by a previous marriage). The older brother ranked highest socially, the brother-in-law lowest. When special foods like fish were available for a communal feast, it was usually held at the older brother's house.

On this occasion, as on most others, each married couple sat together as people chatted while the fish soup was cooking. Then they separated into male and female groups: one group was composed of the three men and the brothers' twelve-year-old nephew, the other the women and younger children. The older brother's wife dished out a large plate of fish soup and set it before the men along with a bowl of manioc. The men began to eat the manioc but ignored the soup until the older brother took a spoonful of broth. After a moment the younger brother took a spoonful, then the brother-in-law, and finally the nephew. They continued eating manioc until the older brother took another spoonful of broth; then again, in the same sequence, the others did. This orderly cycle continued until the broth was gone; then another pause ensued until the older brother broke off a small piece of fish and ate it. Then the others followed suit in the same order until the fish was gone. All this was done in a matter-of-fact way, without discussion.

Meanwhile the women and children were sharing from a common pot. As among the men, individuals helped themselves to manioc without restraint. But the fish soup was carefully doled out by the women, ensuring a fair distribution. When the eating was done, husbands and wives turned back toward one another and soon shifted position, bringing the nuclear families back together.

This small episode teaches us two important facts about the social organization of a Machiguenga hamlet. First, despite the fundamental individual freedom of the separate households, they accept a measure of hierarchy and control so that precious resources such as fish can be distributed with a minimum of resentment or dispute. An abundant food like manioc does not occasion such care. Second, the social nature of the fish—that it ultimately belongs to the group and not to the person who caught it—is apparent in the dissolution of the nuclear families into hamlet-level men's and women's eating groups. As soon as the socialized fish has been consumed, the nuclear family units reconstitute themselves, for they remain the primary units of Machiguenga society.

When households collaborate, it is usually to obtain or distribute special foods. A single family may do all its own hunting, fishing, foraging, and growing of pineapples, papayas, and other favorite foods. But these are often available only sporadically, and then in unwieldy quantities. Sharing can not only reduce a sudden windfall to manageable proportions but also ensure that similar windfalls in other households will be shared, thus making special foods available more frequently to more people. The good feelings surrounding such exchanges help alleviate the constant small frictions that arise from daily competition over scarce resources, and are the primary social glue holding a Machiguenga hamlet together.

As we have seen, evidence of hierarchy appears in this egalitarian society in the distribution of the fish soup. But there is no paradox. The Machiguenga household itself is hierarchically ordered, primarily on the basis of age, although occasionally an especially productive member may outrank an older but less productive one. Complex cooperative tasks are managed smoothly because a clear chain of command and compliance exists. When children grow up and form separate households, these lines of authority tend to reassert themselves when group cooperation is required.

The three households in the anecdote of the fish soup express their hierarchical structure in many ways. For example, a higher-status household receives far more visits from a lower-status household than it pays in return: the older brother's household receives about six visits from the younger brother's household, and nine from the brother-in-law's, for every visit it pays them. Likewise, the brother-in-law's household pays a great many visits to the younger brother's household, which almost never pays a visit in return (A. Johnson 1978: 106–9).

Lines of authority and prestige between households materialize in cooperative ventures. The most cooperative task among the Machiguenga is fish poisoning, which may involve from two to as many as ten households. Here a leader always coordinates the activities: men build dams to slow the water, and women construct weirs to catch the drugged fish as they float downstream. Each of these activities involves a complex division of labor, and timing is important. The level of water in the river, the number of workers needed, the provision and preparation of the poison, the exact moment it is introduced into the water—all require coordination by senior men and women who are used to authority and toward whom others are compliant.

In the early phases of the work, as in the multihousehold meal, husbands and wives separate into same-sex groups and work apart. Once the poison has been introduced into the water, however, husbands and wives rejoin one another at preselected points and gather fish for their own households. Sometimes a household that provided much labor will find few fish in its stretch of river. In the later exchange of fish these differences will be evened out to some extent, but no authority or institution exists to allocate the catch fairly, or even to define what "fairly" might mean.

If disputes arise within a household or hamlet, they are resolved locally by a senior family member. For example, a man was attempting to catch a stunned *segori*, a troutlike fish of excellent flavor whose roe are especially valued. It eluded him and disappeared into a pool. A minute later his seven-year-old nephew caught the fish, a look of pure pleasure lighting the boy's face. But the uncle saw and said, "Here, that's my fish. I was chasing it!" The boy refused to hand over his prize until his other uncle, a highly respected man, ordered him to do so. Later the boy caught his own segori, and his happiness was restored. But had he not, his disappointment would have been seen as an unavoidable outcome of the need to acknowledge seniority and keep peace between households.

Periodically, particularly during a full moon, members of a hamlet will plan a beer feast. The women spend several days making manioc beer while the men devote themselves to hunting and fishing. Members of more than one hamlet may attend if invited by a respected man or woman. With feelings and tongues loosened by the abundance of beer and meat, many political issues, such as forming cooperative fishing groups, claiming garden land, or teasing rule-breakers, are aired. A man who is organizing a fishing project will seek cooperation and in that capacity may set the tone for some of the discussions. Or a man of wit may become a center of attention as he directs caustic gibes at some unfortunate who has offended him. But no clear leader is to be found, and the conversation ebbs and flows as this topic or that is picked up, passed around, and dropped.

For extensive horticulturalists like the Machiguenga, cooperation between households will always have both costs and benefits. Sociability, security, and the distribution of windfalls all make cooperation attractive, but at the expense of a certain autonomy in deciding how to serve one's own interests. The tensions that arise may grow into resentments, but standards of courtesy and respect keep these from being freely expressed. During the drunkenness of beer feasts, hostilities break out in intense, humiliating joking and in verbal and physical fights. These may ventilate feelings and restore equilibrium, but often they lead to a sense of injustice and a decision to leave the hamlet. On the whole, the Machiguenga fear aggression and much prefer disengagement. In most cases, one who feels intense anger simply flees (*ishiganaka*). He may later return to stay, or he may gather his family and move away. Slowly, over time, troubled relations will be soothed, and in a later phase of the cycle—especially when wild food is again abundant—the same households, and perhaps some new ones, will reestablish their hamlet and enjoy cooperative living again.

Hamlet groups do not own corporate property, nor are they as groups validated by the ceremonial occasions that we will discuss at length in Chapters 6 through 8. Except for a loose sense of a home range, as described for the !Kung (Case 2), no territoriality can be said to exist. Individual families own garden plots that they have carved out from the natural forest, but only as long as they cultivate them; the plots revert to common lands during fallow. All natural resources of the forests and rivers are open to all Machiguenga, although a foraging group generally keeps its distance from another's home range.

In summary, the Machiguenga illustrate the conditions under which horticulturalists may maintain a family-level economy and social organization. In an area where competition from other groups is low and where valued wild foods are scarce and widely scattered, the Machiguenga function very effectively in small, scattered households or hamlets. By the simple device of overproducing certain edible roots, they can live for years at a time as independent, self-sufficient households.

On the other hand, they find advantages in cooperating with other households in poison fishing and sharing windfalls of wild food. Within and between households, natural hierarchies exist that establish chains of command for coordinating labor and food distribution. But such leadership, and the splitting of married couples into separate men's and women's groups that sometimes occurs when wild foods are procured or consumed, are always temporary. The autonomous household regains command when the specific event is over.

Change is coming rapidly to the Peruvian Amazon, and the Machiguenga have felt its impact to varying degrees. Eight years after the research reported here, Baksh (1984) studied a Machiguenga village formed under the "Native Communities" policy of the Peruvian government. About two hundred people agreed to live together under the direction of a charismatic Machiguenga leader who focused their wish to have access to modern technology, especially medicines and steel tools. They had the unusual opportunity to settle an area rich in wild resources that had been depopulated for many years following Western contact. Although they formed separate households and hamletlike neighborhoods within the village, they agreed to cooperate in planting cash crops to earn money with which to "advance ourselves," as they said.

At first things went smoothly. Villagers would remain in the community four days per week working on communal projects, then scatter to favorite fishing spots for a three-day weekend they referred to as "vacations." But soon they found that the local fishing streams were becoming depleted, and travel time to ever more distant fishing spots was rising dramatically: the average travel time to fishing spots doubled every six months during Baksh's research. Disputes became so common that they threatened to split the community. In the end, the leader resolved matters by moving the whole village to a new site farther downriver where fish were still abundant.

In the quarter century since the first researchers visited Shimaa, large numbers of Quechua-speaking farmers from the Peruvian altiplano (descendants of the communities once ruled by the Inkas) have been migrating down to the Kompiroshiato in search of land to farm. The Machiguenga have responded by forming their own native community and closing off their side of the river, avoiding outside contacts wherever possible. Visitors who take a raft across the river to Shimaa are politely but firmly asked to turn around and go back. The people of Shimaa continue to practice subsistence agriculture supplemented with crops of coffee and cacao, and to hunt and fish in the local forests. They still weave their own clothing, although now their households are more likely to display colorful plastic basins and the occasional radio or sewing machine.

Downriver, however, where motor-powered river transportation is possible, changes have been far more dramatic (Henrich 1997). The Camisea natural gas project (Camisea 1998) has brought tons of modern equipment and new job opportunities to Machiguenga communities. At the same time, the better transportation has meant closer involvement with market opportunities. Most Machiguengas in these lower-elevation regions now live in villages, grow cash crops, and work at least some of the time for wages. They have enthusiastically embraced market opportunities and now express a strong desire for cash income.

The results of denser settlement in villages and of growing crops for market as well as subsistence have been a predictable intensification of the traditional system. Garden land close to the village has been over-exploited, leading to growing travel time to distant garden lands; one village that experimented with shortening fallows found that when they lowered the fallow period to less than fifteen years, they could no longer grow crops in a new garden for more than one year (Henrich 1997: 340).

A growing trend is to build fences to declare private ownership of especially good plots of land near the village, but this causes much resentment among some community members. Wild foods such as fish and game have become an extremely minor part of the diet now. Dietary deficiencies in protein have been recorded in some communities, as well as high rates of illness from malaria and other infectious diseases. The current pattern of intensification is leading to much longer work days and is environmentally unsustainable. At current rates, by 2005 the Machiguenga will have deforested all the village lands originally allocated to them under the Peruvian native communities program (Henrich 1997: 346).

The case we described earlier in this chapter, therefore, is the one that prevailed before recent times, in which families are scattered and no sizable patch of territory is inhabited for long. Yet wild resources are everywhere at a low level, for no good fishing spot or hunting trail is abandoned for long. Living under a competitive mode of subsistence, any community larger than a family simply depletes local resources that much faster, requiring more rapid abandonment of a site or else the disruption of the community with increasingly frequent disputes.

We may anticipate later chapters by noting that when there is nowhere to run, when the environment is too full of competing families, some other means of resolving disputes becomes necessary, and the most likely at this level of political development is warfare (Carneiro 1970b). The seeming abundance of the Machiguenga economy, therefore, does not imply underpopulation. Indeed, the speed with which even a small local increase in population can lead to depletion and hardship indicates that the Machiguenga are living closer to environmental limits than is at first apparent.

Case 4. The Nganasan of Northern Siberia

We now examine briefly a family-level forager society in which domesticated animals play a significant economic role. Here again domestication as such—in this case animal domestication—is not a sufficient condition for socioeconomic development beyond the family level. Among the Nganasan, small family herds of tame reindeer served almost exclusively as a way of facilitating the foraging way of life. With pressure from an expanding European population, however, new conditions arose that encouraged the Nganasan and similar groups to increase their herds of tame reindeer at the expense of wild reindeer. And it was this process, a reaction to population pressures rather than to the attractions of domestication, that eventually led the Nganasan to form larger, more economically complex social units and exert a tighter political control over resources.

The Environment and the Economy

The Nganasan (Popov 1964, 1966) inhabit the frozen, windswept tundra of the Taymyr Peninsula in the northern extremity of Central Siberia. They are found from the northern limits of the forested tundra north across a hilly plain to the Arctic Sea. The landscape is locally variable, with dry, rocky hills, grassy slopes, swampy lowlands, and numerous lakes. Trees are rare; shrubs, lichens, and sedges are the main vegetation. The fauna of greatest importance to the Nganasan are reindeer, polar fox, fish, and various species of geese and ducks.

On the Taymyr Peninsula the temperature falls below freezing on 263 days of the year. The summer is short, and frosts are likely to occur in late spring and early fall. Owing to the intense summer sun, however, the tundra blossoms in July and August, when it is visited by great flocks of birds and swarms of biting insects. At this latitude (75°N), well north of the Arctic Circle, there is about a month in summer when the sun never sets, and another month in winter when it never rises.

Reindeer, or caribou, are the central focus of the Nganasan economy. For most of the year reindeer are scattered in small groups, but they aggregate in large herds in the fall for the migration south, and again in the spring for the return north. In the summer and fall reindeer grow fat on grass, sedges, leaves, and fungi. Over the winter, however, they depend on lichen and their own stored fat for survival. The availability of lichen limits the population of reindeer, probably more so than predation by wolves or, under traditional methods of exploitation, by humans (Ingold 1980: 20, 35).

Human settlements are widely scattered, with population densities below one person per fifty square miles, and population movements are responsive to reindeer movements. Unlike wolves, which can follow the reindeer herd at its usual speed (from ten to forty-odd miles per day), slower humans must use stratagems to ambush the reindeer or lure them to destruction. The most popular and productive of these are communal hunts in the spring and fall at places that reindeer are known to visit. During these hunts large numbers of reindeer are trapped, killed, processed, and, in the fall, stored for winter consumption.

Migrating reindeer stop at certain lakes and cross rivers at favorite crossings; old hunters, who know these places and the best times for hunting, take charge of organizing the hunt. Men are prohibited from hunting at such sites except during the communal hunt, so that the game will not be frightened away by excessive contact. In October 1936, Popov (1966: 20) observed a migrating herd so large that it took several days for the "dense mass" of reindeer to cross the frozen Pyasina River.

Reindeer prefer to gather near lakes or rivers into which they can flee for safety when attacked by wolves. The Nganasan take advantage of this by using dogs to drive reindeer into the water, where hunters in dugout canoes spear them. Another strategy uses flags made of poles from which flap strips of leather. Since the flapping intimidates the reindeer, simply by placing poles every fifteen feet or so the Nganasan construct long funnel-shaped fences along which they can drive the reindeer into corrals where hunters lie in wait.

Groups of men often leave the seasonal camps for days at a time, returning with quantities of animals for the already busy women to process. When herds are very large, women will join in the hunt. But usually a strong division of labor separates the men as hunters and makers of hunting implements from the women as domestic food processors and makers of clothing and storage containers. Where animals are concerned, men hunt reindeer whereas women and girls care for the domestic herds; more often than not, after a man has killed an animal, women are sent to bring it home (Popov 1966: 28).

Particularly in the fall, the take from communal hunts can be prodigious. People gorge themselves on food in the late summer and fall, and process the surplus for storage. They dry the meat and render the fat for storage in containers fashioned from skins and internal organs. They prepare the hides for tents and clothing. To a greater degree even than the Shoshone, the Nganasan must store large amounts of meat and fat in order to survive the long winter ahead. They have two simple rules for eating: in the spring "eat as little as possible," and in the fall "eat as much as possible."

Other foods are important in some seasons. The annual cycle of food production is approximately as follows. With the spring thaws Nganasan families disperse and move north, away from their winter hamlets, to hunt reindeer, partridge, and ducks. With the advent of the summer fishing season in June and July, small, scattered family groups enjoy a relatively settled life until late July and August, when they come together for communal hunts of geese, which are then molting and can be taken in large quantities with nets. Like the reindeer, these are rendered and their fat stored for winter consumption.

In late August the move back south begins, interrupted periodically by reindeer drives until November, when the Nganasan settle once more in winter hamlets. Over the winter some hunting of scattered individual reindeer and polar foxes continues, along with ice fishing. During this time the Nganasan make clothing, repair tools and sleds, and pursue other sedentary activities. Early spring, before the thaws have come and when stored foods have run out, is a period of scarcity and hunger both for humans and for the animals they eat.

The routes of human migration are fairly well established. A hunter often leaves the frozen carcass of his catch lying alongside a trail that he knows his family will be passing a month or two later. In order to protect the carcass from wolves and polar bears, he may cover it with rocks and pour water over them. The water quickly freezes, making a secure icebox in which food remains stored until needed.

The Nganasan's movements reflect the whereabouts of their quarry. For most of the year, reindeer, fowl, and other game are widely scattered, and the Nganasan follow them in groups of one or two families. At other times, when reindeer or geese are locally available in large quantities, families congregate to exploit that opportunity. Periods of stable settlement—in summer near favorite fishing spots, in winter near ice-fishing spots and (more important) near pasture for domestic reindeer—alternate with periods of movement in pursuit of migrating reindeer.

Tame domestic reindeer are used chiefly for transportation. The Nganasan family, although mobile, is not light on its feet. In the fall and the long winter, a family requires several reindeer to pull large sleds piled high with the heavy tents, clothing and skins, food stores, and firewood that are essential to surviving the harsh Siberian winter. Tame reindeer also pull the light, fast sleds on which hunters pursue small herds of wild reindeer in the winter, and can be trained to act as decoys to lure wild reindeer within range of camouflaged hunters. Additionally, though only when the alternative is starvation, a household may slaughter its domestic reindeer. So reluctant are the Nganasan to slaughter a tame reindeer that they consider shedding its blood a sin; thus they kill the animal by strangulation, a difficult task.

It takes labor to pasture domestic reindeer and protect them from wolves, and in the winter a family may have to move when nearby pastures of lichen become exhausted. Nganasan households traditionally kept fewer than ten reindeer, enough for winter transportation and hunting but not so many as to require frequent moves.

Warfare is not reported. Stories of hunger and famine do occur, however, in which men came to blows over caches of food during the hungry spring season. Men nowadays do not know of such cases and admire those fierce ancestors who would fight over food. But it appears that the common response to the spring scarcity is to join a hamlet group and share stored foods until the scatter to summer resources can begin. As with the !Kung (Case 2) and the Machiguenga (Case 3), scarcity may provoke personal violence, but organized intergroup aggression must have been discouraged because of the importance of broad interpersonal and intergroup ties in spreading risks.

The scarcity of resources in the far north might suggest the likelihood of intergroup trade, but what scant information we have indicates that until recent times the Nganasan were essentially self-sufficient. As we shall see, however, that situation changed; an extensive trade of animal products for technological items developed historically as part of a general intensification of resource use.

To summarize, the critical problems faced by the Nganasan are the extreme scarcity and unpredictability of resources in the Arctic environment. Because of these problems population density remained very low until historic times, and a family-level existence could be maintained. Cooperation between families was needed only for large-scale hunting and for the sharing of stored foods.

Social Organization

The autonomy of nuclear family groups and multifamily clusters is a strong ideal among the Nganasan. Nuclear families often live separately in their own small tents. Possessions for individual use are treated as private property: as with the Shoshone, only very large items like the nets used in reindeer drives are owned by a group. Families share with each other, to be sure, but each keeps careful track of its contributions. Popov (1966: 108) comments on "their extraordinary frugality with food products. In the spring when the people who are short of food go for help to their better supplied neighbors, the latter give them a meager amount: two or three cracknels or a small piece of meat the size of a fist. However, no one is offended by this, for food at this time of year is of great value and precious to everyone."

When two or more families share the same tent, one man and his wife are accepted as leaders of the tent and occupy the place of honor at the right of the entrance. Other residents of the tent inform the leaders about their own economic activities. Popov does not mention whether separate families keep separate larders, but it does seem that sharing a tent implies at least a degree of communal food supply. In winter a large tent (of up to thirty feet in diameter) may house as many as five families. Clusters of tents are common, as' are clusters of stone and earthen huts. Still larger aggregates occur temporarily when geese or reindeer are abundant.

Where several families share a tent, each occupies its own portion of the tent, within which men, women, and children have their assigned places according to commonly accepted principles (e.g., the men are nearest the central hearth). The parking place for each member's sleds is also established, indicating the degree to which individual behavior must be structured in the multifamily coresidential group.

In the larger groups the unequal distribution of skills may lead to a division of labor. A good fisherman may be a poor sled-maker and vice versa; hence exchanges between them are natural, if by no means free and easy. Popov writes:

Collective consumption does not in any way . . . mean that food products, tools of production, or everyday objects are freely lent; on the contrary, strict accounts are kept of everything. A hunter's family, for example, will share the meat of a killed wild reindeer with neighbors. . . . But the hunter's neighbors who receive a potful must give help to the hunter's household, by means of their own labor or reindeer. They are obliged to tend his domesticated reindeer, clean his fishnets, lend him their sledge reindeer, and even occasionally supply him with a gun and ammunition. If a hunter did not receive help from his neighbors, he considered it his right not to share a potful with them.

For all this emphasis on individual ownership, concessions must be made to the needs of the group. For example, as we have seen, experienced hunters are allowed to regulate communal reindeer drives, and individual hunters agree not to hunt in ways that would threaten the group's success. Exemplifying the competitive mode, when camps or hamlets break up in the spring, families reach an agreement about which trails, streams, lakes, and so forth each will exploit, in order to avoid unnecessary overlap and competition.

With these exceptions we find no evidence of political activities beyond the household level. There is no group territorial control over resources except in the sense of a home range that a group occupies by tradition or mutual agreement; understandings concerning winter fishing spots are perhaps the strongest forms of resource control. A dominant man may attract hangers-on who will work under his direction, but they do not depend on him for access to resources and may strike out on their own at any time. The Nganasan operate on the !Kung principle that "we are all headmen."

In sum, the Nganasan reveal the basic pattern of a family-level economy. Living in an environment of scattered resources, they pursue food sources opportunistically, moving much of the year in single-family households in pursuit of reindeer and other wild foods. Then periodically they congregate to harvest seasonally abundant foods such as migrating reindeer herds and flocks of molting geese. Stored meat and fat from these harvests are essential to their survival through the arduous winter and spring. Families remain obdurately independent even in their winter camps and hamlets, and are always free to separate from the group to follow an independent course. The family herds of reindeer are small and facilitate the foraging way of life: tame reindeer provide transportation, help in the hunt, and serve as insurance against starvation.

Recent history has seen significant changes in the economy of the Nganasan, leading to their transformation from reindeer hunters to true reindeer pastoralists. Essentially, as population expanded northward, consuming more and more of the temperate forests, the demand for the animal products of the far north increased drastically. By the end of the nineteenth century, the Nganasan found that they could sell reindeer and furs in an ever-growing market, and with the proceeds they could afford to buy guns, canoes, nets, traps, iron pots, tea, tobacco, and supplementary foods.

As the demand for reindeer meat grew, it became advantageous to manage reindeer production by increasing the size of domestic herds, which could be pastured on lands from which wild reindeer were being depleted by overhunting. Tame reindeer are clearly marked by coded notches carved in their ears and will not be hunted by other Nganasan. The consequences of this transformation to true pastoralism have been several. The costs of production rose, since private herds had to be protected from wolves and poachers. Many more animals were herded: whereas formerly eight or nine reindeer was a large number for a family herd, now fifty animals are considered a small herd. In the winter a family with a large herd must move frequently in search of pasture. Hence the semipermanent hamlets of sod houses built near fishing spots have now been abandoned in favor of large, heavy tents that must be cumbersomely dismantled, transported, and erected in a new location every few weeks. It is even necessary to seek out and transport fodder in winter for the domestic herds.

Camp size has increased, and kin relationships have become formalized around property in herds. Dowry payments and patron-client relations have emerged as important features of social life. With larger camps has come increased capital investment in such technology as large nets for the communal hunts of reindeer and geese. And reindeer hunting and the sale of reindeer (both domestic and wild) are now monitored by a community extending far beyond the limits of the family group (see Ingold 1980).

The transformation of the Nganasan from reindeer hunters with small domestic herds into large-scale reindeer pastoralists was a response to a great increase in the demand for reindeer meat in an expanding market. Once reindeer were being hunted for sale rather than household consumption, it became necessary to own more of them, since the numbers of unowned (i.e., wild) reindeer were being rapidly depleted. With changes in the provisioning of winter fodder the numbers of reindeer that could be maintained in this environment, especially in winter, increased, a form of intensification of production. The resulting increases in the scale and complexity of social organization are clearly responses to the underlying economic change.

Following the Russian Revolution, the communist government attempted to collectivize its Siberian minorities, including the Nganasan. They had some success among sedentary fishing populations in coastal regions, but the Nganasan fiercely resisted these efforts, which they rightly saw as an effort to destroy their self-sufficient, nomadic way of life and impose unwelcome new standards of behavior (Sergeyev 1956: 498). Their resistance was slowly undermined by gradual communist missionization (Forsyth 1992: 309–10; Sergeyev 1956: 497), abetted by the continuing colonization of the region for mining. By the 1970's the Nganasan constituted only about 4 percent of the population of their former territories (Forsyth 1989: 87–88). They had become increasingly settled, had converted to Soviet-style herd management practices (Sergeyev 1956: 505), were dependent on bread, sugar, butter, and other imported goods, and were starting to urbanize (Popov 1964: 580–81; Savoskul 1989: 116).

As of this writing, however, the likelihood is increasing that some Siberian herders like the Nganasan will return to an adaptation similar to the one described by Popov (Bennett 1997). With the breakup of the Soviet Union, the flow of wealth and technology into the Siberian wilderness has drastically declined, and with it the wage employment that had drawn men away from herding in the first place. "Family brigades" of six to ten members once again manage small herds on long seasonal migrations. Even as international investors lay plans to exploit the region's mineral wealth, small groups of traditional herders—some reluctantly, others willingly—are "going back to the totally tribal way our forefathers lived" (quoted in Bennett 1997: 16).

Conclusions

Although they possessed the technology of food domestication, neither the Machiguenga nor the Nganasan made use of it, before recent times, to organize beyond the family-level economy. The clear tendency is for small social units to be scattered uniformly across the landscape as long as the wild foods on which they depend are widely scattered. Aggregation is temporary, for the purpose of cooperation in getting food, as in the Machiguenga poison fishing or the Nganasan reindeer hunt, or sharing food, as in the seasonal hamlets of both groups.

Family autonomy is evident in a number of ways. Productive capital such as tools, weapons, herds, and gardens is individually owned, and its use by others is regulated and carefully reckoned. Similarly, a family keeps its own food supply, sharing food only reluctantly with families of the same hamlet. The ultimate autonomy of the family, of course, is its freedom to move, to detach from other families and pursue its own interests with minimal interference.

Evidently pressure on resources brings about a greater dependence on domesticated foods and an increase in community size and economic integration. Internal population growth, encroaching populations from outside, access to new technology (e.g., shotguns) that facilitate intensification, and the opportunity to earn cash by intensifying production all make for a greater dependence on domestication. With this change comes larger communities and a new level of social stratification involving tighter control over resources in behalf of the larger group (as distinct from the perceived self-interest of the separate families that make up the group). Families as such are not particularly happy about this development, but accept it because they have no alternative.

Part II

The Local Group

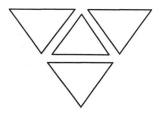

FIVE

The Local Group

IN CHAPTERS 5 TO 8 we examine the local group, the institutions of which organize politically autonomous human groups of roughly one hundred to five hundred members. The local group has an evolutionary history. Its organizing principles and mechanisms are cultural artifacts developed for specific purposes and maintained out of tradition and utility. Local groups can be coresidential as a village, or dispersed as hamlets, or even as mobile pastoralists, depending on the specific nature of their social organization and underlying economy. The development of local groups is often linked to the Neolithic revolution, associated with the domestication of plants and animals, but perhaps equally revolutionary was the development of formal social institutions that channeled human interaction in new ways.

Although in the local group the family remains of primary significance in everyday living, its economic behavior cannot be understood without reference to considerations that extend beyond the individual family and even the territorial limits of the local group. Each local group is fashioned by embedding from as few as two to as many as twenty subgroups, each an extended or grown-up family unit familiar to us from the family level. Each subgroup is organized from within by flexible close biocultural relationships, but it is the task of the local group to organize and regularize interactions, rights, and obligations between these subgroups. The cultural mechanisms that maintain the local group combine emergent patterns of leadership with extensive ceremonialism. These cultural artifacts allow families to live together and coordinate their activities despite countervailing pressures to split up and go their separate ways.

The settlement pattern of the local group is comparatively sedentary. Hunter-gatherers continue to aggregate and disperse throughout the year, but they often form seasonal villages and live in them for months while eating stored foods. When depending on farming, villages or hamlet clusters locate near productive lands and remain there for many years consecutively. For defensive purposes and to define social groups, villages or hamlets may be surrounded by palisades. Dance grounds and ancestral burial grounds focus group ceremonies. Pastoral groups, however, owing to their dependence on the herd, are even more mobile than some foragers, having to move their animals frequently so as not to overgraze pastures. As a consequence, pastoralists tend toward small egalitarian groups unless forced—usually by external aggression—to form larger groups.

Local group societies are abundantly familiar to anthropology. Their institutions—corporate kin groups, status rivalry, and ceremonial associations—guide many activities: with whom to marry, to cooperate and share, to make friends or enemies, and to identify as a people. The local group controls access to the land, fights to defend it, cooperates to exploit it, and provides access to mates. One's very survival is based on membership in such a group; viewed from within, it would be hard to imagine any collection of people in the world more important than the members of one's local group.

Local groups themselves are linked to other local groups by extensive regional networks of personal friendships, exchanges, alliances, and ceremonial cycles (Dalton 1977). These networks are decentralized institutions that balance complex and unstable political relationships of competition and cooperation. At their greatest extent, they can take on the character of regional collectivities, managed via major ceremonies by local group leaders, that anticipate the evolution of regional polities that we will describe for chiefdoms.

Still, the degree of internal structure of the local group may be easily overdrawn. As part of our evolutionary heritage, the dynamics of daily life continue to be worked out in small families. Most decisions about the use of resources, the organization of production, the distribution of food, and specifics of association and cooperation take place within the family and between close relatives and friends. As much as these are influenced by rules and traditions, the pragmatics of daily life in families mean that most work, social interactions, and recreation are quite spontaneous and flexible.

The main characteristics of the local group, according to the culture-core checklist of Chapter 1, are these:

1. *The environments* associated with local groups can be highly variable, from high Arctic coasts to tropical forests, but they tend to be more productive than for comparable family-level groups on the one hand,

and more marginal than for chiefdoms and states on the other. Resources are often abundant seasonally (but not year-round), or capable of significant intensification (but usually not permanent cropping, although the Central Enga [Case 10] are an instructive exception).

2. *Population* is similarly intermediate. Among farmers, it typically ranges from 1 to 20 or 30 persons per square mile, well above levels achieved by family-level societies. The Enga are again exceptional, their densities ranging from 85 to 250 persons per square mile and requiring a specific explanation. Among hunter-gatherers and pastoralists, population densities must be much lower, constrained by the available wild resources of animals, fish, and pasture. Among the coastal Tareumiut (Case 6) or the fishermen of the Northwest Coast (Case 9), population densities are highly concentrated on key resources, but overall populations are generally less than 1 per square mile. Among pastoralists, the productivity of the pastures limits the density of animals and herders; densities are usually about 1 to 3 per square mile.

3. *Technology* consists primarily of personal tools, such as the digging stick and harpoon. But some key technologies, especially for intensified hunting and fishing and for animal-herding, are owned by individuals and used by a larger group under their control. These include fishing weirs, whaling boats, and animal corrals.

4. *Social organization of production* has two levels, each with characteristic sets of functions: (a) the family level, involving daily subsistence, child-rearing, frequent socializing, and informal aid; and, (b) the local group, involving cooperation in large-scale work tasks, risk management, war, and ceremony.

5. *Warfare and territoriality* are common among most local groups, with ownership of group lands highly charged and often carefully demarcated. In lower density local groups such as the Yanomamo (Case 5), raids build an outward image of fierceness to keep enemies at a distance from home territories. For higher density groups such as the Tsembaga Maring (Case 7) or the Central Enga (Case 10), territorial boundaries are sacred and defended in organized battles against any intrusion. Among pastoralists at the local group level, raiding of animals is a constant threat and defense of herds and pasturage is essential. Even among foragers, their most productive seasonal resources, such as fish runs, are highly prized and defended. The larger technologies (weirs, canoes) are personally owned and managed.

6. *Political integration* is strong within the local group, defined by a combination of ceremonial activities and leadership. The local group, furthermore, albeit autonomous and responsible for defense of its own territory, is always linked to other local groups by networks of mar-

riage, exchange, and alliance. These regional systems, despite the absence of centralized rule, may be quite strongly integrated into collectivities of leaders who compete and coordinate with each other through the prestige economy.

7. *Stratification* in the local group takes the form of leaders whose status rivalry creates the intergroup collectivity. But these leaders do not have exclusive control of resources and hence the power to oppress. Individuals, usually men but supported and directed by women, distinguish themselves by their fierceness or diplomatic skill to become recognized leaders for their local group. Some leaders control more resources than others, but their lot is to work harder and lead by example. The scale of leadership varies from headmen to Big Men, but both kinds of leader are frequently polygynous and thus have higher reproductive success.

8. *Sanctity* especially takes the form of invoking, honoring, and placating ancestral spirits who stand for the local group and its subgroups. Ceremonies honor the ancestors for their benevolent contributions to fertility, food production, and success in battle. Ceremonies serve to define the local group and its corporate entities, and to create and maintain regional intergroup relationships to obtain allies, regulate conflict, make marriages, and trade for needed and desired products. Many of these ceremonies are calendric, performed regularly on annual or multiyear schedules, and are considered essential for success in all important affairs.

Comparing the local group level with the family level, much appears to be the same, while some things change dramatically. As we review the cases in Chapters 6, 7, and 8, the most dramatic contrasts with the family level appear in the frequency of warfare and the rise of ceremonialism and leadership. These in turn contribute to a change in emphasis in gender relations: whereas a strong division of labor continues the close economic interdependence between wives and husbands within the household, now a cultural emphasis on men's bravery, aggression, and display of status contribute to a public imagery of male superiority and a corresponding devaluation of women's activities and attributes.

We start our examination of the local group level by summarizing the change in the institutional character of society, what has been referred to as the domestication of the human species. To explain this profound social transformation, we look at the relevant theories of warfare and economy that form the basis of our theory of the evolutionary dynamics that caused the social transformation.

The Domestication of the Human Species

The Neolithic revolution of some ten thousand years ago was a profound change in human history, second only to the origin of culture itself (Childe 1936, 1942). Although first described for the Middle East and Europe, similar changes are found to have taken place worldwide and largely independently in Africa, Asia, and the Americas. In *The Neolithic Revolution*, Cole (1959) describes several major technological changes:

> origins of plant cultivation
> domestication of animals
> ax-trade and forest clearance
> new transport with boats and carts
> crafts, including pottery and weaving
> villages
> houses
> tombs

The implication of progress is strong in this list: evidently by such means humans liberated themselves technologically from the harshness of nature. The domestication of plants and animals allowed for new subsistence security, that in turn allowed people to settle down and enjoy the material well-being of village life. Yet doubts about progress remain: given human creativity, why weren't such technological achievements made much sooner? As early as forty thousand years ago, for example, it appears that Upper Paleolithic hunters and gatherers had a basic understanding of the principles of plant cultivation (Maryanski and Turner 1992: 91). And contemporary foragers seldom seem eager to settle down to village life, which in practice may be more demanding of labor and of personal sacrifices.

The Neolithic revolution was more than a list of technological advances. It was a social revolution—our domestication—a transformation as much conceptual and social as economic: "Domesticated people are those who live (and mostly work) in houses grouped together in hamlets, villages and small towns as distinct from people of the past and the present who only use temporary dwellings" (Wilson 1988: 52). As mobile foragers, organized at the family level, humans maintained an open society based on personal intimacy, and enjoyed "the only true form of liberty, liberty from the interference of others" (Wilson 1988: 52).

When humans settled down and built houses in villages, their cognitive and spatial worlds changed. In a manufactured landscape, people live and interact in built spaces that relate individuals and their daily routines to each other and to overarching communities:

By living in a built environment people create for themselves, quite unknowingly, problems that affect the senses vital and essential to the conduct of all other activities instrumental in survival, subsistence, and well-being. . . . Once people become domesticated they must confront and are confronted with a structure arising, as Durkheim would say, sui generis, out of those conditions—the structure of the relations between people as neighbors and as hosts and guests. (Wilson 1988: 112)

These are thus neighborhood societies, in which people share formalized environments that divide and join personal space and activities. Spaces are private or public, connecting people and separating them, defining sacred and profane contexts. Perhaps most important, these relationships are not fluid. They exist often through the lifetimes of single individuals and even across generations. One is born into a social world to which one must adapt in order to survive and prosper.

Within the pessimistic wing of social evolutionists, this transformation represents anything but progress for human well-being:

The abandonment of hunting and gathering involved the construction . . . of sociocultural cages that infringe on human needs for parity, freedom, mobility, and individualism. Of course, as big-brained hominoids, humans are remarkably flexible; and when forced to settle down in larger numbers, they could do so. The principal tool for this adaptation was the elaboration of kinship units from relatively autonomous nuclear (and at times extended) units into lineages that trapped individuals in a web of kinship. This line of structural elaboration was the easiest, especially when economic surplus was modest. But compared with the mobility and freedom of hunters and gatherers, the constraints of unilineal descent rules, dictating as they did family composition, residence, domestic and economic activity, authority, and marriage, represented a truly dramatic change. Perhaps the change occurred so gradually that people were unaware of the structural cage in which they were enclosing themselves, but once constructed, this highly circumscribed existence stood in contradiction to our ancestral heritage and its refinement during thousands upon thousands of years of hunting and gathering modes of adaptation. (Maryanski and Turner 1992: 110)

The situation these authors so vividly depict is the building of social institutions, the cultural artifacts that form the basis of the local group. In our cases, we will see that groups create and constrain possibilities within institutional frames. A dominant theme is the role of the ancestors. Associated with local groups are cemeteries, places where ancestors continue somehow in connection with living descendants. A person is defined largely by descent and kin relations that determine personal rights in land, marriage, and obligations to others. The world is inhabited by the ghosts of ancestors who are helpers, but whose disapproval is feared. Groups are materialized in annual and periodic ceremonies that celebrate the group and honor the ancestors for their help. The new sense of ceremony marks the intrinsic dependence of the individual's subsistence quest and reproductive hopes upon the local group.

Theorizing the Local Group

Using cultural media, humans have fashioned institutions that extend sociability in extraordinary ways. Here we focus on several dramatic and novel characteristics of local groups involving warfare and male supremacy, kinship and reciprocity, and leadership and ceremony.

Warfare and Male Supremacy

Warfare prevails in most local groups, especially among horticulturalists and pastoralists. Sahlins (1968b) describes how, without an overarching regional integration, local groups ("tribesmen") inhabit a world of political anarchy wherein all groups are potentially at war with all others. Service's category "tribe" (1962) covers most local groups, although he emphasized the regional organization of clans and other cultural institutions—"cross-cutting sodalities," he called them—at the expense of local group autonomy in most political affairs. The Yanomamo (Case 5), Tsembaga Maring (Case 7), and Central Enga (Case 10) represent a continuum in the evolution of tribal societies toward increasing density of population and intensity of warfare (Johnson 1989).

Is warfare between local groups an outcome of human nature? As we noted in Chapter 1, humans are phylogenetically prepared to be aggressive under some circumstances: they competitively seek to obtain food, shelter, and mates to support themselves and their offspring, and will defend these prizes against all comers. But it is not so clear that this explains warfare: family-level communities, in which these same tendencies apply, manage to live rather peacefully by comparison.

Peace becomes impossible, however, as the subsistence economy intensifies. In social evolution, we have seen that the first response to resource competition—at very low population levels—is to scatter and avoid conflict. Men may fight one another over this resource or that, but the overall pattern is to maintain peace through disengagement. As landscapes fill in and opportunities diminish, competition inevitably rises, but the family's first thought is not to create a regional political structure to resolve conflict. Rather, applying conservative logic, families do what they have always done: try to locate the best resources before others, and, if they are scarce, occupy them exclusively. If competitors try to dislodge them, those in possession must dig in, especially if other resources are now also occupied by other families. The result is that as population rises, competition increases, and so does aggressiveness.

The frequent outcome of this iterative process of increasing circumscription (Carneiro 1970b) is what Harris (1977: 65) calls the "male supremacy complex": male monopoly over weapons, training of males for combat and bravery, female infanticide, training of females to be the passive rewards for masculine performance, patrilineal bias in property and descent, prevalence of polygyny, competitive male sports, intense male puberty rituals, ritual uncleanliness of women, bride price, and other male-centered institutions. These behavior patterns are not human universals, although many are found apart from local group societies—in most military services, for example, and in other male-oriented communities such as athletic teams and fraternities. The male supremacy complex in its fullest development is brought about by endemic warfare where the lives and well-being of members of the local group are under constant lethal threat, where empirically from one-fourth to one-half of all male deaths result from homicide, and where defeat results not only in male casualties but also in the capture of wives and daughters and the displacement of the whole group from its ancestral lands.

These profound consequences of unregulated warfare have been well described for highland New Guinea (Feil 1987; Langness 1977). Initiated males of a local group form a strong male comradeship for mutual defense of the clan's land. They constitute "a secret male cult featuring sacred flutes (*nama*), violent male initiation rites, the total exclusion of females and uninitiated children, ritual feasting on pork and other desired foods, beliefs about male superiority, the ancestors and ancestral power" (Langness 1977: 3). The male bonding can express hypermasculinity by way of homosexual relationships that are believed to make men strong and to avoid the supposedly enervating effects of women (Herdt and Stoller 1990). These men are all from the same clan, their women marrying in from other, potentially hostile, clans. Contact with women is polluting.

Modulating the harsh gender antagonism is the central economic role of women in the domestic economy. Among nonindustrial societies, it is local groups with a horticultural subsistence base in which women make the largest direct contribution to food production (Sanday 1973: 1691). Women, who also manage the household economy and do the actual work of raising pigs as wealth, then become essential for successful ceremonial performance and political maneuvering. Despite the male-centered public displays of the political economy, both men and women understand the profound day-to-day economic importance of women.

Kinship and Reciprocity

Institutionally, the formation of clans and lineages distinguishes the organization of the local group from the less formalized organization of the family level. Kinship becomes a calculus that defines personal relationships and group associations, rooted in what Malinowski (1944: 55) calls "the reproductive principle of social integration." Biological relationships (breeding, parenting, nurturing) underpin emergent cultural constructs of marriage, descent, and socialization, upon which the institutions of the local group are founded. A vast literature in social anthropology analyses these institutions, of which the prototypical form is the descent group, such as the agnatic descent groups that Fortes (1949) discovered at the core of the "web of kinship." Why do descent groups assume such prominence at the local group level?

Clans and lineages in most local group societies are corporate—they own something, most crucially land. They delimit group territories by controlling access to scarce, highly productive resources. The corporateness of the descent group arises from increased competition over resources and the consequent need for strength in numbers to regulate and defend access. In a world without regionwide legal institutions to guarantee access, the corporate descent group declares the legitimacy of its members' claims, justifying them by reference to ancestral ties to the land.

Membership in the corporate group entails specific rights to land and assistance that are vested in the individual (Bell 1998a), and specific duties to participate in and materially support major ceremonial events and warfare. The individual's good standing in the group requires many reciprocities of the sort discussed in Chapter 2: obligatory gifts at life-cycle celebrations, payments for marriage or dispute resolution, food and labor to underwrite feasts. Although structured in the language of generosity characteristic of gifts, these are in fact obligations of group membership (Bell 1998b). In substantivist terms, membership in the local group is an aggregate of economic relationships embedded in the social institutions of the group.

Common descent is a cultural construct built upon and closely linked to the powerful biological constraints of kin selection. Being cultural, it is able to transcend the relatively weak capacity of biology to extend an individual's sense of loyalty, trust, and common interest beyond the family level. But in reality, in the way most people live at the local group level, the individuals with whom they have the most intimate ties and pressing obligations tend overwhelmingly to be close biological kin, roughly within the genealogical distance of first cousins. Although the corporate kin group utilizes every symbolic and ceremonial means at its disposal to extend the sense of group obligation outward by activating ancestral ties (ever more distant links of common descent), the tendency of corporate groups is to be inward-looking, as bent on excluding some as on including others.

In order to overcome the narrow inwardness of groups built on the principle of common descent, local groups use a variety of institutional means to create cross-cutting affiliations between descent groups. The two most powerful and pervasive of these are marriage and debt. For groups like Fortes's Tallensi, incest rules require individuals to seek spouses from a descent group other than their own. Hence, children have relatives in both the mother's and the father's descent groups, brothers and sisters end up living in different descent groups, and so on. In contrast to the lineal calculus of descent, these ties are personal cognatic networks of kinship: "There is no compulsion about these ties; they are not visualized in terms of binding rights and duties, but as being at bottom voluntary" (Fortes 1949: 281). These egocentric networks are to an extent like friendships: individuals choose which ones to emphasize (through visits, meal sharing, cooperative work, and so on), not unlike the broad regional networks of family-level societies (Johnson and Bond 1974). And they appear to function in similar ways: Dalton (1977) describes how such networks bind local groups together and create opportunities for trade, marriage, alliance, and movement. Such networks are expansive: the goal is to create opportunities and flexibility. They counteract the exclusionary loyalties of descent.

In addition to the personal networks created by marriage, the exchange of spouses plays a central role in a larger process of creating debt and credit between local groups. Marriages are typically viewed as a gift of a bride or groom from one descent group to the other. These gifts have the classic character of prestations, entailing obligations to give, receive, and repay. To accept a gift is to agree to be in debt, and this debt creates or reinforces a social connection. Often, the debt created by marriage is not reciprocated for years, even a generation. Among the functions of the leader of a local group is to remember these debts and credits and to guide group behavior toward fulfilling obligations and maintaining social ties with other local groups.

If we imagine a fishnet held up to view, the vertical strands (the warp of a textile) would be the lines of descent embodied in corporate groups, and the horizontal strands (the woof) would be the cross-cutting linkages created by marriage: that is the web of kinship. The web is enhanced still further by other prestations: lavish feasting with grandiose displays of generosity (creating debt) are the most famous, but smaller exchanges of utilitarian objects, payments of wealth to mollify injured feelings, and sharing windfalls of produce all do their part to strengthen the web of kinship.

As Fortes describes, the web of kinship has a virtually unlimited potential for expansion, one link at a time. The linkages are maintained by balanced reciprocity (Chapter 2): links hold to the degree that over time there is a sense of balance or fairness in the relationship. Often, the relationships require the reciprocal exchange of wealth objects that symbolize, and indeed materialize, the relationships that constitute the network (DeMarrais et al. 1996). Each wealth object has a history, a social life that encapsulates the social bonds of the manufacture of the object and the network through which it has moved (Appadurai 1986).

Leadership and Ceremony

At the family level we found a comparative scarcity of leadership and ceremonial occasions. Where they did occur they were ad hoc, vanishing with changing circumstances. Not so the local group, where the prevalence of warfare and other conditions requires suprafamily groups, and these in turn depend on the initiatives of leaders and the group-building functions of ceremonies.

Ecologically, the leader has been viewed as a social technology that develops to solve problems beyond the capacity of the family (Harris 1977; Service 1962). Perhaps the most important of these problems is endemic warfare. Feil (1987) describes the evolution of leadership in highland New Guinea via agricultural intensification, increased frequency of competition and warfare, and the development of regional political systems to moderate the severity of conflict. Beyond warfare, leaders help solve problems in risk management, technology, and trade.

Politically, a basic role of the local leader is to organize and represent the group in intergroup ceremonies, where his followers advertise their personal valor, wealth, and attractiveness in displays of dance and dress. The leader compels their material support by reminding all that he acts in their name. His prestige is their strength, able to be transformed into whatever the group may need in order to defend its interests in a highly competitive environment.

Among the dramatic transformations occurring with the rise of the local group is the door it opens to individuals of unusual ambition for power. In theory, any community will have its share of "aggrandizers," a term that refers to

any ambitious, enterprising, aggressive, accumulative individual (elsewhere referred to as accumulators, or "triple A" personalities) who strives to become dominant in a community, especially by economic means. The term subsumes Great Men, Head Men, Big Men, elites and chiefs. (Hayden 1995: 18)

Unlike family-level societies like the !Kung, however, who admire the self-effacing meekness of a cooperative and generous compatriot and who joke that "we are all headmen over ourselves," the local group leader proclaims his eminence to all who will listen. What opens the door to aggrandizers is the new problems they come to solve in the local group: people need them, and they take advantage of such opportunities for control to advance their personal interests.

The leader's position is always tied to ceremonial performances that define the group's internal nature and external ties. While ceremonies remain few in the household and the hamlet, ceremonial cycles pervade all affairs involving the local group and its relations to other groups. Ceremonies, financed as they are by the intensification of production, become the context for all social production. The ceremony is the structural essence of the local group, defining its very existence. Here we see the creation and enforcement of formal suprafamily ties, the public proclamation and validation of the group's political status regionally, and the advertisement and exchange of property ownership by means of primitive valuables or money.

Because of the importance of public ceremonies in conferring prestige, especially in Big Man systems, some have termed the economy supporting them the "prestige economy" (Herskovits 1952: 464–65). Yet, since in these societies (as elsewhere) political and economic power reside not in wealth as such but in the control of access to resources, labor, and economic goods, the prestige economy and the political economy are in fact one and the same. An individual and his support group gain prestige in competitive intergroup ceremonies to the degree that the leader can demonstrate his ability to mobilize supporters to provide goods, labor, and warriors. His group's ceremonial performances demonstrate economic and military might and the group's ability to commit resources to intergroup enterprises. In effect, prestige is latent power, the promise of power.

A central feature of ceremonial performance in all local groups is the public materialization of the group as a body. Family-level societies have little need for such affirmation, since the family's interdependence is evident daily in cooperation and sharing and is rooted in primary kinship ties. It is different when the interdependence is between hundreds of people who may not know each other intimately or like each other very much. Individuals may not perceive their dependence on others and may not be well disposed to submit gracefully to the sacrifices that group life demands. The ceremony not only provides the opportunity to heal factional wounds through dances, contests, and feasts; it also focuses the attention of all on the material exchanges that are its integrating core.

Especially in regionwide intergroup collectivities, ceremonies provide a public proclamation of ownership, ancestry, and successful transmission of rights. On the Northwest Coast (Case 9) and in the New Guinea highlands (Cases 7 and 10), a major aspect of ceremonial behavior is the public display of crests, emblems, tokens, valuables, and property markers. In a world without courts and documents, the ceremony is the forum in which to legalize property rights.

The ceremony is also imbued with sanctity. To sanctify something is to invest it with supernatural power and significance, to make it awesome. As Rappaport (1979) has shown, ceremonies in local groups sanctify behaviors that have great adaptive importance: the feast honoring the ancestors is in fact the central ceremony that affirms or negates military alliances, defines new rights over horticultural land, initiates or ends cycles of warfare, and reduces overpopulation in the pig herd. Sacred spirits are called forth by offerings of food, chanting, playing the sacred flutes, and dancing in masks. The awe attaching to them makes violations of ritually sanctified agreements and understandings dangerous. To defy the spirits is to invite disaster. Sanctity, therefore, reinforces the ties that bind the local group. It works against the corrosive effects of short-sighted, self-centered, impulsive behaviors such as violence, theft, and adultery that could (and often do anyway) shatter group cohesiveness.

In Chapter 2 we learned that among Wolf's household funds, the subsistence fund dominates budgets at the family level. At the local group level, however, the ceremonial fund joins subsistence as a major household expense. As social relationships become more extensive, "all social relationships are surrounded by . . . ceremonial, and ceremonial must be paid for in labor, in goods, or in money" (Wolf 1966a: 7). Each family must generate a surplus, characteristically mobilized by local leaders, to be used in the emergent political economy to underwrite feasting, display, and competitive gift-giving. In this way local group ceremonies, called forth by the exigencies of economic intensification and warfare, begin to affect basic productive decisions in the subsistence economy.

To supply both funds, staple goods continue to be produced within the family. But now a large portion is periodically amassed, displayed, and consumed during the ceremonies that define the local group and its relationship to other groups. The competitive displays of food at these ceremonies measure directly the productive potential of the group and thus the attractiveness of its members for marriage, trade, and alliance.

Exchange and the use of primitive valuables also play a significant role in the ceremonial fund. Primitive valuables such as shells and feathers make the body beautiful, as they do in family-level societies, but they may also make it more fearsome militarily. And the valuables themselves have "social lives" (Appadurai 1986). Each object comes with a history of transactions that tells how its current owner is positioned in the social network. Valuables materialize the abstract network of social relationships that each individual and group must build in order to survive and prosper.

In most situations involving local groups, the valuables are broadly exchangeable for other objects including subsistence items; they are not separated into separate "spheres of exchange" (Earle 1982; cf. Bohannan 1955). They serve as a medium of exchange and as stores of value. In the Big Man cases, the gift-giving and display of valuables take on the character of status rivalry in an emergent political economy.

The Primary Dynamics of Local Group
Economy and Society

Our challenge is to understand how intensification causes institution-building at the local group level. Intensification, the engine for change, continues to be driven by increasing population densities that bring about competition and corporate group formation. Competition in turn creates linked local and regional political rivalry that further intensifies production to fuel ceremonial competition. According to the model in Figure 3, population growth and subsistence intensification together create specific economic problems that require new institutional forms of integration. The extraordinary diversity of natural environments and human means of intensifying production at the local group level leads to distinctive problems and alternative institutional solutions. These evolutionary processes are not unilinear but multilinear, meaning that the specific causes, conditions, and outcomes of social formation vary according to local environments and histories.

Still, certain regularities can be described for the three broad adaptive types of foraging, farming, and herding, despite the ample cultural variability to be found within each type. Most foragers are organized as family-level societies, as are some farmers and herders. What causes the development into local groups in the three subsistence types? Since the specific economic conditions in each type differ significantly, so too do the institutional forms. This can be seen in the contrasts among the forager groups (Shoshone, Case 1; !Kung, Case 2; Eskimo, Case 6; and Northwest Coast Indians, Case 9), agriculturalists (Machiguenga, Case 3; Yanomamo, Case 5; Tsembaga Maring, Case 7; and Central Enga, Case 10), and herders (Nganasan, Case 4; Turkana, Case 8; and Kirghiz, Case 11).

Among foragers, the primary cause for the evolution of local groups appears to be technological necessity. As Oswalt (1976) argues, hunting and fishing technologies required to capture elusive prey are quite complicated and may require organization above the family level to build and operate them. Even among the Shoshone, camps come together periodically to hunt jackrabbits and other animals in large drives using nets and corrals. Intensification among foragers often focuses on highly productive resources and the special technologies to exploit them. In contrast to inland Nunamiut Eskimo, who are a family-level society, for example, the coastal Tareumiut hunt whales from large boats. Local leaders own the boats, organize crews with a division of labor, and maintain storage of the rich harvests. On the Northwest Coast, intensified use of the marine environment makes desirable such technologies as large canoes, fishing weirs, storage cellars, and drying racks, items beyond the means of independent families. Leaders exhort people to work, oversee the placement and maintenance of equipment, and direct its use. They are also the guardians of the food produced, part of which should be regarded as the socialized production of the local group via the leader, not simply the aggregate production of individual households. The trend to large-scale technologies among intensive foragers is especially evident where seasonal variation and food storage are important. This contrasts dramatically with horticultural groups, whose productive technology is no more beyond the family's capacity than it is for plant foragers.

Risk management also requires local group formation among some foragers. Hunting is unpredictable and requires even family-level communities to share risks throughout the camp. The local group level Tareumiut manage risk by harvesting and storing whale meat and blubber, abundant only for the short spring season. Thanks to cooperative boat crews and the coordinated efforts of boat owners, huge surpluses of food are produced, stored, and shared over the lean winter months, allowing the Tareumiut to boast, "We don't let people starve." When local stores fail, food may be available via the links that householders and boat owners have established through ceremonial feasting with other whaling villages along the coast, and even with nomadic caribou hunters from the interior.

Risk management has been elaborated into a fine art in the Northwest Coast. Through the political allocation of rights of usufruct, given physical expression in tokens and emblems, Big Men control the exploitation of temporary abundance, attempting to ensure that as much as possible is consumed or stored. They even issue tokens allowing access to the next whale stranded on their beach. With their capacity for storage in cellars, smoke-houses, and watertight boxes, and their frequent ceremonial displays and distributions, they spread the risks of failure across many local groups at the same time that they maximize the surplus available for political rivalry.

Warfare is less a concern among most foragers. When the intensification of resources creates strong differentiation in productivity, however, conditions arise that are similar to those in agricultural societies. Fighting among local groups on the Northwest Coast is over the most predictable and richest salmon rivers and perhaps over the technology that improves their yields.

Among farmers, the primary cause of the development of local group institutions appears to be warfare: competition over preferred land and developed agricultural plots. Families become members of corporate groups—lineages and clans—that guarantee access to fields, and these groups join together to form village-sized groups for mutual defense. The Yanomamo are in several ways intermediate between family level and local group level: low population density, relatively ample land resources, fragile village structure that fragments from internal disputes, and a small polity size (60 to 250). The primary subsistence contrast to the family-level Machiguenga is long-term cultivation of banana and peach palm trees, investments in land worth fighting for. When fighting is not an immediate danger, Yanomamo groups tend to fragment into hamlet-size units that retain ceremonial ties to other hamlets in the event that the threat of war requires them to reunite.

For the Tsembaga in the highlands of New Guinea, where good land is scarce, the local group (about two hundred people) and its tiny territory (about three square miles) are the only guarantees of safety and subsistence. The local group is composed of several corporate groups ceremonially integrated for defense. Other groups are politically independent but may ally through individual interpersonal ties of marriage and exchange and through intergroup ceremonies—the web of kinship. The Central Enga also have the complex of competition, warfare, corporate clans, local defensive groups, and intergroup networks and ceremonies. Their much higher population density, however, and intense competition over permanently cropped farmlands, have led to an increased reliance on intergroup allies and the creation of a regional collectivity of Big Men who seek to build personal prestige as they regulate intergroup warfare.

Among herders, the primary causes of the evolution of local groups are risk management and warfare, with trade sometimes a factor. A Turkana family's animals are shared out among kinfolk and friends, spreading the risks of failure. When pastures in the plains are temporarily lush, Turkana families come in from areas of more permanent pasture to graze the green grasses before they are lost to drought, and thus they maintain a mobility not unlike that of the family level. Similarly, among the Kirghiz, the khan owns most of the group's herd, which he manages to benefit both his own wealth and the subsistence of his followers. He gives out animals according to a family's management skills, absorbs some of their risk by replacing dead animals, and demands more care in their husbandry. Among herders, the number of animals that a family can manage effectively is quite small, often too small for herd survival, and so each family must be tied into a larger social unit that shares the risks of individual losses.

Nomads tend to have strong warrior traditions, in which young men, who are initiated together, are the community's defenders. They must protect their own herds and raid outside for animals to restore herd losses or to make bride wealth payments. Since animals are mobile and easily purloined, intergroup raiding is a significant cause of local group formation based on male age grades. The segmentary lineage (Sahlins 1961) is a flexible political system in which pastoral groups can increase or decrease in effective size depending on the level of threat from external groups (Irons 1979); when such threats are weak or absent, local groups of pastoralists tend to be small, and they may even resemble family-level groups on the ground.

For the Kirghiz, external trade became their basis for survival in a world of agrarian states that controlled movement and territory. Barth (1956) argues that pastoralists adapt to environmental conditions unsuited to agriculture, but in close association with agriculturalists who need the products of their herds. Much of the Kirghiz food came from settled farmers, and the khan managed the external trade in animals that guaranteed the flow of cereals from farms, and tools and clothing from the cities.

SIX

The Family and the Village

WE HAVE ARGUED THAT the benefits of a larger community must outweigh the costs before people will form one, or join an existing one. As we see in the cases in Chapters 6 and 7, the intensification of the subsistence economy, itself an outcome of rising population and technological innovation, creates specific problems that can best be solved working in larger groups. The nature of the problems varies according to the environment and how it is utilized technologically. The dominant form of intensification is the domestication of plants and the beginnings of farming, represented in the archaeological record as the Neolithic revolution. This change can be quite gradual and in itself does not require the development of the local group. But the growth of agriculture revolutionizes the subsistence economy, eventuating in a worldwide increase in population densities that creates problems whose solution lies in larger communities and a more settled existence.

Two broad benefits arise from larger groups involved in farming: sharing of food (and other resources), and defense. The need to protect families and their lands from enemy raiding places intense pressure on local groups to increase in size both by living within a village-size group and by entering into intergroup alliances. Because people who share defense are likely to share food, and because food-sharing (commensality) is among the most powerful ways of building alliances, it is not easy to disentangle and measure the relative importance of defense and pooling in increasing group size. Reliance on one for security is likely to lead to reliance on the other, mutually enhancing the value of the local group to its constituent families. This pattern is especially evident among the Yanomamo, the subject of this chapter.

Settling down in an agricultural village, however, also involves costs. Simple logistics are more difficult: a concentrated population requires families to live farther from their farmland, and all the resources (game, firewood, building materials, etc.) are more quickly exhausted, requiring longer trips to obtain them. Living in the cramped conditions of the village also increases the transmission of disease, the likelihood of theft, and the suspicion of sexual intrigue. Finding ways to live together is not easy, as the Yanomamo club fights illustrate.

The emergence of regular ceremonies is a dramatic element of village life. The village defined by its surrounding walls and fences is focused on its dance ground. Ceremonial life is a means of building social institutions that help organize people into local groups larger than the family, an artifact of human culture not based in intimate biological relationships. The Yanomamo illustrate the fragility of such social institutions. The group is always liable to fission, struggling to hold together by the need for group defense and on the lookout for allies outside the group to help out in war and its aftermath. In the intervillage feast, a delicate balance is set as participants remain uncertain to the last whether a feast will end in friendship and support or in treachery and death.

Case 5. The Yanomamo of the Venezuelan Highlands

The Yanomamo have become a test case for materialist theory, primarily because of the difficulty of explaining their peculiar form of warfare (Chagnon and Hames 1979; Harris 1974). The central issue has been and remains this: Do the Yanomamo, who appear to fight frequently, impulsively, and with extraordinarily high rates of mortality, fight over scarce material resources or for other, nonmaterial reasons (Lizot 1989)?

In his original descriptions of the Yanomamo, Chagnon (1968a, 1968b) emphasized that they fight for many reasons: for women, who they say are scarce; for revenge of suspected sorcery and of real past injury; and because the political system is too weak to prevent warfare. Harris (1974: 102; 1979) correctly pointed out that such an eclectic view did not provide a satisfactory explanation for Yanomamo warfare. In his opinion the Yanomamo were competing over hunting lands, and in particular over access to scarce supplies of dietary protein. Chagnon replied (1983) that whereas the Yanomamo do indeed view meat as both highly desirable and rather scarce, his data showed them to be adequately supplied with protein in the diet (Chagnon and Hames 1979).

Recently Chagnon has espoused the bioevolutionary concept of "inclusive fitness," marshaling evidence to show that success in war, intimidation, and political maneuvering correlates with success in reproduction: in the simplest terms, Yanomamo men do not fight just over women but over the "means of reproduction." Aggressive men, within limits, succeed in leaving more offspring than men who allow themselves to be intimidated and dominated. Thus as the debate between Harris and Chagnon over the causes of Yanomamo warfare has matured, it has tended to coincide with the debate, discussed in Chapter 2, between theories focusing on reproduction and natural selection (Chagnon, evolutionary biology) and those focusing on production and adaptation (Harris, cultural materialism). We will argue that both are plausible explanations based on biological motivation, and that a full appreciation of Yanomamo warfare must include both.

In this chapter we argue that it is indeed competition over resources that ultimately explains Yanomamo warfare, including (but not limited to) competition for mates and for hunting territory. The challenge is to explain why such competition, which in some form is virtually universal at all levels of sociocultural complexity, results in the specific style of Yanomamo warfare, a form intermediate in the evolutionary spectrum between the relative absence of warfare among family-level groups and the more organized and routinized forms of warfare that we shall encounter in later chapters. Although much like the peaceable Machiguenga (Case 3) in their adaptation to a tropical forest, the Yanomamo have crossed the fateful threshold from a cultural emphasis on control *over* aggression to an emphasis on control *by means of* aggression.

The Environment and the Economy

The Yanomamo (Chagnon 1983), also known as Yanoama (Biocca 1971; Smole 1976) and Waika (Zerries and Schuster 1974), traditionally inhabit the highlands of the headwaters of the Rio Orinoco and Rio Negro in Venezuela and Brazil. Although this region is generally considered part of the tropical forest lowlands of South America and its peoples are often considered Amazonian, these highlands are different from the tropical lowlands that surround them. Most studies of the Yanomamo describe communities that have recently migrated from the highlands into "virgin" lowland territories (Smole 1976: 226), communities significantly different from the highland Yanomamo on whom we focus here (see map B in Migliazza 1972: 17).

The Rio Orinoco originates in the Guiana Highlands, a landscape of rocky promontories and ridges with uplands of ancient granites and metamorphic rocks heavily weathered and eroded into an intricate and irregular sequence of hills and valleys. Except for a spotty distribution of alluvial deposits, the soils are poor: "None of these uplands of sedi-

mentary rocks is suitable for agriculture. Throughout the Guiana Highlands, it appears that agricultural advantage is limited to the valley
bottoms and that these are not of remarkable fertility" (Sauer 1948: 320;
see also Lathrap 1970: 42).

The region traditionally occupied by the Yanomamo ranges in altitude from about one thousand to four thousand feet. The higher elevations (up to six thousand feet) are used less frequently for foraging and
tend to be "uninhabited, covered by scrub and brush and very rocky"
(Smole 1976: 32–33). We may visualize the region as an island rising
above the sea of tropical rain forest that spreads outward along the rivers of the Orinoco and northern Amazon drainages. The highlands are
cooler and drier than the lowland rain forest, and support a unique bi-
ota (Anduze 1960: 186–87; Chagnon 1983: 55).

Anduze (1960: 173) noted that whereas game abounded along the
river at lower altitudes, it became increasingly scarce higher up, a fact
he attributed partly to intensive hunting by the highland Yanomamo.
Smole (1976: 41, 131) also notes that wild foods in general and game in
particular are less abundant in the highlands. Fish are also scarce and
add less to the diet of highland Yanomamo than to lowlanders (Chagnon 1983: 102). Thus the Guiana Highlands are not merely an island in
the physical sense, but a distinctive ecological zone characterized by
poor soils and scarce wild foods (Hames 1997a: 3–5).

The Yanomamo have long inhabited the Guiana Highlands and may
even be descendants of original "foot nomads" of those parts, who inhabited a much larger region until they were displaced by expanding
Cariban and Arawakan groups (Atlas 1979: 320–21; Smole 1976: 17–18;
Wilbert 1966: 237–46). The Yanomamo language is apparently unrelated to Arawakan and Cariban, and the culture is quite distinct. The
Arawakan and Cariban groups were canoe peoples of remarkable
strength and ferocity who dominated the navigable rivers with an
economy centered on bitter manioc, fish, and game hunted in the comparatively rich lowland forests. Most often, where the Yanomamo were
in touch with such groups, it was the Yanomamo who were either subservient, if contact was peaceful, or killed and driven off if contact was
hostile (Chagnon 1983: 61; Smole 1976: 228, 230).

An example of "competitive exclusion" (Barth 1964), the Yanomamo
occupy an ecological niche distinct from that of their lower-elevation
competitors: they do not use canoes, they consume little fish, and they
generally avoid water whenever possible. Their economy is also distinct in its emphasis on plantains and sweet manioc. According to
Smole (1976: 13–14), the Parima region of the Guiana Highlands is "one
of the last great cultural redoubts of the South American continent. . . .

Most of the traditional Yanoama territory is inaccessible by water navigation, effectively protecting its inhabitants from outsiders." When we examine Yanomamo warfare and "fierceness" later, we should remember that the Yanomamo primarily occupy a difficult refuge zone historically surrounded by powerful antagonists.

Following the European colonization of the Americas, riverine groups like the Arawakans and Caribans were highly vulnerable because they occupied rich environments easily accessible by boat. They were enslaved, decimated by disease, and finally incorporated within the expanding frontier of Western civilization. By contrast, the Yanomamo seemed to draw into their highland shell even more completely, perhaps chiefly as a way of avoiding disease, which they equate with white men (Biocca 1971: 213; Chagnon 1983: 200).

At least by the nineteenth century, however, the Yanomamo had acquired steel tools and plantains, after which their population rapidly increased (Chagnon 1983: 61). Since the 1940's, a number of Yanomamo have ventured out of their highland redoubt to colonize larger rivers at lower elevations. These groups are best known worldwide because of the wide exposure to Chagnon's case study and his films with Timothy Asch (Chagnon 1992). In this region population pressure was initially comparatively low owing to the collapse of the Arawakan and Cariban populations, and the fact that malaria and yellow fever were endemic and had undoubtedly acted as a barrier to Yanomamo migrations in the past (Smole 1976: 228). As a result, an unpopulated no man's land or buffer zone had grown up around the Yanomamo. Good garden land was available in this zone, and game animals were both abundant and virtually unafraid of men, since they were so seldom hunted (Steinvorth-Goetz 1969: 195). Chagnon reported abundant game in this region in 1968–71.

A problem for proponents of resource scarcity as a cause of Yanomamo competition and warfare is that these colonist communities not only continued to practice warfare in the face of resource abundance but may have been even more violent than before (Chagnon and Hames 1979: 912). If they now had abundant resources, why fight? For two reasons. First, the migration is recent, and we would not expect warfare to disappear instantly upon a change in resource abundance— old hatreds remain, as do attitudes ingrained from childhood. Second, and more to the point, the resource abundance of the lowlands was short-lived, a common occurrence throughout Amazonia where colonists enter formerly uninhabited regions (Baksh 1984). Within a matter of years local resources were becoming scarce (although farmland remained available). Ten years after Chagnon's first research in the area, for example, the game had been hunted out by the Yanomamo and others, and Chagnon likened the region to a desert (1983: 157, 202).

For these historical reasons, population densities among the lowland Yanomamo are often quite low (below 0.3 person/square kilometer), whereas they tend to be significantly higher (over 2.0 persons/square kilometer) in their traditional highland setting (Hames 1983: 425). Smole (1976: 48) summarizes the situation as follows: "Mean population density over their entire territory is approximately 0.5 person per square mile. Since such a calculation is based upon heavily populated highlands as well as virtually empty lowlands and uninhabited high highlands, the effective density is much higher locally. Observation of the extent to which portions of the high Parima have been transformed into savanna leads to the suspicion that only a few decades ago, if not centuries, population densities there were considerably greater than they are now."

Like the family-level economies we reviewed previously, the Yanomamo economy provides a sufficient livelihood at comparatively low cost. In particular, the diet of the highland Yanomamo contains ample supplies of protein (Chagnon and Hames 1979). Yet the resources they depend on for a high-quality diet and for what they see as the basic necessities of life are scarce, and as a result they experience crowding. To a limited extent the crowding is a result of warfare, which forces the Yanomamo into large villages for defense and hastens the degradation of the environment within reasonable traveling time from the village. This is paradoxical because, as we shall argue, the warfare itself is an outcome of scarcity and competition over resources.

Wild Foods and Hunting. The Yanomamo are dependent on wild foods for nutritional diversity and for the spice such foods add to meals that are primarily made up of garden produce. They have eclectic tastes and relatively few restrictions on what may be eaten (see Taylor 1974). Their foods include crabs, shrimps, and occasional small fish from mountain streams, frogs, ants, termites, insect larvae, hearts and fruits of palm, other fruits, and various roots. Indeed, although large game is the meat preferred by highland Yanomamo, because of its scarcity they probably depend as much on insects as on game (Smole 1976: 163). Some fruits are preserved by drying and are then stored in caves (Biocca 1971: 76; cf. Smole 1976: 237), and some groups prepare special "breeding grounds" in which large numbers of frogs will reproduce to be harvested (Smole 1976: 247).

This general scarcity of food and the diversity of foods sought is characteristic of the subsistence economy as we analyzed it in Chapter 1: over time, the most abundant and favored foods become so scarce that less favored foods come to be viewed as comparable in worth. In this sense, the highland Yanomamo are better described as gatherers than as hunters. While living in villages they have a hard time satisfying their desire for wild foods. So they frequently leave their villages and form hamlet-size extended family groups to forage in less densely populated areas of their territory and even in the remoter sections of neighboring territories.

For periods of time these small foraging groups go on trek. Leaving their secure villages and gardens, they depend heavily on wild foods. As their trekking may take them in the vicinity of old gardens that may still have edible food in them, especially peach palms, they need not depend entirely on wild foods. Should they happen upon a windfall of some wild food, however, they will send word back to relatives, inviting them to join in the unexpected bounty. Thus it happens that frequently throughout the year a village is either completely empty or else inhabited by a small fraction of its total population.

Yanomamo groups vary in how much wild food they eat. The inhabitants of large, sedentary villages may be militarily secure but regret the comparative absence of wild foods in their diet, whereas small, mobile groups enjoy access to wild foods but are vulnerable to raids and may be driven from their territories. In one case reported by Helena Valero, a Brazilian girl brought up by the Yanomamo, a powerful group of villagers captured the women of a small foraging group. When the captives fled, the village women called after them angrily: "Go on, go on! Go back to eating wild fruit and bad fruit. Stupid women for running away! If you had stayed with us, you would have eaten *pupugnas* [peach palm fruits] and bananas from our *rocas* [gardens]. Now you'll have to work hard enough to find wild fruit in the woods!" But the forager women were not impressed, calling back: "We haven't come to ask you for fruit and bananas" (Biocca 1971: 34–36). Indeed one group, the *Gnaminaweteri* ("solitary people"), received its name because of its preference for a peaceful, mobile life in small groups, a culturally recognized strategy of "hiding" (*baimi*) to escape its enemies (Hames 1997: 8).

Certain species of game are the only animals the Yanomamo designate as "real food"; the major garden foods, plantain and peach palm fruit, are also "real food." Only real foods can form the basis of meals during intervillage feasts and ceremonies. Thus when a feast is anticipated large groups of men leave the village for about eight days (the length of time required for freshly harvested green plantains to ripen in the village), returning only after they obtain sufficient supplies of game. Among the most prized species are the tapir and the peccary (both very meaty animals), the agouti, the armadillo, and secondarily certain monkeys and birds (Smole 1976: 182). In these expeditions the men range far from their village and often into hunting lands of adjacent friendly villages. The preferred hunting areas are usually at higher elevations, where neither gardens nor villages are located and hence where game is not so frequently hunted. But even when hunting is done for household use and not for a feast, hunters often expect to be gone for several days. By contrast, the typical hunting trip among the family-level Machiguenga (Chapter 4) lasts five to seven hours.

In other respects the highland Yanomamo and the higher-elevation Machiguenga have much in common. Neither group gets as much wild food as it wants, and no highland area exists in either region that is not systematically and continuously foraged. Even in the only zone both groups avoided, the recently settled lowland fringe where once-dreaded canoe Indians and recently the more dreaded whites lived, game is scarce. Chagnon (1983: 157) reports the results of a hunt for a feast held by the Bisaasi-teri in 1965, fourteen years after they had moved into the lowlands. Although a large group of men spent a week hunting, they returned with only seventeen monkeys, seven wild turkeys, and three large armadillos, scarcely enough to feed a hundred guests for several days and supply them with meat to carry home after the feast. The Yanomamo understandably have a special term for "meat hunger" as distinct from other hunger (Smole 1976: 175), and even in the lowlands "meat is always the most desirable food and is always considered to be in short supply" (Chagnon 1983: 119; cf. Harris 1974: 102–3).

Coupled to this pervasive sense of scarcity is perhaps a more important sense of imbalance. Some locales are perceived as better for game than others, and most of these probably *are* better. These locations are coveted and, one can assume, defended actively from outside hunters. According to Chagnon (1983: 70), "The Yanomamo prefer to remain in one *general* area a long time, especially one that has a reliable source of game within a reasonable walk from the village. My research has revealed many cases of the same village remaining in one area for 30 to 50 years, leaving it only when the military pressures on them are overwhelming."

Gardens. Near the villages, plots for slash-and-burn agriculture are cleared from the forest. The centrifugal attraction of wild foods is counterbalanced by the centripetal pull of the gardens, which are as highly productive as the Machiguenga's gardens (Smole 1976: 150–51). The highland Yanomamo make effective use of those scarce lands that are suitable for horticulture, growing a number of foods and other materials without which they simply could not exist in anything like their present numbers.

The soils the Yanomamo clear for gardens are "fertile, friable loams" (Smole 1976: 24), often capable of supporting a village population in the same general location for many years. But large areas of the highlands are unsuited to agriculture: in these areas "soils tend to be sandy and at least mildly leached" (Smole 1976: 37). Even the "friable loams" are often very acidic (pH 4.5), which limits the production of some crops. In addition, many areas have slopes too steep for gardening. The higher altitudes (above thirty-five hundred feet) are marginal for agriculture, and the lower altitudes are avoided for health reasons. Finally, extensive areas of the highlands, though at a good altitude, are sterile savannas of absolutely no economic utility (Smole 1976: 37).

As among the Machiguenga, the selection of good garden land is a major concern. Potential sites for new gardens are a popular topic of conversation between the men during hunting trips (Chagnon 1983: 60). The best lands (*ishabena*) should be covered by a forest of large trees; be at the proper altitude; have sufficient slope for good drainage and for different crop associations at different elevations in the same garden, but not an excessively steep slope; have heavy, dark soil; be big enough to support the population of a village; and be near pure drinking water (Smole 1976: 26, 107–10, 116, 132, 239). Such ideal conditions are rare and patchy. As a consequence the Yanomamo are very unevenly distributed throughout the highlands, with great concentrations in areas with the best garden sites and few if any settlements in other areas. Once located in an area of good soils, the Yanomamo tend to stay, clearing garden after garden until whole regions are checkered with old and new sites, blending into open savannas that appear to be manmade.

Altitude, as we have seen, is an important factor in Yanomamo horticulture, and gardens at a given altitude will not often fill all a household's needs. Crops such as plantains, peach palms, and tobacco prefer low, humid soils, whereas crops such as arrow cane do better at higher elevations. Since all these crops are essential to the Yanomamo, we find not only frequent trade between villages at different altitudes but also the cultivation by enterprising family groups of gardens at different altitudes in addition to their main garden close to the village.

Warfare adds further to the complex interplay of factors that determine where the Yanomamo will place their gardens. The members of a village prefer to have their gardens close to the village, where they are easier to defend, and that may lead them to plant in less desirable land (Smole 1976: 107, 244). But the opposite also occurs (Smole 1976: 239):

"[The Docodicoro-teri] had become so dissatisfied with gardening on the low, alluvial terraces near the safety of the *shabono* [village] that they cleared a large new garden high in the mountains about four miles to the south. This brought them much closer to their enemies (the Bashobaca-teri), but they took the risk because they felt there was no place closer to the *shabono* that was as good for growing the *cowata* plantain."

The major food crops of the Yanomamo are plantains, sweet manioc, peach palm fruits, tarolike cocoyams (*Xanthosoma*), and yams (*Diosco-rea*). Plantains, a very efficient source of carbohydrates and by far the major food in their diet, must be transplanted by cuttings from the roots. This requires a tremendous effort if a new garden is to be distant from the current one, or if a group must move suddenly and will have to transport the larger roots that produce a crop more quickly. Both these conditions are most likely to occur when a group has been defeated in war.

Plantains produce only once in a period of months and cannot be stored. They are planted at different times, as a man's labor permits, so that the plants ripen at different times, spreading the harvest throughout the year (Chagnon 1983: 71). But it is difficult to foresee exactly when and in what quantities plantains will ripen, so that sometimes there are no plantains even where the average production is ample for the population. Friendly villages even out such local fluctuations by inviting each other to feast when their own supplies are excessive (see Biocca 1971: 27, 45; Smole 1976: 104, 106, 129, 141–42). Smole (1976: 193–94) suggests that there are no actual surpluses of plantains, since all those not eaten by their growers are eventually consumed in feasts. With minimal care, plantain gardens continue to produce food for many years.

Sweet manioc, cocoyams, and yams help fill the periods when plantains are insufficient. The fruits of the peach palm (*Guilielma* sp.) are seasonal, tending to ripen in January and February (Anduze 1960: 215); with twice the protein of plantains and manioc and ten to forty times the quantity of fat, they are a highly prized food. According to Chagnon (1983: 70–71), "This palm is an exception to my earlier generalization that it takes a great many palm fruits to get a full belly. Peach palm fruits (*rasha*) have relatively small seed (some have no seed at all) and a very large amount of mealy flesh, about the texture of boiled potatoes, rich in oil, and very tasty." These palms also have an exterior wood so hard that it is nearly impossible to drive a nail into it. The Yanomamo use this wood to fashion their bows, several types of arrowheads, and their fighting clubs (*nabrushi*).

Along with plantain, peach palm fruit is a "real food," and hence suitable fare for feasting. In Chagnon's words (1983: 71), "Families usually plant one or several of these trees every time a garden is cleared, and the trees produce very large crops of fruits for many years after the gardens have been abandoned. Thus, by remaining in a general area the peach palm crops can be easily and conveniently harvested, and yield enormous quantities of tasty, nutritious fruit." Since peach palms grow better at lower altitudes, and since their fruit is seasonal, they are less commonly served at feasts than plantains and are enjoyed less frequently in villages at higher elevations. But the availability of peach palm fruits in old gardens at a distance from the village permits families to forage for extended periods away from the village when plantains are scarce and wild foods become important in the diet (Smole 1976: 155).

One difference between Yanomamo and Machiguenga gardens must be emphasized. The Machiguenga garden's useful life is only a few years at most. Yanomamo gardens, by contrast, with their stands of peach palm (and to a lesser degree plantain), are major capital improvements that yield harvestable food many years after their initial cultivation: perhaps five years for plantains and over twenty years for peach palms. Old gardens are an important resource for the Yanomamo. Because of old gardens a village's territory increases in richness through time and is not to be abandoned lightly.

Scarcity in Yanomamo Ecology. We have referred to various forms of scarcity among the Yanomamo: scarcity of large game animals, of top-quality agricultural land, of preferred wild plant foods, of particular foods or raw materials that do not grow well in their gardens, and periodically of their most favored agricultural products, plantains, and peach palm fruits. The most dramatic and significant evidence of scarcity in the highlands, however, is the destruction of the forest by over-intensive agriculture that has resulted in widespread savannas. This condition is most severe in the areas of densest, longest-term settlement (Smole 1976: 203, 208). In most cases these savannas are the remnants of old gardens. Many have the regular shapes and straight edges of gardens, and some adjoin old gardens that may be savannas in the making. The cooler, drier highland climate may hasten the development of savannas in some highland areas. But as Smole (1976: 208–9, 254) makes clear, areas that were rich garden lands within the memory of living Yanomamo are now sterile savannas.

Smole (1976: 210) describes three "zones of impact." Near the village the environment has been completely domesticated in a "fragmented zone of intensive use," and savannas often border the villages (Fig. 7).

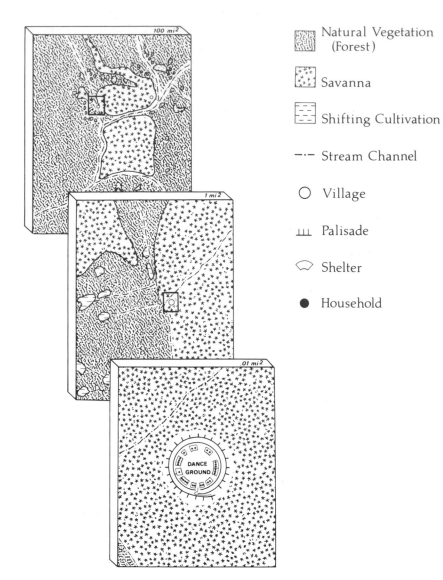

Natural Vegetation
(Forest)

Savanna

Shifting Cultivation

—·— Stream Channel

○ Village

⊥⊥ Palisade

▽ Shelter

● Household

Fig. 7. Settlement Pattern of the Highland Yanomamo. Family groups cluster together in small villages for defense. Despite a fairly low population density, the environment has been severely degraded and economically barren savannas dominate the landscape.

Within "easy reach" of the village, say a one-day trip, is a "zone of intensive foraging" from which wild foods are substantially depleted; this zone regenerates after the village has been relocated. Beyond that is the much less intensively used "zone of hunting and sporadic collecting." The savannas, of course, are a fourth zone, and one that is growing.

Another aspect of scarcity is the local distribution of certain highly desired products. For example, the plants that provide the hallucinogenic drug *ebena* are unevenly distributed, and many villages are unable to procure their own; the same is true for arrow cane, curare, bamboo for quivers, and peach palm. Villages near abundant supplies of these plants specialize in preparing them as items for trade (Arvelo-Jimenez 1984; Chagnon 1983: 46–50; Smole 1976: 70–71). The unequal distribution and unreliable productivity of many products make trade an important economic activity among the Yanomamo.

Social Organization

Yanomamo society resembles Machiguenga society in that the family is primary and kinship is the basic means by which social life is integrated and structured. As we shall see, however, the Yanomamo have a further level of social integration not found in family-level societies: village and intervillage alliances.

The Household. The family household is the basic economic unit of the Yanomamo. Although, in contrast to the family-level societies, single households always live in large groups, the Yanomamo household retains significant autonomy. Within the village each family's space is carefully demarcated and contains its own hearth, sleeping area, and goods. Similarly, although villages appear to have large communal farms, each man's separate garden is clearly demarcated and protected by strict rules against theft. Despite the vastness of the forest and the spaciousness of the village, with its large central clearing, Yanomamo families crowd into tiny spaces, where they hang their hammocks side by side or even stack them one above the other. According to Smole (1976: 67), "It is not at all unusual for a family of five to occupy a space of approximately ten by twelve feet, which means that an individual has about 25 square feet of living space." In these close quarters children learn to control their selfish impulses, and in particular to be generous (Biocca 1971: 137–38, 159). Children are indulgently reared, although some "fierce" (*waiteri*) men fly into rages and impulsively beat their wives or children, occasionally injuring them seriously. Parents are reassured by having children, especially sons, to care for them in their old age, and a woman's only defense against an abusive husband is to have her brothers nearby to protect her (see Biocca 1971: 95).

The Teri. The smallest groups observed living alone among the Yanomamo number thirty to thirty-five people, about as many as the largest groups normally found among the Machiguenga. No Yanomamo household can live apart from some form of larger group, called a *teri,* which is an extended family or collection of extended families occupying a single village. All *teri* are named, usually after a feature of the landscape, for "the teri name is geographic" (Smole 1976: 52, 57).

The village, or *shabono,* is essentially a large circle of lean-tos with joined roofs of palm leaves sloping up from the ground to a height of fifteen to twenty feet. The center is open to the sky, and the ground is reserved for public events, as when the village hosts a feast for an ally. The individual households are laid out around the circle of the dance ground and under the slanting roof. The slanting roof of the village encloses and fortifies the teri; people can enter and leave only by a narrow gate.

The *teri* often comprises two intermarrying patrilines, each similar in size to a single Machiguenga hamlet (cf. Wilbert 1972: 46). Thus in the Parima highlands the average *teri* contains seventy to seventy-five members. The men of such a *teri* are either brothers or brothers-in-law, fathers or sons, or uncles or nephews. In larger *teri,* however, many men are only classificatory kin; they are not biologically close and tend not to interact very much. True brothers, bound by strong family feeling, and true brothers-in-law, who have actually given women to each other's group, are very close: they live in adjacent parts of the *shabono;* plant their gardens side by side, sharing the different microecological zones of the garden area; and leave the *shabono* together on hunting and foraging ventures (Chagnon 1983: 67, 131; Smole 1976: 67, 94, 158, 188–89). Villages of more than a hundred members tend to be unstable and temporary. The larger *teri* comprise several smaller *teri* that have come together into a single large *shabono* for security in wartime. While there, they take on the name of the *teri* identified with that territory. The solidarity of a Yanomamo *teri* depends on the density of kinship and marriage ties among the members. Chagnon (1983: 110–45) shows that although the classificatory kinship system pairs many men as "brothers" or "brothers-in-law," a man's closest associates are those to whom he is most closely related genetically and by marriage. Powerful emotions and social sanctions prohibit theft, insults, and violence between close relatives.

A *teri* increases its solidarity when its members intermarry, a strategy that not only knits distant kin more closely together as affines but also increases the actual degree of genetic relatedness between members. Since close relatives side together in a fight, villages whose members are closely related fight less among themselves and can grow to a larger size, a distinct advantage in times of war. Chagnon shows that the Shamatari, who are greatly feared along the Rio Orinoco (Anduze 1960: 122), have an "average relatedness" equivalent to that between biological first cousins. That is much more relatedness than the neighboring Namoeteri achieve, and allows the Shamatari to live in larger, more stable, and hence more dangerous groups than the Namoeteri.

Although Yanomamo kin groups have been referred to as "lineages" (Chagnon 1983: 127; Smole 1976: 13) and as "clans" (Anduze 1960: 2–28), these labels suggest more structure than is actually present (Jackson 1975: 320–21; Murphy 1979). Yanomamo kin groups may have a patrilineal bias, but lineal descent from common ancestors is not either a major emphasis or a principle for reckoning property rights in any rigorous way. Nor is there any clear residence rule (Smole 1976: 236). Small *teri* are stable, cooperative groups by virtue of their close ties of kinship and marriage, but they are not formally kin groups.

In a very real sense, the *teri* is a biological group. Mutual support within this group takes many forms, among them assistance in tasks requiring several people, the sharing of meat, and providing help when a family member is incapacitated. As Chagnon (1983) has argued, this genetic closeness translates into interpersonal support in fights within the village and determines the lines along which the village splits when internal hostilities cannot be resolved. Small *teri* leave a village temporarily to forage, or to live alone permanently, or to join other groups. As long as they remain members of the same *teri*, households share the natural resources of the *teri* territory. Their old and new gardens, however, like their part of the village, remain their own, and no one else may enter unless invited. Households are tied in nets of kinship and marriage to others whom they trust and are loyal to. As a *teri* grows, these bonds become insufficient to hold it together; fights occur, and the *teri* breaks up into smaller groups.

At some times close allies live together in the same *teri*; at others they live apart in separate *teri*. Within a *teri* their loyalty to one another is based on actual genealogical closeness, ties by marriage, and day-to-day sharing and cooperation, and those same principles apply to trade relations and military alliances between *teri*. Beyond that, relations between *teri* rest chiefly on geographical propinquity, the sharing of temporary food surpluses, trade in specialized items, and mutual defense.

Yanomamo occupying adjacent regions try to maintain friendly relations and generally succeed, despite an accumulation of small tensions due to theft, adultery, insults, and other pervasive complaints (Lizot 1989). If war breaks out between two neighboring groups, one will move to a distant location, usually before much fighting takes place. Often neighboring groups are former members of a *teri* that has broken up; its members now inhabit separate *shabono* and have different names, but relations between them remain amicable. Such groups visit frequently (Chagnon 1983: 43), invite one another to feasts, share kinship and marriage ties, and in wartime are likely to move into a single *shabono* again.

We have seen that supplies of the major staple, plantain, and the nutritionally important peach palm fruit are somewhat unpredictable. Since plantains and peach palm fruits must be eaten when they ripen or they will spoil, when these foods are abundant a feast is held and the members of friendly *teri* are invited. Neighbors are the most likely to come, but word is also sent to relatives in distant *teri*, who may be willing to walk for several days to visit and share food. Naturally the guests are expected to reciprocate when they have similar surpluses. This system is so successful that few plantains or peach palm fruits ever go to waste (Smole 1976: 40, 187).

Researchers familiar with the Yanomamo have great respect for them as traders, a respect that borders on awed exasperation. They are relentless in demanding things they want and are almost impossible to refuse (Chagnon 1983: 14–16; Smole 1976: 100). They are especially aggressive with strangers, whom they value only for what they can get from them. According to Chagnon (1983: 15), who found himself bullied into making unintended "gifts," "The loss of the possessions bothered me much less than the shock that I was, as far as most of them were concerned, nothing more than a source of desirable items."

Trade is important to the Yanomamo, and since it often involves exchanges between distant and comparatively unrelated villages, aggressive bargaining is common. As we have seen, the ecological basis for trade is regional specialization, but trade is also a significant part of the web of alliances that promote peace in a region. Some division of labor between villages exists even when no ecological differences exist, simply to give villages unique items to trade and thus incorporate them in the trading network (Chagnon 1983: 149).

Whenever members of one *teri* visit another, they expect to trade. Men do most of the visiting and will visit only a *teri* where they have relatives. After eating and socializing, the guests make the rounds of the village demanding gifts (Biocca 1971: 158, 192). Hosts are expected to be generous; guests do not express thanks, since the gift is expected and "to ask for something is to flatter its owner" (Smole 1976: 237). If hosts are not generous, guests become angry, and their resentment can lead to intergroup hostilities and warfare. To avoid appearing stingy, men may hide their extra machetes, best arrows, or other valuables in the forest when guests are expected (Smole 1976: 102). Hostile "guests" may provoke their hosts by arriving uninvited, eating more than their hosts can afford, and generally demanding unreasonable gifts, as though to test their hosts' readiness to draw the line (Chagnon 1983: 164). Thus trade can contribute modestly to friendship between *teri* but may also sow seeds of disappointment and antagonism. Ceremonies and leadership, as we shall see, help to minimize these dangers.

In sum, the Yanomamo economy is centered on the same family-level groups we examined in the previous section, although food-sharing and trade between communities are here more important. As group size increases, the integration of families into the larger group is increasingly fragile. Yet the larger village group does exist. Why? Largely, as we see it, for defense against enemies.

Yanomamo Warfare

The Yanomamo are a paradoxical people. Loving and nurturant family members, they can flare into dangerous outbursts of violence. Frightened of warfare and fully aware of its consequences, they nonetheless allow bitter hostilities to arise and persist over years at the expense of human lives and economic efficiency. They are generous yet envious, honest to a disarming degree yet capable of the ultimate in treacherous deception.

Our students who have seen the Yanomamo films of Asch and Chagnon (Chagnon 1983: 221–22) are invariably fascinated but frequently disturbed and puzzled. How can people be like that? they ask. Some outside observers have even wondered if the Yanomamo are fully human (cf. Chagnon 1983: 205). Indeed they are, as we hope to show in this section, and perhaps particularly human in their vain effort to find more "rational" solutions than interpersonal violence to the predicaments they face.

We must not imagine that the Yanomamo enter into violent conflict lightly. The threat of violence worries them, and they have developed a graded series of responses (discussed below) for heading off its more severe manifestations. Even so, Chagnon (1983: 5) reports that in the lowlands at least one-quarter of all adult male deaths result from interpersonal violence. Smole (1976) finds warfare less prominent in the highlands, where some groups have reportedly enjoyed peace for a generation or more. But Helena Valero's account leaves little doubt that the Namoeteri and Shamatari experienced frequent homicides and raids even before they migrated into the lowland contact zone along the Rio Orinoco (Biocca 1971).

Yanomamo of all ages grieve mightily when their dearest relatives are killed (see Biocca 1971: 247, 251, 258–61). Even those not immediately affected by death in the family, however, are affected by a state of war. Labor costs rise markedly as men are killed or wounded, dispatched to build or repair palisades, or posted as watchmen on distant trails to give early warning of an attack. Small *teri* must move together into a single large village, increasing not only their travel time to their gardens but also the possibility that those gardens, and all the labor invested in them, will be lost (Smole 1976: 137).

Any death by violence among the Yanomamo, including death by disease that is regarded as having been caused by sorcery, sends a shudder through the Yanomamo community, testing alliances and highlighting conflicting loyalties. Allies of the contending parties are often fearful of being drawn into the violence, for if their side proves to be the less powerful, they will have to abandon their lands and start over again in a distant region (Smole 1976: 235).

Chagnon (1983: 73–77, 111, 146) documents a general decline in the quality of life during warfare. Although in peacetime the Yanomamo are diffident and careful regarding fecal wastes (Anduze 1960: 228), in wartime they are afraid to leave the village and will defecate into leaves and toss them over the palisade, polluting the immediate environs of the village. Crowded into a village with many comparative strangers, people bicker and squabble endlessly until the threat of violence from within nearly matches the threat from without. When anger threatens to burst into violence, older men and women, as well as the angry man's brothers and wives, attempt to cool him down with such words as these:

Oh my son, you must not shoot. You have two male children; one is growing up, the other has only recently appeared. Why do you think of killing? Do you think that killing is a joke? If you kill today, tomorrow your sons will be alone and abandoned. When a man kills, he often has to flee far off, leaving his children behind him, who weep for hunger. Do you not yet know this? Do not remain angry. . . . Do not let yourself be conquered by anger. (Biocca 1971: 218)

In the face of such reasonable advice, why do Yanomamo men kill?

The Nature of Yanomamo Warfare. We have seen that the Yanomamo of the highlands are living in locally dense populations, enjoying a relatively comfortable life but aware that the best resources are scarce.

Each man is a member of a family that owns valuable resources in old gardens; shares a larger foraging territory with other close family members; and has or hopes to acquire a wife and children, or perhaps two or more wives. He can see that other men also perceive these resources to be scarce and do their best, through intimidation backed up by the threat of outright violence, to acquire or keep them at his expense. Looking ahead, he can see that his access to needed garden land and other territorial resources must be guaranteed. He can stabilize his position only by participating in an alliance with close relatives by birth and marriage, and by showing himself ready to defend his "family estate" by violence if necessary.

This situation puts a premium on men who are strong and fearless. If a man is not temperamentally suited to that role himself, he must seek out and become attached to such a man. The pattern we have seen among family-level groups such as the Machiguenga and the !Kung, where overly aggressive men are ostracized or killed by the group, cannot work here. The level of competition has risen to the point where fierce and aggressive men, the *waiteri* men, despite their dangerous natures, are eagerly sought after and invited into the group. Their violence intimidates potential enemies, who are well advised to steer clear. Unfortunately, however, *waiteri* men are prone to violence and increase the number of violent incidents within and between *teri* that disturb the peace and make war more likely.

Yanomamo violence has an impulsive quality. Men (and sometimes women) will become enraged and strike out at near kin. Later they will feel regret, but no one seems to hold a grudge if the harm is not great (Biocca 1971: 308). As noted earlier, the Yanomamo have devised a graded series of mechanisms to control violent impulses. Angry men make lengthy speeches at each other. If these do not serve to dissipate the rage, they enter into chest-pounding duels in which first one, then the other, stands stoically while being struck at full force with a closed fist. If they are more angry still, they may enclose rocks in their fists to intensify the blows.

Beyond this, men fight with clubs (or the flat sides of machetes and axes). These fights are structured events with an audience of supporters and leaders, kin of the combatants, who monitor the fight to see that it does not explode into homicide. The combatants must exchange blows in alternating order. If a man falls, a kinsman replaces him. Leaders may intercede and direct some hangers-back to take their turns and share the responsibility for what has become a test of courage between the two groups (Chagnon 1983: 164–69).

The Yanomamo say, "We fight in order to become friends again." In this sense the club fight and other duels are "the antithesis of war" (Chagnon 1983: 170), for they occur under carefully controlled conditions and their main purpose is to manage the competitive and hostile feelings between groups before they lead to homicide.

When these mechanisms fail, there is nothing to be done but kill (Chagnon 1983: 174). The successful Yanomamo raid is one in which an enemy is ambushed alone and killed without any of the raiding party being harmed (Chagnon 1983: 185). An especially angry or fierce group may surround a village and wait: since little food is stored in the village, men must eventually emerge and may then be shot. Direct attacks on villages are very dangerous, for well-armed men inside can see the approaching enemy. The attackers therefore position themselves behind trees at the edge of the clearing and fire arrows into the village. A ten-foot palisade makes direct shots impossible, so they must arch their arrows, making a direct hit a matter of chance. It is during such attacks that women are occasionally wounded or killed.

Yanomamo warfare is remarkably personal: not *teri* against *teri* so much as man against man, including the man's family and property (i.e., his "estate"). Men call out insults to each other, claiming their readiness to kill and using the opportunity to utter each other's personal name, a deadly insult. Men are careful to avoid harm to their relatives who live with the enemy. When arrows fall, people examine them and recognize the enemy archer by the unique design of his arrows. If someone is killed, care is taken to identify the killer. The killer must then undergo a ritual of purification, and through gossip everyone, including the deceased's relatives, learns his identity.

Waiteri men who have killed large numbers of men are hated and pursued by their victims' kinsmen. When threatened they may stand in the village clearing, inviting their enemies to shoot. If the threat is a bluff, the enemies will withdraw; if not, the *waiteri* man may be shot. The more times a man has killed, the larger the number of vengeful relatives there are to conspire against him (see Biocca 1971: 186ff). It is no wonder, then, that *waiteri* men tend to die by violence more than other men (Chagnon 1983: 124; Lizot 1989: 31).

The ultimate in Yanomamo warfare is the "treacherous feast." Powerful hatreds lead one group to feign friendship for another, invite its members to a feast, then fall on them and kill as many as possible. One group was massacred only during the third feast by a group that had made "friends" with them during two previous feasts, lulling them into carelessness. This outcome is uncommon, however, since such a degree of organization is difficult for most Yanomamo. *Teri* disunity is usually such that some members have no idea that others are planning to kill their guests. When they find out, they may warn the intended victims, but so confusing is their world that the victims may not believe their warnings (Biocca 1971: 53–54, 190).

Social Responses to Warfare. Chagnon (1983: 148) vividly portrays the Yanomamo as masters of the politics of "brinkmanship." Each group must establish its reputation for toughness or it will be bullied and exploited, yet groups that are too fierce frighten other groups and have trouble finding allies. In the most dramatic instance, the men of two groups who wish to ally must face each other in duels in which they attempt to prove their indomitability by giving and receiving painful blows; yet they must not allow themselves to be provoked to kill or cause serious injury lest they destroy the possibility of an alliance and create new enemies instead.

"Brinkmanship" is an apt term if we do not infer too much purpose or policy behind it. The duel or club fight is in truth the outer limit of the political economy, beyond which the means of social integration are far outweighed by mistrust and hostility. The Yanomamo do not create these fights as deliberate policy; on the contrary, they do everything they can to expand the circle of peace and cooperation outward from their communities, and the fight is the tangible sign of their inability to expand it further.

The dramatic differences we see between the Yanomamo and family-level societies are the formation of villages and the expanded role of ceremonies and leaders. These differences are to be understood as responses to the prominence of warfare and the threat of violent death.

The construction of a *shabono* is a good metaphor for the relationship between family and village. To a visitor the *shabono* appears to be a communal structure, yet each household constructs its own shelter; it is only because shelters are built adjacent to each other, and with the goal in mind of creating a closed circle, that the finished *shabono* appears to be communal.

Yanomamo villages grow to more than one hundred members, and regional clusters of villages may even total several hundred (Smole 1976: 55, 231). Between the smallest *teri* of thirty members and the largest *teri* of perhaps three hundred, any intermediate size may occur. In fact the size of the *shabono* varies consistently within limits (Chagnon 1968a, 1983). On the one hand the village must have at least eighty to one hundred people to allow for adequate defense. A larger village is militarily stronger: more resistant to attack and more successful in raids. But on the other hand, as we have seen, the larger villages are the most subject to destructive social frictions. Village headmen work constantly to smooth out the many hostilities, but a sense of common economic interest in such a large group is mostly absent.

Within and beyond the village take place ceremonies that simultaneously express seething tensions and seek to resolve them. In Yanomamo ceremonies several purposes are served: food and other goods are distributed to equalize seasonal and geographical variations in abundance, social relations between old allies are reinforced, and possible new alliances are explored. All these functions depend to a degree on the skill of leaders.

Invitations to a feast are not issued by one *teri* to another, but by a specific individual in one *teri* to specific individuals in other *teri*. These individuals are the headmen of their own family groups, and may or may not have larger followings. Some will accept the invitation; others, for a variety of reasons, may refuse. The groups being integrated by a feast are not large villages but bits and pieces of several villages. Socially the feast is a mosaic composed of only some of the larger number of family groups in a region.

One way to define a Yanomamo *teri* would be as a group that follows a common leader, or *tushaua*. In the smaller *teri* the *tushaua* is simply the head of the dominant family, but in larger *teri* one man generally stands for the group, is addressed on behalf of all group members, and issues commands to do the group's work. That his commands are often ignored, and that other headmen in his group, also called *tushaua*, offer other advice or lead their groups in other directions, are signs that his authority is limited by the autonomy of small *teri*, a remnant of the !Kung attitude that "we are all headmen." But the *tushaua* is a force to be reckoned with in Yanomamo society, with important functions for and impact on the group. He does not intrude much into the domestic economy, except by influencing where a *teri* settles and plants its gardens. His major role is managing intergroup relations, keeping the peace where possible, and leading the men to war when necessary.

A *tushaua* attempts to resolve disputes within his *teri*. He proposes solutions to problems and attempts to reason with the parties involved in disputes. He often invokes general principles, such as: "You have too many wives already—there are men here who have none." And he intervenes to control dangerous situations: "Let him speak! Let no one point his arrow at him; let everyone keep their arrows in their hands" (Biocca 1971: 37, 110). Leaders are also expected to be more generous than others (Biocca 1971: 216), and for that purpose they plant gardens of above average size (Chagnon 1983: 67). As the official host for intervillage feasts, the *tushaua* is at the center of the integrative efforts those feasts represent.

On the other hand, a *tushaua* is expected to be a leader in war. He orders the palisades built and posts guards along the trails from enemy *teri*. He calls for men to join him in battle, tells them where to camp and how to avoid detection during a raid, and takes the lead in the actual fighting. Yanomamo men often seem reluctant to fight or to stand firm in the face of continuous resistance (cf. Biocca 1971: 59). A leader is expected to take the first shot at the enemy and to risk his own safety.

Thus, leaders "are simultaneously peacemakers and valiant warriors. . . . The thin line between friendship and animosity must be traversed by village leaders" (Chagnon 1983: 6–7). That is a delicate balance to strike, and leaders approach the task in various ways. Some are mild-mannered, cool, and competent; others are flamboyant and domineering (Chagnon 1983: 26).

A leader who has killed too often generates such a network of vengeful enemies that he is not likely to live long. According to Helena Valero (Biocca 1971: 193), when the *tushaua* Rohariwe was invited to what he anticipated could be a treacherous feast, he said: "I think they will kill me. I am going so that no one may believe that I am afraid. I am going so that they may kill me. I am killing many people; even the women and old ones are angry with me. It is better that the Namoeteri kill me."

A certain pessimism or sense of futility, then, is felt by the man who has killed too often (cf. Biocca 1971: 226–47). It is as though he senses that the violence has gotten beyond his control, and in a deeper sense that may be true. Chagnon (1983: 188) documents a case in which the relatively mild mannered leader of a defeated group, now bullied and despised by the "friendly" *teri* that gave them shelter, had to become more violent in order to defend his group. He was forced into fierceness against his will by the implacable pressure of fierceness around him.

Proximate Causes of Yanomamo Warfare. Chagnon's data (1983) emphasize the capture of women as the major motivation for war; Smole (1976: 50, 232) sees suspicion of sorcery and the consequent wish for revenge as central; and Helena Valero provides ample case examples of both of those motivations (Biocca 1971: 29–41, 98, 133, 186–88, 293). Since these are immediate causes, given by the participants themselves, we call them "proximate causes" (cf. Hames 1982: 421–22). As clues to the conditions and events that precipitate war, proximate causes are invaluable guides to understanding the process of growing antagonisms and violent outcomes.

As explanations of warfare, however, proximate causes are generally unsatisfactory. For one thing, people engaged in warfare often list many different reasons for fighting, leading only to the conclusion that war has many causes, some unrelated to others. We believe, by contrast, that Yanomamo warfare, and warfare in general, can best be understood within the framework of a single theory.

A second shortcoming of "proximate causes" as an explanation of Yanomamo warfare is that whereas the same sources of interpersonal conflict are present in all the family-level societies we reviewed in Chapters 3 and 4, in none of those societies do sexual jealousy or revenge wishes result in endemic raiding. Similarly, in the villages of complex chiefdoms and states that we will examine in Chapters 11 through 13, these motivations are powerful but do not lead to local warfare, and the warfare that does occur in those societies is qualitatively different from Yanomamo warfare. We postulate, then, that Yanomamo warfare has some deeper cause or causes, a question to which we shall return after examining three proximate causes:

1. Since the Yanomamo are often viewed as "the fierce people" (Chagnon 1983: subtitle), it might appear that warfare is an inevitable consequence of their psychology. Especially dominant in warfare are *waiteri* men—violent, aggressive men who have come to characterize the Yanomamo to many anthropologists. They are protective toward their own kin and allies but are exploitative toward others outside their orbit of cooperation and trust. Strong groups bully weak groups and appropriate their women and other resources. For example, having driven off a group of men from their village, *waiteri* warriors taunted one of the angry fleeing wives: "So much the worse for you, that you have no arrows and you have a husband who's afraid!" (Biocca 1971: 33, 108–9.)

Groups must appear fierce or lose the respect of others and be bullied (Chagnon 1983: 148–51, 181). A broken and defeated group, the Pishaanseteri, tried to recruit a brave man, Akawe, to bolster their reputation: "You are *waiteri*; you are famous everywhere; you have killed Waika, you have fought against Shiriana. . . . If you kill a Shamatari, we will give you one of our women; you will stay here with us" (Biocca 1971: 316). As this story implies, many, if not most, Yanomamo men are actually frightened of violence. They put up a fierce front, but when the dueling or fighting is about to begin they hang back or find excuses (Chagnon 1983: 183). A truly *waiteri* man, one not afraid to die and prepared to kill, is necessary to a group that wants to build its reputation for violence.

Although the psychology of aggressive men is integral to the dynamics of Yanomamo warfare, as an ultimate cause it is not helpful because, in keeping with Boas's principle of the psychic unity of humankind, we would expect a roughly similar proportion of brave/fierce men to be born into any human community. Why don't they create similar patterns of warfare everywhere?

2. The Yanomamo frequently give revenge as their motive for raiding other groups (Biocca 1971: 40). Yet revenge as an ultimate cause of warfare presupposes the violence it is supposed to explain: one homicide is assumed to lead to another in a perpetual cycle of revenge. But why do family-level societies like the Machiguenga manage isolated homicides without further violence, whereas the Yanomamo cannot? Furthermore, as we shall see, the Yanomamo use ceremonial occasions to remember the dead and renew their passion for revenge. Why do they go to such lengths to keep alive motives for war when the costs of warfare are so high?

3. Yanomamo men frequently announce their intention to raid other groups and steal their women (Biocca 1971: passim). When Chagnon (1983: 86) mentioned to some Yanomamo men Harris's theory that they fight over hunting territories, the men laughed, saying, "Even though we do like meat, we like women a whole lot more!"

Yanomamo raiders try to avoid killing women and girls, and more than once spared Helena Valero's life; "Leave her: it's a girl; we won't kill the females. Let's take the women away with us and make them give us sons" (Biocca 1971: 34). The women they value are women of childbearing age. Old women are not worth fighting over; indeed, an old garden is called an "old woman" because of its barrenness. Being virtually immune from harm in war, old women are very useful for carrying messages between enemies and retrieving the dead during battles.

Many Yanomamo men experience difficulty obtaining wives (Biocca 1971: 41; Chagnon 1983: 142–45). Obtaining a wife often involves negotiations between the man and the girl's parents, and men with high social standing and strong kin networks are most successful. Hames has shown that polygynous households tend to be those of leaders, and that such households receive the lion's share of exchanges of food with other households, one of the reasons that women are willing to become second wives of such men (Hames 1996). Husbands tend to be much older than their wives, and, as a result of polygyny, many young men are without wives. Raids are in part efforts by young men to obtain wives for themselves and to begin a family. Since captured wives may escape, or may be stolen back by their original husbands or carried off by still other men in subsequent raids, there is an endless cycle of raids and counterraids. Although in some areas there seem to be enough women for men seeking wives (Smole 1976: 50), Yanomamo everywhere do capture women when at war, and competition among fierce men for available women is characteristic.

The difficulty with this as an ultimate explanation of Yanomamo warfare, however, is that whereas everywhere there is some kind of competition among men over fertile women, this competition does not everywhere lead to warfare. Why, then, do the Yanomamo permit or require aggressive men to rout or kill each other in order to obtain reproductive rights over women?

The Ultimate Cause of Yanomamo Warfare. Each of the three proximate causes we have identified—basic ferocity, revenge, and capture of women—is inadequate as an ultimate cause of Yanomamo warfare because it is a universal human characteristic, not peculiar to the Yanomamo. Where the Yanomamo differ from the family-level societies we have examined is in having crossed the threshold from sporadic violence, deliberately isolated and contained, to endemic violence that feeds upon itself in a never-ending cycle of new homicidal acts.

This higher level of endemic violence among the Yanomamo is directly related to interpersonal and intergroup competition over scanty resources, of which we find evidence in their greater concern with the definition, defense, and violent capture of territory. Conflicts over access to and distribution of scarce resources keep interpersonal hostilities simmering among the Yanomamo. And it is the comparatively simple political structure—for the Yanomamo remain close to the family level of sociocultural integration—that accounts for the frequency with which these hostilities boil over in impulsive violence, cruelty, and treachery.

A good deal of interpersonal friction arises from the ownership and distribution of resources. Yanomamo are enjoined to be generous with friends and relatives; being ungenerous is taken as a sign of hostility and breeds mistrust. Yet rules guarantee all individuals control over their production. To enter another's house or garden, even only to take firewood (Chagnon 1983: 68), is considered theft and infuriates the property owner. Hames (1997b) reports, "I nearly saw a riot break out in Mishimishimabowei because someone claimed that an ongoing distribution of cooked peach palms were harvested from his trees." When demands are placed on them, the Yanomamo are faced with the choice of acceding and giving up things of value, or of taking a stand and risking the disappointment and enmity of others.

Distributions of food within a *teri* are continual sources of bickering and jealousy. If they are not countered by the positive feelings and rein-forcing experiences of close family life, they can give rise to grudges that accumulate into bitter resentment; and in the volatile atmosphere of a Yanomamo village during wartime, persistent resentment can lead to violence (Biocca 1971: 84–86; Smole 1976: 244).

Jealousy and suspicion between *teri* are even more productive of violence. Members of a *teri* do steal from other *teri*'s gardens and hoard their own trade goods. Women often grumble about the greed of other *teri*. To quote Helena Valero (Biocca 1971: 206), "Meanwhile the Namo-eteri women began to say that the Mahekototeri had many things, many machetes, but that they did not give them away; that when they came, they ate so much and their stomachs were never full; that the more they ate the more they wanted to eat; that they themselves were angry with them." In this case, although the Namoeteri headman wanted an alliance with the Mahekototeri, the women's grumbling prompted a faction of the Namoeteri to warn the Mahekototeri that an attack was imminent, ruining the opportunity for an alliance. In more serious cases, for example when a garden has been seized or destroyed, women will harp at their men and incite them to kill (Biocca 1971: 219).

Because the Yanomamo have been most often compared with more complex groups in Africa and New Guinea, their actual degree of ter-ritoriality has been underemphasized. The Yanomamo are significantly more territorial than any of the groups we examined in Chapters 3 and 4. Each *teri* is associated with a geographical space, generally bounded by prominent features such as rivers or watersheds (Smole 1976: 26–27, 231). Because neighboring *teri* are friendly, members move freely in the extended zones of hunting and foraging distant from the *shabono*.

As we have seen, when a friendly *teri* joins others in one village for security it takes the name of the group in whose territory the village is situated. But it remains the proprietor of its own territory; members continue to plant gardens there, and they return there when the large *teri* breaks up (Smole 1976: 234). Why are the Yanomamo attached to territories that are more distinctly defined than the home ranges of family-level societies?

The answer is that territories are valuable possessions, full of neces-sary raw materials for present and future needs as well as such capital improvements as plantain gardens and peach-palm trees. That is the main reason why the Yanomamo do not move to villages far from their old ones except when routed by their enemies (Chagnon 1983: 70).

Although getting rid of hostile neighbors is rarely offered as a proximate reason for raiding another *teri*, warfare does frequently lead to the permanent displacement of a *teri* from the immediate neighborhood of its enemy (Biocca 1971: 98, 103, 209; Smole 1976: 235–36). When hostilities cease, however, and the people of the displaced *teri* have confidence in a lasting peace, they may take the opportunity to move back into superior lands closer to their former enemies (Smole 1976: 93–94).

Yanomamo warfare is not directly aimed at seizing territory as such. In some highland areas warfare is relatively uncommon, and many groups have been stable for generations. But that is because they have formed territorial alliances and present a formidable obstacle to their enemies.

In areas where warfare is more common, an uprooted group may aggressively displace a weak group because of its own desperate need for new territory. In one instructive example, after the Namoeteri under their leader Fusiwe split into four separate *teri*, one of them, the Pishaanseteri (Bisaasi-teri), built their *shabono* provocatively near the Namoeteri garden. The Namoeteri proper were now a small group, and when the Pishaanseteri began stealing their crops and destroying their tobacco plants, some Namoeteri counseled Fusiwe to abandon the garden. But Fusiwe became enraged, saying, "They are asking me to kill them."

The two groups tried to defuse the growing hostility by a club fight. Afterward, Fusiwe stated: "No, I am not angry. You have struck me and my blood is flowing, but I bear no wrath against you." The Pishaanseteri leader's brother, however, replied: "You must go away; you must leave this *roca*; here we must live. Go and live with the Patanaweteri; we must be the masters of this place." As hostilities escalated, the Pishaanseteri enlarged their ambitions: "We wish to kill the Patanaweteri [including Fusiwe's Namoeteri]; we alone will remain, we, the Pishaanseteri, the most *waiteri* of all." They did kill Fusiwe and scatter his group, but a conspiracy of many *teri* now hostile to the Pishaanseteri eventually joined to massacre most of them at a treacherous feast. The survivors then set out on a long search for new territory that finally ended in the Orinoco lowlands (Biocca 1971: 217–50, 302; see also Chagnon 1983: 152–53).

In sum, we hold that Yanomamo warfare is a tragic failure. It is tragic in the classic sense that it is not anybody's fault but rather the inevitable outcome of contradictions in human character under the specific conditions of Yanomamo life. In a Yanomamo myth, humans were created when one of the ancestors shot Moon in the belly. In Chagnon's words (1983: 95), "His blood fell to earth and changed into Men, but Men who were inherently *waiteri*: fierce. Where the blood was 'thickest,' the men who were created there were very ferocious and they nearly exterminated each other in their wars. Where the droplets fell or where the blood 'thinned out' by mixing with water, they fought less and did not exterminate each other, that is, they seemed to have a more controllable amount of inherent violence." Control of violence is central to the Yanomamo: they know that uncontrolled violence leads to anni-hilation. Their warfare is not adaptive but, rather, is the failure of ad-aptation. The Yanomamo are strong-willed family members with es-tates of real material importance to defend. Their sense of self-interest leads them into alliances that distribute seasonally scarce wild and do-mesticated produce and extend the region of peace surrounding them. But that same sense of self-interest is offended when allies are not gen-erous (Chagnon 1983: 163), and a feeling that one is being taken ad-vantage of sets in. In order to position themselves for competitive ad-vantage in a scarce environment, men must give the appearance of fe-rocity and be prepared to back it up with action.

This sets the stage for *waiteri* men to dominate the scene. Men that in family-level societies would be taught restraint or expelled from the group, among the Yanomamo gain extra wives and a following of men. But, being *waiteri*, they are truly fearless and expose themselves and those around them to danger: despite efforts to restrain them, they lose control and maim or kill other men, bringing the wrath of their victims' families down on themselves and their close relatives and inflicting on everyone the costly consequences of a state of war. There is seemingly no alternative, since less combative groups are bullied and exploited by stronger groups who covet their women or want to displace them from their lands. The fact that in the highlands good farmland is scarce and improved with peach palm trees, both old and new, means that flight is not a realistic response to aggression.

In this sense, the ultimate cause of Yanomamo warfare is what Car-neiro (1970b) has called geographical circumscription. The Yanomamo of the highlands are surrounded by a lowland into which it has been impossible to flee until very recently. Their highlands are a poor envi-ronment of limited possibilities, one in which the control of territories encompassing past, present, and future resources is essential to an ade-quate quality of life. With nowhere to run, the Yanomamo were forced to stand and defend themselves, grouping into villages and alliances, defining their territories and rigorously distinguishing friend from foe.

The Yanomamo have often been compared with more complex groups such as those we describe in later chapters (e.g., Chagnon 1980; Ramos 1972: 127–31). Such a comparison is one-sided, for it emphasizes the relative abundance of wild resources enjoyed by the Yanomamo and the spontaneity and individualism of Yanomamo warfare, making it seem primitive, irrational, and lacking in political structure in comparison with more organized forms of warfare. In comparison with the family-level societies we have examined previously, however, we are impressed not with what the Yanomamo lack but with what they have achieved: villages, leaders, kin solidarity, and ceremonies that dissipate hostilities and create bonds of trust and dependence.

Conclusions

The Yanomamo are in essential ways like a family-level society. The greatest degree of economic interdependence is found in the *teri*, territorial groups and owners of improved agricultural lands who anticipate the corporate kin groups of later chapters. But because the Yanomamo are crowded in their landscape in comparison with true family-level societies, a fundamental and far-reaching transformation has taken place: they can no longer avoid resource competition simply by moving elsewhere, and brave, aggressive men are now treated as valuable allies rather than as dangerous outcasts.

Competition and fierceness are an explosive compound that endangers the *teri*'s well-being. The Yanomamo understand this and do all they can to avoid war. But the inevitable disappointment, sense of injustice, and suspicion that arise from exchanges between non-kin often overcome the limited economic benefits of intervillage trade, leaving *teri* vulnerable to attack by hostile and remorseless enemies seeking wives or lands for themselves. A *teri* that does not itself become fearsome in defense of its estate, embracing and rewarding brave, violent men, has no place to hide and no future.

SEVEN

The Village and the Clan

IN CHAPTER 5 we examined the causes of economic and political integration beyond the family level. In Chapter 6, with the Yanomamo, we saw how the need for defense of the family estate, both as a region of improved garden lands and as a set of women in whom men claim reproductive rights, brought about village life. We also found that risk-aversive food sharing and intercommunity trade reinforced the patterns of alliance and leadership that emerged from defensive military arrangements.

In this chapter we continue to explore the complex determinants of suprafamily economic integration. The value of Steward's notion of multilinear evolution becomes apparent in the three cases of this chapter. The engine for change continues to be intensification driven by population growth and channeled by specific conditions in the environment and the technology used to exploit and transform it. In environments with rich wild resources, especially maritime ones, intensification of hunter-gatherer-fisher economies is often possible. The technology to fish offshore and in rivers and to capture large sea mammals can be quite complicated, involving special boats, lances, lines, weirs, and the like. The Coastal Eskimoes, our first case, are closely related to inland groups organized at the family level, but their complex technology of the whale hunt requires substantial capital investment in equipment and a division of labor in the chase. Leaders, the owners of the whaling boats, are important, and small villages form around their residences. Trade is also important, but warfare much less so than for horticultural societies organized at this scale.

In other environments the outcomes of intensification can be quite different. Looking at the continuing process of intensification among horticultural groups, we find that the Maring illustrate the group-building role of territorial defense uncovered in the Yanomamo case, but under a greater population density that brings the importance of property in land clearly to the fore. Noteworthy are the formalized Maring clans, kin-based corporate groups that are so common at the local group level. Clans claim title to land founded on sacred rights, and they defend those rights against predatory neighbors.

Finally, in environments marginal to agriculture, especially in grassland savannas either natural or man-made, intensification characteristically results in the development of subsistence pastoralists. Among the Northern Turkana, local groups are essential to defend the herds against raiding and to provide common access to pasture used opportunistically by all segments. Population does not center in a village for obvious ecological reasons, and loose and highly scattered networks create a local group as a means to spread the risks of herding (from both natural and human predators) and to maximize flexible and opportunistic movement to pasture and water.

With the addition of these three cases to the Yanomamo, we may examine in further detail how each of the four processes of economic integration—defense, risk aversion, capital investment in technology, and trade—creates economic interdependence even in societies only somewhat more institutionalized than family-level societies.

Case 6. The Eskimos of the North Slope of Alaska

The North Slope Eskimos offer a remarkably clear example of factors that lead to the formation of a village-level economy. This case is especially revealing because although all North Slope Eskimos belong to the same cultural and linguistic group, only those living on the coast and engaged in cooperative whale hunting (the Tareumiut) have a developed village economy. The inland Eskimos (Nunamiut) are typical family-level foragers; much like the Nganasan (Case 4), they aggregate in groups beyond the camp level only for semiannual caribou drives or, less commonly, to pass the winter in the security of a settled neighborhood.

The Environment and the Economy

The Tareumiut, or "people of the sea" (Spencer 1959), and the Nunamiut, "people of the land" (Gubser 1965), occupy separate niches in the North Slope habitat, a region of some seventy thousand square miles all within the Arctic Circle, descending from the Brooks Range north through foothills and coastal plains to the Arctic Ocean. Despite its desolate appearance as a treeless tundra, the North Slope offers a wide range of animal foods for a small, scattered foraging population.

Along the coast are whales, walruses, seals, and polar bears. Inland are the highly valued caribou, along with grizzly bears, mountain sheep, moose, and ptarmigans. Ordinarily there is adequate food to sustain aboriginal population densities of about one person per twenty square miles; but there is a wide seasonal fluctuation in the availability of foodstuffs, and there are unpredictable annual variations in the migration patterns of the most important game mammals, the caribou and the whale.

Both on the coast and inland the spring migrations of whales and caribou are times of anticipated food abundance. As the polar ice pack breaks up, whales migrate close to shore where boatmen can hunt them. Inland, the caribou aggregate in herds of hundreds or thousands that flow through passes in the Brooks Range to pasture in the meadows of the North Slope. As summer approaches, the migrations end and game scatters. The snows melt, and although the region is a true desert, receiving only about six inches of rain per year, moisture evaporates slowly. Hence the landscape is a maze of bogs and pools resting on permafrost. During a two-month period of twenty-four-hour sunshine in summer the land blooms and all land animals fatten, but the first snow may fall in late August; by early October the land has frozen over. In the fall there are smaller migrations of caribou, and occasionally whales.

By November, winter brings the "hungry time." Winter has its advantages: at temperatures of –10°F to –30°F the snow and ice are well suited for sleds and foot travel; there is much leisure time and, in settled areas, intense socializing. But winter is a difficult time for hunting, since the game can see, hear, and smell for great distances across the barren snow and are difficult to stalk. Gubser (1965: 260) reports that a man can hear another's footfalls in the snow for distances of well over a mile. Game animals are widely scattered and may not be seen for weeks on end. People are accordingly forced to eat less desirable foods such as fish, which is felt to be lacking in oil and hence inferior, or even fox. (Foxes are normally hunted or trapped only for their pelts, their meat being discarded or fed to the dogs.) "With their level of technology and in the environment in which they lived, it was impossible to ensure a sufficient surplus of food to last each family throughout every winter" (Chance 1966: 2).

For the Nunamiut, as for the Nganasan, a household's food supply depends almost entirely on successful hunting, and the diet is dominated by caribou meat and fat. Caribou hides, antler, sinew, and bone provide most needed materials, including the makings for tents and clothing. Women procure firewood (a major resource scarcity), fetch water (which is melted from blocks of snow in winter), prepare food, and manufacture clothing.

Most of the year the Nunamiut roam in individual families or extended family camps that often split into individual households and go their separate ways for a time before reassembling. During this same period caribou also travel in small, widely scattered groups, which the Eskimo conceptualize as nuclear and extended families.

When the spring and fall caribou migrations occur, several camps assemble in predetermined areas for cooperative hunts. As with the Nganasan, successful hunters are called on to organize the collective activities of the caribou drive. But much hunting at this time remains individual, and in years when large caribou herds fail to materialize the Nunamiut simply disperse in pursuit of small herds.

Although summer is a fairly easy time, the take of caribou in the spring and fall is rarely enough to last through the winter, and that poses a dilemma. On the one hand, a family may remain in the vicinity of other families for the winter; since people are required to share food when asked, no one will starve as long as his neighbors are well provisioned. On the other hand, scarce supplies of game and firewood are quickly exhausted in the vicinity of a settled community, and inconvenience, hunger, and the constant importunities of neighbors may drive an enterprising family into the lonely tundra, where it need not share whatever food and firewood it obtains. Alternatively, such an isolated family may find nothing to eat for weeks at a time and may starve.

Warfare as organized intergroup aggression does not exist among the Nunamiut, although it was found in some other Eskimo areas (Nelson 1899: 327–30; Oswalt 1979: 194–97). As in other family-level societies, fighting and occasional homicide take place, especially over women. A man might try to seize a woman, especially if her kin are perceived as weak, and extramarital affairs and fiercely jealous husbands are common (Spencer 1959: 78). Despite a pattern of strict control over anger and aggression within the family (Briggs 1970), homicides resulting from disputes between families do occur and must be revenged, with feuding as a result. Strangers, too, are regarded with suspicion and may be pummeled and humiliated if they enter the home range of another group without permission. Still, networking both for trade and to manage risk is of great importance and helps to counteract these divisive tendencies.

The Tareumiut economy is very different, although, like the Nunamiut, they do some foraging and hunting of caribou, especially in the

TABLE 6

North Slope Eskimo Trade

From coast to inland	From inland to coast
Oil	Caribou hides
Skins (seal, walrus)	Pelts (wolf, fox,
Pottery	wolverine, sheep,
Wooden vessels	musk-ox)
Stone, slate	Horns and antlers
Bags	Caribou legs
Ivory	Pitch
Driftwood	Manufactures of wood
Boat frames	and stone
Muktuk (whale skin and	Pemmican and berries
fat)	

summer and the fall. The Tareumiut live in sturdy sod houses in permanent winter villages of two hundred to three hundred members located far apart along the Arctic coast. The economy is centered on whales. A successful village can take fifteen or more whales in a spring season, producing hundreds of tons of meat and blubber. Unlike the Nunamiut, who dry surplus caribou meat and store small quantities for later consumption, the Tareumiut arduously dig ice cellars out of the permafrost and store large quantities of frozen food for the winter.

In addition to whales the Tareumiut also take quantities of walruses and seals, but they must have whales to survive. An adult eats seven to eight pounds of meat per day. Dogs, which are necessary for transport among both Eskimo groups (like the tame reindeer of the Nganasan), must also be fed. Spencer (1959: 141) cites a report that in 1883 a group of thirty people was observed to consume 18,500 pounds of meat in seventy-five days, an average of about eight pounds per person each day. Despite huge takes of meat and fat in good years, famine is an ever-present threat. When in some years the whales fail to follow their customary routes, the Tareumiut depend more heavily on walruses and ultimately on seals, whose meat is not favored but is most reliably in supply (Chance 1966: 9, 36).

The two Eskimo groups are intimately bound by the need for trade. The Tareumiut need more caribou for tents, clothing, and tools, and the Nunamiut covet seal oil for fuel as well as food. In addition many other products are traded (see Table 6): for example, the Nunamiut consider whale blubber an excellent food, while the Tareumiut seek fox, wolf, and wolverine pelts for clothing. Trade at a great distance is important to the Eskimo economy and is often surprisingly well organized. For example, the Tareumiut prepare precut strips of seal hide in standard bundles of twenty as a popular trade item.

Social Organization

Among both Eskimo groups the nuclear family is the basic residential and productive unit. Two or three families might build houses next to each other, and occasionally two houses might share a common entrance tunnel, but food is stored and cooked separately. There is a great emphasis on harmony and unity in the primary family group. Spouses are chosen in part on the basis of their compatibility with other family members; indeed, the most common reason given for suicide is that the victim could no longer tolerate living with a "troublemaker." Kin ties remain the strongest basis of social relations beyond the household. Kin are free to visit and ask help from one another, but kin have the strongest relations when they live nearby.

Nunamiut social rules require food sharing within the hamlet group and between exchange partners. Yet ownership of food is carefully noted, and all hunting weapons are identified by personal marks to avoid disputes over who killed which animal in communal hunts. Even spouse exchange is permissible, being viewed as a form of reciprocity in men's property rights over their wives' sexuality. The most respect goes to calm, hard-working, generous men who have no wish "to place themselves above the heads of others."

Local groups among the Nunamiut are known by the name of their usual home territory; for example, the inhabitants of the Utokak River area are called Utokagmiut. Perhaps two hundred to three hundred people will identify their home range in such an area. Since strangers may be physically abused if they enter another home range, people establish partnerships throughout the inland region so as to make possible visiting and hunting outside their own home territory. Each household member has a unique set of friendship ties that may be activated when needed, ties that are frequently reinforced by the exchange of gifts, trade items, and sexual access to wives. These voluntary dyadic ties are of great importance in integrating households beyond the immediate neighborhood.

The Tareumiut and the Nunamiut enter trade partnerships with each other and meet in designated places each summer for trade. As many as five hundred people might congregate at such temporary marketplaces or "trading emporia" (Spencer 1959: 198). The quantities traded are often large: for example, two men might trade hundreds of caribou skins for dozens of pokes of seal oil. Not everyone participates directly in this trade, but when traders return home they find a ready demand; distribution soon takes place throughout the community via kin and friendship ties.

The village economy of the Tareumiut is based on cooperative whaling and the distribution of stored food. Although kinsmen prefer to work on the same boat, nonkinsmen must often work together as boat crews, and several boats from one village may cooperate in taking a whale. Whale hunters form voluntary associations under the leadership of an *umealiq* ("boat owner"; pl., *umealit*), who organizes the labor necessary to acquire and maintain a large whaling boat. The *umealiq* must be a knowledgeable and successful whaler to acquire and hold a following, and he must be able to integrate the diverse personalities of specialists (helmsman, harpooner) into a smoothly functioning unit. Followers must trust their *umealiq* and fellow crew members, because a capsized boat in Arctic waters rarely has survivors (in fact, few Eskimos know how to swim). The *umealiq* ensures that the whale is properly butchered and distributed among the hunters.

An *umealiq* must provide for the security of his followers even in a bad season. All families have ice cellars for storage, but an *umealiq* has a larger cellar, corresponding to his greater responsibilities. This cellar serves as a sort of social security fund from which his followers may draw supplies. In the early spring, before the whale hunt, he cleans out his cellar and feasts his followers with the remnants of last year's catch. In addition he is expected to provide clothing and other items to his followers in exchange for their loyalty. Furthermore, an *umealiq* establishes ties with other *umealit* in the village, from whom he can call up reserves of food when his own boat has a run of bad luck. Thus the Tareumiut remain together throughout the winter, enjoying a degree of food security unknown among the Nunamiut, whom they criticize for occasionally abandoning aged or infirm relatives during a lean winter. They say of them: "They are just like animals, they let everybody die" (Spencer 1959: 95). Finally, the *umealiq* plays an important role in economic integration beyond the village level. Men who trade frequently and in large quantities tend to be called *umealiq* whether or not they own a boat.

The highest development of intervillage dependence among the Tareumiut is found in the Messenger Feast, an important ceremonial occasion with considerable elaboration. An *umealiq* who believes he has available—in his own stores and in those of his allied *umealit*—a large surplus of food and other wealth, invites the *umealit* of other villages for a potlatch-style feast (see Chapter 8). These feasts include footraces and other forms of ceremonial competition, and are marked by large displays of competitive generosity. At a later date the guests are expected to reciprocate with a feast of their own. We shall reserve our analysis of the potlatch for Chapter 8, here simply noting that the Messenger Feast functions to distribute large surpluses throughout the coast (and inland) and to finance interpersonal and intercommunity competition.

Eskimo social life is imbued with competition and comparison, but among the Nunamiut social pressure to be "honest and patient" keeps the powers of would-be leaders in check. According to Chance (1966: 73), "Nobody ever tells an Eskimo what to do. But some people are smarter than others and can give good advice. They are the leaders." Competitive athletics, acrobatics, dancing, singing, and joking are pastimes for the long winter night, but the emphasis is on each displaying his own strengths and showing admiration for the strengths of others. That is what we have learned to expect from family-level societies.

"Eskimos are not 'self-effacing': they are honest about their own talents and achievements. Their emphasis rather is on the control of aggression" (Chance 1966: 65–66, 78). When hostile feelings threaten to erupt into aggressive action, it is safest to leave for a while until feelings cool. Habitually aggressive men are ostracized from the community, a strong measure given the difficulties of surviving alone in the winter. Nonetheless, when hostility does lead to homicide, the victim's kinsmen unite for revenge, instituting an interfamily feud that can be difficult to stop in a system with no political controls beyond the family level.

The Tareumiut, in sum, illustrate the situation in which warfare is less important to multifamily cooperation than risk-aversive food sharing and capital investment in food-producing technology. The absence or lesser scope of such conditions among the closely related Nunamiut is reflected in their status as true family-level communities. The focus of the Tareumiut political economy is clearly on the *umealit*, leaders who coordinate the manufacture, use, and maintenance of the whaling technology and the distribution of the massive catch it makes possible. As surely as among the Yanomamo, who cannot live except under the defensive umbrella provided by their brothers and brothers-in-law as commanded by their *tushaua*, Tareumiut families could not survive apart from the cooperating group of relatives and associates brought together in the boathouse under the direction of the *umealiq*.

Recent Change

Although subject to many sources of change, including formal classroom education, military service, construction of military facilities, and oil exploration, the North Slope Eskimos remained largely subsistence-oriented into the 1960's, when oil was discovered at Prudhoe Bay.

Shortly thereafter, in 1971, the Alaska Native Claims Settlement Act (ANCSA) redefined Eskimo lives by imposing and encouraging new forms of political and economic organization. The Eskimos, for example, immediately formed the entire North Slope into a borough with power to tax the oil revenues from Prudhoe Bay, to receive state funds for city services, and to sell municipal bonds on Wall Street (Chance 1996: 3). This allowed Eskimos to determine who was hired for municipal services and to pay competitive wages.

At the same time, the structure of ANCSA required that native lands and resources be managed as a corporation and for a profit. This had the effect of favoring the development of "a growing elite group of Iñupiat (along with a sizable contingent of non-Native managerial, fiscal, and legal associates)" (Chance 1996: 3). There now exists a tension between the more egalitarian borough—oriented toward public service and recognition of the importance of family, kinship, subsistence opportunities, and native cultural integrity—and the profit-making orientation with bottom-line values tending toward social stratification and the assimilation of Eskimos into U.S. society (an explicit intention of the congressional framers of ANCSA).

A surprising proportion of the Eskimo economy is still oriented toward family subsistence based on exploitation of natural resources: as late as the mid-1980's the majority of the diet in three villages studied by Jorgensen (1990: xvi, 310) was obtained from naturally occurring sources. As men were drawn into wage work, women expanded their participation in food production, even entering hunting, an activity formerly restricted to men (Jorgensen 1990: 308). Closely integrated family groups share resources and are linked through mutual aid and the exchange of gifts. Members of these groups express strong sentiments in favor of this subsistence economy.

At the same time, households have become dependent on outside income, and now enjoy or suffer the ups and downs of the oil market. With high prices, they became enthusiastic consumers of store-bought goods and heating oil. As prices declined, they retrenched and sought low-cost alternatives. To turn back to their former independence now appears out of the question (Jorgensen 1990: 287–313).

Case 7. The Tsembaga Maring of New Guinea

The Tsembaga, an archetypical acephalous society (Rappaport 1967: 8, 10), are one of about thirty politically autonomous Maring groups living in the highland fringe of central Papua New Guinea (Buchbinder 1973; Clarke 1966, 1971; Lowman 1980; Rappaport 1967). Some seven thousand Maring speakers live in the montane zones of the steep Jimi and Simbai Valleys that border the Bismarck Range, tending swidden gardens, raising pigs, and foraging for wild foods. Until the 1950's the Maring remained beyond direct Western contact, and their ethnography offers a rare opportunity to view a tribal society as it functioned in a world of stateless groups.

Even more so than the Yanomamo, the Tsembaga live in a crowded landscape with hostile warring neighbors, are organized into clans and local groups, and have elaborate ceremonies. Higher population density has led to intensification and direct competition for land, resulting in persistent warfare among neighbors for lack of regional mechanisms to mediate intergroup disputes. To counter the threat of incursion, battle, and possible death, each family must join both a clan, as a mechanism for asserting rights to land, and a local group, for cooperative mutual defense. Ceremonies help to symbolize, unite, and institutionalize these larger groups, and also enable the Tsembaga to reach out regionally for allies.

The Environment and the Economy

The Tsembaga live in a rugged, mountainous environment that is economically marginal for highland New Guinean people. The best lands in the highlands are found in the fertile valleys where the Enga (Chapter 8) and similar groups live, at considerably higher population densities based on more intensive agriculture. The broken terrain where the Maring live is in some senses a frontier or refugee region compared with the highland core. Here in the highland fringe, the topography is steep; elevations plunge from 7,000 feet on the mountain crests to about 2,000 feet along narrow valley floors. Below 5,000 feet slopes average about twenty degrees but become steeper higher up. Small streams cascade down the slopes to join the main river at the base. The climate is generally tropical and humid. At 4,750 feet, Rappaport (1967: 32–33) recorded 154 inches of annual rainfall well distributed throughout the year and a uniformly warm temperature ranging from 60–65°F at night to 75–80°F during the day. Temperatures are lower at higher elevations, and the mountains become enveloped in clouds.

Two primary forest zones have been described by Clarke (1971) for the Maring region. Above 5,000 feet large *pandanus* trees dominate the plant community. Below 5,000 feet remnant forest stands show a more diverse forest community, with trees more than one hundred feet in height and a scrubby herbaceous undergrowth. Most of the primary forest below 5,000 feet has been cleared for gardens, and this area now is a patchwork of active slash-and-burn agricultural plots and secondary forest growth. Primary forest is restricted mainly to the lowest elevations near the rivers and to the highest elevations.

Population density in the Maring region is considerably higher than that of the Yanomamo. Overall density is about 35 people per square mile (7,000 people in two hundred square miles), and Figure 8 shows an environment filling up with settled hamlets. Rappaport (1967: 14) records about 200 Tsembaga in their territory of 3.2 square miles, or about 60 per square mile. Looking at the problem diachronically, Lowman (1980: 15) describes a cycle of population growth and decline that interrelates resource pressure, warfare, marriage patterns, and disease. Both regionally and diachronically, this dynamic cycle of social evolution runs its course. As a local group builds its prestige, its members amass wealth and become attractive as mates; an inflow of women builds the reproductive capability of the group and it flourishes, only to overextend the use of the environment, fragment socially, and contract in size and influence. The Tsembaga, recently defeated in battle, are probably on the decline, and Rappaport estimates an earlier peak population of between 250 and 300 (80 to 95 per square mile).

Population density is a key variable in our evolutionary model. Clearly the Tsembaga are more closely packed than any family-level society, but their relatively low density when compared with Big Man systems in New Guinea's Highland Core (Chapter 8) is equally important. Why is their density not higher? Mainly, it seems, because of environmental and epidemiological factors (see esp. Lowman 1980). The steep mountain slopes are vulnerable to erosion and nutrient depletion, which limits opportunities for intensification, and at lower elevations endemic malaria has restrained population growth. In some sense population density will always be high relative to the available resources, but some environments, such as the Maring homeland, cannot sustain intensification without severe degradation; thus population densities are lower.

The Tsembaga's subsistence economy is predicated on a population small enough to be supported with a diversity of domesticates and some wild foods. Plant foods, consisting of tubers, other vegetables, and fruits, make up nearly 99 percent of the total diet by weight (Rappaport 1967: 73), with the tubers, namely taros, yams, and sweet potatoes, providing the starchy staple. This diet is much more varied than that of higher-altitude New Guinean groups such as the Mae Enga (see Chapter 8), and under ordinary circumstances it is adequate (Rappaport 1967: 74–75). Young children and women also get some protein from rats, frogs, nestlings, and grubs. Meat, although a very

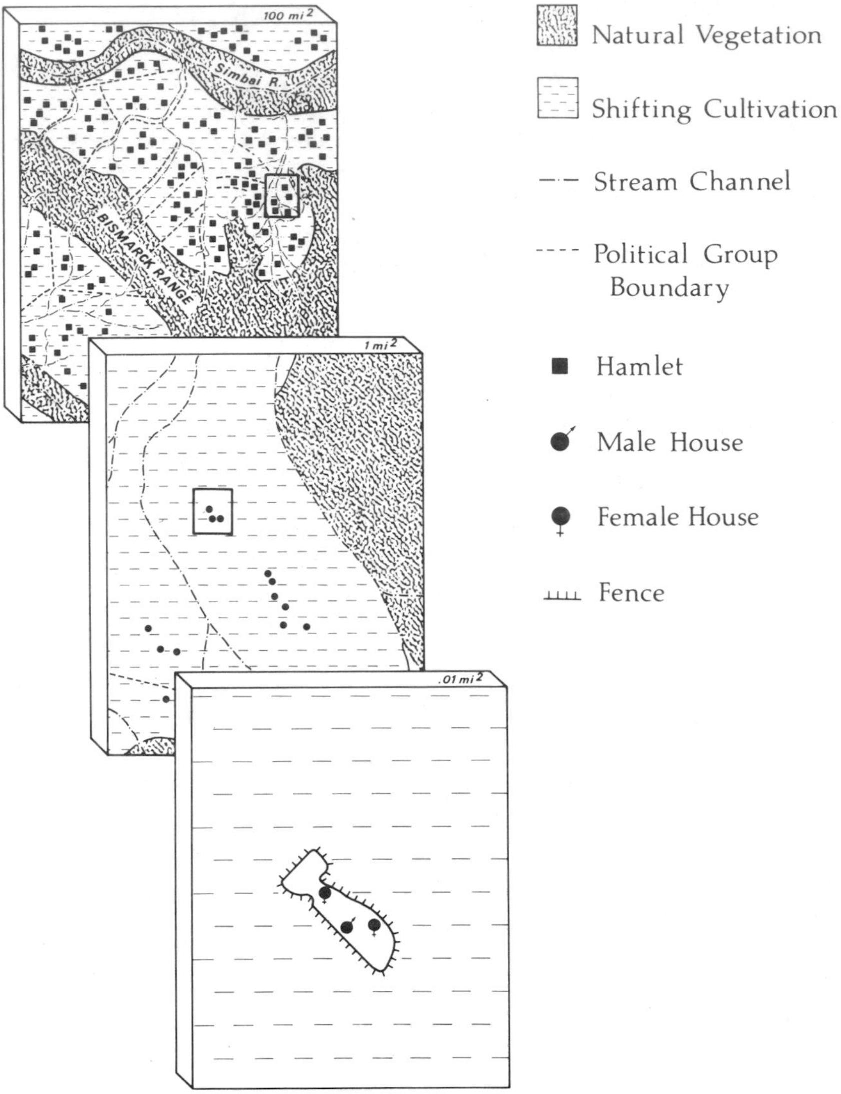

100 mi²
Simbai R.
BISMARCK RANGE
1 mi²
.01 mi²
Natural Vegetation
Shifting Cultivation
Stream Channel
Political Group Boundary
Hamlet
Male House
Female House
Fence

Fig. 8. Settlement Pattern of the Maring. Except for mountain ridges and valley floors, the landscape has been transformed into a mosaic of gardens and secondary growth. Scattered hamlets are protected with fences because each local group's territory abuts enemy lands.

minor part of the diet, is obtained by hunting wild pigs and marsupials and from domesticated pigs and chickens.

To supply this dietary mix the Tsembaga have created a complex environmental mosaic that is a cultural artifact. At all times they seek to have available a mixture of vegetation at every stage of succession, from newly cleared fields to forest fallow. They maintain this ecological diversity by using a long-fallow cycle in horticulture, which in turn is made possible by their comparatively low population density and limited production requirements. With a simple technology, forests are cleared for swidden fields, domesticated pigs are herded, and wild foods are foraged.

Shifting cultivation in the secondary forest (elevation 3,000 to 5,200 feet) is the dominant production strategy. Tsembaga gardens provide a diversity of crops: taros (*Colocasia* and *Xanthosoma*), sweet potatoes, yams, bananas, manioc, sugar cane, various greens, and other vegetables. At higher elevations sweet potato becomes increasingly important in the gardens, providing up to about 70 percent of the yield by calories.

According to Rappaport (1967: tables 3 to 5), lower-elevation swidden fields yield about 12.8 million calories per hectare, higher-elevation fields about 11.3 million. Based on estimates of the energy costs of clearing, fencing, weeding, harvesting, and transporting (but not food processing), the ratio of yields to costs are 16.5:1 for the lower gardens and 16:1 for the higher gardens. These ratios are virtually identical, a point not emphasized by Rappaport but exactly what we would predict for a subsistence economy trying to minimize production costs.

The preparation, planting, and harvest of a swidden garden are done by a man and a woman working jointly. Men are mainly responsible for initial clearing, fencing, and some planting. Women then do the bulk of the planting, weeding, harvesting, and transporting of the harvest. Generally the garden is the cooperative work project of a nuclear family, although men and women do make gardens with unmarried siblings, unmarried in-laws, and widowed parents (Rappaport 1967: 43).

After a field has been cleared, the brush is burnt and the field fenced to protect crops from roaming pigs. Planting takes place immediately after burning, and the standard pattern of intercropping creates a complex artificial plant community with complementary species of different height, speed of growth, and depth of root. Most important for the Tsembaga is the relatively long period of yield created by such a planting design. Most yields from yam, manioc, sweet potato, and taro are available throughout the period from twenty-four to sixty-six weeks after planting. Some vegetables are available sooner, and other crops, notably sugar cane and banana, continue to yield for another year or longer.

After the main harvest period the field reverts gradually to secondary growth as the harvest of the longest-yielding crops continues. At the same time a couple will prepare a new field, usually adjacent to the previous one. A progression of old fields forms a swath across the landscape. At lower elevations the fallow cycle is about fifteen years long, at higher elevations up to forty-five.

Silviculture is an interesting secondary agricultural strategy practiced by the Tsembaga and other Maring (Clarke 1971; Lowman 1980: 59–62; Rappaport 1967: 55–56). Two species of trees are commonly planted as individually owned orchards in the lower elevations of the Tsembaga territory. *Ambiam* (*Gnetum gnemon*) provides an edible young green leaf, and *komba* (*Pandanus conoideus*) provides a fruit that, like the Yanomamo peach palm, is rich in oil as well as protein and niacin (Hipsley and Kirk 1965: 39). A group defeated in warfare will have their trees destroyed, making it harder for them to live in the territory when they reoccupy it. The group that defeated the Tsembaga cut down their groves, and that may be why they make less use of tree crops than do other Maring populations (Rappaport 1967: 55).

The Tsembaga raise not only pigs and chickens but also captured cassowaries (Lowman 1980: 78–97; Rappaport 1967: 56–71). Pigs are by far the most important domesticated animal; although they account for less than 1 percent by weight of the Tsembaga diet, they are a major source of proteins and fats. They are primarily a ceremonial food, eaten at major intergroup pig slaughter ceremonies and at health crisis ceremonies.

Pigs are owned and managed by a male-female pair, commonly a married couple. Men obtain the pigs in trade and from the wild; women are responsible primarily for raising them and tending the gardens that feed them. Mature pigs are largely allowed to forage unwatched, but are kept bound to their family by daily rations of garbage and sweet potatoes. Herds remain small, in part because the practice of castrating males means that females can be impregnated only by wild pigs, and in part because ritual slaughters keep their numbers down.

Vayda et al. (1961: 71) suggested that pigs in New Guinea act as living storehouses for surplus food produced in good years, making it possible for that food to be eaten in bad years in the form of meat. But Rappaport (1967: 59–68) has shown that pigs are a poor storehouse for energy, since they require about one calorie of energy expenditure by the Tsembaga for each calorie returned in food. Indeed, each pig eats about 0.15 acre's worth of sweet potatoes when the herd is at its maximum density; as Rappaport emphasizes, that is the size of garden required to support one human! Thus the Tsembaga's massive expenditure of labor on pigs is clearly not to store calories but to obtain critical supplies of protein and fat. Pigs are also primitive valuables; the exchange of pig meat by the Tsembaga in politically important ceremonies anticipates developments in the political economy that we will describe in Chapter 8 for the higher-density Big Man societies of New Guinea's central highlands. Political rivalry among men is supported by the labors of their wives raising the primary capital in the forms of the pig herds.

Hunting and gathering, so important in societies like the Machiguenga and the Yanomamo, are marginal to the main diet of the Tsembaga. Forests provide building materials and dietary variety, but extensive farming diminishes the forest area and thus the supply of wild foods. Wild pigs and marsupials continue to provide protein and fat, but their overall contribution to the diet is very small. Human exploitation has made the region's natural resources increasingly difficult to obtain. The Tsembaga economy is marked by the scarcity of key resources. Prime agricultural land is limited and overused. Wild resources, especially meat, are badly depleted, and pigs, produced for fat and protein, are costly to feed. In this situation of overall scarcity, competition is intense.

Warfare is an infrequent yet ominous threat to the daily lives of the Tsembaga, whose small territory is surrounded by enemy lands. Actual episodes of warfare are regulated by the ritual cycle and probably engage a given group directly only once every twelve to fifteen years (Rappaport 1967: 156). Battles in the open test the two sides' strength; when a numerical imbalance is seen, the more powerful group will charge and kill anyone they can catch. As Rappaport (1967: 110–17) observes, the proximate cause of warfare recognized by the Tsembaga is revenge for past killings. But as with the Yanomamo, the ultimate cause is competition for resource-rich territories, which are in short supply and from which a group that cannot gain sufficient military strength will be permanently displaced.

Trade is an important part of the Tsembaga economy. It involves salt, axes, and other items that some groups have access to only by trading, as well as a full range of valuables, such as pigs, feathers, and shells, that are used in social exchanges and ritual displays.

Social Organization

The settlement pattern of the Tsembaga is dynamic, with a multiyear cycle of aggregation and dispersion synchronized with the cycle of conflict and ceremony. During periods of ceremonially recognized truce, settlements are dispersed through the territory of a local population as individual households and small hamlets. Although generally scattered, residences remain at the middle elevations where agriculture is most productive; low elevations (which are malarial) and high elevations (being too high for agriculture) remain uninhabited. When the truce ends and war may commence, families move to form a concentrated villagelike settlement around the traditional ceremonial ground. Rappaport (1967: 173) sees this concentration as part of the preparation for the major *kaiko* ceremony (described below), but it can also be viewed as a defensive preparation for the expected war.

War comes, and the next stage in settlement reflects its outcome. A victorious or nondefeated group gradually disperses again as the pig population builds up and problems with pigs increase. A defeated group abandons its territory and disperses through the lands of other local groups. It may later try to resettle its territory, but in that event its military weakness requires it to concentrate its population in a defensive settlement. When the Tsembaga returned to their territory following defeat, the whole group of about two hundred people lived together in a loose village aggregate covering perhaps twelve to fifteen acres. The explicit reason for maintaining residence together, despite the increased distance to their fields and the damage to nearby gardens caused by pigs, was fear of their enemies (Rappaport 1967: 69).

Settlement in the Maring region responds to opposing forces. Populations come together for defense and related ceremonial activities; they then disperse for easier access to more distant fields and to avoid the destruction of agricultural crops by pigs. This dynamic of concentration and dispersion is like that described for simpler societies but extends over a longer time period and has the critical added factor of deadly warfare that forces people together.

The Maring generally, as typified by the Tsembaga, consist of hierarchically nested groups that are constantly forming by segmentation and coalescing from necessity. The different levels of organization and the economic and political functions of those levels have been discussed by Lowman (1980: 108–28) and Rappaport (1967: 17–28). For our discussion we recognize a somewhat simplified set of four main levels of organization: the domestic household, the patrilineal household cluster, the clan, and the local territorial group.

The domestic household (Lowman 1980: 111–12) corresponds to the hearth unit composed of a married man and woman with their unmarried children and perhaps additional close relations. Members cooperate in economic activities and share food cooked in a single pot. The division of labor, mainly by sex and age, cross-cuts the household and creates a potentially independent subsistence unit. Men and women share work in gardening and husbandry, and eat together from their common produce. The woman lives in a separate house with her unmarried daughters, young sons, and pigs. Living in the men's house but still part of one household are the man, his older sons, and his unmarried brothers. These males have been initiated; they have passed ceremonies of instruction and ordeal to make them men. They must live apart from women, although they eat and work with them. Men must fight together to defend their land, their women, and their honor.

The patrilineal household cluster is a hamlet-size informal grouping composed of domestic units whose males are linked in explicit and known genealogical relations; its male members are no more distant than first cousins. Typically the males live in a single men's house and interact frequently, but the group is unnamed. The group functions as a unit because of the closeness of its internal kin ties and its members' mutual support in economic, ceremonial, and political undertakings. Households live close together; they often share an earth oven, and a protective fence surrounds the hamlet compound. Not far away are the household's gardens. Available for sharing among members of this minimal residential grouping are land, plant cuttings, and agricultural produce. In social and ceremonial activities, patrilineal relatives often act together, for example in preparing a bridewealth payment or in sacrificing pigs to specific ancestors. Membership in this group is not sharply defined, and new groups form constantly by segmentation.

The clan—which unlike the first two groups is not found in family-level societies—is a formal, named, and ceremonially defined social unit that is very important to the Tsembaga. Membership in a Maring clan is putatively patrilineal, although actual genealogical relationships among members are not always traceable. Some immigration is permitted, especially when land is available and added members would strengthen a group's position. Immigrants are fully incorporated into the clan within two generations (Lowman 1980: 116); for all intents and purposes, ritual participation with the clan group defines membership. The clan is exogamous.

The clans recorded for the Maring in 1966 had an average size of seventy-five (Lowman 1980: 120), about the size of a Yanomamo *teri*. The two hundred Tsembaga were divided among five clans that actually formed three groupings (two small clans were united with one larger one). The clan does not normally form a coresidential village, but it functions as a unit in economic, political, and ceremonial activities. Economically it controls a territorial strip that runs vertically from the mountain crest to the river and incorporates all the ecological diversity of the Tsembaga area. Formal boundaries to this territory are known and marked, often by natural features such as streams or ridges. Clan members individually hold improved agricultural lands such as swidden plots and groves, and the lands of the patrilineal subgroups form noncontiguous clusters scattered at different locations in the territorial strip. Most important, the clan defines ownership rights and restricts access to land. Clan members may exchange land with each other, and extensive land exchanges between two neighboring clans represent a major step toward fusion into a single territorial unit.

The clan is also central to all ceremonial and political events. It organizes and serves as host for ceremonies in the central *kaiko* cycle; indeed, participation together in these ceremonies, especially the planting of the *rumbim* following war, operationally defines the group. The clan owns a fighting-magic house and its own set of fighting stones that are actually prehistoric stone tools (Lowman 1980: 1–18; Rappaport 1967: 125). Its ritual leader in war is responsible for the house and its stones, and helps coordinate the ceremonies that coalesce the clan into a single fighting unit. Such "war shamans" (Lowman 1980: 119) hold the highest position of leadership among the Maring, and the history of the clan is largely their history.

Ideally a clan corresponds to a territorial division, although, as we have seen, smaller clans may merge with larger ones. The creation of this suprafamily corporate group with leadership and ceremonial integration is a significant departure from family-level society. A still more significant departure is the ritual integration of most Maring clans into a codefensive territorial group of clans.

The local group or clan cluster of the Maring is a grouping of two to six clans that numbers from 200 to 792 people and averages 380 (Lowman 1980: 125). The Tsembaga, with 200 people, are at the very bottom of this range, reflecting their weak political position following a recent defeat in warfare. The clan cluster is not named and has no overarching ritual leaders or war houses, but its constituent clans are tightly interrelated by marriage and exchange. The main ceremonies—the planting of the *rumbim* that establishes a truce, the planting of the stakes that define a clan's territory, and the slaughter of pigs to repay allies and ancestors for their assistance—are synchronized to prepare the clans to act together in territorial definition and defense. Analytically, this local group is a kind of "village," and under some circumstances related to its defense its constituent clans will actually come together into a coresidential grouping. As indicated in Figure 8, these local groups are the significant political entity, beyond which is war.

Beyond the local group no institutional structure exists, although there are frequent interactions. Individuals build networks of interpersonal ties through marriage and exchange outside their local group. These ties act as means of personal and group security: they are used to obtain spouses, trade goods, allies in warfare, and refuge in case of defeat. Since these external contacts are both made and reinforced on ceremonial occasions, a person's participation in intergroup ceremonies is central to his networking strategies.

Among the Tsembaga all external relationships on which the local group depends are based on individual ties mediated by group ceremonial presentation. Although a man depends on his group for access to land, for economic support, and for mutual defense, he must achieve special prominence in his group to have access to a regional network that affords contacts, security, and trade opportunities beyond what the local group may provide. The opportunity to shine comes in ceremonies in which men bedeck themselves with fine feathers and shells and display themselves in group dances. Rappaport (1967: 186) describes in detail the elaborate dress and individual display at the main *kaiko* ceremony:

Adornment [in the public dancing] is painstaking and men often take hours to complete their dressing. Pigments, formerly earth colors of native manufacture, more recently powders of European origin, are applied to the face in designs that are subject to frequent changes in fashion. Beads and shells are worn as necklaces and garters of small cowries encircle the calves. The best orchid fiber waistbands and dress loin cloths enriched with marsupial fur and embellished with dyed purple stripes are put on. The buttocks are covered with masses of accordion-folded leaves of *rumbim* called "*kamp*" and other ornamentals. A bustle, made of dried leaves obtained in trade, which rustles during dancing, is attached on top of the mass of *kamp* leaves.

Most attention is given to the headdress. A crown of feathers, eagle and parrot being most common, encircles the head. The feathers are attached to a basketry base, which is often hidden by marsupial fur bands, bands made of yellow orchid stems and green beetles, or festoons of small cowrie shells. From the center of the head rises a flexible reed, two or even three feet long, to which is attached a plume made either from feathers or an entire stuffed bird.

A man's success in competitive display reflects his own prestige, which in turn increases (or decreases) the overall desirability of his group as an ally.

The Maring ceremonial cycle is described at length by Rappaport (1967: 133–242; 1971) and Peoples (1982). In briefest outline, hostilities between local populations of Maring are endemic, and open warfare is periodic and violent. When it is decided to end open fighting, either because of a major defeat or because of many deaths without a clear outcome, a truce is instigated and ceremonially marked by the ritual planting of the special *rumbim* plant. Then, following a period of five to twenty years during which the plant grows, warfare is considered impossible. The pig herd is allowed to grow in preparation for the *kaiko*. When a consensus is reached that it is time to initiate the ceremony, which is designed to repay the assistance of ancestors and allies in past combats, the first step is to plant stakes that mark off the territorial boundaries of the local clan or clan cluster. If a defeated group has not reoccupied its territory and planted its *rumbim*, the stakes of the victorious clans will be laid out to incorporate the new land; otherwise, the stakes define the same territories as existed before the war. Then the *rumbim* is uprooted and a major intergroup ceremony is performed at which the group's pig herd is slaughtered and eaten. This ceremony ends the truce; no institutional mechanism is in place to restrict hostilities, and the local groups await the outbreak of war. When this occurs, as it inevitably does, allies recruited through the interpersonal regional networks come together to support the warring groups.

What are we to make of this odd cycle? Three positions are presented by Rappaport, Lowman, and Peoples.

As a cultural ecologist, Rappaport (1967, 1971) sees the *kaiko* ceremony as a homeostat, or system regulator, which in the absence of group leadership benefits the group by regulating the distribution of human population, the size of the pig herd, the exploitation of wild marsupials, and other variables. Whether or not the participants know it, the ceremonial cycle causes the group to take actions necessary for its survival.

Lowman (1980) disagrees. Rather than a neat pattern of "regulation," she sees periods of rapid population growth and collapse related to a group's success in warfare, marriage, and immigration on the one hand, and eventual severe environmental degradation with overpopulation on the other. Supporting that position, Clarke (1982) argues that any semblance of regulation or equilibrium among the Maring is a result of their simple, individualistic technology and of severe malaria at lower elevations (see Lowman 1980).

Peoples (1982) presents still a third view: namely that ceremonialism is most important in warfare as a means of obtaining and maintaining allies. Peoples addresses the issue of whether the *kaiko* primarily serves "group advantage" or "individual advantage," concluding that these two perspectives are not necessarily opposed but can be combined for a more complete understanding of the *kaiko*.

Although our emphasis is somewhat different from that of Peoples, we agree that the ceremonial cycle offers both group advantage and individual advantage. Group advantage seems quite clear. The ceremonies are the main way to obtain allies or support outside the group. Given the existence of the ceremonial complex in New Guinea, whose origin has never been clearly explained, participants in the *kaiko* ceremony have a competitive advantage that allows them to expand at the expense of nonparticipants. This group selection is linked to competitive exclusion in warfare and the "social extinction" of groups lacking the organizational trait (Peoples 1982: 299).

Individual advantage seems equally clear, since in addition to the ongoing networking advantages the ceremony offers, its participants can plausibly equate success in warfare with the number of allies recruited through the ceremonial cycle. Group advantage and individual advantage are thus identical in this instance.

Beyond any consideration of advantage, the ceremonies institutionalize the local group. Participation in the ceremonies defines membership in the group and its relationship to the ancestors. The ceremony is thus an event to materialize the group and enact the relationships among its members, following formal procedures. When we speak of Maring social groups, we must conceive them in terms of their *kaiko* ceremonies and the associated cultural landscape.

The Tsembaga exhibit both continuity with simpler, family-level societies and important institutional developments beyond the family level. The household and the household cluster remain central for most aspects of production and consumption, but the increasing complexity of life has given rise to two new levels of integration, the clan, of perhaps seventy-five people, and the territorial community, of several hundred, which unite families with distant kin and non-kin for purposes of corporate ownership and mutual defense. These institutions are maintained by impressive ceremonies but do not have leaders in the modern sense; indeed, Tsembaga clans have no recognized leadership position except for that of war shaman (Rappaport 1967).

The importance of the corporate clan and the territorial group, ceremonially integrated, marks the beginnings of what Childe (1936) would have called a Neolithic Society. What caused the development of these institutions? Now people exist in a cultural world of institutions that have the physical form of a village or clan territory, a landscape of group relations that acquires meaning in the historical narratives the ceremonies embody.

The most dramatic changes in basic lifeways from, say, the Machiguenga to the Tsembaga are in population density and warfare. In our theory a significant increase in population density leads to a shift in subsistence toward agriculture, restricted access to and competition over limited resources, small group territories, and endemic warfare (cf. Brown and Podolefsky 1976). That is what has happened to the Tsembaga. Their diet is now almost exclusively vegetarian and agricultural, and their environment is almost totally transformed and managed by human groups. Lands are scarce, clearly demarcated, and jealously defended, with the clan restricting access. The territorial group, composed of several clans, must number several hundred for defense purposes, but the territory is small, only a mile or so across, and surrounded by enemies. Access to any resources not available within this small area must be through intergroup trade. The threat of warfare can never be dismissed.

The institutional elaborations of clan and territorial group appear as logical extensions of an exclusionary policy necessitated by the pressure of population on resources. Ceremonies, so important to the Tsembaga, function to define these groups and to interrelate them with other groups for mutual defense. The "domestication" of humans into interdependent social groups and the growth of the political economy are thus closely tied to competition, warfare, and the necessity of group defense for individual survival.

These contrasts with the Machiguenga are of sufficient importance that they should be visible in the pattern of how people spend time. Although time allocation data are lacking for the Tsembaga, a recent study of the Kapanara, a highland group living at a similar population density, allows us to make a rough comparison (Grossman 1984). In Table 7 we see some important differences from the Machiguenga pattern of time use (Table 5). As expected, the time devoted to hunting, fishing, and collecting is much less among the Kapanara, who instead spend four times as many hours in livestock care (pigs, of course) as do the Machiguenga. Also, in contrast to the Machiguenga, Kapanara women do much more agricultural work than the men, who are heavily engaged in public ceremonial and recreational activities. In this case we also see a considerable investment in commercial activities (cash cropping and wage labor), new activities that reflect the growing commercialization of the New Guinea highlands in recent decades. Commercial work was undoubtedly less common when Rappaport studied the Tsembaga than it is today, but some of the time that now goes toward commercial projects may then have gone into production of food, including pigs, for ceremonial (as opposed to subsistence) purposes.

Yet the contrast between the Machiguenga and the Tsembaga should not be overdrawn. As Lowman (1984) has emphasized, there is a broader regional dynamic in Maring society: the highly institutionalized and ceremonialized Tsembaga are not typical of all Maring, but only

TABLE 7

Kapanara (Papua New Guinea) Time Allocation

(Hours per day)[a]

Activity	Men		Women	
Food production				
Hunting	0.2		0.0	
Fishing	0.0		0.0	
Collecting	0.2		0.3	
Agriculture	1.8		3.1	
Livestock	0.2		0.2	
		2.4		3.6
Food preparation		0.8		1.5
Food consumption		0.4		0.4
Commercial activities				
Cash cropping	1.0		1.2	
Wage labor	0.6		0.1	
		1.6		1.3
Housework		0.2		0.1
Manufacture		0.4		0.3
Social				
Child care	0.1		0.4	
Public ceremony	0.4		0.2	
Public recreation	2.5		1.8	
Education/information	0.5		0.3	
		3.5		2.7
Individual				
Hygiene	0.2		0.3	
"Nothing"	1.2		1.0	
Ill	0.1		0.3	
		1.5		1.6
Other		1.2		0.7
TOTAL		12.0		12.2

SOURCE: Grossman 1984.
[a] 12-hour day (women's total differs owing to rounding).

of Maring in the higher-density and longer-occupied areas. Groups that have settled frontier areas where densities are lower and competition less intense are organized in simpler ways and are more like family-level societies. They live in hamlets without strong clans and have less elaborate ceremonies. Like the Yanomamo, the Maring range along a continuum from family-level to local group organization depending on local variations in resource availability, population density, and intergroup competition.

Case 8. The Turkana of Kenya

As mobile pastoralists who raise animals primarily for household consumption, the Turkana exhibit the individualistic, family-centered economy now familiar to us for groups like the !Kung or the Nganasan. But their comparatively high population density, and the high risks they face from drought, disease, and raiding, compel them to organize and mobilize family and camp groups into neighborhoods and regional associations to spread risks and provide defense. Despite their extraordinarily fluid and opportunistic movement through an unpredictable environment, their local groups show a degree of structure and integration not found in family-level societies.

The Environment and the Economy

The Turkana are mobile pastoralists of the eastern Rift Valley of Kenya (Gulliver 1951, 1955, 1975). The northern part of their region, on which our description will focus, is hot and dry; rainfall averages from six to fifteen inches per year and is highly variable. A good year for pasture comes only once every four or five years, and one year in every ten a severe drought seriously depletes the Turkana herds. Rainfall is heaviest from April through August but may come suddenly at any time in cloudbursts that fill pools and small watercourses for a few days before the water drains off or evaporates. Owing to the highly unpredictable state of resources, the Turkana adaptation is not easy to characterize. For them "there is no 'best area' nor 'best exploitation strategy,'" but rather continually shifting responses to shifting circumstances (Dyson-Hudson 1989: 181).

The Turkana environment varies from "arid"—thorn-brush and grassland—to "very arid"—dwarf shrub rangeland of "low potential" (Patton 1981: 2). In the northern region, mountainous areas and borders of watercourses offer the best grazing lands, and population tends to concentrate in those areas in the middle and late dry season. But most Turkana prefer to live in the open plains and will move there as soon as the rains permit. According to Gulliver (1951: 44), the immediate principle governing Turkana migration is that "browse or graze which will not last long should be used before that which will persist, so that maximum use can be made of the total vegetation." As we shall see, this results in frequent moves by individual homesteads and a continuous aggregation and dispersion of households as local conditions change (cf. Dyson-Hudson 1989: 169).

Gulliver estimated the Turkana population in 1949 at about eighty thousand, spread over about twenty-four thousand square miles. The average population density is accordingly 3.3 persons per square mile, with the dry plains supporting only about 1 person per square mile and the moister mountains much higher densities. But densities vary locally throughout the year as the flexible Turkana take advantage of opportunities in a constantly changing landscape. In 1949 Gulliver visited a temporary mountain "neighborhood" of twenty square miles in which four hundred people lived (twenty per square mile) along with two thousand head of cattle, twelve hundred camels, and four thousand sheep and goats.

For most of the year the Turkana's main foods are milk and meat. The major livestock are cattle, camels, sheep, goats, and donkeys, the last being used primarily for transport but the other four being important in the diet. Cattle, and to some extent sheep, require grass for grazing, and hence must be pastured in the best-watered regions, generally the mountains. Camels and goats, by contrast, do well on thorny, brushy "browse," and hence can feed in areas too dry to support cattle; moreover, camels, with their ability to go five or more days without water, can pasture on lands far from water and hence unusable by cattle, which require watering every other day. The pastoralist exploits these differences by dividing his herds in complex, opportunistic ways to make complete use of whatever resources are available at the moment.

Wetter and drier periods occur unpredictably throughout the year and from one year to the next. The Turkana herder must constantly assess conditions and develop strategies accordingly. In wet periods animals graze freely, milk is abundant, and there is plenty to eat; extra milk can even be preserved by separating and storing the butterfat and by drying the skim milk on skins spread in the sun. In dry periods, animals become thin and milk is scarce. In these periods women gather wild plant foods to round out the diet. Pasture limits population, but it is water that ultimately limits pasture. Rivers periodically dry out and year-round springs are few. Water can be obtained by digging in riverbeds during dry periods, but in bad years water holes can be deep: "many women deep" in Turkana terms, since it requires a chain of women to pass buckets from water level up to ground level.

In addition to meat and milk, animals supply most of the homestead's other needs: leather skins for sleeping mats, roofing, drying pans, shields, containers, clothing, and cordage. Women do most manufacturing and food processing, and in rare good years they may tend small sorghum or millet gardens near the wet-season pastures (in a few areas of the plains). Since young men do most of the herding, older men spend much of their time together in the shade, discussing their herds and the state of pasture.

Pastoralism is the only possible way of life in much of East Africa, thanks to the comparatively high population density and the extreme marginality of the region for rainfall agriculture. The central feature of pastoralism is the concentration of subsistence in movable property— that is, the family herds. Since the Turkana herds are the envy of neighboring groups, raiding for animals is a constant threat, and many aspects of Turkana social organization are designed to minimize or at least control that threat.

Unlike pastoralists such as the Kirghiz (Case 11) and Basseri (Case 14), the Turkana do not have strong exchange bonds with agricultural populations. A careful sixteen-month nutritional study of four Turkana families found that they "obtained 76% of their food energy directly from livestock through meat, milk, and blood; 16% through selling or bartering livestock for sugar, sorghum, and maize; and the remaining 8% from wild animals and plants" (Dyson-Hudson 1989: 169). Here the social web of ties serves primarily to solve problems of risk rather than to integrate the Turkana into a regional economy of specialized producers.

Social Organization

The basic production unit is the homestead or camp (*awi*), consisting most often of a man, his wives and children, and a small number of other dependents, with a separate sleeping and cooking hut for each wife. The camp is usually enclosed by a fence of thorn brush into which the family herds are led each night and protected from raiding. Each day the herds are taken to pasture by boys and young men, who keep a loose watch while foraging wild foods for themselves or playing together. When pastures are distant boys may sleep out with their herds, and many pass much time alone and away from their homesteads. In some cases, according to Gulliver, a male househead assigns different wives and their sons to different segments of the herd. For much of the year in such cases, and even for years in succession, each wife (along with her children) lives apart from the others and from her husband, being visited by him in rotation.

Homesteads are largely self-sufficient and autonomous. For much of the year single homesteads or small hamlets are deliberately scattered to avoid competing with other Turkana for pasture and water. Families may aggregate to make use of the short-lived pastures that spring up in the wet season, and as the dry season progresses they may aggregate again near rivers and in the mountains, where water and pasture are more reliable. The Turkana, however, view themselves as plains dwellers; they describe the mountains as cold, difficult to walk in, and overrun by lions and leopards, and they look forward to the time when they can return to the plains. In a good year, when pasture and water are abundant in the plains and a few millet gardens are producing, homesteads that have been apart for months or even years are reunited. The relatively dense aggregations of homesteads (up to forty) that occur in good years, although temporary, are in some ways like villages. There is much feasting and exchange of meat and milk, and major ceremonies are performed.

Dyson-Hudson and McCabe (1985: 79–80) describe the degree to which Turkana groups form out of myriad individual decisions:

Kinship, both agnatic and affinal, is an important basis for cooperative relationships. However since livestock are a readily partible resource, and since the frequent moves of camps and splitting of the major *awi* into satellite camps allows the breaking of old bonds and the establishment of new ones, a man has great latitude to choose to live with people he likes. A woman also has some choice: she can live with her father, her brother, or her grown sons, as well as with her husband. Flux and flexibility characterize [their] social networks.

Although the Turkana lack highly structured kin groups, territories, and a formal political system, they do establish and maintain large networks that amount to a kind of effective community for each homestead. First, hamletlike groups of close relatives or friends live and move together for part of the year. Second, such groups cluster within convenient walking distance of one another, and men in such a cluster meet often to take turns distributing freshly slaughtered meat and to share information on herds and pastures. These two levels of social organization (Gulliver calls them primary and secondary neighborhoods) provide the individual househead with a network of friends through which food and information flow, friends from whom he may beg insistently as a good Turkana should (Gulliver 1951; Patton 1982) and who will cooperate with him in defense against raiding. Although a family is free to move at will, in practice families tend to move with their neighbors and settle near them at new locations.

The Turkana also establish and maintain strong friendship ties at a distance by means of livestock exchanges. True friends are generous with one another, even though they may meet once a year or less. Having friends at a distance helps spread risk: if natural disaster should decimate the herds in one area, each homestead has friends scattered throughout Turkana land to whom they can turn for food and stock to replenish their herds. The sporadic wet season aggregations in the plains are opportunities for homesteads, neighborhoods, and even distant friends to reinforce their networks. During these aggregations, marriages and age-set ceremonies consolidate existing ties and create new ones.

Dyson-Hudson (1989: 187) provides an illustration of the importance of social ties in successful herd management:

Between July 1979 and February 1981, a period of intensifying drought, Angor (a herd owner with five grown brothers on whom he could rely) divided his livestock into six sub-herds, with separate satellite camps for the weak and the strong non-milking small stock, as well as for all the cattle and for the non-milking camels. In contrast Lori, who had only one (unreliable) younger brother in his *awi*, had one satellite camp for the non-milking camels, and depended on a distant agnate to herd his cattle. Angor was a successful herd manager, having parlayed a small foundation herd to a large livestock holding; whereas Lori's large foundation herd dwindled, and by 1983 was reduced to too few animals to support his family. However, Lori's failure to divide his livestock into satellite camps during the drought was probably evidence of his poor management abilities (in not establishing reliable herding partnerships which would have enabled him to do so), rather than the cause of his catastrophic livestock losses during the study period.

In the past, extensive networks were also undoubtedly a response to warfare and defense needs. Raids against other tribes were a normal means of replenishing or increasing one's herds, and through their networks the Turkana could participate in the spoils of raiding parties or seek help against enemy raiders. Even under pacification, at the time of Gulliver's study men carried spears when traveling, and raiding and banditry have recently once again become common (Dyson-Hudson 1989: 179–80; Dyson-Hudson and McCabe 1985).

The main cement of Turkana social organization, however, is the exchange of livestock. A nuclear family's herds are all owned and managed by the father; and although their daily care falls to women and boys, spread over the countryside, there is a strong sense of the essential unity of the family and its herd. Some hamlet groups are the remnants of old extended families whose senior male has died: in such cases the brothers and in-laws continue to live near each other, and, because their herds once had a common owner, the men continue to feel part of one family. Often, as we have seen, the hamlet-size group also includes friends.

The ties in an individual's network are strengthened by gifts and loans of livestock. The Turkana are closely attached to their stock: they name each animal and know the names not only of their own stock but of their neighbors'. A gift or loan of livestock to a friend is thus a highly personal and symbolic act that will not be forgotten; it lays the foundation for future exchanges. A loan also helps spread risk by placing some animals from the family herd in different microecological zones and subjecting them to different styles of herd management.

How extensive is Turkana social structure? On the one hand, there are indicators of "tribal" integration. The Turkana say, "We are all brothers," and respect this tribal identity by rarely raiding or using spears against one another (bandits, *igorokos*, are exceptions). They know and acknowledge the "territorial" names of their regions. They also belong to clans, some of them small and localized, others widespread throughout Turkana land. In past times, apparently, whole regions of Turkana mustered thousands of warriors against non-Turkana enemies.

Yet in their daily life the Turkana are not conscious of themselves as a tribe. They have no tribal, territorial, or clan leaders, no corporate groups, and no genealogical reckoning beyond the grandparent level. They are highly individualistic and tend to migrate within circumscribed areas; even close-knit extended families usually separate at times in response to their individual needs. A great many factors, among them the availability of pasture, the mix of livestock, the amount of labor available to the family, the current location of kinsmen, and the threat of raids, influence migration and set up a complex motion of family units in and out of larger "communities" (Gulliver 1975).

We may view Turkana social structure—embodied in rules, weak though they are, concerning mutual respect, territoriality, clanship, age-sets, and bridewealth—as providing a set of opportunities for the individual Turkana homestead. Since a highly unpredictable environment makes the serious depletion of herds a constant possibility, family autonomy, however powerful a cultural ideal, will not work in practice; suprafamily ties are essential. Out of all the possible ties of kinship, marriage, friendship, and neighborhood, the Turkana select some rather than others for emphasis, and solidify them through exchanges of livestock and seasonal feasts. In this way each homestead is essentially free to exploit constantly changing resources yet retains an extensive social network that can be activated in times of insecurity and danger.

Conclusions

Let us now briefly consider the formation of village-level institutions in terms of the fundamental evolutionary processes of intensification, integration, and stratification.

Intensification of the subsistence economy is a prominent feature of the four cases discussed in Chapters 6 and 7. Higher population pressure on food resources causes significant changes in the diet and in the amount of work necessary to meet dietary requirements. In areas with soils suitable for cultivation, the dominance of slash-and-burn agriculture in food production is clear. We have documented population pressure on the land among the Yanomamo, but the Maring, with a population density of up to eighty persons per square mile, are the extreme case. Virtually the whole environment of the Maring has been transformed by the agricultural cycle; wild foods are now comparatively minor, probably well below 1 percent of the diet by weight. Protein from meat sources comes largely from domesticated pigs rather than hunted animals, and it is obtained only at the cost of considerable labor.

In areas where agriculture is more marginal or impossible, specific environmental conditions offer a variety of alternatives for intensification. The Turkana, in the dry East African savanna, combine mixed pastoralism with occasional agriculture. The Eskimos in the extreme Arctic can depend on the whale, a high-yielding but seasonal resource that requires storage. Intensification in the subsistence economy can therefore take a number of forms, including increased dependency on agriculture, extensive herd management, and specialized hunting. Different environments and histories create distinctive ways that a group can intensify, and these different subsistence strategies result in distinctive problems and institutional means of solving them. Multilinear evolution, the development of parallel but distinctive forms of complexity, results from such underlying contrasts in the subsistence economy.

Integration involves the development of suprafamily structures that link families to corporate groups (clans and lineages), organize the corporate groups into residential aggregates corresponding to villages, and interconnect these local groups in extensive interpersonal networks of exchange and personal support. An essential feature of these higher levels of integration is the reliance on ceremonies to define groups and their interrelationships. Another feature, less prominent but always present in some form, is status rivalry and group leadership in the person of the headman responsible for specific ceremonial and economic tasks.

Why do suprafamily organizations with ceremonialism and leadership develop? The answer is implicit at the family level. In the chapters dealing with family-level organization we described a basic contrast in interfamily relationships corresponding to the subsistence strategies being used. For food gatherers resources are basically predictable and their procurement is largely an individual matter; since interfamily relationships are basically competitive, population is generally dispersed, coming together primarily to exploit periodic windfalls of plants or game. For hunters, by contrast, resources are more unpredictable and procurement tasks may require cooperation among several families; camp-level groups are accordingly formed, and families maintain exchange networks to other camps.

This contrast between basic subsistence modes continues to characterize societies at the local group level. There is no single answer to this question: rather, the different conditions of intensification created different needs and mechanisms for integration. In agricultural groups the primary cause of organizational elaboration appears to be defensive needs. For both the Yanomamo and the Tsembaga, a relatively high population density leads to competition between local populations for the control of such productive resources as prime agricultural land and foraging territories. The formation of the corporate group, the *teri* or clan, makes it possible to bar the group's land to outsiders and regulate its use by clan members; and the organization of clans into a ceremonially synchronized territorial group makes it possible to defend the territory against neighboring groups.

The more narrowly economic causes of group formation seem much less central in agricultural populations. At the local group level of organizational complexity, agricultural technology is simple and does not require cooperative group activities. In the Yanomamo case the seasonal scarcity or oversupply of plantains and peach palm fruits argues for intergroup arrangements. But even in their case the risks are not high, and the economic functions of the *teri* seem clearly secondary to its defense functions. What appears to happen is that economic activities such as commodity exchanges are handled institutionally in the same way as alliance building, and act to reinforce the more basic relationship.

In hunting and fishing economies, economic causes are more prominent in promoting group formation and regional networking. Among the Eskimos village organization is directly necessary to the whale hunt; networking within and beyond the village is equally necessary because of the unpredictability of the food supply. Among pastoralists such as the Turkana, an intermediate condition exists. The animal herds are mobile and easily stolen in a raid. At the same time, the animal herd that an individual family can manage is small and vulnerable to disease and other losses. Risk is critical. The regionally dispersed Turkana community provides mechanisms for both defense and risk management. The organizational character of the local group follows the specific problems of intensification, and the significance of local leaders can be quite variable.

Stratification involves the differential control of productive resources, and little evidence for it exists at the local group level. By and large, individuals acquire and exploit their own resources. Except in cases of economic cooperation where a leader controls the necessary technology, as in the Eskimo whale hunt, and in the immediate instance of warfare, where attack and defense (including their economic aspects) are coordinated by prominent men, leadership carries no connotation of economic control.

Yet within the more complex social organization of these societies, as contrasted with family-level societies, are undeniably contained the basic elements of status rivalry. Individuals compete with each other for prominence and recognized status in the displays and games found in all these societies, notably in the group dancing at the *kaiko* ceremonies of the Tsembaga and in the Eskimo song contests. As we have seen, this competition has important economic implications, for it contributes to an individual's success in forming networks. And tied as it is to underlying economic and political factors, it foreshadows the development of competitive leadership, which we discuss in the next chapter.

EIGHT

The Corporate Group and the Big Man Collectivity

WE NOW EXAMINE the factors that favor the rise of economically powerful "Big Men" among subsistence-oriented producers. The Big Man is a local leader, one who makes decisions for the local group and represents it in major intergroup ceremonies. As Big Man systems we will consider together the highly dynamic Big Men of Highland New Guinea and the somewhat more institutionalized "chiefs" of the Kirghiz of Afghanistan and the Indian fishermen of the Northwest Coast of North America. Although the systems are structured differently, they are remarkably similar in terms of social, political, and economic behavior.

In the past, the emergence of Big Men has been attributed to surplus food production, as seen especially in their competitive feasting (Hayden 1995). Although surplus production is certainly necessary to support Big Men's activities, we must still ask why food producers forgo leisure in order to generate a surplus in the first place. That is, why are people willing to accept the burden of supporting Big Men, their expensive feasting, and public displays of wealth and status?

Big Men characteristically manage the economy beyond their own local group. They organize and direct the intergroup ceremonies, accompanied by large-scale, coordinated gift-giving, that are critical for a group's prestige and desirability as an ally and exchange partner. They organize external trade and may be important traders. In general, the Big Man acts as a group's spokesman, dealing with other Big Men to organize political and economic relations in the loose association of communities known as the intergroup collectivity.

The Big Man's decisions on behalf of his group inevitably entail a certain loss of family-level autonomy among his followers. True, the

Big Man must please his followers or lose their support, but while in power he restricts their options by dominating systems of production and distribution.

In the three ethnographic cases that follow, we continue to examine different lines of evolutionary change that respond to underlying differences in the subsistence economy and its intensification. These potential pathways are represented by the hunter-gatherer Northwest Coast Indians, the horticultural Central Enga of Highland New Guinea, and the pastoralist Kirghiz of Afghanistan. All cases reveal the importance of external relations in the development of strong leaders, but the particular combinations of warfare, trade, and diplomacy differ. In accordance with the pattern identified in Chapters 6 and 7, the importance of leadership in defensive matters is of primary concern in the horticultural case (Central Enga), while other economic matters are of more importance among Northwest Coast groups (where the subsistence economy depends on fish and animal resources) and among the trade-oriented Kirghiz.

Case 9. Indian Fishermen of the Northwest Coast

The native societies of the Northwest Coast of North America hold an immense fascination for the Western observer. Their beautiful art, their elaborate technology, the unexpected extent and complexity of their political life, and above all their competitive, entrepreneurial, and seemingly "capitalistic" economy strike many responsive chords. That these parallels to modern society should be found among hunter-gatherers employing a "stone age" technology has led many observers to question whether any evolutionary theory can explain Northwest Coast economic life.

In this section we shall examine the relations between environment, technology, the social organization of production, and the political economy on the Northwest Coast in an effort to explain this seemingly aberrant economic system.

The Environment and the Economy

Most observers agree that the Northwest Coast environment is capable of providing amply for a hunter-gatherer population (Drucker and Heizer 1967). The coast is significantly more productive than the interior, and population densities and village sizes are larger. Despite local variations in the abundance of certain foodstuffs, the general pattern of food procurement is similar throughout the region, which runs from the Olympic peninsula to southern Alaska. Communities on the coast are oriented toward marine and estuary resources. The seacoast offers eleven saltwater fish, including halibut, cod, herring, and flounder; sea mammals, including sea otters, sea lions, porpoises, and occasionally whales;* waterfowl and shore birds; mussels, clams, and other shellfish; and seaweed and other plants.

In the interior, a comparable diversity is found. Seasonal runs of salmon and candlefish are major sources of food. Although the density (biomass) of game animals is low, their diversity provides "a hunter's paradise" (Oberg 1973: 8). White-tailed deer, mountain goats, bear, moose, bighorn sheep, caribou (in the north), and other species may be hunted for furs as well as meat; geese, ducks, and other fowl abound in some seasons; and a wide variety of berries, roots, and other edible plants are available.

Owing to the unusual productivity of the natural ecosystem, population densities along the Northwest Coast reach one to two persons per square mile, and much higher in specific locales, perhaps the highest density achieved by any ethnographically known hunter-gatherer people (an archaeologically known population, the Calusa of Florida, may have been several times more dense [Marquardt 1992]). Although at such densities we expect population pressure on wild resources, it is not certain that Northwest Coast peoples have experienced any significant food scarcity (Codere 1950; Driver 1969; Drucker and Heizer 1967).

Considerable evidence, however, suggests that the people expect and fear food scarcity and make serious efforts to avoid it. For one thing, the people themselves tell tales in which communities in the past suffered from hunger (for example, Boas 1910: 139; *People of Ksan* 1980: 13). For another, enormous amounts of food are stored for winter, a time when food is scarce and hunger a real possibility. We know also that the region's supply of wild foods varies greatly from year to year. Just as the Eskimo and the Nganasan can never be sure how many caribou will come their way, so Northwest Coast people cannot be sure of the supply of salmon, which can be hugely abundant one year and quite scarce the next for reasons completely beyond the control of local fishermen (Donald and Mitchell 1975, 1994). Finally, some groups, such as the Kwakiutl (Boas 1966: 17), work hard to intensify the production of gathered resources, for example by clearing areas in which edible plant species such as clover and cinquefoil are collected or by burning over berry patches and grazing areas to raise their yield.

The evidence suggests that truly huge surpluses are likely to occur

---

*Whales are seldom hunted, except by the Nootka. A beached whale is a great windfall and the occasion for a feast.

only seasonally and in the good years. Given the food requirements of the region's comparatively large population, scarcity and even famines episodically threaten during the winter months.

Despite the size and complexity of Northwest Coast societies, individuals in small family groups procure their own food for most of the year. Depending on local circumstances (whether coastal or interior, large river or small, etc.), the annual round is approximately as follows.

In March and April, people from separate local groups come together for the great candlefish runs. Candlefish are oily: it is said that one can insert a wick in a dried candlefish, light it, and burn it like a candle. In the early spring millions of candlefish run, and intense labor is invested in harvesting them and rendering their oil, which is then stored for home consumption and trade. The oil is a valuable preservative and additive to dried foods and a key source of calories needed to keep warm in winter. Being storable, it plays such an important part in the political economy that its attraction for people is "like the lure of gold" (*People of Ksan* 1980: 89).

In the late spring and the summer people scatter in family and camp groups, similar to those of the Nunamiut and the Shoshone, to hunt, fish, and collect roots and greens. Coastal groups forage for shellfish and seaweed along the shore and hunt sea mammals in small canoes in coastal waters and among nearby islands. This period is described as one of ease and plenty.

In August and September the tempo of production speeds up as berries come into season and the salmon runs begin. Berries are collected in large quantities, carefully dried on finely crafted racks, and packed in large boxes, sometimes covered with oil, for winter consumption. Salmon runs, like candlefish runs, require a heavy investment of labor to catch and then preserve the fish. In both cases the bounty in good years is more than the people can handle; as a result, the greater the labor invested, the larger the harvest, with little or no declining productivity.

Once this period is past, people aggregate in winter villages, where they pass the season manufacturing and repairing boats, tools, clothing, and the like. There are some hunting expeditions, but people live mainly on stored foods. This is a period of intense socializing and ceremonial activity. By early spring people are tired of stored foods, many of which have begun to deteriorate and are no longer palatable. They are eager to move out of the winter village and resume family-level foraging.

The Indians of the Northwest Coast are masters of woodworking. They build large, sturdy houses, canoes both small and large, and some fish weirs so large that wooden "pile drivers" are used to set the main posts. On a smaller scale they build smokehouses and sheds furnished with drying racks and tables. Of major economic importance also are large boxes made of cedar planks carefully hewn and lashed together. These are watertight and may be used for cooking by filling them with water and adding hot stones from the fire, or for storing oil, berries, seaweed cakes, or other foods.

Prodigious amounts of food can be stored in the smokehouses and in earthen cellars covered with wood and sod (*People of Ksan* 1980; Stewart 1977: 145). Being sedentary each winter, households store quantities of berries, oil, and dried and smoked fish and game, along with pelts, bone, and horn used in manufacture. Some households thereby accumulate substantial wealth in capital and consumer goods. This capacity for wealth, and for the growth of differences in wealth between individuals, ranks the societies of the Northwest Coast among the most complex of known hunter-gatherers (Arnold 1996a). Clearly, then, the importance of storage in the Northwest Coast economy is a precondition to the development of social differentiation (see Suttles 1968).

The considerable accumulated wealth and highly productive localized fisheries were natural targets for raiding; and warfare was in fact present and at times brutal. According to Barnett (1968: 104), "The Kwakiutl say that before the white man came they fought with weapons; now they fight with property. This is a consequence of white interference with their wars, slave taking, and headhunting."

In the late eighteenth century, at the time of the first important contacts with whites, warfare was apparently endemic on the Northwest Coast. Body armor in the form of heavy leather cloaks or "coats of mail" made from wooden slats bound by sinew were widely used, and the technology of battle-axes and clubs was well developed (Gunther 1972: passim). From all indications "true warfare, aimed at driving out or exterminating another lineage or family in order to acquire its lands and goods, was a well-established practice in the North" (Drucker 1955: 136). Warfare could involve long-distance raids aimed at capturing booty and slaves, but competition over resources lay behind much of it. In Drucker's words (1965: 75), "There is considerable evidence that the coast carried the maximum possible population in prehistoric times, particularly in the northern half of the area. That is, the ample natural food resources were fully exploited within the limits of the native technology. The traditions are replete with accounts of groups driven out of their homes and lands, and of the hardships suffered before they found new homes."

A group that could not maintain its strength against powerful neighbors was lost. Drucker (1965: 81) describes one group as being so "ground to bits" between two powerful neighbors that its members traveled in small groups and ate their food raw for fear that their fires would attract roving war parties. "Both sets of enemies were trying to exterminate these people, to take possession of their rich fishing and hunting grounds." At the same time an elaborate system of exchange bound together local populations with special resource opportunities. In particular, as with the Eskimos (Case 6), extensive trade existed between coast and inland groups.

To summarize briefly, the Northwest Coast Indian populations were confronted aboriginally with an exceptional complex of problems related to their intensive hunting, gathering, and fishing economy. The natural environment offers abundance along with unpredictable fluctuations. In some of its areas resources are abundant; in others they are comparatively scarce. Many resources are also highly localized in their distribution. The economy of the Northwest Coast Indians therefore encompassed a remarkable combination of elaborate fishing and storage technology, occasionally fierce warfare, and considerable trade. We now consider their equally remarkable social organization.

Social Organization

Five levels or units of social organization can be discerned: the family, the house group, the lineage, the village, and the supravillage "intergroup collectivity" (Newman 1957). The focus of the family and the house group is on subsistence; house groups form and fragment through the annual cycle as subsistence prospects dictate. By contrast, the lineage, the village, and the larger collectivity are concerned with the political economy and focus on capital investments, ceremonials, exchange, and warfare.

The family is the elemental economic unit, acting independently during summer foraging. Most tools, clothing, food, and manufactures are individually produced and owned and do not concern any larger group. But families are organized for much of the year into "house groups," with an estimated average size ranging from seven (Rosman and Rubel 1971: 130) to twenty-five (Donald and Mitchell 1975: 333), roughly the size of the family hamlets discussed in part 1. House groups pool resources and often eat from a common cooking box.

The house group is not a lineal descent group, yet kinship, traced bilaterally though often with a patrilineal or matrilineal emphasis, is the major determinant of membership. The oldest male of the house group is generally considered its head or chief, yet he is not necessarily of higher social rank than the other adult males in the larger political economy. He and his closest kin constitute a more or less permanent residential core, with less closely related persons moving in and out opportunistically as local resources and labor needs fluctuate. This pattern at the household level reflects a larger division in Northwest Coast societies between elites, who are closely bound to productive resources through politically reinforced ties of ownership, and commoners, who roam more or less freely throughout regional territories, "respecting" different Big Men in succession by residing with them for short periods (Newman 1957: 9–12).

House groups have many communal features. The house itself—permanent, secure, and provisioned with stored foods—understandably attracts its members back each winter. Much of the productive capital of the group, including fish weirs, dams, oil-rendering apparatus, drying racks and sheds, and canoes, is produced jointly and held in trust under the househead's control. Labor in fishing, oil-making, berry-picking, hunting, sealing, and trading is contributed equally by the members of the house. Labor contributed to a Big Man, for the construction of his weirs and dams or the maintenance of village streets, is a joint effort of individual house groups.

Women's labor was central to the household economy. The following description of the Tlingit is representative (Emmonds 1991: 165):

The man was the worker in stone, bone, metal and utensils, and all the implements and tools used in the labor of both sexes. He was the carver and painter. He made all of his weapons, the frames for skin dressing and blanket weaving, and the frames for snowshoes, as well as ornaments of ivory, bone, and shell. He made the musical instruments [drum, rattle, tapping sticks], gambling devices, and wooden hats, helmets and headdresses used in ceremonies. He supplied firewood and the large slabs of cedar bark used for various purposes.

The woman cared for the little children and trained the girls. She tanned and dressed the pelts, made the clothing, spun the goat's wool for blankets, prepared the roots, grass, and plant stems used in sewing, weaving, and making blankets, baskets, and nets. She received, prepared, smoked and cured the fish [perhaps her most important contribution], but often assisted in hanging them on the drying frames and in packing them for transportation. She gathered berries, edible roots and plants, clams and other shellfish and seaweed, cured or prepared them for use. She prepared the food at meals and apportioned what was served. She worked in split porcupine quill and bead embroidery. Medicinal plants were also within her province, since she was the leech and midwife. The manufacture of fish and seal oil was principally her work, but the man assisted. . . . The woman's position in the household was assured. She was the treasurer that carried the keys of the chests that contained the blankets, clothing, and in later years, money. . . . [Her role in trade was great:] She not only could veto any bargain made by her husband, but also made the goods which she traded herself or gave away at potlatches.

Women's production of dried salmon was the economic base of both subsistence and luxury wealth. A wealthy woman of high rank could also build her own house and potlatch in her own right. And female shamans are reported to have had as much power as the male (De Laguna 1983: 81).

Beyond the house groups are units variously named *numayma*, lineages, and clans. Such groups acknowledge kin relationships among their members and are set apart by the possession of distinctive tokens, crests, and other markers. When all members of a lineage live in a single village, they are coholders of rights in specific resources such as streams, berry patches, and offshore islands. But membership is fluid: many people are eligible on kinship grounds to join two or more groups, and will join the one most advantageous at the moment. It is also possible for a non-kinsman to buy into a group.

The named lineage can extend across village boundaries. Such a lineage is not a corporate and territorial group, but it may offer valuable links throughout a wide region in which trade and ceremonial exchanges are important. Lineage ties also provide some security in an area where warfare is endemic and destructive.

Large villages contain more than one lineage and may have as many as five hundred to eight hundred members. The property-owning core of the village population is more or less stable because of the large investment in houses and productive capital. The house is considered sacred, the permanent residence in which ideally one is born, marries, and dies. Since the winter village is the site of these houses and of the major ceremonies and feasts, the Kwakiutl say, "The summer is secular, the winter sacred" (Boas 1966: 172).

Yet as we turn to consider how villages are integrated into a single regional economy, we must remember that the village is only loosely united. Its members are primarily loyal to their own house group, and suspicion of others, especially for theft, is rampant (cf. Boas 1910: 70, 138, 148, 153). As we shall see, many chiefs vie for the support of the villagers, and even their loyal followers must be constantly browbeaten to yield up their precious subsistence products to the political process.

The key to the Northwest Coast political economy is the Big Man or chief. Public life provides many opportunities for expressing differences in rank, and for testing and reordering rank. Ultimately a Big Man's rank is a reflection of his wealth—that is, of the amount of wealth he can accumulate from the group that acknowledges him as leader. To be sure, his functions are complex and extend into areas only partially related to economic life, such as marriage, life-cycle observances, and kinship structure. Viewing just those functions of the Big Man that are central to the economy, however, we can understand a great deal about how Northwest Coast political economy operates and what it does for people. Several points are apparent:

1. The Big Man represents a group, and for many purposes is that group. His wealth is the group's wealth, and his rank expresses the cumulative rank of his following. Thus participants in a ceremony often stress that the Big Man is acting not in his own name but in "our name."

The Big Man is invested with titles and emblems representing the group's territories and wealth objects. In a house group or a local group these titles refer to specific fishing grounds, berry patches, sealing rocks, and the like (the ocean and inland hunting regions are not controlled in this fashion). When a Big Man integrates other local groups with his own, he typically buys their emblems or seizes them by force, so that he becomes, albeit in a restricted sense, owner of the group's resources. Although a Big Man may obtain control of a group by force, perhaps even murdering its original leader, in the long run he must depend on its loyalty, which he must earn by bravery, managerial skill, and generosity.

2. The Big Man organizes a complex economy characterized by large-scale capital investments and an elaborate division of labor. His house contains specialists, such as canoe-makers, harpooners, and carpenters, who are supported from his store of wealth. Although he owns these specialists' products, his followers routinely use them in obtaining, processing, and storing food.

In family-level societies it is difficult to organize the construction of large-scale works like dams, weirs, and defensive structures. A leader is needed to persuade people to do work that does not directly benefit the family, and the Big Man uses his wealth and influence to that end.

3. The salmon fisheries, although very rich, may be overexploited except on the larger rivers. Weirs can literally close off a smaller stream. The Big Man, as ceremonial specialist, must decide when to open the season; fish may be allowed through the weirs for use by upriver groups and to spawn. To some degree, the ritual cycle regulated by the group leaders provides a critical management function that overrides the tragedy of the commons (Morrell 1985; Pinkerton 1985).

4. The Northwest Coast Big Man must maintain greater stores than others, for which purpose he invests in storage structures. These and the larger buildings needed to house specialists constitute what Netting

(1977: 36) describes as "substantial houses full of weighty possessions." Actually, as with Big Men elsewhere, most of the wealth that comes into his house quickly goes out again to meet his followers' expenses, pay debts, make loans, and so on. The basic principle is: Wealth not invested is idle wealth.

5. To support his activities the Big Man requires a share of his followers' production. A successful hunter or fisher must give one-fifth to one-half of his catch to his Big Man (Boas 1921: 1333–40). If he does not, he will receive few favors in the future and may even be roughed up (ibid.: 1334).

In turn the Big Man spends or redistributes his income, returning part of it to his followers through feasts and other generous acts and using part to pay his specialists for their products. Some of these products are directly useful (e.g., canoes and storage facilities); others enhance the prestige of the Big Man and his group (e.g., totem poles and house decorations). Finally, part of the Big Man's income goes to increase his store of prestige goods such as beaten copper valuables and blankets, which are used in ceremonial exchanges.

6. Where warfare is common the Big Man also maintains a retinue of warriors. A brave and well-armed Big Man is a source of security to his followers—or a source of worry if they fail to meet his demands.

7. Big Men are the prime movers in large, interregional ceremonies like the potlatch. Most ceremonies occur in the early summer or in November and December, following the major periods of food storage. An infinite number of occasions can justify ceremonies, among them the numerous life-cycle events of a Big Man's family—births, naming ceremonies, etc. What determines the actual occurrence of a ceremony, however, is the amount of wealth a Big Man has accumulated. Only if his wealth is ample will a Big Man host a ceremony, since other Big Men will be quick to ridicule him if his feast is less than sumptuous. A primary goal is to advertise group success and thereby attract the labor the Big Man needs to exploit resources and increase the wealth at his disposal.

Ceremonial occasions are economically complex. Politically they are occasions for Big Men to compete for prestige by giving away, and even destroying, wealth. Envy and humiliation are integral to the feast. According to Boas (1921: 1341–42), Big Men may exhort their followers thus:

I depend on it that you will stand behind me in everything when I contend with the chiefs of the tribes (villages). . . . I want to give a potlatch to the tribes. I have five hundred blankets in my house. Now you will see whether that is enough to invite the tribes with. You will think that five hundred blankets are not enough, and you will treat me as your chief, and you will give me your property for the potlatch, . . . for it will not be in my name. It will be in your name, and you will become famous among the tribes, when it is said that you have given your property for a potlatch, that I may invite the tribes.

The Big Man and his following seek "to flatten" the name of another group by "burying" it beneath piles of gifts. But a similar feeling of competition exists between a Big Man and those of his own followers who may seek followings to rival his. When a potlatch is proposed, each of the Big Man's followers responds to his proposal, standing and speaking in order of rank. One may speak as follows (Boas 1921: 1343): "I am annoyed by our chief, because he asks us too often for property for his potlatch. I shall try to make him ashamed. Therefore, I shall give him one hundred blankets, that we may bury his name under our property. I wish that you give for the potlatch fifty, or forty, or ten pairs of blankets; and from those who are poor, shall come five pairs of blankets."

All this is conducted openly for all to hear and see. Indeed the hosts offer gifts to the audience of a potlatch as a form of payment for "witnessing" the exchanges between Big Men (Barnett 1968: 93). The need for witnesses is to publicize the economic productivity of the group represented by the Big Man, and, as Newman (1957: 86) indicates, to validate or "legalize" transfers of property control from one headman to another.

Despite the emphasis on blankets and coppers as standards of value, the majority of items given away or destroyed at a potlatch are foods, tools, boxes, other useful goods, and services (Barnett 1968: 76, 85–88). These items represent the surplus available for such uses in this storage-oriented society in years of abundance. In years when food is scarce, by contrast, a Big Man would be humiliated to host a potlatch; and of course none are required until the host is ready. In general, groups with the best resource bases are the largest and wealthiest and have the wealthiest Big Men (Donald and Mitchell 1975: 334–35).

Guests who are given storable items save them for their own future ceremonial needs, or use them to pay off debts or make loans between ceremonies. Food is consumed at the feast or carried home. But the potlatch does not guarantee that food from the rich is transferred to the poor (J. Adams 1973): in bad years the rich meet their own needs first out of limited stores, whereas in abundant years even the poor have ample food. In especially abundant years "grease feasts" are held during which competing leaders pour boxes of fish oil on the fire and burn them in a lavish competitive display of wealth.

8. Big Men can also obtain food for their supporters in bad years in

exchange for items of wealth accumulated in good years (Vayda 1961: 621), assuming of course that some other group has food to exchange. Valuables thus permit at least some distribution of food from well-supplied to hungry areas, and stores of wealth objects serve as savings accounts or social security deposits against local famines. Boas (1898: 682, quoted in Barnett 1968: 4) likened such wealth to a life insurance policy, since it could be inherited and would protect young children should they become orphaned. The security provided by storing wealth in this way is central to people's willingness to submit to a Big Man's demands, since only elites have access to such wealth.

The owner of valuables not only has access to another group's stores but can also grant another group the right to participate in a seasonal or unexpected food surplus in the owner's territory. Thus a headman who "owned" a particular beach gave out tokens entitling the bearer to a share of blubber from the next beached whale to appear on his beach (Newman 1957: 82). And thus also outsiders could obtain rights to fish for salmon or candlefish along privately owned streams when the owning group had fish to spare during a good run. By the ownership and allocation of rights of access, labor can be moved opportunistically yet not chaotically from windfall to windfall, from one short-term surplus to another, reducing the loss of food that is common when small forager camps come upon temporary surpluses beyond their ability to consume.

9. In addition to the exchange of food for valuables, trade also occurs at a distance, notably between the coast and the interior. Such trade is not conducted by members of individual households but is usually organized by Big Men, who through their political activities have established ties to Big Men in other ecological zones.

It is important not to exaggerate the degree of rivalry between Big Men. The language of potlatching is aggressive, and the self-serving speeches are intended to make others ashamed. But Big Men are tough and not easily crushed by mere polemics, and they respect the debts they incur through ceremonial exchanges and attempt to pay them back. Over time they build ties of respect and trust (Barnett 1968: 112; Rosman and Rubel 1971: 170) that can be called on in times of need.

As with the Yanomamo (Chapter 6), these ties serve also to create regions of peace within which aggressive competition between populations can be regulated and turned to constructive purposes. In fact, the evidence suggests that when peace was enforced by whites following contact, rivalries that once would have led to open conflict came to be expressed in particularly acrimonious ceremonial competition. Once again, then, warfare must be attributed to the failure of the political economy to integrate communities that lack strong ties of kinship and exchange. At times even the potlatch ceremonials are turned into Yanomamo-style treacherous feasts by enemies who simulate peacemaking efforts in order to lure wary victims to their destruction (Drucker 1965: 80).

Prior to pacification, among the fruits of war were captives, generally referred to as slaves. The term "slave" is problematic, since war captives were usually ransomed (ibid.: 51–52; Suttles 1968) and tended to be viewed as complete outsiders to their host communities (Kan 1989: 95). Nonetheless, captives were often held indefinitely and in some cases became major sources of labor for elites who themselves did little or no productive labor. As such, slaves were valuable: they were a major goal of some warfare, and could be bought, sold, and given as precious gifts at potlatches (Mitchell 1984). In some cases slaves made up as much as 20 to 30 percent of a community's labor force, and their status was fixed and passed on to their children (Donald 1984), who were considered inappropriate marriage choices by the host community. In such cases, "slavery" does not seem an inappropriate label.

There is much debate over whether there are economic classes in Northwest Coast societies (Ruyle 1973). In addition to the contention that slaves constitute an exploited labor class, the argument has also been made that elites form an upper class who use control over property to command the labor of others (Arnold 1996a: 63; Hayden 1995: 64–65). As titleholders who control resources, hold publicly recognized high rank, and pass both property and rank on to their offspring, some Northwest Coast elites could be considered chiefs rather than Big Men. In that view, there would be three classes in stratified Northwest Coast societies: chiefs, commoners, and slaves.

Ruyle (1973) calls this "incipient stratification." We retain use of the term Big Man, however, because it is clearly appropriate for the vast majority of communities on the Northwest Coast, where leadership is local (usually appertaining to a large household and only occasionally a village), where "hereditary" rights are nearly always contested, and where emblems of rank are readily bought and sold. Even the Tlingit word for chief is *lingit tlein*, "big man" (Kan 1989: 83). But the likelihood of incipient stratification in some Northwest Coast societies is consistent with a multilinear approach to sociocultural evolution. Too often the possibilities for political complexity and stratification among hunter-gatherers have been neglected because of a deep-seated typological assumption that hunter-gatherers are inevitably egalitarian (Arnold 1996b).

The Big Man on the Northwest Coast embodies the suprafamilial economic interests of his following. He holds and defends title to their resource base, organizes cooperative labor for projects benefiting the group, generates and maintains large capital investments, stores food and wealth against hard times, maintains economic specialists and exchanges their products for shares of the production of nonspecialist households, exercises or delegates military responsibility, and manages intervillage and interregional ceremonies and exchanges that integrate the economy far beyond the family level.

The interregional group, Newman's "intergroup collectivity" (1957), is in fact an association of Big Men in which no single paramount leader dominates, although some are stronger than others by virtue of their resource base and their political, military, and managerial skills. Through public ceremonies they negotiate the continual exchange of power for prestige and prestige for power, which amounts to the exchange of wealth (blankets, coppers) for economic goods (food, technology, labor) and vice versa.

This elaborate and extensive political economy is made possible by an abundance of wild foods concentrated locally and seasonally. But it is also made necessary by high population densities (with a continuous high demand for food), unpredictable fluctuations in food supplies regionally and seasonally, and warfare and raiding for the control of desirable resources. The political system may be viewed as a mechanism for mobilizing a family-centered populace to increase its security against famine and war by producing foods and manufactures beyond their personal needs. Much of this surplus is directly invested in public works and social security by Big Men. The rest is spent in self-promoting displays that maintain their Big Man status in the face of continual competition.

Our use of the ethnographic present in this narrative (in an effort to be consistent with other cases) will seem odd to readers who recognize that it has been many generations since Northwest Coast societies operated in the fashion we describe. By the late eighteenth century, fur traders were engaged in extensive trade with Northwest Coast societies that had already enjoyed far-reaching aboriginal trade relations among themselves (Wolf 1982: 182–92). As expert traders, Big Men eagerly embraced the expanded possibilities for trade, motivated to accumulate and control ever greater wealth. This open embrace of market participation had several effects on the political economies of the Northwest Coast.

1. By enlarging the economic control of Big Men, it enhanced social inequality.

2. Market demand increased the value of surplus production, which in turn increased the value of labor and thereby made slave-raiding for workers more common than before.

3. Contact encouraged the formation of larger political groups (confederacies) that instituted ever more elaborate potlatches to determine group rank within the confederacy. A great elaboration of potlatches, including unprecedented quantities of valuables such as blankets and coppers, probably led anthropologists to overestimate the scale of these events prior to contact.

4. Catastrophic loss of population due to introduced diseases, accompanied by a steady encroachment on native lands by Euroamerican settlers, marginalized the Indoamerican natives and fundamentally altered their subsistence and political economies.

Case 10. The Central Enga of Highland New Guinea

The Central Enga of New Guinea's Highland Core are in many ways like the acephalous Tsembaga Maring described in Chapter 7, but there are certain dramatic differences between the two that help us understand the further development of the political economy. The process of intensification is particularly salient in this case and will be emphasized in our discussion. As we have seen with the Tsembaga, population growth leads to intensification, intensification to warfare, and warfare to the formation of clans and local groups. Among the Enga, whose population density is double that of the Tsembaga, intensification has resulted in permanent sweet potato gardening on prime land: there is no other reliable way for such a large population to get enough to eat. Warfare is accordingly oriented toward seizing prime land, its frequency has risen, and this increased frequency has sped the rise to prominence of Big Men. Local leaders orchestrate the exchange and alliance networks of the regional collectivity on which the local group's survival ultimately depends.

The Environment and the Economy

The Central Enga, including the Mae and Raiapu Enga, live in a mountainous region west of the Hagen range in Papua New Guinea, a region of high population density in contrast to the lower-density "fringe" area occupied by the Tsembaga. We have selected them for discussion because excellent data are available on the economy, ceremonialism, and sociopolitical organization of the Mae Enga (Meggitt 1964, 1965, 1972, 1974, 1977), on the subsistence economy of the closely

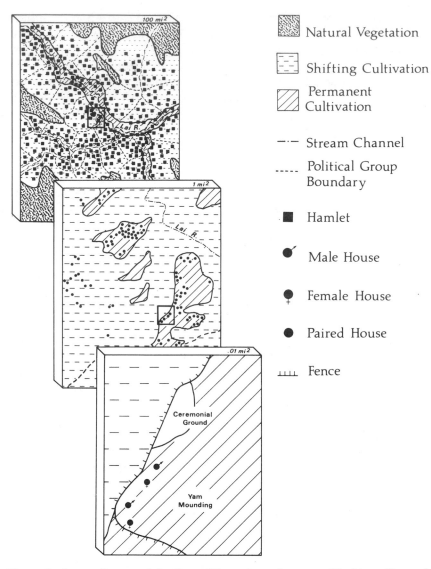

▨	Natural Vegetation
⊡	Shifting Cultivation
⧄	Permanent Cultivation
–·–	Stream Channel
····	Political Group Boundary
■	Hamlet
♂	Male House
♀	Female House
●	Paired House
⊥⊥⊥	Fence

Fig. 9. Settlement Pattern of the Central Enga. Apart from uncultivable gullies and ridges, the landscape is filled with gardens. Population is dense and hamlets are everywhere, but they cluster near sweet potato gardens and in defensible locations. Each local group has a ceremonial dance ground.

related Raiapu Enga (Waddell 1972), and on the regional *tee* exchange (Feil 1978, 1984).

The Central Enga, like other Highland groups, had been isolated from direct Western contact until quite recently (Meggitt 1965: 2). Their earliest recorded contact was in 1933. A patrol base was established in their territory in 1942, and in 1948 missionaries and miners arrived. The first ethnographer to study the Enga, Mervyn Meggitt, came in 1955, only twenty years after sustained contact had been initiated.

The Central Enga live in an area of highland rivers and open intermontane valleys. Their land ranges in elevation from about thirty-nine hundred feet in the grassland valleys to as high as seventy-nine hundred feet. Rainfall averages 108 inches a year, and there are 265 days with some rain. Summer (November to April) tends to be a little wetter and warmer than the annual average (50° to 80°F), winter (May to October) a little drier and cooler (40° to 70°F). Droughts occur in the winter, which can be a time of food shortage.

Plant communities and microclimates vary markedly from one elevation to another. Below forty-six hundred feet lie the dense rain forests of the lower valleys, virtually uninhabited because of malaria. The zone from forty-six hundred to seventy-five hundred feet was originally a midmountain and valley forest; now cleared for agriculture, it is a mosaic of gardens and fallow plots. Alluvial fans edge the valley floors and are farmed intensively; three-quarters of the population is concentrated there. Above, from seventy-five hundred to ninety-five hundred feet, is a zone of beech forests that shelter game and are important foraging areas for pigs. Still higher is a subalpine cloud zone of little economic use.

Much of this environmental diversity occurs within a remarkably compact region, the steep mountain slopes standing directly above the valley floor. As a result the lands of a Central Enga clan, although typically very small (encompassing from one to two square miles), cut vertically across all the zones and incorporate a part of each. The intense use of the environment, however, has greatly diminished the former diversity of plants and animals, and much of the region now consists of grasslands and permanent garden plots. A clan territory among the neighboring Raiapu Enga was only about 5 percent forested (Waddell 1972: 14).

According to Meggitt, the population density in the core area of the Central Enga ranges from 85 to 250 persons per square mile, near the maximum for Highland New Guinea groups. Figure 9 shows an environment crowded with settlement and heavily transformed with long use. Much higher than the densities of the simpler horticultural societies described in earlier chapters, this man/land ratio has obvious implications for the subsistence economy.

The economy of the Central Enga, described most fully for the Raiapu Enga (Waddell 1972), is dominated by an intensive form of agriculture involving mounded sweet potato production, some slash-and-burn farming, and considerable pig husbandry. Because the environment has been degraded by the intensive agricultural use, wild foods are limited and contribute insignificantly to the diet.

The dominant subsistence strategy is year-round sweet potato gardening. In a sample Raiapu community, 62.5 percent of the garden land was in permanent sweet potato production (Waddell 1972: table 8). The field is made up of mounds about nine feet in diameter, and the sweet potatoes are grown in the soft soil of the mound. Following the harvest the mound is pulled apart and earth pushed back around the mound; in the center is placed green manure, consisting of the old sweet potato vines, leaves, and other mulch. When this mulch has begun to decompose, the mound is rebuilt and is ready for replanting. With such artificial fertilization the mounded fields can be kept in constant production, and there is no fallow period, a significant intensification as compared with shifting agriculture (Waddell 1972: 44).

Most of the mounded fields are situated in the lower fans and valleys, where the slope is less than 10 percent (Waddell 1972: table 9). On the steeper slopes shifting swidden gardens produce a wide variety of crops including yams and bananas (Waddell 1972: tables 13 and 14). These gardens are similar to the shifting fields of the Tsembaga, which in some ways duplicate natural floristic conditions and use a long fallow cycle (of ten to fourteen years) to restore fertility. Swidden production is more important for dietary diversity than for calories, with the gardens constituting only about 20 percent of the total agricultural land (Waddell 1972: table 8).

Unlike the Tsembaga, the Central Enga do not cultivate trees for food. Some cultivated tree species, however, provide materials used in building and fencing and for other purposes (Waddell 1972: 40), materials obtained from uncultivated trees before the deforestation of the region. And Meggitt (1984) reports the intensive cultivation of the *Casuarina* tree to meet the tremendous need for firewood.

Pigs are everywhere in the Highlands and usually outnumber humans (Waddell 1972: 61–62). They forage for food in the hills, but like humans they depend mainly on cultivated food, especially sweet potatoes (Waddell 1972: 62). The adoption and intensification of sweet potato were closely tied to the intensification of pig production, which has primary political motivations (Feil 1984: 229).

As we have seen, the energetics of pig raising are astonishing and its cost to the farmer is high. Waddell (1972: table 28) estimates that 49 percent of all agricultural produce goes to the pigs—more than is eaten by the Enga themselves! Some 438 hours per person per year are devoted to raising food for pigs, which provide less than 2 percent of the total diet by weight: the net gain to the human is incredibly low, only about forty calories per hour, or about one-twentieth of the calorie production of a *single* sweet potato plant. Of course the protein and fat derived from meat, limited from other sources, are essential to the Enga; they must raise pigs. But the high cost of doing so dramatizes the loss that people incur when intensification makes it necessary to replace hunting with husbandry.

As elsewhere, intensification has also produced major changes in the diet itself: with the shift to permanently cultivated fields, the diet has shifted almost exclusively to agricultural products. Sweet potatoes make up as much as 90 percent of the food consumed by the Chimbu and other groups. As a result, Highland populations "experience a high incidence of protein-calorie deficiency among infants and a general deficiency in the protein intake" (Waddell 1972: 122) and are at risk from nutritional deficiency diseases. The Raiapu Enga (Waddell 1972: 124–25) alleviate this potential health problem by growing a variety of vegetable foods in their shifting gardens (including several introduced species, such as peanuts), and today by purchasing food, such as canned fish, that provides both protein and fat. At present the diet appears adequate, except perhaps for young children.

Warfare is the most immediate threat to the Enga, and an ever-present one: there was a war every two or three years in the relatively small region studied by Meggitt (1977). Each small local group's territory is surrounded by enemies or potential enemies, and war can break out at any time. Mortality is high, with an average of four deaths per conflict. Thus population losses are severe, and groups must maintain a high growth rate to remain politically viable.

Although a wide variety of proximate causes for warfare are given (from rape and theft to conflict over land), Meggitt (1977) argues convincingly that the underlying cause is competition for land. Wars are commonly between neighbors who are in direct competition; a local group will attack and defeat a weaker group and quickly annex its land. The Enga themselves recognize that wars are caused by competition for agricultural land, especially the limited amount of prime land used for the permanent, intensive cultivation of sweet potatoes. Over half of all Enga wars are explicitly acknowledged to be over land.

Trade in food and raw materials has been relatively minor for the

Enga, except for exchange in stone axes, salt, and—especially—pigs. Pigs are their main protein source and have become the primary political currency in local and regional relationships (Feil 1984). The emergence of the political economy is linked directly to the subsistence economy in the labor-intensive raising of pigs, and of the sweet potatoes needed to sustain them.

Social Organization

Settlement Pattern. The Central Enga have no villages (Meggitt 1965: 3; Waddell 1972: 30–39). Homestead farms, traditionally consisting of paired male and female houses, are spread through a clan's territory, although they tend to cluster on the alluvial benches most suited for sweet potato farming (Fig. 9). The houses are often located between the sweet potato fields and the upper slopes, with their swidden gardens and fallow growth grazed by the pigs; it is a location that minimizes movement costs, a major labor expenditure in gardening (Waddell 1972: 179). Traveling time to the sweet potato fields is usually less than seven minutes; to the swidden fields, it is twenty-four to thirty minutes.

Why did the Central Enga not form villages like those seen elsewhere in the Highlands, such as among the Chimbu (Brown 1972)? Presumably for cost reasons: to form a village is to increase the distance to agricultural fields and thus the costs of farming. The Tsembaga formed villages anyway, for defensive reasons, and that certainly makes sense for Highland groups such as the Chimbu, among whom warfare is endemic. Why not, then, for the Enga?

Although the answer is not immediately clear, several differences between the groups may be noted. The Enga's hamlets minimize production costs in transportation; the Chimbu's villages maximize protection against sudden attack. If the importance of defense is the same for both groups, the difference in settlement patterns probably corresponds to a difference in production costs. The Enga depend on mounded sweet potato gardens that utilize bench land spread out along river courses; the dispersed nature of their prime land may make village life prohibitively expensive for them. The Chimbu depend on drained field systems concentrated in the flat valley bottomlands; the concentrated nature of their prime land may make village life feasible for them. Also, the bench land of the Enga is heavily dissected by erosion so as to create ridges that are naturally defensible. We should emphasize, however, that the organized local group found in both the Enga and Chimbu regions is much more important than the presence or absence of villages. Villages are good indications, especially for archaeologists, of local group formation; but dispersed hamlets may also be organized politically into local groups where environmental conditions make hamlets economically preferable to villages. When people do not live in villages, the local group can be given an alternative physical form that materializes the group institutions. Among the Enga, group identity is focused on the ceremonial dance grounds.

Turning to social organization proper, we consider four levels of organization: the household, the clan segment, the clan with its Big Man, and the intergroup collectivity. As in our previous case, organization at the two lower levels responds to subsistence problems and centers on food procurement activities and the division of labor; organization at the higher levels responds to problems in the political economy and centers on defense and economic interdependence.

The Household. The primary social and economic unit is normally the family (Waddell 1972: 20), typically the elemental family with an average of 4.5 members: a woman, her husband, and their children—and of course their pigs.

The Central Enga perform most subsistence activities individually; work groups rarely exceed two or three persons (Waddell 1972: 103). Gardening, especially in the sweet potato fields, is highly individual and does not require or encourage large work groups. Women perform the routine subsistence tasks of farming, especially in the sweet potato gardens, cooking, and child care. The gardens and homes are considered their domain (Meggitt 1965: 246). They provide 92 percent of the work in the sweet potato fields and 80 percent of the work in the swidden gardens, excluding the important "male" crop of yams (Waddell 1972: 98). Men's work is more irregular and includes the periodic clearing and farming of swidden gardens, care of the yams, housebuilding, and numerous public activities (Waddell 1972: table 25).

For the neighboring Mount Hagen groups, A. M. Strathern (1972) argues that a woman's role is in (re)production, a man's in exchange. Similarly among the Enga, women are the primary farmers, cultivating the fields and harvesting sweet potato; they must also manage the household's work to provide food and other care for both children and pigs. Older children, in turn, watch the family's pigs and younger children. Men's most important activities involve ceremonial-based intergroup exchange and territorial defense. Enga men and women collaborate in both household and political affairs (Feil 1984). Men act in the public display and giving of wealth, but the pigs, the primary source of wealth, can be produced only by women. The Big Man and his wives are thus partners in all political maneuverings.

Land is owned directly by the household. At marriage a man receives land from his family estate and establishes an independent household. This land, typically including both sweet potato fields and swidden lands, is then managed by the husband and wife working together. Although transfer of ownership of the land is restricted and requires the consent of concerned patrilineal kin, the household otherwise retains control of its land.

The amount of land farmed by a household is a direct reflection of its size: the larger the number of consumers in the household, the greater the land area under cultivation (Meggitt 1974: n. 43). In short, the extent of agricultural activity is determined largely by the subsistence needs of the household.

Despite the intensity of the subsistence economy, the traditional technology is simple and personal, relying heavily on the woman's digging stick and net carrying bag and the man's stone ax. Each family has its own tools, which it either makes or obtains by trade.

This sketch of the household and its subsistence economy fits closely Sahlins's model (1972) of the Domestic Mode of Production. The household is the primary unit of production and consumption; it has direct control over the main factors of production—labor, land, and technology—and gears production to meet its own needs.

Despite the economic interdependence of the sexes, men fear women and express a deep antipathy toward them as threats to maleness and health (Meggitt 1964). Men and women inhabit separate lives. The women's residence, the basic household center, houses the woman, her children, and her pigs. The men's house among the Mae is ideally the residence of the males from one patrilineage (Meggitt 1965: 20, 22), but among the Raiapu the man's house is individual and paired with his wife's (Waddell 1972: 34). Among the Mae, therefore, household clusters appear to consist of a number of women's houses around a men's house; in contrast, the Raiapu show a pattern of isolated farmsteads with separate men's and women's residences.

As we discuss below, in eastern New Guinea the division between men and women can be even more extreme (Feil 1987). Men often form close-knit coresidential groups defined by initiation rites including ritual homosexuality. These male groups are important in battle, and their distribution correlates with the frequency of unregulated warfare (Langness 1977). Among the Enga, however, the opposition between the sexes is bridged by the partnership essential for the outward-looking political maneuvering that we describe shortly and that helps regulate warfare.

Each wife's household is a separate domestic economy. Because women do most production work, a man who seeks to increase his agricultural production so as to finance his political ambitions can do so by marrying many wives. As we shall see, however, access to wives depends on the accumulation of considerable wealth through affinal exchanges, and on access to productive land.

The Clan Segment. Households are organized into patrilineal groupings that are segments of the territorially based clans. Although Meggitt's structural analysis (1965) is perhaps too rigid, we describe the operation of what he sees as two levels of group formation below the clan, namely the patrilineage and the subclan.

Patrilineages are "people of one blood" named for a founder from whom descent is traced (Meggitt 1965: 16). The founder is usually said to have been the "father's father's father of older living men" (ibid.: 16–17), and actual kin relationships among lineage members are known. Meggitt refers to the patrilineage as "a quasi-domestic grouping" (ibid.: 17) whose existence is not readily apparent to an outsider. For the Mae Enga the men's house is typically composed of the members of a patrilineage (ibid.: 20, 22), but this men's house has no ceremonial importance (cf. ibid.: 235).

The patrilineage is a group of households with closely related male heads that help each other in specific economic and social situations. The few activities requiring labor outside the household typically involve men from a local group for such things as clearing swidden gardens, building fences, and building houses (see Waddell 1972: 106). A person's patrilineage "brothers" are responsible for helping him when he needs help (Meggitt 1965: 244); should he be disabled, for example, they will prepare his gardens and rebuild his house for him. "Brothers" are also a man's most reliable source of support in arranging marriage exchanges and the like.

Patrilineages range in size from four to sixty-eight members, with a mean size of thirty-three (Meggitt 1965: 5–18). In our terms this is a hamlet-size group of much the same sort as other hamlet groups we have discussed: essentially an extension of close kin bonds to achieve subsistence and security goals that are important to the smaller and more vulnerable nuclear family but beyond its reach.

The subclan, by contrast, is a larger unit, organized along political and ceremonial lines, whose members are putatively descendants of a son of the clan founder. A subclan owns a dance ground and a sacred grove of trees, and it plays a major role in external exchanges and in political matters. The Mae Enga social system imposes heavy payments, such as bridewealth payments and death payments, on individuals upon ceremonial occasions (see Meggitt 1965: 110–27). These obligatory payments require contributions from a supporting group, the subclan. Similarly, as we shall see, the primary support of a man's climb to Big Man status comes from his subclan.

Although the individual is the focus of bridewealth payments and other social exchanges, such exchanges, with their accompanying public display, also reflect back on the subclan group as a whole. As with the Tsembaga, a man needs a broad regional network of interpersonal ties to provide him with wives, nonlocal trade goods, security in case of local disaster, and political support in competitive exchanges. A man's subclan plays an essential role in helping him establish his regional network. In return, the successes of any subclan member in regional networking increase the status of the subclan and its members' desirability as partners for persons in other groups. Because individual status translates directly into group status, the support given by subclan members is clearly part of a more general strategy for building up their own personal networks.

Competition among subclans occurs over dominance in the political affairs of the clan. The subclan is also the point of cleavage for the formation of new clans by segmentation. Subclans among the Mae Enga range in size from 45 to 145 members, with a mean of 90 (Meggitt 1965: table 7), about the size of the Tsembaga clan grouping.

The Clan and Its Big Man. The clan is politically the most important group among the Central Enga. Defined by its carefully demarcated territory (Fig. 9), the clan is a defensive group, protecting the claims of its members against outsiders. The clan is also politically autonomous, being the largest group to act as a group in both warfare and ceremony. It is led by a Big Man, who speaks for it in external affairs and works internally to mobilize it for ceremonial and political action.

The clan is first and foremost a corporate entity, restricting access to land. It is putatively patrilineal, with rights to land in clan territory reflecting a reckoning of male descent lines thought to derive from a common founding ancestor. Where good land is in short supply the rules for allocating such land place a premium on lineal descent. Individuals who are not patrilineal kin can become attached to a clan and gain access to land, but only where the clan has ample land and needs more settlers for security reasons. The clan is supposed to be, and largely is, exogamous, with wives coming from other localized clan groups as part of a regional system of exchange and alliance. Meggitt (1965: 9) estimates average clan size for the Mae Enga as 350 persons (ranging from 100 to 1,000), roughly the size of the Tsembaga territorial group.

As a group the Enga clan owns a main dance ground and plot with an ancestral-cult house (Meggitt 1965: 227). The dance ground, thought to have been cleared by the founding ancestors, is the focus for ceremonial exchanges with other territorial clans involving death and homicide payments and the dramatic competitive exchanges of the *tee* ceremonial cycle. Like the village elsewhere, the landscape of ceremonial constructions of the Enga is the physical form, or structure, of the local group.

Apart from ownership of the ceremonial ground and joint defensive action, the clan asserts itself as a discrete group in certain ceremonies, in the clan meeting, and in the action of its leader, the dominant clan Big Man. In a number of ceremonies, notably the *sadaru*, group identification is made explicit. The *sadaru* is the ritual exclusion of bachelors, in which males are instructed in defense against female pollution (Meggitt 1964; Waddell 1972: 87). This occasion involves "four nights of seclusion and instruction in a special house erected in a remote part of the territory. . . . At the 'emergence festival' when the bachelors return fully adorned and chanting from their mountain retreat, members of the host clan distribute food to the large number of visitors present" (Waddell 1972: 87).

The bachelors are a cohort of male patrilineal kin, united as a group in this seclusion, who become the next generation of household heads and political actors. They are presented publicly at the main dance ground by their clan to visitors from neighboring clans who are to be their affines, trade partners, allies, and of course potential enemies. The fineness of this display of the clan's future prospects is important to the process of clan members' economic and political maneuvering in the region.

Although the right of the household to independence is valued, as expressed in the statement "Each man makes his own decisions" (Sackschewsky 1970: 52), there are times when the group must act together, as in warfare and *tee* exchanges, and in these matters the clan meeting is crucial. All active males of the group affected, a clan or subclan segment, meet to discuss the issue and come to a consensus. Nonkin have very limited rights in such a meeting; women and children are excluded. The consensus reached by the meeting applies to all those who participated in it.

Leadership, a key ingredient in group action, is seen clearly in the clan meeting and related ceremonial and political events. The Big Man, though his status is highest, need not be the one to call the meeting, nor is his word considered binding to the group. Rather the Big Man is a man of renown—known for success in political and economic affairs and listened to because of his demonstrated ability to influence individual action, his control over wealth and exchange, and his public speaking ability. Feil (1984: 3) emphasizes that Enga Big Man status de-rives especially from minimally institutionalized *tee* exchanges, based on individualistic alliances of friendships and the exchange of pigs.

The Big Man is both an individual entrepreneur and a group spokes-man. In the first role he uses the resources available to him through the manipulation of his extensive interpersonal network based on mar-riage, alliance, and exchange. By aggressive and calculated action he comes to control a high percentage of the exchange and production of valuables, notably pigs, which are important in all social exchanges. In the second role, as spokesman for the group, he exhorts its component units to work together for the group's survival and the general good of all its members.

The selection of the clan Big Man demonstrates this dual nature (Meggitt 1967). As we have seen, each clan is composed of a number of subclans. One emerges as Big Man from among the men of a subclan on the basis of personal qualities of leadership and calculation, and with support from patrilineage brothers, to deal with matters requiring sub-clan action, such as the collection of marriage exchange payments and the initiation of ceremonies. Subclan leaders then compete with each other for leadership of the clan and the status of primary Big Man. In part a man's ability to achieve and hold this status depends on the size of his immediate support group—that is, his close relatives. But he must also broaden his support to receive assistance from other subclans and ultimately from other clan members. He does this by such means as offering to help raise marriage payments for a member of another sub-clan, thereby placing that person and his patrilineal relatives in debt to him. Another would-be clan leader may make the same offer, or a more generous one. That is the way the two compete for supporters.

A push-pull energizes the activity of group leaders. Subclans and clans must have an effective leader to serve their interests in interclan relationships involving marriage, exchange, and defensive alliance. A group thus pushes a potential candidate forward. In turn the attrac-tiveness of real control over wealth, power, and women (for it is the Big Man who is polygynous) motivates the leader to act in such a way as to maximize his personal power and reproductive success.

The clan as a unit exists chiefly to cope with the external relation-ships of warfare, defense, alliance, and exchange. To understand the clan and its leader is thus to understand their place in the regional sys-tem of competition and cooperation. We will therefore first briefly sketch the nature of regional interaction before returning to the place of the clan, the ceremonies of integration and interrelationship, and the emergence of the Big Man.

The Intergroup Collectivity. Frequent and vicious warfare characterizes interclan relationships. All people outside the clan are potential
enemies, and all land outside the clan's small territory is potentially
hostile. Perhaps half a mile beyond a person's home lies an alien world
fraught with the risks of sudden death. According to Meggitt (1977: 44),
"In the past all movement outside one's own clan territory was hazard-
ous, and in general men made such excursions only in armed groups
and for compelling reasons, in particular to attend distributions of
wealth, to negotiate exchange transactions, to trade, and to assist
friends and relatives in battle. Casual social visiting by lone men was
not common, not only because it exposed the wayfarer to the dangers of
ambush and murder en route, but also because it violated Mae notions
of personal privacy and group security."

The threat or promise of warfare is central to all clan decisions. A
large clan, with power in numbers and a shortage of land, looks for an
excuse to attack a weaker neighboring clan and seize its land. A small
clan, weak in numbers and vulnerable to attack, must encourage settlement by nonpatrilineal relatives to swell its defense force. Since the
losers in war lose everything, a household's control of essential resources depends on its clan's political power and success.

A group's ability to defend its territory or seize new territory depends primarily on how large a fighting force it can field. This depends
both on its own size and on how many allies it can recruit for a confrontation. Clan size is determined in part by demographic factors; the
individual fertility of members can have a dramatic effect, with some
clans growing rapidly while others are declining. As we have seen, one
strategy available to a small or declining clan with land to spare is to accept nonpatrilineal kin as members (cf. Meggitt 1965). By contrast, strict
patrilineal kin rules, whereby a man receives land only from his father's
clan, are maintained if the group is large and its density high. This correlation between the percentage of patrilineal kin and population density supports the more general proposition that lineality increases with
subsistence intensification.

Successful clans tend to become larger, in part because a clan's success in regional exchange and warfare increases its members' ability to
obtain wives and thus the clan's reproductive potential. As a clan's
numbers swell, overuse of local resources begins to degrade the ability
to produce the all-important pigs. Success quite literally breeds both
success and failure, producing relatively rapid upswings and down-
swings in a clan's fortunes.

It was once widely assumed that warfare acts as a negative feedback mechanism to regulate demographic growth. Thus as population

grows resource shortages occur and warfare over resources increases, producing a rising mortality that keeps the population down. This appears not to happen among the Central Enga (see Meggitt 1977: 112), where people try to have as many children as possible so as to provide males as warriors and females for the regional exchanges that are critical to alliances. In effect, an increase in warfare has intensified the pressure to expand population.

Another important factor in arranging alliances is a clan's reputation as a reliable and beneficial confederate. Success in obtaining allies is tied to success in a set of related ceremonies of exchange involving marriage, death compensation, life-cycle displays, and the regional *tee* exchange cycle. In each ceremonial setting the reputation of the individual and the group is displayed publicly by group size, personal adornment, and the exchange of primitive valuables. This is seen most clearly in the *tee*.

The *tee* is a cycle of competitive exchanges that link up many Central Enga clans (Feil 1978, 1984; Meggitt 1972, 1974). Its main participants are a number of clans linked as an exchange line but with a number of alternative paths (Meggitt 1974: diagrams 2 and 3). Other clans peripheral to this main line are joined to it through personal exchange relationships with clan members of the main-line clans.

Starting at one end of the chain, initiatory gifts of small pigs, marsupials, pork, salt, axes, and other valuables are given as individual exchanges from one partner to the next down the chain of clans. After this pattern of giving has continued for a time, individuals from the clan at the initiating end begin to demand repayment in pigs. As this signal passes through the system, individuals start to amass pigs to be given away alive at a series of massive ceremonial occasions accompanied by display and oratory. This series of ceremonies, which involves major interclan presentations, begins at the opposite end of the chain and proceeds in a wavelike action to the beginning, taking six to nine months to complete. The clans that begin the main gifting ceremonies then start to demand repayment, and those at the opposite end start slaughtering perhaps half the pigs that they had amassed and giving the pork in an elaborate interclan ceremony to the next clan in line. All gifts from members of one clan to the next clan in the chain are thus displayed and given together to maximize the visual effect of scale and to identify the coordinated group action. These clan-level ceremonial presentations are coordinated by the clan Big Men.

The Big Men also orchestrate the interclan negotiations to end hostilities between local groups and to make homicide payments. When it becomes clear that fighting has gone on too long with mounting casualties and no clear outcome, the Big Men must call for a large meeting of the opposing groups to exchange quantities of pork, to settle claims for homicides, and thus to reestablish peace (Meggitt 1977: 20). Most important in this peace process is the payment of homicide compensation. Each death in battle must be paid for by the enemy who killed the man and by the ally who encouraged him to fight. To end a war, responsibilities for each casualty must be assigned and the compensation payment made. For any individual, obviously, payment received for the death of a kinsman should be large but the payment given for a killing should be small. With such opposed interests between warring factions, ending a fight is not easy. But the Big Man can arrange satisfactory payments by arguing that they must be generous to reflect well on the group's prestige. At these meetings the rhetoric of the Big Men is militant as they vilify their opponents, but their action is clearly to appease and mediate and thus to reestablish the status quo of the regional collectivity.

The Big Man's role in these ceremonies is to coordinate the clan's presentation of gifts and payments, making those gifts and payments, and the occasion itself, as impressive as possible. Thus he puts on a show that reflects well, first on the Big Man as leader and organizer, second on his clan as a powerful group, and third on individual clan members who seek to maintain and expand their networks of in-law exchanges and trade partnerships.

The survival of the group depends directly on its profile in these competitive exchanges. Who will become an ally to an unsuccessful clan, a partner to an ineffective Big Man, or an in-law to a nonparticipant? Prestige gained in the *tee* translates directly into successfully obtaining allies, trade partners, and wives. Success in the *tee* thus brings about success in other social and political realms and ultimately affects the survival of the group and its participating households. In fact, the *tee* and warfare are opposing principles (Feil 1984: 5). The development of the regional *tee* exchange, although motivated by a need for allies in war, creates a network of friendships that regulates regional connections. The *tee* becomes the embodiment for the regional collectivity that coordinates interpolity relationships and lessens the daily threat of war.

The Enga clan sits in a hostile social environment among armed neighbors who are eager to seize its land. Its productive and reproductive success depends on its defensive posture as a group and its recruitment of allies. These in turn depend on its success in the organized intergroup relations orchestrated by the clan Big Man and presented in the dramatic intergroup ceremony.

In the group ceremony and the economic and political maneuverings of the Big Men we discover a well-developed political economy. Goods are mobilized from the constituent households to support a set of actions that are basic both to the rise to power of an individual Big Man and to the long-term political survival of the local group.

In the life history of 'Elota, a Solomon Islands Big Man, Keesing (1983) observes that interclan regional relationships in the Solomons did not result in constant wars; as long as a clan was considered powerful, it could live at peace most of the time. Although an offense against the clan must be met with anger and a show of aggression, it was usually thought prudent to accept compensation in wealth rather than take violent action. A measure of balance in political power, carefully maintained and portrayed in ceremony by the region's Big Men, was the basis for peace.

In his comparative study of the evolution of New Guinea societies, Feil (1987) describes contrasting institutional formations. In the western New Guinea Highlands, population densities have risen to very high levels with a long history of intensive agriculture, and the threat of conflict has encouraged the creation of systems of ceremonies and exchange that establish interpolity relationships and provide mechanisms for political negotiations among local groups. Although local groups are always potential enemies, they can diffuse much conflict through negotiation, exchange, and ceremony. Warfare is thus restricted by the regional collectivity of Big Men (see Langness 1977).

In contrast, in the eastern New Guinea Highlands, the more recent intensification of agriculture and expansion of population only followed the recent introduction of sweet potato, which led to growth in population that caused high levels of warfare. But the conflict is as yet unregulated by competitive and compensatory systems of feasting and exchange. Here the local group is relatively disconnected from other local groups. Because women are not economical partners in the political process of raising and exchanging pigs, the local group's composition emphasizes the close-knit, inward-looking cadres of related males who defend themselves and their land; relationships between groups (involving marriage) are not held to be significant. Without the regional collectivity based on ceremonial feasting and exchange, warfare is unregulated and local leadership is more ephemeral.

The reason for strong leaders among the Enga seems straightforward: the local group could not function well without them. It seems odd at first, especially considering the very high population density and the intensely competitive attitude of Big Men, that a single regional Big Man has not emerged from the competition and transformed the society into a chiefdom. The fact is, however, that a chief cannot govern effectively without economic control, and the conditions for economic control are absent in the Highlands: storage is unnecessary, technology is simple, and technology and trade are broadly based rather than concentrated. In contrast to the chiefdoms to be examined in Chapters 10 and 11, an Enga chiefdom would have no way to exert control over the basic factors of production. True, the emerging political economy of the *tee* rests on pig production, but the labor-intensive and dispersed nature of pig husbandry neither invites leadership nor permits regional control over production by emergent leaders. The *tee* ceremony, where Big Men jockey to influence exchange, is a realm of pure competition, impossible for a single entity to control.

Case 11. The Kirghiz of Northeastern Afghanistan

Within a single generation the Kirghiz of northeastern Afghanistan were transformed from a predominantly family-level herding society into a society with strong local leaders. The conditions that brought about this swift and dramatic evolution are clearly identifiable and shed considerable light on the other Big Man systems described in this chapter.

The Environment and the Economy

The Kirghiz (Shahrani 1979) are nomadic pastoralists of the Pamir zone of Afghanistan, near the borders of China and the Soviet Union. They inhabit broad, flat intermontane valleys at altitudes of over twelve thousand feet, above the limits of agriculture. Average annual precipitation is below six inches, and there are fewer than thirty frost-free days each year. Vegetation is sparse, and the environment is made especially inhospitable by the persistent harsh winds.

Historically, the Pamir lay on the Silk Road, the trade route connecting China with the Middle East. It is not devoid of resources. When Marco Polo passed through on his way to China, he was impressed by the abundance of large wild sheep (prized by modern sport hunters as "Marco Polo sheep"), and there are mountain goats, Tibetan wolves, brown bears, marmots, hares, and turkeys. Mountain streams feed marshes and lakes where pasture is seasonally abundant. Peat bogs provide fuel for cooking and heating.

Formerly the Pamir was a favorite summer pasture of the Kirghiz. In July and August the days are hot, and pasture grows lushly in alpine meadows on the valley floor. But over the long winter the pasture dries out; the meadows are covered by snow, and the winds are bitterly cold. In past winters the Kirghiz retreated with their herds to lower pastures in China and Russia. But the Soviet Union closed its borders in 1938 and China followed suit in 1949, leaving the few thousand Kirghiz nomads in Afghanistan the only ones outside Soviet and Chinese control (Paksoy 1984: 56–57; Shahrani 1984: 31). This political change forced them to intensify their use of the Pamir in order to live there year-round.

The Kirghiz of the Pamir now number approximately eighteen hundred persons living at a population density of roughly one per square mile. This group pastures a mixed herd of some forty thousand sheep and goats (in which sheep outnumber goats by three to one), four thousand yaks, and small numbers of camels and horses. As among the Turkana (Chapter 7), herds of different composition have different requirements and can make use of contrasting microenvironments. Sheep and goats are always herded together because they complement each other's feeding habits; since sheep graze and goats browse, they do not compete directly for food. In the winter sheep have the advantage of being able to paw away snow to reach the frozen undergrowth, and goats stay close to them to find food. In the summer, when sheep by themselves would tend to graze too long in one spot and so destroy pasture, goats move on quickly, the sheep follow them, and overgrazing is minimized. The Kirghiz recognize this complementarity and deliberately maintain mixed herds.

Yaks are native to the area, well adapted to the cold and the high altitude, and able to exploit pasture that the other species cannot. The Kirghiz herd only about four thousand yaks, but because of their large size and rich milk they make a major contribution to the diet.

Like the Turkana, the Kirghiz are careful to use short-lived pastures first, leaving the more permanent pastures as security for the scarcest times. In the winter, whenever a bit of pasture is exposed by the wind, herders move quickly to exploit it before it is covered by new snow. The south side of the valley is in shade much of the time; the north side is sunny. Since the prevailing winds blow from north to south, during the long winter the south side is in shadow and piled high with drifted snow. At this time the Kirghiz are scattered in small family groups throughout the north side of the valley. The best pastures are found there and on the valley floor near water, but both are used as sparingly as possible in the winter. Only in the spring, when sheep and goats give birth, do the Kirghiz move their herds into the richest pastures in order to strengthen their animals for birthing.

In the summer, families move to the south side to make intensive use of the short time in which those pastures are available. This is a time of abundance. There is little competition over pasture, and settlements are larger. Then as fall approaches they move onto the valley floor for a month or so, slowly making their way north to the winter encampments.

Since the closing of the borders, the Kirghiz have begun to intensify their use of pastures. They allow the richest, best-watered pastures to grow all summer, and then harvest and store fodder for winter. Led by their khan, they have begun also to irrigate pasture land and to fertilize with dung.

The Kirghiz produce much of their own food. Meat and dairy products are important in the diet, particularly in the four or five warmest months. Milk is processed into yogurt and "sour milk," which, when salted, can be frozen and stored for winter. Cheese is made and dried for storage, and butter can be clarified and stored for several years in bags made from goat or sheep stomachs. Meat is eaten frequently, especially on multicamp ceremonial occasions. Wild foods are of little importance except among the poorest families, and vegetables are rarely eaten. Trade in foodstuffs, however, is essential to the household economy, as we shall see.

Although one might expect the animal herds to be a strong temptation to raiders, raiding does not appear to exist. Why? Apparently there are two reasons. On the one hand, the khan is powerful enough locally to resolve disputes among the Kirghiz themselves. On the other hand, the existence of powerful states capable of regulating borders and punishing outlaws prevents external peoples from attacking Kirghiz herds. In fact, prior to the border closings, the Kirghiz had been among many tribal groups that ran raids against Russian invaders: characteristically, the Russians called them *basmaci* (bandits), whereas they called themselves *mucahit* (holy warriors, *mujahideen*; Paksoy 1984: 57).

At the time the borders were closed, the demand for animal products in the agricultural areas of Afghanistan had grown markedly. Afghanistan's population growth seems to have required considerable expansion in agriculture at the expense of open lands that once pastured wild or domesticated animals. Each year the Kirghiz export about five thousand sheep and goats, two hundred yaks, seven thousand kilograms of clarified butter, and many hides, ropes, felt blankets, and the like, acquiring in return agricultural produce, tea (which they consume in prodigious quantities), metal and wood products (including yurt frames), opium, and many other outside goods. Their dietary staples are now mainly wheat and other grains obtained through trade.

To summarize, the intensification of pastoralism has resulted in a number of significant shifts in the Kirghiz economy. These include incurring the considerable risks of raising stock year-round in a marginal environment, using new methods of intensification such as irrigation and fertilization, and exchanging animal products for agricultural produce and other goods available from a settled agricultural population. As with the Nganasan (Case 4), the development of this exchange on a systematic basis has made the Kirghiz into specialist producers in a broader market economy.

Social Organization

The basic social unit of production is the household. An average Kirghiz household consists of 5.5 persons, 120 sheep and goats, 12 yaks, 1 horse, and 1 or more dogs. A single herdsman can manage a herd of several hundred animals by himself, and a herd of over 100 sheep and goats is sufficient to meet basic subsistence needs. The household usually inhabits a yurt constructed from wood and straw and wrapped in large felt covers. Recently, however, families have begun to build winter homes of stone and earth, constructed on land claimed as property by the household or kin group.

Eighty percent of Kirghiz households are nuclear, some with unmarried or elderly members attached; the rest are either extended families or polygynous. The household is an integrated unit sharing a single hearth, and is largely independent. A senior man acts as its spokesman, but all adult members, male and female, have a voice in economic decisions. Typically two or more households form a group known as an *aiel* (camp) or a *gorow* (corral, indicating a common shelter for their herds). These camps grow larger in summer and smaller in winter. They usually consist of patrilineally related households, but in any case they are fairly stable units that claim territory and share responsibilities for hospitality. The camp has a leader, a wealthy and respected man who mediates disputes within the group and represents it in intergroup ceremonies and conflicts.

Men and women share responsibility for major decisions within their domestic group: "Women in Kirghiz society are quite assertive in all matters of importance to the domestic unit, though their role varies a great deal from household to household. Among the poorer households, male-female equality is in evidence in domestic affairs but in richer . . . units males tend to dominate" (Shahrani 1979: 141). Kirghiz marriages are overwhelmingly monogamous, with only a few rich herders (7.5 percent) able to support two wives. Men do all the heavy labor (transporting goods for trade, digging irrigation ditches), and with their sons do most of the work associated with herding, including construction, leatherworking, and collecting dung for fires.

Women spend most of their time inside or near the yurt, milking animals and preparing milk products, spinning, weaving, and carrying water. "Scores of other tasks—feltmaking, ropemaking, dismantling the yurt, packing and setting it up again, and milking require the participation of all members of the household. Looking after lambs, kids and calves are chores usually assigned to young boys and girls, when they are available" (ibid.: 141). Beyond the camp, patrilineages and neighborhoods form loose cooperative and ceremonial units. Patrilineal relations are important in marriage, particularly among the wealthy, who see endogamy as a way of keeping wealth within the larger kin group. Since the closing of the borders, kin relations have taken on added significance as groups of kinsmen lay claim to territories and regulate their use, becoming as a result corporate kin groups.

The border closings have greatly increased the stratification and political centralization of the Kirghiz. Formerly they moved freely through the Pamir largely as independent family camps, although leaders existed for specific functions in ceremonial exchange and dispute resolution. But after 1950 camps and kin clusters laid claim to strips of land transecting the valley to ensure their access to all the microenvironments they need for year-round subsistence. And with the construction of permanent houses, corrals, and irrigation works, the ownership of carefully defined plots of land has become common.

In terms of theory, a key change has been the dramatic rise in the unequal distribution of wealth and property. Formerly, such wealth differences as existed were primarily a matter of age: young couples with small herds would join the camps of wealthy relatives for whom they could work while building their own herds. In time, they could expect to accumulate their own property and take their place in an egalitarian world of household herders. But as a result of the rapid transformation into a chiefdomlike political system, the predictable has occurred: increasingly, the economic means of existence—animals and pasture—are owned by an elite group of wealthy households.

Hence, two-thirds of all households now own few or no animals, and a mere 5 percent own 80 percent of all sheep and goats. A few men with exceptional skills in managing both animals and people have gained control of the herds. Their tents are surrounded by those of dependent households who obtain access to animals through the patronage of the wealthy men If their own animals fail to survive a harsh winter, a not infrequent occurrence, the wealthy man provides them with food and new animals.

This control of herds by an elite is a response to the intensification of production in the Pamir. When households could leave the zone during winter, they did not experience such a great risk of losing their animals. The wealthy man now functions as a risk-avoider who scatters animals throughout the Pamir. When disaster strikes in one place, he moves in resources from another, becoming a main source of security for his dependents. He also identifies poor herders and corrects their mistakes, or else withdraws his support.

A further element in the centralization of power by leaders has been their role in external trade, from which they derive significant wealth. Wealthy leaders of camps and lineages engage in this trade for much of the winter, when they travel to agricultural areas for barter. The khan, the acknowledged spokesman for the whole Kirghiz group in the Pamir, actively develops trade relations with outside markets that provide pastoral products to the Afghan urban population. He operates with his people's wholehearted support because the non-Kirghiz itinerant traders are accused of cheating the Kirghiz and exploiting them by encouraging the use of opium.

Modern Change

Earlier this century, the closing of the borders with China and the Soviet Union led to a local intensification of production, whose consequences may be summarized as a series of interlinked changes:

1. More careful management of existing pasture, storing for winter use the rich pastures formerly enjoyed in summer.

2. Capital investment in technology, such as irrigation works and more secure buildings to shelter humans, animals, and fodder.

3. Efforts to define property relations over campsites and pastures, leading to more disputes and the involvement of elites in resolving disputes.

4. Increasing stratification as herd control and management has become centered in the hands of a small elite who, like Big Men, act as risk-spreaders, skilled managers, and patrons to dependent households.

5. The growing importance of trade to the household economy, placing emphasis on elite households that act as brokers between poorer households and the competitive and uncertain world of the market.

Since Shahrani's study in the 1970's, modern change among the Kirghiz has taken still more dramatic turns. In the 1970's, Russian "hunters" began appearing in the Pamir, armed, unlike the usual sports hunters, with AK-47 assault rifles. They represented Soviet efforts to secure an area fraught with tensions between the Soviet Union and China, Afghanistan, and Pakistan. After the 1978 Soviet-inspired military coup in Afghanistan, a Kirghiz leader, Haji Rahman Gul, united the remaining free Kirghiz and in 1981 led them on a dramatic long march through roadless terrain into Pakistan (Shahrani 1984: 32). By 1985 the only inhabitants of their former home were Soviet and Afghan soldiers (Nyrop and Seekins 1986). But the hot lowlands of Pakistan were entirely unsuited to the Kirghiz cultural adaptation, and over the next four years their herds were depleted and more than one hundred Kirghiz had died.

Longing for the old life in the Pamir, but denied all hope of return by the Soviet invasion of Afghanistan in 1979, Haji Rahman Gul began to search for another homeland, seriously considering Alaska until refused by U.S. authorities. In 1981, however, he approached the Turkish embassy, where the Kirghiz's Turkic heritage found a sympathetic response; the Kirghiz, loyal to their now-primary leader (Paksoy 1984), were relocated to a village in eastern Turkey. Indeed, similarities in climate and culture in this distant village made the Kirghiz feel comparatively at home and they courageously began their herding existence once again.

For this small group of Kirghiz nomads, the political and economic uncertainties may appear to be over, at least for the moment. The same cannot be said of the estimated 2 to 3 million nomadic pastoralists and the millions of others who are suffering from the tragic war in Afghanistan. The Kirghiz odyssey is indeed a sad commentary on the plight of millions of nomadic pastoralists who, for the sake of their cultural integrity, managed to adapt for centuries to extremely unfriendly natural environments, only to be destroyed by the revolutions of this century which, ironically, promised or promise to liberate humanity. (Shahrani 1984: 34)

Conclusions

In Chapters 6 and 7 we examined village-level groups in which group leaderships as such played no significant part. For the groups in this chapter, leaderlessness is no longer an option; strong leadership is required to integrate the village-size community into a regional economy, especially in the "intergroup collectivities" of the Enga and the Northwest Coast fishermen. (The Kirghiz differ because they are surrounded, not by numerous communities of roughly equal size and power, but by extremely powerful national economies that force the Kirghiz khan to be more a broker between his people and the superordinate political economy than a Big Man in the classic sense.) In order to understand the causes for this growth beyond the comparatively acephalous village-level economy, let us examine the three dimensions of intensification, integration, and stratification.

The intensification of production is a powerful agent of change among the Northwest Coast fishermen, the Enga, and the Kirghiz, although its specific form varies from case to case. On the Northwest Coast intensification has made it possible to harvest the often stupendous seasonal or unpredictable supplies of candlefish and salmon, to store these foods against periods when food is scarce, and to distribute local surpluses to areas that are temporarily experiencing shortages. This achievement, which depends upon such capital investments as traps, weirs, drying racks, storehouses, and watertight boxes, reduces the amount of wild food that escapes capture and thus allows the total population density to increase to remarkable levels for a hunter-gatherer people.

With the Mae Enga intensification has meant a shift toward total domestication of the environment. The forests have been cut and wherever possible turned into permanent fields. Production has come to focus on a single highly efficient crop, sweet potatoes. The most dramatic rise in production costs is seen in pig husbandry, where half the sweet potatoes go to compensate for the loss of wild game that elsewhere lives off the land and to support the emergent political economy of the regional collectivity.

The Kirghiz, a pastoral people used to following an extensive migration route through seasonally rich pastures, were suddenly forced to occupy a single comparatively poor area along that route. They have responded by fertilizing, irrigating, and harvesting and storing fodder in order to survive throughout the year, whereas formerly all they needed were a few good months of summer pasture.

The different forms of intensification create somewhat different organizational needs and hence variants on the Big Man system. In the forager economies of the Northwest Coast, leaders are needed chiefly to manage the high risks involved in the pursuit of migratory species, to supply equipment needed for the periodic large-scale procurement and processing of wild food, and to negotiate alliances and peacekeeping arrangements. The group leader also directs the major intergroup ceremonies, which are essential to a group's prestige and its members' ability to form regional exchange networks, and is obligated to support followers who experience economic difficulties.

Among the pastoral Kirghiz, where technology is relatively simple, leaders are needed chiefly to spread risks and to conduct the external trade on which the subsistence economy depends.

The horticultural Enga need leaders primarily for political maneuvering and the regulation of war. The group leader of the Central Enga is a politician par excellence, orchestrating the group performance at intercommunity ceremonies in such a way as to keep old allies and obtain new ones. In the New Guinean world of constant intraregional warfare, the leader, as negotiator of intergroup alliances and of intergroup peace, is essential to the group's survival. The formation of corporate groups, as discussed in Chapters 6 and 7, is the first step in restricting access to productive resources. The next step is to establish the collectivity that helps regulate warfare and regularize a regional land tenure system; this can be done most effectively by a new segment of acknowledged leaders bound to each other through exchanges of prestige goods.

Among the Northwest Coast fishermen and the Enga, as among the Tsembaga and Yanomamo, warfare represents the outer edge of the political economy. In the current cases the population is larger and more interdependent and the political economy more complex. Yet in all these cases, simple and complex alike, warfare is not so much the outcome of deliberate policy as the breakdown of policy, proceeding from leaders' ultimate inability to restrain, in the interest of the greater good, the competitive and acquisitive impulses of strong, family-centered individuals.

Depending as it does on differential control over strategic resources, stratification is clearly evident, albeit in incipient form, in Big Man societies. In all cases the Big Man controls resources, such as smoked fish, pigs, or herds of sheep and goats, that help him to spread the risks of food production far beyond the family level. In other ways the Big Man's economic control varies among the three cases: control of technology in the hunter-gatherer economy, control of long-distance exchange in the pastoralist economy, and control of intergroup exchange ceremonies in the horticultural society. But in each case leadership involves economic management and manipulation for individual as well as group advantage. As we shall see in Chapters 10 and 11, the further evolution of the political economy institutionalized as chiefdoms depends on more elaborate forms of economic control.

Part III

The Regional Polity

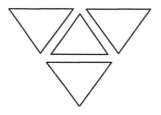

NINE

The Regional Polity

REGIONAL POLITIES ARE political institutions that organize human groups ranging in size from as few as one thousand people to modern-day China with more than a billion. It has really been only in the last five thousand years that regional polities have developed and come to organize the vast majority of humankind. One of the most dramatic long-term trends in human history is the declining number of independent polities in the world (Carneiro 1977). During Neolithic times, there were probably more than 100,000 independent political units of family or local group scale. Through expansion, conquest, incorporation, and geopolitical treaties, this number has been reduced to the mere 160 sovereign states in the United Nations. Rapidly emerging regional blocs suggest still smaller numbers of economically integrated communities in the future. The formula is simple: as world population has grown, the number of independent polities has decreased. Yet this negative correlation is counterintuitive: why aren't more independent polities created by segmentation of groups as their populations grow? That is the question we will seek to answer in the next five chapters.

We have identified the following levels of cultural evolution: the family, the local group, the Big Man collectivity, the chiefdom, the archaic state, and the nation-state (see Table 8). These labels do not signify perfectly discrete levels or plateaus, to one or another of which all known cultures must be assigned; rather, they designate stations along a continuum at which it is convenient to stop and make comparisons with previous stations. "Chiefdom," for example, is a convenient abstraction for a culture that is still evolving from (and contains elements of) the Big Man collectivity or the local group, and for one that may be well along the road to becoming a state. Since the evolutionary continuum represents a transformation of many variables at once, local conditions and history produce many variants that appear "more evolved"

TABLE 8

The Size of Communities and Polities in Evolutionary Perspective

Polity type and case	Size of community	Size of polity
Camp		
Shoshone	30	30
San	20	20
Hamlet		
Machiguenga	25	25
Nganasan	30	30
Local group		
Yanomamo	150–250	150–500
Taremiut	150–300	150–300
Tsembaga	200	200
Turkana	20–25	100–200
Big Man collectivity		
NW Coast Fishers	500–800	500–800
Central Enga	350	350
Kirghiz	20–25	1,800
Chiefdon		
Trobriand Islanders	200–400	1,000
Hawaiian Islanders	300–400	30,000–100,000
Basseri	200–500	16,000
State		
Inka	±400	14,000,000
Brazil	±300	80,000,000+
China	±300	600,000,000+
Java (Indonesia)	±300	100,000,000+

NOTE: The cases of medieval France and Japan (Chapter 12) are excluded because they cover a long period over which population size and political integration changed dramatically.

in some respects and "less evolved" in others when compared with their neighbors on the continuum.

We begin with a typological concern: with such a wide array of polity sizes organizing very different economies, there must be a dizzying array of different types of regional polities. For analytical purposes, however, the range is quite limited, constrained by specific economic conditions. Here we organize the diversity along two dimensions—scale and subsistence. The scale of regional polities increases from simple chiefdoms (with populations in the thousands), to complex chiefdoms (populations in the tens of thousands), to regional states (populations in the hundreds of thousands), and finally to empires (with populations in the millions). The subsistence base for most regionally organized societies is agriculture, often highly intensive (employing, for example, irrigation or terracing), although at the end of the chapter we consider alternatives based on both foraging and pastoralism.

Given the task of describing the whole range of human societies from small scale to large, we originally selected our case studies to represent a world prior to the rise of the mercantile and industrial states that have dominated the scene in recent centuries. Their story involves the somewhat accidental rise of the "West" (really Europe, North America, and Japan) out of apparent backwaters of history (Blaut 1993). Some of the peoples we studied were shattered by those states (e.g., the Shoshone, Case 1; the Inka, Case 16); others were powerfully shaped by them (the villagers of Kali Loro, Case 19). Indeed, all of our cases have been affected to some degree by this major transformation of human society, and we have outlined these changes in a number of our cases. In Chapter 14 we juxtapose those cases to show how our analytical framework can be extended to the dynamics of nation-states, imperial systems, and the emerging global collectivity.

Regional polities are fashioned by embedding and transforming family and local group communities. Even in regional polities, the family remains the locus of everyday living. Most decisions about productive activities are made in households or in familistic groups of related households; the family organizes work in the gardens, marketing, and even wage labor. And yet in both chiefdoms and agrarian states the family's options are increasingly constrained by broader economic and institutional realities. Their economic behavior cannot be understood apart from the local communities and regional polities that contain them.

Peasant communities like those we examine in Brazil (Case 17), China (Case 18), and Java (Case 19) have been a main locus of study for anthropologists, who sometimes exaggerated the degree to which they were independent and self-contained. While community studies made abundantly clear the degree to which families allowed the local community to shape their lives in every respect, it took time to recognize how far the community's economy and politics in turn were shaped by its place in the regional polity. Regional polities, to greater or lesser degree depending on their scale and internal integration, constitute the world of law and legal force that guarantees order among communities within the polity, as well as a coordinated response to the outside world of competing and cooperating states.

The settlement pattern of chiefdoms and states is typically sedentary and hierarchical. For the Trobriand chiefdoms (Case 12), the medieval states of Europe and Japan (Case 15), the Inka empire (Case 16), and most peasant communities (Cases 17, 18, and 19), the primary unit of settlement is the village—a socially recognized community, ritually focused on a plaza, shrine, or graveyard, and subject to elite control.

Separated from other villages across the landscape so that households remain close to productive lands, the village has usually been occupied continuously across many generations, its history seemingly eternal to its members, its ancestors still a presence in everyday life.

The village settlement distinguishes insiders (those with community rights and obligations) from outsiders—whether members of other villages or outlaws. The sense of neighborhood is strong, but villages are rarely defended. Rather they depend on the overarching power of the chiefdom or state for security, and their lack of defenses underscores their subordination to regional power. The occasional appearance of local militias to maintain law and order is a certain sign that the regional polity is weak and ineffective, a condition that occurs cyclically in the rise and fall of chiefdoms and agrarian states.

In polities with market systems, towns and cities are organized hierarchically to serve the demands of the market and effective regional administration (C. Smith 1976). In these centers of political and religious power, lords and masters occupy their awesome residences, temples, and administrative buildings. Government activities, and the marketplaces with their associated craftsmen and workshops, draw workers and visitors from the surrounding countryside. The seats of economic, religious, and political power are typically defended by special fortifications, arrayed in multifaceted hierarchies of central places set atop a sustaining mat of agricultural villages.

In the development of regional polities, a wide range exists in the degree of bureaucratization. Chiefdoms are usually seen as nonbureaucratic. Comparatively small in scale, their leaders, like the village leaders of the Trobriand Islands (Case 12), have very generalized roles, acting as managers, judges, warriors, and priests. Although a chief may delegate specific chiefly duties to another, like the Hawaiian land manager (Case 13), the delegate is not part of a separate administrative institution but reports directly to the chief he represents. Even in many states, such as the medieval states of Europe and Japan (Case 15) and the Inka empire (Case 16), the structure of the state administration is based on personal (often kinship) bonds reminiscent of chiefdoms. But with the development of large and modern nation-states as described in Chapter 13, the scale of operations requires an elaborate set of bureaucracies for administration and control.

The following culture-core variables characterize regionally organized polities:

1. The environment now usually includes (a) rich resources like irrigated land or bottom alluvium, or (b) opportunities for trade resulting

from water-based transport or proximity to markets and trade routes. The environment has been radically transformed by intensification—cleared forests, plowed meadows, drained swamps—and artificial facilities are everywhere. The carefully parceled landscape, with lines of ownership spelled out, promotes control over access to productive resources and transport.

2. Population density is characteristically high, although, as we have come to expect, a wide variety of densities reflects differences in the underlying economy and how it is intensified: from the Trobriand Islanders with 100 persons per square mile to Taitou with 400 and Kali Loro with 1,850. Among pastoralists, even those organized as chiefdoms, population density remains quite low. This can be seen in the Basseri, with only 2 persons per square mile, who occupy marginal lands outside of zones that can be used for agriculture, but whose territories seasonally interweave and coexist with agricultural communities.

3. The technology of intensive agriculture includes major capital improvements (such as irrigation canals, flood control dikes, terraces, and drainage). Where trade is important, capital investments can be found in canoes and ships, piers and ports, wagons, bridges, and roads. Ownership of the technology is an opportunity for control of both production and distribution.

4. The social organization of production is hierarchical, subject to regional patterns of specialization and stratification. While daily production is often still organized within the household, much of the transformation of the landscape, including such activities as the construction and maintenance of irrigation systems, requires the mobilization at least of entire local communities. Some local development and regional markets depend on administration and finance by regional elites. In the larger polities, ethnic divisions often coincide with regionally specialized economies integrated through trade and markets.

5. Warfare and territoriality remain central, but the goals change. The nature of war shifts fundamentally, from competition between local groups over land and other resources—in which enemies are killed or driven off—to conquest warfare that seeks to expand the political economy by capturing both land and labor and bringing them under elite control. The increasingly professional military serves both to expand (or protect) the polity in the competitive external political arena and to outlaw violence between communities and against the state. Land ownership implies the right to share in production (the fund of rent), the basis for finance of elite institutions and projects.

6. Except in the cases of the smallest chiefdoms, political integration

is expanded spatially to incorporate large regions and thousands of subjects. The political system thus brings together people who may know little of each other and have little fellow feeling. In states particularly, this involves multiethnic populations that have very different histories and identities that must somehow be cultivated and balanced within the power structure. It is the building of regional institutions of power—the chiefdom, the state, church hierarchies, and bureaucracies—that most defines the emergence of the regional polities. All depends on means of financing the new institutions of government.

7. Stratification in the regional polity is pronounced—some would say it is its definitive characteristic. With the emergence of complex chiefdoms and states comes the division into classes: a ruling segment that owns and manages much of the wealth and productive resources and a commoner segment that works in the fields and at other productive tasks. The stratification may include a belief in elite racial, historical, and religious superiority. Gender inequality also can become quite marked. Materially, the many divisions and hierarchies are represented in dress, culture, quality of housing, burials, and the like. The regional polity is a world of divisions and distinctions that both reflect and legitimize economic domination.

8. Sanctity in the regional polity is deployed most dramatically, in sacred ceremonies intended to create a sense of common origins, purpose, and destiny among strangers and to sanctify the class divisions of society. To be sure, shamanism, magic, and ancestor worship still play vital roles in families and neighborhoods, and worship at village shrines or ceremonies to honor patron saints continues to reinforce relationships at the local group level. But it is the ceremonies of the regional polity that materialize the polity in displays of military might, beautiful religious celebrations, dramatic performances, and public punishments and sacrifices. Their effect is to impress the audience with a power far beyond their ordinary experience, a power that attracts them while at the same time demonstrating the futility of any attempt to rebel or escape. If sanctity at the local group level is mainly about highlighting and reinforcing the ties that bind families into groups, at the level of the regional polity sanctity is mainly about encouraging the compliance of commoners with elite policies and privilege.

In contrast with the family and local group levels, the most dramatic difference in the regional polity, from the standpoint of the household, is the distance to the highest levels of leadership and political power. That is one reason why Kroeber (1948: 92) called peasants "part-societies with part-cultures": much of their social, economic, and cultural context is created and determined far from the household—in the marketplaces, towns, castles, and temples, and in the power struggles of elites. In contrast to the intense importance of the web of kinship in the local group, peasant households are more atomized, isolated to a degree by their individual participation in the market and their one-on-one ties to elite patrons.

The complementary division of labor between husband and wife continues to underscore the economic interdependence at the base of marriage. But among peasants in the regional polity, land and other wealth tend to be transmitted in the male line, residence is patrilocal, and there is a clear-cut ideology of male dominance (Michaelson and Goldschmidt 1971). These patterns are strongest in families with wealth, where an emphasis on producing male heirs places a premium on chaste daughters who will become fertile and faithful wives. But the ideology of male dominance pervades all regions and classes. Newly married couples may strongly wish for a separate hearth and home of their own, yet this often comes into conflict with older parents' desire to maintain patriarchal control of their sons' household economies and to be cared for in old age.

The Political Revolution: The Origins of Civilizations

The Urban Revolution is the third profound change in human history (Childe 1936, 1942). The growth of cities involves the development of regional political landscapes with centers of population, administration, religion, and economy. Urbanism, however, is itself but one of many interrelated processes that result in complex society. Here we focus on one basic dimension of this revolution—the expansion of a political economy that mobilizes a surplus from agrarian communities to finance the new elite institutions of chiefdoms and states.

Why do local agrarian populations go to the extra effort of producing a surplus with which to finance projects that are largely beyond their control and that may have little impact on their lives? The broadest answer is that long-term intensification of production creates opportunities for control that position elites to demand a share of production. We have already seen how intensification in the subsistence economy, as feedback between population growth and technological change, creates new problems (such as increased risk, and the emergence of warfare), requiring new social technologies, examples of which include extended kinship, debt and credit, ceremonial cycles, and leadership. A further elaboration of this process is the creation of opportunities for control.

To see how this process works, we look at the institutionalization of power relationships. In *How Chiefs Come to Power*, Earle (1997) investigates the emergence and elaboration of chiefdoms in three independent historical and archaeological examples: Hawaii (Case 13), Highland Peru (Case 16), and Denmark. In each case long-term growth in human population required subsistence intensification that resulted in dramatic anthropogenic changes to the environment—the clearing of forests and the construction of fields and other productive facilities. Intensification created specific opportunities for control. Although alternative pathways to complexity became evident, the process was remarkably similar in each instance, albeit based on control over different sources of power.

The primary sources of power derive from the economy, the military, and ideology (compare Mann 1986), and each can be seen as an outcome of intensification. In the economy, various conditions resulting from intensification require management as they create opportunities for differentiated power. The first is risk: more intensive economies are locally more risky and require elements of regional risk-spreading. The second is technology: the building of irrigation systems or other facilities creates capital improvements to the landscape. The third is trade: in the "secondary products revolution" (Sherratt 1981), intensive agriculturists begin to consume animal products provided by pastoralists living in agriculturally marginal zones. As described by Barth (1956), a regional economy emerges that binds together different polities with different subsistence economies, and chiefly wealth can be generated by managing the trade between populations (e.g., the Basseri, Case 14).

As for the military, as the economy is intensified, competition for the most productive resources and for objects of trade creates an armed force in the form of a warrior elite. Warriors defend the group's territory against external threat, and, as far as the local community is concerned, establish a regional peace. The new regional order guarantees rights of access to resources for commoners, but those rights come at a cost: the warriors (and the chiefs or lords they represent) extract a rent for land, which is now owned by the elites. The warriors take on a double function, enforcing the established stratified order (with differential access to the means of production) and extending, through conquest, the political domain of their chief or lord.

Ideology establishes a powerful source of legitimacy that validates the economic and military arrangements the local economy has become dependent upon. In regional polities, ceremonies continue to function as group charters, as they did at the local group level, but they are now

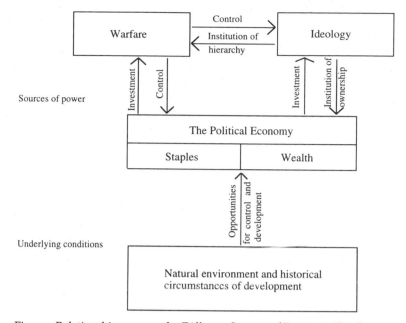

Fig. 10. Relationships among the Different Sources of Power in Chiefly Power Strategies (Source: Earle 1997: 204)

performed at several levels, most significantly imbedding the local community within the overarching political structure of chiefs and lords, who assert special status with respect to the gods and the universe. That status makes the elites essential in the ritual practice on which the continuity and fertility of the community is believed to depend. Ceremonies come to define relationships of dependency and domination.

Figure 10 illustrates how the underlying conditions of the subsistence economy permit control over production and distribution, which in turn results in the mobilization of a surplus used in the political economy. Surplus in the political economy can then be reinvested in the infrastructure of the economy to expand surplus production. In turn, surplus channeled through the political economy is used to support an emerging warrior elite that exerts control over both the economic infrastructure and the ideological superstructure. At the same time, the surplus supports the elaboration of the ideology that includes formal religious institutions and large-scale ceremonial occasions. The ideology establishes the rules of order in the regional polity that legitimize social stratification.

Theorizing the Regional Polity

To understand the regional polity is to understand the ways in which leadership becomes institutionalized and extended to dominate populations of thousands, and ultimately millions, of people. Much of the theoretical debate about how this happens has followed a cleavage between the ecological and the political dimensions of power as touched on in Chapter 1 (Earle 1987). On the ecological side, theorists emphasized how the leaders of regional polities manage the subsistence economy. Service (1962) saw the evolution of chiefdoms as caused by the emergence of a regional redistributive economy managed by chiefs. In his view, chiefs receive goods from economically specialized communities in order to allocate them where needed. Sanders (1956) also related the evolution of states to distribution, this time in markets that require a central state authority to maintain the regional peace on which markets depend. Wittfogel (1957) saw the state as prerequisite to the construction and maintenance of regional irrigation systems; much like later industrial technologies, he argued, the productive scale of irrigation requires central management of large work forces.

On the political side, Fried (1967) argued the Marxian idea that stratified societies emerge to maintain differential access to the means of production. When irrigation and other agricultural facilities become available, food producers quickly become dependent on them. Mann (1986), for example, describes how the irrigation systems of Middle Eastern civilizations effectively caged the commoner population, whose choices in those desert climes were few. Such facilities are easily seized by an emerging military elite and used for their support (Gilman 1976, 1981). In this view the institutions of the stratified society centrally concern the functions—laws, courts, records, titles, police, prisons—that maintain elite control of wealth and property.

Ecological and political theories of the emergence of complex societies are equally necessary because intensification both requires local management of the subsistence economy and at the same time creates opportunities for control over access to resources. We turn to these theories in greater detail now, looking at the economic, military, and ideological sources of power.

Theories of the Economy

A key issue in the political economy of complex society concerns where the surplus comes from. Leslie White (1959), for example, argued that cultural evolution followed technological advances in energy capture; with each innovation, a greater abundance of energy would support more people, liberating them for a wider range of activities. This surplus theory of social complexity argues simply that technological progress permits ever greater surplus production, from which flow the achievements of civilization—the arts, formalized religion, writing, craft specialization, urban life, and regional governments:

[The Urban Revolution] was initiated in the alluvial valleys of the Nile, the Tigres-Euphrates, and the Indus about five thousand years ago with the transformation of some riverside villages into cities. Society persuaded or compelled the farmers to produce a surplus in foodstuffs over and above their domestic requirements, and by concentrating this surplus used it to support a new urban population of specialized craftsmen, merchants, priests, officials, and clerks. (Childe 1942: 18)

A sophisticated food production technology was thought necessary to generate the surplus that financed social complexity.

Pearson (1957), however, in his famous article "The Economy Has No Surplus," criticized the surplus theory of social evolution. Arguing as a substantivist, Pearson turned the logic of the surplus theory on its head, maintaining that it is impossible to define a fixed "subsistence level" beyond which surplus becomes available for development. All societies, he believed, have the potential to produce in excess of any biological necessity (Wolf's caloric minimum), but whether or not they actually do so—and whether they devote that excess to greater household consumption or to public expenditures—depends on the social context in which the production system is imbedded. Since in the substantivist view the economy is ultimately an operation of social institutions, economic goals are set by the society. Surplus could not have created complex society, because society itself creates the surplus in the first place!

Working from an ecological viewpoint, Harris (1959) broke out of this chicken-and-egg dilemma by starting from the assumption that the primary goal of social institutions is to maintain human populations in particular environments. Although agreeing with Pearson that surplus was socially driven, Harris argued that surplus is never superfluous; indeed, it is essential for the long-term survival of a population. For example, more variable, unpredictable environments require more surplus to guard against disastrous fluctuations in harvest. As an example, he described how "surplus" yams on the Trobriand Islands (Case 12) are displayed centrally in the chief's village, and in a good year may be allowed to rot. But the overproduction is a necessary hedge against crop failure in an unstable island environment—in bad years few yams are left to rot. The redistribution of surplus by a chief is a kind of insurance policy, made necessary by intensive farming in a region where harvests are always uncertain and vested in social institutions. It is equally fair to say that the surplus is created by society and that the surplus sustains society.

The transformation from the local group to the regional polity means for the household that its production goals must expand to meet the demands of the regional political economy, generally in the form of payments to elites. In the household budget, the subsistence fund is as necessary as ever. As in the local group, the ceremonial fund is also essential; each household must maintain its place in the community's social structure. To substantivists like Pearson, the ceremonial fund is a sign that the peasant economy is embedded in society; for Harris, as for Wolf (1966a), it is a necessary expenditure on social relationships vital to the household's long-term success in subsistence and reproduction. But with the development of regional polities, households must also supply a fund of rent—payments to chiefs, overlords, or religious and governing institutions who claim ownership of land and productive technology. The household must pay shares of its produce, corvée labor, and other forms of rent and taxes to retain rights to use subsistence plots and other resources. This surplus, which is often a quarter to a third of all household production, is extracted from each commoner household to finance the institutions of the new society.

Specific economic systems characterize the development of chiefdoms (redistribution) and states (markets). Polanyi (1957) describes redistribution as the socially prescribed giving of goods and services to a central figure, who then redistributes them. Surplus, in these terms, would be the culturally determined part that commoners owe (and pay into) the center from whence it is redistributed to meet broader social needs. As seen among the Hawaiian chiefdoms (Case 13), redistribution was the organized political economy that mobilized resources to finance the expanding chiefdoms (Earle 1977).

Polanyi regarded market exchange, in which prices are set by supply and demand, as a late development in human history associated with the rise of capitalism. But others have noted that most states have market systems (Claessen 1978: 542). Marketplaces are those neutral grounds where people from the countryside, and from other polities, can come to exchange goods and services in barter or for cash. States are important for markets because they provide the infrastructure (roads, ports), institutional framework (money, property rights), and regional peace upon which market exchange depends. But why are markets so important to states?

The evolution of chiefdoms and states depends on the availability of resources to support chiefly and state institutions, and these must come ultimately from the fund of rent. Systems of finance take two distinct forms: staple finance and wealth finance. Both forms have long histories in simpler societies: staples provide sustenance and wealth marks status everywhere. But it is with the evolution of regional governing institutions that control over the production and distribution of these goods becomes fully centralized.

Staple finance (D'Altroy and Earle 1985; Earle and D'Altroy 1989) is a form of redistribution, a system in which staple goods (especially food) are required from individual households as a payment to the center. With staple finance, leaders mobilize food surpluses—just as local groups do to support ceremonies—and distribute them to those working for the chiefdom (or state). The primary institutional form of complex societies that use staple finance is corporate (Blanton ct al. 1996); the ruling elites own the land, from which they receive shares of food produced by commoners in exchange for use rights. This ownership is materialized by a constructed landscape of power that includes monuments, storehouses, roadways, and barriers. Corporateness is represented dramatically in group ceremonies that identify people with the land and other resources, under the sacred guidance of the ruling elite.

The primary advantage of a staple finance system is its simplicity. The surplus is used directly to compensate a "nonproducing" sector of elites, their managers, warriors, and artisans, as well as commoners working on corvée projects. Many chiefdoms rely on staple finance, and states can as well, as seen in early medieval societies (Case 15) and even the Inka empire (Case 16). Such complex, stratified polities may exist without a strong market system, but they require large central storehouses. The primary disadvantage of staple finance is logistical; the bulkiness and weight of the staples make them difficult to move any distance (D'Altroy 1992). More often than not, such polities are fairly small, perhaps less than thirty miles across, and nonurban.

Wealth finance (Brumfiel and Earle 1987; D'Altroy and Earle 1985) refers to the controlled production and distribution of valuables or currencies. With the emergence of chiefdoms, prestige goods often move in a separate sphere of exchange, such that they are no longer easy to exchange for staple goods (Bohannan 1955). This limits commoners' access to the objects and enables elites to control the prestige economy (Earle 1982). Primitive valuables, like the *kula* objects of the Trobriand Islanders, establish a person's status, confer the rights and obligations associated with the position, and mark prestige ranking. They can act as

a political currency to compensate a person for service. Many chiefdoms, especially those without highly intensified agricultural facilities,
rely on wealth finance using valuables.

The primary institutional form of wealth finance in chiefdoms is the
network in which individual status and position are determined by social, economic, and political relationships (Blanton et al. 1996). Networks are materialized by wealth objects that are exchanged and displayed in public ceremonies; the exchange of prestige goods is the medium in which fluid and extensive confederacies develop.

In states, the development of currency correlates with the development of markets that take on a new integrative function of profound
significance. True currencies are valuables that have become adapted
as media of exchange and stores of value. They tend to be divisible into
denominations of various sizes, and freely convertible (i.e., fungible) in
exchange for goods, as in the all-purpose money of modern market
economies. They are used for payment and purchase in state societies
with markets. Most states use currencies, often originally in conjunction
with staple finance.

The primary advantage of wealth finance is its ability to be centralized. Because prestige goods and currency are highly valued (especially considering their portability), wealth in rent or tribute can be moved
across considerable distances and stored centrally. Such means of finance require little space and do not lose value through spoilage.
Wealth is easily centralized and defended in vaults at administrative
centers.

The primary disadvantage of wealth finance is that the means of
payment (the wealth) cannot be used directly to support those working
for the chiefdom or state. You cannot eat prestige goods or currency;
they require markets in which the wealth can be converted into staple
goods (Brumfiel 1980). When markets are disrupted, wealth loses
value. Yet, truly large states can develop only by using currency systems for taxation and payment, converting the currency through the
market to support a large, nonagrarian, urban sector. That is why states
are often defined as urban, market-oriented societies.

Theories of the Military

How warfare and the military relate to the rise of complex societies
continues an earlier theme. As we saw for local groups, population
growth and subsistence intensification increase competition between
communities over land. The local group seeks to defend its members'
use rights to land, and eventually to build intergroup collectivities that

provide allies and regulate warfare. But what happens as population continues to grow and resource use is further intensified?

Carneiro (1970b, 1981) has investigated the relationships between warfare and the establishment of regional polities. He argues that both chiefdoms and states are warrior or militaristic societies. No one voluntarily submits to a regional order; populations must be conquered and forcefully incorporated within it. As population grows and fills the landscape, people can spread out into unoccupied lands, intensify local production, or seize lands from others. Eventually, however, growing populations become geographically and socially circumscribed. There is nowhere to go: all open terrain has been occupied and claimed, and people are bound closely to their land, which must be defended against neighboring groups. Intergroup competition and warfare place a strong group selective advantage on leaders who mobilize and coordinate warriors and negotiate for allies to defend territory. The harsh reality is that populations with effective military leadership displace less militarily organized populations (see Carneiro 1967).

In chiefdoms, warriors are specialists attached directly to chiefs and used for conquest and enforcement; typically, the chief portrays himself as the lion-hearted master warrior from whom all benefits and protection flow. In states, the military can become a large and highly structured institution for both imperial expansion and internal rule. In both cases the military is charged with seizing and holding the productive resources upon which the political economy depends (Haas 1982). The military, successful in conquest, then becomes an avenue to privilege and an enforcer of inequality.

Theories of Ideology

Ideologies are systems of belief created and strategically manipulated by certain social segments, most notably the ruling elites of chiefdoms and states, to establish and maintain the legitimacy of their position in society. Ideologies involve public performances that recount religious theology and social narratives. For example, prior to Dutch imperial conquest, the countryside of Java was settled by peasant communities, antecedents to Kali Loro (Case 19). These communities existed within large states that maintained religious systems and ceremonial complexes to establish continuity and rule by traditional kings. For the neighboring Balinese states, Geertz (1980) argues that the polity (*negara*) was quite distinct from instrumental state institutions such as bureaucracies or militaries. Rather, he refers to them as "theater states" that stage elaborate calendrical and cyclical ceremonies. In these, the historical narrative of the state unfolds in a performance justified by religious dogma and materialized in ceremony, liturgy, sacred text, monumental architecture, and inscriptions. The power of state religion is brought to bear to sanctify the narrative of the state and the power relationships it codifies.

Mann (1986) believes that the development of social complexity can involve the creation of different social segments, each accessing different sources of power. If we assume that power may originate from different places, the economy, the military, and religion, then it seems plausible that they may remain partially independent of each; divisions may exist between sacred and profane powers or between the military and the landowners. Although leaders will want to bring the different power sources under their control, their ability to do so will always be problematic. The development of states does not merely involve increased centralization but may also result in a fragmentation of separate and potentially opposed power sources. As described in Chapter 10, instead of a single center of power, we can find a "heterarchical" system made up of partly overlapping power hierarchies that balance each other (Ehrenreich et al. 1995).

The Primary Dynamics of the Regional Polity

To understand how and why humans, best adapted to small-scale groups, should have constructed regional polities, we return to the basic motor of intensification. In addition to the continuing pressure from relentless population growth, the political economy is itself growth oriented, giving intensification a new dynamic. Although central management serves the local community and binds it to the political superstructure, a primary motivation for management now becomes maximizing surpluses for the ruling institutions. Leaders are highly motivated to increase their control over the economy through growth, enhancing their standing in the highly competitive political world of chiefdoms and states.

Leaders must establish a delicate balance. They seek to mobilize as much as possible from the households of the subsistence economy, but within realistic limits. They must not place the productive infrastructure at too much risk. Although elites, believing themselves inherently superior, typically have little sympathy for their commoners' plight, they understand as a practical matter that commoner households must be allowed access to an adequate subsistence base to support themselves and to supply the labor needed to generate surplus for the superstructure.

Ultimately, they must beware of setting off a peasant rebellion. Although the ideology of chiefdoms and states legitimizes the domination of the rulers, peasants have a strong sense of their right to family survival, an aspect of what Scott (1976) calls "the moral economy of the peasant." As Harris (1959) argued, each economy must on average overproduce to guarantee that enough is available during bad years, according to Leibig's Law of the Minimum. In a peasant economy, all surpluses potentially belong to the owners of the land, but the amount mobilized varies according to the success of the harvest. In good years, much can be paid in rent to the elites, who are then free to invest it in more land, technology, security schemes, or fancy lifestyles. But in bad years, the elites must cut back on what they mobilize so that the peasants' "moral" right to self-support is guaranteed.

In agrarian Europe (Case 15), for example, elites feared peasant rebellions. Because the peasants substantially outnumbered the lord and his retinue, the lord would have to withdraw to the castle when rebellion threatened. As long as the amount of surplus extracted allows for continued family maintenance, however, peasants are inclined to support the existing order, which guarantees their livelihood. If this guarantee is broken, as it has been in recent times with expanding rural labor markets (see, e.g., the sharecroppers of Boa Ventura, Case 17), peasant unhappiness can breed revolt (Johnson 1999; Scott 1976).

The cross-cultural development of regional polities continues to illustrate the processes of multilinear evolution. Intensification of production causes problems whose solutions offer opportunities for control, but the varying conditions that allow for control cause evolution to follow separate paths. Specifically, agriculture, foraging, and pastoralism follow different lines of development toward the regional polity.

Most chiefdoms and states are based on intensified agriculture, and we have already outlined the key features of their evolution. A wide range of environments offer conditions suitable for sustained agricultural intensification that permits both high population densities and the generation of surpluses for financing institutions. Intensification of agriculture creates two major problems that require different forms of management. Where investments in capital facilities such as irrigation or drainage are not possible, intensification usually takes the form of careful management of the fallow cycle, to deal with the problems created by short fallows in tropical ecosystems. In the Trobriand Islands (Case 12), chiefs manage the agricultural cycle of dryland farming by a combination of land allocation and agricultural ritual, and they encourage the storage of food that in bad years is essential for the communities' survival and in good years supports chiefly competitive feasting.

In locations permitting the development of highly productive agricultural facilities (irrigation systems, terraces, drainage, and the like), improved lands become the property of elites who can extract a surplus from agricultural workers who have nowhere else to turn. Such systems of finance supported the complex chiefdoms of Hawaii and the Inka empire.

With the emergence of the agriculturally intensive regional polity, the goal of warfare becomes conquest. True, agricultural intensification enhances land value and hence the likelihood of aggression over land within the polity, and the ability of a warrior chief or lord to protect land rights supports his efforts to gain loyal subjects. But wars are fought between chiefs for control of territory and for populations to rule, war being the result of a desire to increase income via the fund of rent.

Under specific conditions, chiefdoms and states can develop on a foraging base. Among foragers the primary condition making this possible is a highly productive environment that allows for comparatively high population densities and the generation of surpluses. These conditions may exist in maritime environments where rich populations of fish and sea mammals can support dense human settlement. Among the Indian fishermen of the Northwest Coast (Case 9), strong local leaders developed where a complicated technology of boats, fishing weirs, and drying and storage facilities made intensification possible. Like agriculture, such capital improvements can significantly raise the productive potential of a locale. These facilities are owned by leaders who finance their manufacture, organize their maintenance, and protect them from neighboring groups. Control over these facilities offers the leaders a means of mobilizing resources for the competitive political displays that organize crucial intergroup collectivities. These Big Man systems are not an uncommon condition for "complex hunter gatherers" described both archaeologically and ethnographically (Arnold 1996a; Price and Brown 1985), but the productivity and control necessary to support chiefdoms and states is rarer.

Still, under unusually productive conditions, foragers have developed regional polities. Arnold (1996b) argues that the ownership of boats formed the economic basis of control in forager chiefdoms like the Chumash Indians of southern California. The intensification of the maritime economy led to extensive trade, employing seagoing canoes to connect island economies rich in animal resources with mainland economies rich in plant resources. In addition to greater efficiencies of production through specialization, the trade provided a hedge against disasters. Among the island Chumash, for example, the highly productive marine economy could fail because of conditions like El Niño that increase water temperature and lower the availability of fish and other marine animals. The wild seed and animal resources from the mainland could then be traded to the island groups in exchange for their shell "money" acquired in trade during good years.

Foragers have developed ceremonially integrated regional polities in comparably rich environments: the protected Florida coastal bays of the Calusa (Widmer 1988); the slack-water environment of the early prehistoric Poverty Point chiefdoms (Gibson 1994); and the riverine-uplands of the prehistoric Ohio Adena. These archaeologically known examples, lacking significant agriculture, included early and elaborate mound complexes that document regional integration and a mobilization of labor. Along coastal Peru, the extraordinary rich marine re-sources supported the elaboration of complex chiefdoms out of which Andean civilization developed (Moseley 1975; Quilter et al. 1991). Here the beginnings of agriculture involved not food but cotton, used to make fishing tackle and the woven wealth of clothing. Control proba-bly resulted from both ownership of the technology of intensive ex-ploitation and defense of the most productive environmental zones.

Among pastoralists, the primary condition for stratification appears to be proximity to agrarian chiefdoms or states (Beck 1986: 9–17; Irons 1979). Pastoralists occupy lands that cannot be intensified by agricul-ture, but the herded animals yield valued resources. Under these con-ditions, pastoralists become specialists producing animal products (meat, hides, plow animals, milk, and cheese) for trade with farmers who produce cereals. It is a much more efficient use of land to feed a dense population from cereals than, as the Turkana do (Case 8), from meat and milk.

In these intensive systems, where pastoralists move about among the farm populations, exploiting fallow farmland as well as marginal pas-tures where farming is impossible, pastoralists trade expensive animal products for inexpensive farm produce. A regional exchange system develops integrating peoples of sharply contrasting lifestyles and usu-ally of distinct ethnicity (Barth 1956). The development of such trade has been called the "secondary products revolution" in prehistoric Europe, where it was among the economic bases for social complexity (Sherratt 1981).

In pastoral societies associated with agrarian states we can see most clearly the tension between familistic and local autonomy on one side and the efforts of regional polities to impose control on the other. Pro-ducing animal products for settled farmers does not in itself require a regional polity level of control. Mobility allows pastoralists a degree of freedom that settled farmers do not enjoy. Farmers and elites equally consider such freedom dangerous and seek to limit it. Pastoralist groups like the Basseri (Case 14) may even increase their mobility beyond what is required on purely ecological grounds simply to enjoy the freedom and military advantages it gives them in dealing with the regional polity (Irons 1979). Without the military threat posed by the agrarian state, it is doubtful that the Basseri would even have reached a chiefdom level of complexity (cf. Fried 1967: 240–42).

In fact, the nomadic pastoralists of Asia and Europe frequently became specialist warriors. As we learned for the Turkana (Case 8), warrior training is common among pastoralists as a means of defending the family herds and of obtaining new animals through raiding. Even when trading with settled farmers, the pastoralists of the Old World, disdaining the soft life of farm and city, would often constitute a military elite capable of turning against and dominating settled populations. The Mongols of central Asia are the most dramatic historical example of a pastoralist state (Morgan 1986). The military might of the Mongols allowed them to conquer much larger agrarian societies and co-opt the agrarian surplus production to support their pastoralist state. Mongol armies surged out of the Asian steppes to dominate the ancient Chinese agrarian state and create the largest land-based empire ever to exist.

TEN

The Simple Chiefdom

THE EVOLUTION OF CHIEFDOMS is marked by the development of regional political institutions. Chiefdoms integrate several local groups within a single polity (Carneiro 1981), and quite extensive confederations can form chiefly collectivities that coordinate political and religious affairs (M. E. Smith 1985). For the first time, the polity, defined as a group organized under a single ruling individual or council, extends beyond the village or local group. Often the community associated with the ruling chief is unusually large in comparison with nonstratified societies; however, the more dramatic difference is in the size of the population that is united politically.

Archaeologically, chiefdoms succeed the simpler community organization of early Neolithic society. With chiefdoms we see the beginnings of truly large-scale constructions, such as the mound groups of the Olmec (Bernal 1969; Earle 1976) and of the Mississippian (B. Smith 1978), the ziggurats of the Ubaid (Wright 1984), and the henges and cursus of the Wessex chiefdoms (Renfrew 1973). These impressive early monuments testify unambiguously both to the central organization of a labor force and to the function of a site as a regional ceremonial and political center. To judge from the ethnographic examples discussed in this chapter and the next, chiefdoms range in population from the low thousands to the tens of thousands, making them an order of magnitude larger than simpler polities (cf. Feinman and Neitzel 1984).

A polity of this size requires a new level of integration that bridges the local communities. Two contrasting regional forms of chiefdoms have been described: hierarchies (Earle 1978, 1987) and heterarchies (Ehrenreich et al. 1995). Within chiefly hierarchies, a ruling aristocracy occupies local and regional offices with generalized responsibilities in social, political, and religious affairs. Community chiefs act much like local leaders, but they are also responsible for activities that articulate with the regional polity. Regional chiefs coordinate and direct a wide range of activities, from warfare to ceremonies, that cut across the local communities, and chiefly offices form reinforcing chains of status wielding authority and power.

Within the chiefdom the regional organization is based on an elite class of chiefs, often considered descendants of the gods, who are socially separated and ritually marked. The organization is explicitly conceived as a kin-based, communitylike organization expanded into a regional governing body. The chiefs are related to each other through descent and marriage, and the idioms of kinship and personal bonds remain central in the political operation of the chiefdom. The tie between the developing economic system and developing social stratification is plain to all, and the chiefs come to dominate the economy as well as the social and political realm.

Within chiefly heterarchies, a similar aristocratic sector exists, but elites are not organized into a single central hierarchy. These different hierarchies are associated with different sources of power, making heterarchies politically more decentralized. Such systems characterize many complex and large-scale societies in Africa (McIntosh 1999); they are ritually elaborated but not institutionally solidified into single polities. In fact hierarchies and heterarchies should best be considered ends along a continuum for chiefdoms that reflect multilinear developments of complexity based on contrasting political economies of finance and means of legitimation.

In chiefdoms, both staple and wealth finance exist (Earle 1997). Staple finance, as in Hawaii (Case 13), characterizes many chiefdoms. Intensification of the subsistence economy has required agricultural facilities that are owned and controlled by chiefs and from which the chiefs receive a surplus that is invested in further agricultural intensification, military expansion, and ceremonial elaboration. Wealth finance is seen in chiefdoms where less intensive agricultural systems dominate, as for example on the Trobriand Islands (Case 12), and where pastoralists on the edge of states provide special animal products for cash and agricultural products (Basseri, Case 14). The two types of finance are evolutionarily equivalent, but staple finance offers more stable control than does wealth finance in chiefdoms, which are likely to cycle dramatically.

We must now explain why the regional institutions of chiefdoms, supported by emergent political economies, should develop. Why do individuals and local communities give up their autonomy and submit to the demands of a regional ruling elite? Plainly the ruling elites benefit; they have an improved living standard, greater reproductive success, and power to direct human affairs. But what is in it for the commoner? To answer this question we must look at the two sides of the chiefly contract: service and control.

The services provided by leaders to local groups include the management of large-scale subsistence activities, the conduct of long-distance trade, the storage of food and wealth objects, and the maintenance of alliances through debt-credit relations. At the regional polity level chiefs provide the analogous services, whose nature varies with the form taken by intensification in various environments. Less variable is the nature of control that rests on ownership of critical productive resources, technologies, and religious power. The long-term intensification of the economy increases the need for management, the ease of ownership, and thus the dependency of the local commoners on their leaders.

In the simplest terms, a chiefdom is a stratified society based on unequal access to the means of production. This point, stressed by Fried (1967), is essential for understanding the differences between chiefdoms and simpler societies. A chief's control translates into an ability to manipulate the economy in such a way as to derive from it a surplus that can be invested. He is granted the power to control or monopolize economic management under certain specific conditions deriving from the same factors that we have identified as requiring individual families to group together: risk management, technology, warfare, and trade. As population increases, there comes a time when the local group or intergroup collectivity can no longer be relied on to handle these life-and-death matters.

As described in Chapter 9, chiefdoms develop specific institutional forms reflecting parallel but distinctive lines of social evolution. Starting with basic differences in environmental potentials for intensification, the possibilities for population growth and for surplus production vary from place to place and from economy to economy. The details of intensification determine the ease and means by which the economy can (or cannot) be controlled, and the differentials of control create distinctive power bases for chiefdoms. Most chiefdoms, however, are agricultural, and control over agricultural production makes possible the surplus that finances their emergence and operation, as is illustrated by the example of the Trobriand Islands.

Case 12. The Trobriand Islanders

The Trobriand Islands are a small group of flat coral islands that lie about 120 miles north of New Guinea's eastern tip. In contrast to the large islands of Melanesia, such as the New Hebrides or the Solomons, which provide near-continental environments, the Trobriands' small size, unvaried resources, and physical isolation seem to constrict their human population. As we shall see, however, trade by means of traditional sailing canoes effectively connects the economies of the island world off New Guinea and provides for both local survival and political finance.

Trobriand ethnography has a special place in anthropology because of the seminal field research of Malinowski (1922, 1935), which began soon after pacification. Later studies by Austen (1945), Powell (1960, 1969), and Weiner (1976, 1983, 1992), and important reanalyses by Uberoi (1962), Burton (1975), and Irwin (1983), make the Trobriands a critical case requiring careful consideration in any analysis of chiefdoms.

The Trobriand case is important in coming to an understanding of the transition from a Big Man system to a chiefdom. Many of the characteristics of Big Man systems are present in the Trobriands, but hereditary ranking, institutionalized leadership, and some regional centralization suggest the chiefdoms of Polynesia. Why hereditary chiefs and not just Big Men?

The Environment and the Economy

The Trobriand group consists of one dominant island (Kiriwina, seventy square miles) and several other islands (totaling about twelve square miles). Kiriwina has little topographical relief, with about 60 percent of its land surface being low arable soils and the rest swamps and occasional jagged coral outcrops. Many resources, such as clay and stone, are not available on the islands. There are no streams, and fresh water comes from a subsurface lens. Vegetation consists of gardens, secondary brush, small stands of coconut and betel palms near villages, and small remnants of native vegetation. Malinowski notes that "little is left to nature and its spontaneous growth" (1935: 4). Except for the swamps, the landscape is the product of human use.

The climate is warm and humid. Rainfall is seasonal, with most precipitation falling during the monsoons. Droughts, although not common, are severe and feared. When the monsoons fail, agricultural production also fails, and famine seizes the islands. The population density of the Trobriands is quite high for a horticultural population. Powell (1960: 119) calculates it at about 100 persons per square mile, a figure he says has not changed significantly since the turn of the century. Figure 11 shows the island environment crowded with small villages. In general the population is concentrated near the cultivable land (about 70 percent of the total), where densities exceed 130 persons per square mile. From Malinowski's description (1935) one sees a crowded landscape transformed by human work.

The subsistence economy combines intensive agriculture and fishing. Foraging is restricted to small quantities of shellfish and crabs found along the shores and marshes. The bulk of the diet consists of root crops, especially yams and taro. The main crop is yam, which is planted in September and October and becomes available for harvest in May and June. Fields are typically prepared new every other year, harvested twice, and then allowed to revert to a bush fallow for three to five years before being used again; their fertility is apparently maintained largely by adding ash to the soil. Following the initial cutting and drying, the vegetation is carefully burned. Then a planting pit is excavated, with care to remove all roots and stone, and it is filled with the loosened soil and a seed tuber. During the growth period of about eight months, the yam crop is tended and weeded. Subsistence yams are then harvested as needed, and exchange yams are harvested and stored in special structures for about six months.

Because of the seasonality and fairly short storage life of yams, a lean period exists during which stored yams from an earlier planting and a mixture of other crops are important. Special taro gardens are common. The staggered plantings of yam and taro through the year provide a long harvest period and some security against unpredictable conditions that might destroy a single crop.

Security in the subsistence economy is paramount to the Trobrianders. The islands, without topographical relief to catch rains and without streams for irrigation, are at risk from periodic droughts. Stories of droughts and famine are commonplace, and food is prominently displayed on all ceremonial occasions—at funerals, at marriages, and at community dances. Having food gives people a sense of well-being, security, and pride. Lacking food "is not only something to be dreaded, but something to be ashamed of" (Malinowski 1935: 82).

There are three main ways of dealing with the threat of food shortage. One is to spread food production through the year by staggering plantings. A second, and perhaps the most important, is systematic overproduction. Encouraged by chiefs and garden magicians and reinforced by the strong ethic of food accumulation as a measure of personal status, the household head routinely strives to produce more than enough food to meet his family's needs. Because good and bad years cannot be foreseen, this extra effort not only enables the household to

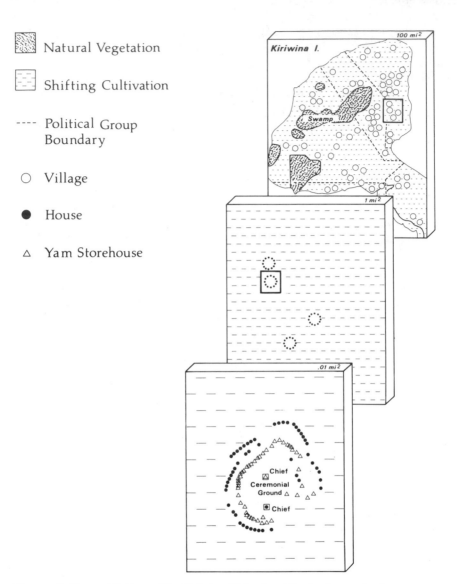

Natural Vegetation

Shifting Cultivation

---- Political Group Boundary

○ Village

● House

△ Yam Storehouse

Kiriwina I.

100 mi²

Swamp

1 mi²

.01 mi²

Chief

Ceremonial Ground

Chief

Fig. 11. Settlement Pattern of the Trobriand Islanders. The landscape has been totally transformed by intensive, shifting cultivation. Small villages cluster together and are often linked to a chief's village, where special ceremonies take place in the central dance ground. Trobriand villages generally contain 13–28 houses; the one depicted here, being a chief's village, is considerably larger.

get by in a bad year but also results in large surpluses in average and good years. The implications of these surpluses for political finance will be discussed later.

The third way, although its effectiveness has been disputed (Powell 1969), is to distribute food between villages as part of the routine of structured gift exchanges and ceremonial distribution. Although such arrangements may be too limited to prevent shortages in the event of widespread crop failure, they probably provide some averaging effect and in the long run cut down the required surplus for the whole system.

The overall intensity of horticultural production required by the population density, by security needs, and (as we shall see) by status rivalry is seen clearly in the planning and regulation of the gardening cycle. Cultivation is done by a village, involving ten or more families. The hamlet head or chief first meets with his garden magician to decide on the location of the large garden section and to allocate plots within the section to individual households. The section is then cleared, burned, fenced, and planted by the men of the village, who usually work together as a group. A garden magician oversees the main steps of garden preparation, plant tending, and harvesting, carefully evaluating the efforts and encouraging the men to exert themselves. In a prominent position in the garden section are "standard plots" (*legwota*) cultivated by distinguished community members; they serve both as the focus for garden ritual and as exemplars for all plots in the section. Whereas in simpler societies subsistence production is largely a household concern, in the Trobriands significant gardening decisions are taken away from the household and centralized in the ritual specialist.

Warfare, although apparently less intense than among the Enga, certainly exists in the Trobriands (Powell 1960). Local groups fight each other at least occasionally, especially during famines but also, as we shall see, for explicit political purposes. The decreasing intensity of warfare reinforces Feil's more general point (1987) that the evolution of regional polities regulates warfare and creates conditions of comparative peace. Chiefdoms and chiefly confederacies are zones of peace that benefit local groups at the same time that they support emergent leadership institutions.

The intensification of cultivation has also led to trade in subsistence products. Soils on the islands are a thin layer over the coral, and a soil's fertility depends on its thickness and development. Some areas, especially northern Kiriwina, are considerably more fertile than others. Productivity on the best soils is nearly double that of average soils and four times that of poor soils (Austen 1945: 18). Communities in highly productive areas concentrate on agricultural production; people in communities with more marginal lands are more likely to specialize in fishing or crafts, trading their products for staples.

Fishing is the most important specialized activity. Except in the best agricultural areas, villages tend to be located on the coast, where both inshore fishing (in the shallow lagoons) and offshore fishing are practiced. Some fish are traded for yams and other produce. The development of this local exchange, sometimes referred to as "fish-and-chips reciprocity," is decentralized and unorganized by chiefs; coastal and interior people trade on an individual basis, using traditional exchange rates. Of course chiefs are indirectly important to trade, since they maintain the intercommunity peace that makes trade possible. Other specialties are also important, notably the manufacture of polished stone axes, baskets, various objects of carved wood, and lime that is chewed with betel nuts to release a stimulant.

Trade with other island populations is important to the Trobriand economy. Certain goods, such as clay pots and stone for axes, are not available on the coral islands of the Trobriands. These imported products are economically significant; stone axes, in particular, are essential to efficient horticultural production. Traded food products, such as sago from Dobu, also add variety to the diet and provide a critical food source in years of severe need. The surplus yams available in good years can be used to obtain valuables in the *kula* exchange (described below), and in bad years the valuables can be exchanged, directly or indirectly, for needed food.

To summarize, the population of the Trobriand Islands faces four critical economic problems resulting from intensive production on small coral islands: a high risk of food shortages; intergroup warfare; considerable local variability in subsistence production, necessitating internal exchange; and a pressing need for external trade for purposes of obtaining food and manufactured products not available locally.

Social Organization

Settlement Pattern. The village of a ranking chief presents the salient unit for analysis, with its characteristic arrangement of household and storage structures (Fig. 11). The village arranges private and public spaces in a way that mirrors the division and integration of the subsistence and political economies. Private space, encircling the village, contains the residences and small storage structures of the member households. The household, with its separate residence, storage building, and work space, is the focus for the domestic economy. The yams from a family's garden plot are harvested as needed and not stored (Weiner 1976); yams received in obligatory exchanges, however, are placed in an enclosed storage structure.

In the center is the public, ceremonial space, where the dance ground, the chief's display storage structures, and the chief's residence are located. On the dance ground are performed ceremonies that define the group's corporate character and display its economic well-being to outsiders. The large central storage structures are constructed with open spaces between side-wall logs to permit viewers to see the concentrated wealth of the chief and his supporters. These stores are used to finance such chiefly activities as the hosting of village ceremonies and the construction of trading canoes. The chief's own house, similar to other houses but larger, is at the edge of the central dance ground, where it appears to dominate the group activities of the village.

Other settlements, without ranking chiefs, have no central public area, except for a simple dance ground. Settlements often form clusters, with a chiefly village dominating. On a more regional scale a few chiefs have come to control larger areas, and their villages are the most elaborated. The settlement system is thus hierarchically organized, with larger public dance grounds, display storage structures, and elite residences found at the political centers. Here ecological and spatial factors play off against each other (Irwin 1983). Within a region, the centrality of a settlement determines the rank of its leader; chiefly villages are located with best access to other villages and thus are able to direct the flow of diverse resources. The overall productivity of a region affects the relative status of its chiefdom.

The Family and the Dala. The household is the basic economic unit of subsistence production and consumption. Average household size is only 3.2 (Powell 1960: 119), primarily organized as a nuclear family with a husband, wife, and those of their unmarried children who have not moved into village bachelor houses. Each household owns its separate house and storage structures and has a separate garden plot in which it grows food for itself and surplus yams for exchange.

The main division of labor is by sex (Malinowski 1929: 24–27). Men do the heavy agricultural activities including clearing land, erecting fences, and planting; they are also the main traders and the specialists in canoe construction and wood carving. Women do the gardening (especially the weeding), collect shellfish, prepare food, care for children, and produce goods that include mats, banana leaf bundles, and skirts made from those bundles (Weiner 1976). By and large, food procurement activities are dominated by men and food preparation by women; craft work is shared but differentiated into male and female crafts. Where communal labor is not involved, the household organizes the basic division of labor in production (Malinowski 1935: 355).

Beyond the household the most important unit is the small village, a residential population of about sixty-five persons who typically represent a *dala* (Weiner 1976). The *dala* is a corporate group that owns a territory used for farming; membership is matrilineal, but residence is virilocal and somewhat complicated. Among those who must reside with the *dala*'s head, or "manager" (ibid.), is his oldest sister's oldest son, who is next in line for hamlet leader. The village also includes some non-*dala* members who receive land from the hamlet head, notably his own sons. The small village is therefore a composite group of matrilineal kinsmen and supporters and their families.

The village is important both economically and politically. Economically, as we have seen, it organizes and manages food-planting activities. Joined to this managed cycle of horticulture is a land tenure system based on group ownership, with rights of allocation vested in the leader (see esp. Weiner 1976). The *dala* owns the land, but the *dala* leader, by controlling its annual allocation, controls effective access to it. A household can obtain land only from the leader, who has considerable freedom in allocating land to non-*dala* members. This link between the control of land tenure and the developing political economy foreshadows the economic basis of the more institutionalized Polynesian chiefdoms. The small village, rather than a simple kin group, has become a flexible political support group.

In addition, the village is organized ritually by its leader. As we have seen, he may designate another villager as his garden magician, but the leader is the "owner" of magic, which is especially important in gardening, and he is the initiator of ceremonies at the dance ground.

The Local Group. Two to six small villages form a local group or village cluster of some three hundred people. This group is highly endogamous; prior to pacification, warfare was prohibited between the constituent hamlets. Intermarriage between hamlets binds the village cluster into a social unit interconnected by many affinal exchanges, notably the annual yam exchanges. Each farmer farms several yam plots, some for his family's needs and at least one for exchange.

When a man's daughter or sister marries, a large payment of yams must be given annually to his son-in-law or brother-in-law. Malinowski (1935) analyzed this payment as compensation to the woman for her rights in the subclan territory, which she gives up when she joins her husband's household; Weiner (1976), as we shall see, has a different hypothesis. Whatever the explanation, the pattern of endogamy and affinal exchanges results in high economic interdependence within the cluster. Although these exchanges do not take place over a region large enough to buffer the group against major economic disruption, they are helpful in the event of local crop failures or the temporary incapacity of a household's workforce.

The most important role of the local group cluster is political. The several *dala* or small villages composing the cluster are ranked socially with respect to each other, and the leader of the highest-ranked *dala* serves as cluster leader. This is apparently a true office, with explicit leadership responsibilities for coordinating group activities in ceremonial and group defense. Although the position may not always be filled, the expectation is always that it will be, in due course, by a deserving candidate. The cluster leader seems to be financed largely by marrying women from the various *dala* and thus obligating his male in-laws to provide a huge quantity of yams, which are then stored in display yam-houses and used to support ceremonial occasions. By manipulating marriage and exchange ties, a chief can bring a support group into what Malinowski (1935) calls a tributary relationship.

As with the Tsembaga or the Central Enga, one justification for this local territorial group may have been defense. Prior to British pacification, warfare was endemic on the Trobriand Islands. The cluster, although itself not a corporate group, was organized as a defensive unit; warfare was prohibited within the cluster and mutual defense required. In the developing political economy, warfare between politically powerful chiefs served to establish and maintain a cluster's privileged position. For example, in 1885 the ruling chief of Omarakana made war on a neighboring chief who had refused to give him a wife and, by implication, accept a tributary relationship; the Omarakana chief won and laid waste the defeated chief's villages (Powell 1960). As we shall argue for the Hawaiian case in Chapter 11, warfare in chiefdoms becomes transformed from simple competition over land to competition over rule and its implied control of land and labor.

Regional Relations and the Chiefdom. The importance of political competition between chiefs for regional control of groups helps to distinguish the Trobriand case from the Big Man systems described in Chapter 8. A high-ranking chief can extend his economic support base and area of political control by marrying women from other village clusters, receiving as a result a flow of yams amounting almost to a tribute payment. According to Malinowski (1935), both the permitted number of wives and the size of yam payments depend on the rank of a woman's husband. If the husband is a high-ranking chief, the yam payment is considerably higher: all male members of the woman's *dala*

are required to provide yams. By marrying many females from many
dala over a broad region, a high-ranking chief becomes the center of an
extensive system of mobilization. The potential extent of this system is
illustrated by the powerful chief of Omarakana in the 1930's, who Malinowski (1935) claims had some eighty wives!

Weiner (1976) notes that the flow of yams to chiefs is balanced by
important reciprocal flows of goods, and notably by the large distributions of "female wealth"—skirts and banana leaf bundles—at the
mortuary ceremonies of the *dala* of a yam-giving man. In essence, a man
receiving yams in his wife's name is obligated to purchase female
wealth for her to distribute at these ceremonies. Her distribution of
wealth at the mortuary ceremony is then a measure of his renown and
reliability in a broader system of ceremonial exchange and display. A
chief and his wives form reciprocal relationships in which wives are essential for political ambition. Kinship obligations and women's ceremonial positions permit the mobilization of a political surplus and
status display.

Sahlins (1963) found two main points of contrast between the ideal
types of the Melanesian Big Man system and the Polynesian chiefdom:
the size of the polity and the nature of leadership. The Big Man polity is
characteristically small (consisting of a few hundred people); larger
units tend simply to segment into independent factions. Leadership is
based on a man's personal demonstration of ability in the course of representing his support group in competitive displays (as in the Enga and
Northwest Coast examples; see chap. 8). A chiefdom is characteristically larger; it is achieved by organizing local communities in a regional
hierarchy based on the inherited rank of their respective leaders. Positions of leadership constitute offices with explicit attached rights and
obligations. Chiefs thus "come to power" that is vested in an office—
rather than building up power, as Big Men do, by amassing a personal
following. Social status in chiefdoms is inherited, based upon an individual's genealogical position in a social hierarchy, and access to power
through office is accordingly confined to specific elite personages.

Leadership among the Trobrianders presents an intermediate form
within the variability of the New Guinean Big Man and the Polynesian
chief (Powell 1960). Both locally and regionally, social status is based on
the established rank of a person's *dala*, which is itself dichotomized into
elite and commoner subgroups. Only a man born in a high-ranked *dala*
can accede to power. The leader of a village's highest-ranked *dala* (if
there are more than one) is the village leader; the village leader from the
highest-ranked *dala* of a cluster is the cluster leader. A cluster leader
from one of the highest-ranked *dala* in the region can then use the

privileges of his rank to acquire multiple wives and extend his power base regionally to form a support group of up to several thousand members. This pattern of inherited status, established political offices, and regional integration identifies Trobriand society as a chiefdom, but with elements of a system based on the Big Man pattern.

External Relationships and the Kula. Beyond the cluster level, a chief's status is based not only on the rank of his *dala* but also on his successful participation in highly politicized ceremonial events, notably competitive yam harvests and *kula* voyages. As we have seen, a high-ranking chief, married into many local subclans, collects exchange yams from a broad support region; each presentation of yams is accompanied by a ceremonial welcome of the presenter and the display of the yams in massive piles before they are stored away in the chief's yam-houses. Yams are both a direct measure of the productive might of a chief's support group and the main capital with which to finance his future political moves. By displaying them in this fashion, in contrast to the private, enclosed storage houses of the commoners, the chief asserts his economic power.

Kula voyages are made for purposes of ceremonial exchange between the Trobrianders and other island peoples. In the Trobriands they are organized by a high-ranking chief and involve the obligatory participation of all canoes belonging to chiefs in his *kula* district. Following a preliminary amassing of valuables and other goods, the canoes set sail, stopping first at a small island where the initiating chief ceremonially distributes food to the participants. On the next day the canoes proceed to the island where the exchange is to take place.

The *kula* is a well-described traditional system of exchange (Belshaw 1955; Leach and Leach 1983; Malinowski 1922). The islands involved, covering a relatively large extent of ocean off eastern New Guinea (roughly 210 miles from north to south, and 270 miles from east to west), exchange many valuables and utilitarian goods. The most important valuables in Malinowski's time were shell necklaces (*soulava* or *bagi*) and conus shell armband pairs (*mwali*). The two valuables circulated in exchange for each other and in opposite directions around the ring of islands: the *soulava* clockwise and the *mwali* counterclockwise (Malinowski 1922: map V). The utilitarian objects included pottery and carved bowls, raw materials such as stone for axes, and agricultural products.

The valuables of the *kula* extend political power in the Trobriands. Severely limited in their exchangeability, they form a separate sphere of exchange (cf. Bohannan 1955). Since *kula* objects are exchangeable only for each other, their distribution can be tracked and controlled by chiefs. With the institutionalization of chiefdoms, prestige goods become increasingly important for status display, and control over their distribution becomes a critical part of the political strategy (Earle 1982).

In a typical, large *kula* voyage, a flotilla of canoes from the Trobriands arrives at an island, such as Dobu, where the Trobrianders line up according to social rank and are ceremonially greeted by the Dobuans. The Trobrianders then disperse among the Dobuan hamlets to meet their trade partners. In some cases a partner has earlier received a gift from a Trobriander and must now reciprocate with an equivalent valuable; in other cases the Trobriander approaches a partner and solicits a desired valuable with gifts of food or crafts. The Dobuan may then give over the valuable, with the expectation of a return gift on his next voyage to the Trobriands.

During the actual handing over of valuables a strict decorum obtains: a show is made of disparaging the quality of a gift received and exaggerating the quality of the gift presented, with a view to increasing the stature of an individual or a group by imputing greater worth to its valuables than to those of its trading partners. At the same time that these valuables are being exchanged, utilitarian goods from the different islands are exchanged by barter. Thus *kula* voyaging creates what is in essence a market, in which people from different regions exchange locally specialized food and crafts with all comers, negotiating exchange equivalence by bargaining.

When their business has been done, the Trobrianders set sail for home, often stopping at several islands on their return. Before landing in the Trobriands the flotilla again stops at the small island, and a special comparative display of the valuables takes place. As described by Malinowski (1922: 375): "From each canoe, a mat or two are spread on the sand beach, and the men put their necklaces on the mat. Thus a long row of valuables lies on the beach, and the members of the expedition walk up and down, admire, and count them. The chiefs would, of course, have always the greatest haul, more especially the one who has been the toli' uvalaku on that expedition." This display is a direct measure of individual success in the *kula*, and after the voyage, word of personal accomplishments and disappointments quickly spreads through the communities.

Competition and display are integral to the political maneuverings of individuals, especially chiefs. By encouraging production and manipulating exchange, a chief publicly demonstrates his political prowess and the economic capability of his support group. Success in both production and exchange depends on initiative and manipulation by all participants. In the *kula*, for example, although valuables travel in prescribed directions, much care and discernment goes into selecting the specific recipient of a valuable from among all those who desire it. In giving his valuables and solicitory gifts, a chief calculates the prospective return both in future valuables as such and in increased status for himself and his group.

Although status is ascribed to a leader according to his *dala* affiliation, his renown can be either augmented or tarnished by his successes and failures in the public display ceremonies. Indeed these successes and failures may alter the ranking of the *dala* itself (Uberoi 1962), as status rivalry adjusts political and social position.

Conclusions

Why did the incipient stratification and institutionalization of political hierarchies evolve in the Trobriands and not in seemingly similar societies? For two reasons, deriving respectively from the political economy and the subsistence economy. First, in the political economy, the social differentiation inherent in the institutionalized leadership on the Trobriands is underwritten by differential access to the means of production and distribution.

External trade, as we have seen, is essential to both the political economy and the subsistence economy, and chiefs are able to monopolize this trade by their ownership of seaworthy sailing canoes (Burton 1975). These trading canoes are technically complex, consisting of a large hollowed-out trunk, a free board, frame, and outrigger, a mast, and a pandanus leaf sail; they are thirty to thirty-five feet long and capable of carrying a dozen men and heavy loads of goods. Making a trading canoe requires the careful attention of a specialist and considerable manual and ritual labor, and only ranking chiefs, with access to yams and valuables, can afford the expense. Thus the control over production and exchange, made possible largely by control over capital, has led to social stratification and a self-perpetuating elite.

Yet as Malinowski (1935) was quick to recognize, chiefs are equally indispensable in the daily lives of the Trobrianders. Characteristically, small islands are ecologically unstable and poor in resources. As a risk management strategy, Trobriand chiefs act as "tribal bankers," investing the surplus made available in a normal year or a good year in capital equipment such as canoes, in foreign trade for nonlocal materials and craft goods, in the political ceremonies that determine individual and group status, and in wealth valuables. In a bad year, when there is no surplus, the chief's management of production guarantees a sufficiency for subsistence needs. Chiefs also, by establishing and maintaining foreign trade relationships through the *kula* exchange system, provide access to markets essential for the smooth operation of the local economy: markets where in good years surplus food can be traded for a wide range of products and in bad years valuables can be exchanged for food.

The power and elite status of the Trobriand chief depends on the centralization and control of the economy. As we have seen, this control stems in part from the requirements of long-distance exchange and in part from the requirements of risk management. Once control was in their hands, chiefs extended it to include monopolies over the production of certain key resources generally desired by the population, among them coconut (important especially for oils, which are scarce in the diet), betel nut (chewed as a stimulant), pigs (a major source of protein and fat), and stone axes (important for clearing land for gardens). Coconut, betel palms, and pigs were apparently owned exclusively by chiefs (Austen 1945; Malinowski 1935), and axes, made from imported stone, were ground by specialists working for chiefs (Malinowski 1935).

In simplest terms, the subsistence economy of the fragile and isolated Trobriand Islands could not be successfully intensified without leadership to manage the production cycle and external exchange. Such conditions in and of themselves do not produce chiefs; rather the intensification process in certain situations offers possibilities for control. In the Trobriands these possibilities include the land tenure system, the storable surplus, and the capital technology of trade. It is by controlling such elements of the subsistence economy that a chiefdom comes into being and perpetuates itself.

ELEVEN

The Complex Chiefdom

THE TROBRIANDS REPRESENT comparatively simple chiefdoms constructed on the structure and ideology of the kin group (*dala*) and its affinal relationships. In this chapter we examine the more complex chiefdoms of Hawaii and the special case of the Basseri of Iran. Since Polynesia encompasses the full range of chiefdoms from simple to complex, from polities of several hundred people to one of a hundred thousand, it is worth discussing the Polynesians generally before examining in detail the unusual, complex chiefdoms of Hawaii, which represent the fullest extent of Polynesia's evolutionary development.

The scattered islands of Polynesia extend from Tonga and Samoa to Easter Island and from New Zealand to the Hawaiian chain. Across this immense region of the Pacific are found clusters of islands, often distant from their nearest neighboring island group. These islands vary in size from the large land mass of New Zealand (which comprises 102,000 square miles) to the tiny coral islets of the Tuamotus just south of the equator, and in climate from temperate to tropical. The larger island groups, such as the Hawaiian Islands and the Society Islands, are dominated by chains of volcanic mountain peaks; they vary in size from large young islands such as Hawaii (4,038 square miles) to small, eroded remnants and coral atolls.

Prior to European contact these isolated lands were colonized and inhabited by the Polynesians, and their common origin made for considerable similarities in language, material culture, subsistence practices, and other traits from island to island. For our purpose the most important element of Polynesian cultures is their sociopolitical organization as chiefdoms. Differences between these oceanic polities help us understand the processes involved in the development of chiefdoms to the very threshold of statehood.

Fundamental to the organization of Polynesian chiefdoms was the principle of social inequality based on inherited status. Each chiefdom was composed of a conical clan with embedded lineages (Fig. 12). The senior line, shown in thick black, was ideally represented by the first son of the first son of the first son, etc. Junior lines were founded by second or third sons, whose descendants formed the lineages of the clan (cf. Kirchhoff 1955). The rank of a man and his descent group was based on his birth order within the household: the second son's descent line was inferior in rank to the first son's, and so on.

In theory, at least, each person and each lineage in the system had a unique rank based on distance from the senior line; the closer to the senior line, the higher the rank (as shown by the numbers in Fig. 12). In practice, rank tended to be restricted to a chiefly group composed of the senior line; junior lines rarely troubled to calculate rank distinctions. Although chiefly titles were usually inherited patrilineally, a line was not exogamous and membership was characteristically cognatic.

Many a junior line, dissatisfied with its inferior rank in the clan, set itself up as an independent local chiefdom. Such chiefdoms competed fiercely for the control of land and commoners, and rank became more determined by genealogical position and by political domination resulting from conquest warfare (Goldman 1970).

At each level in the social hierarchy of groups, leadership was exercised by the chiefly line of highest rank. A chief from a local group's senior line organized and directed group activities. When local groups were organized as regional entities, the highest-ranked local chief coordinated regional ceremonial cycles and military operations.

The Polynesian chief was both a sacred person, closely linked to ancestral gods and instrumental in ceremonials, and a secular leader, responsible for organizing military action, directing economic activities, and adjudicating internal disputes. Since any activity requiring the group to act together was in the chief's domain, his secular and religious aspects were closely conjoined and mutually reinforcing.

In the Polynesian chiefdom, explicit offices of leadership, positions marked by special status, existed whether or not they were filled at any moment. Each group in a hierarchy of nested groups (local community, district, island chiefdom) had such an office, with the offices of subgroups ranked according to status relationships. In Figure 12, numbers 1, 5, 9, and 13 are lineage heads; 5 is subservient to 1 as leader of a larger segment, and 13 is subservient to 9. All are subservient to 1, the paramount chief of the conical clan.

Broadly speaking, each office conveyed to its holder both the right to mobilize labor and goods as needed, to support himself and his relatives and to fulfill his obligations, and the obligation to maintain order

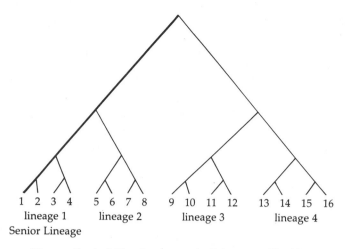

1 2 3 4   5 6 7 8   9 10 11 12   13 14 15 16
lineage 1   lineage 2   lineage 3   lineage 4
Senior Lineage

Fig. 12. Conical Clan Structure of a Polynesian Chiefdom

and productivity within the group. Officeholders were explicitly entrusted with performing ceremonies considered necessary to meet ritual obligations to the gods, maintaining a strong military posture, keeping internal order, and creating and maintaining productive facilities such as irrigation systems, terraced fields, and fishponds.

Polynesian chiefdoms were financed by redistribution, a form of tributary taxation (Earle 1977). By prerogatives of the office, chiefs could amass staple goods produced by commoners. Some of these goods were kept by the chiefs for their personal use, but most were used to compensate people who worked for the chief in the various activities needed to meet the chief's obligations and to maintain the chief's dominating position and imposing lifestyle.

In Polynesia the continuum from simple to complex chiefdoms was well represented (Goldman 1970; Sahlins 1958). Indeed, Polynesian ethnography offers an excellent opportunity to consider how an overarching sociopolitical organization can be maintained despite inherent tendencies to fragmentation. As we have seen, political units often split along lineage lines, with the senior line of a lower-ranked lineage (for example, number 9 in Fig. 12) becoming a separate chiefdom in competition with the original senior line (as represented by number 1). On some islands, such as the Marquesas (Handy 1923) and Tongareva (P. Buck 1932), chiefdoms characteristically fragmented into small polities of a thousand or so. On others, such as Tonga (Kirch 1980) or Hawaii, chiefdoms expanded to incorporate populations numbering into the tens of thousands. What, then, were the conditions that discouraged fragmentation? For it must be these conditions that allowed for the growth in the size of the political system and the development of new institutions to solve the problems created by this new scale.

Case 13. The Hawaiian Islanders

At first contact (in 1778), the Hawaiian Islands had a population of perhaps two to three hundred thousand (Nordyke 1989; Schmitt 1971), divided among four large competing chiefdoms. These chiefdoms, which are considered by researchers (Earle 1978; Goldman 1970; Hommon 1976; Sahlins 1958, 1972) to represent the highest stage of sociopolitical development in Polynesia, are examined here in an effort to ascertain the factors responsible for the evolution of chiefdoms to the threshold of state society.

The complexity of Hawaiian chiefdoms is seen in their social stratification and evolved regional institutions. The society was rigidly divided into two classes, commoners and chiefs. The commoners were the rural cultivators, fishermen, and producers of crafts. Their genealogies were shallow, seldom reckoned past the grandparents' generation, and their ranking and interhousehold organization were informal and ad hoc. A number of related households might live close to each other and cooperate in joint economic ventures, but there is no evidence of a lineage or corporate structure for commoners. Certain commoners were Big Men, in the sense that they were successful farmers and organizers, around whom clustered small groups of households in the community (Sahlins 1992: 208). But the communities, like peasant villages in states, were organized by an egalitarian ethos, set within the regional hierarchy of the chiefdom.

By contrast, the chiefs were organized into various ruling descent groups associated with the major islands of Kauai, Oahu, Maui, and Hawaii. In theory, a person's rank, and by extension his rights to office and support by related chiefs, was determined by his distance from the senior line; this distance was not easily computed, however, because a person received status through both his mother and father, and ruling chiefs accordingly retained genealogical specialists to evaluate individual claims to rank and position. Marriage was important as a way of accruing status for offspring. An elite chief could marry an elite woman only; and a high-ranking chief was polygynous, both within his ruling line, to solidify the political position of his children, and outside his line, to build alliances to other lines. Competition for ruling positions was fierce, and marriage and descent were highly politicized and carefully planned. Women were key political players who held positions as community chiefs, but the paramount chief was always a man, although he could come to power through his wife's inherited rights to an office (see Earle 1978 for the examples from Kauai).

Population estimates for the prehistoric Hawaiian chiefdoms range from about thirty thousand (on Kauai and Niihau) to about one hundred thousand (on Hawaii). Typically, a major island and its closely associated smaller islands were ruled as a single complex chiefdom. Although attempts were made to extend a chiefdom by the conquest of other major islands, these attempts usually failed because of difficulties controlling such large and widely separated populations.

The Environment and the Economy

The Hawaiian Islands consist of seven major islands located in the north-central Pacific, just within the tropics at 20°N latitude. Isolated from all other major land masses by more than two thousand miles, this chain of islands is composed of the peaks of a volcanic mountain range. The geological age of the islands, and thus the extent of their erosion, varies greatly. The large island of Hawaii still has active volcanoes, and its broad, sloping surfaces have few valleys and permanent streams. By contrast, Kauai is heavily eroded with deep canyons that carry water from the central mountains to the sea. Most soils are volcanic in origin, but the most productive soil is the alluvium found in the eroded valleys and along the coastal plains at the valleys' mouths. The amount of alluvial soil varies greatly, depending on the development of the stream systems (see Earle 1980b; Kirch 1977).

Rainfall is another important factor for environmental variation. At sea level the expected annual rainfall in this area of the Pacific is about sixty inches. The distribution of rain is uneven, however, owing to the diverse size of the islands. On the windward side of the islands, rainfall typically varies from about sixty inches at the coast to three hundred inches or more in the central mountains; on the leeward side rainfall is much reduced by a rain shadow and is often less than twenty inches. Variation in rainfall and soils is a critical determinant of differences in local subsistence strategies.

As we have seen, population density for the seven islands at contact has been estimated at thirty-nine persons per square mile. But much of the islands' landscape is steep and broken terrain, and much is too high or too dry for the tropical root crops grown by the Hawaiians. At the low elevations where most of the population was concentrated, usually within a mile of the coast and near streams, densities ran to over two hundred persons per square mile.

As a result of these locally high population densities the subsistence economy depended primarily on intensive agriculture. Irrigation, terracing, and drainage systems were devised that permitted permanent, year-round cultivation. The dominant crop, taro (*Colocasia esculenta*), was grown in irrigated pondfields wherever water and soil conditions permitted (Earle 1980b; Kirch 1977). Pondfields, similar to the rice paddies of southeast Asia, consisted of short ditches from the many island streams that led water to terraced fields, each of which was a small pond with taro planted in the mud or on small mounds. The technology was comparatively small scale and easily managed, and yields were high. A major problem, however, was the concentration of these irrigation systems on the valley bottoms near the sea. A community's agricultural production was periodically wiped out by floods and tidal waves, which indeed continue to plague modern taro systems in the islands today (Earle 1978).

Where irrigation was impractical, short-fallow shifting cultivation was used for taro and in drier locations for sweet potatoes. Other crops included yams, sugar cane, arrowroot, and a number of tree crops, especially breadfruit and banana. Domesticated animals, among them pigs, dogs, and chickens, were also of some importance for protein. Pigs were particularly prized by the chiefs, who appear to have monopolized their husbandry.

Fish were a main source of protein. Men used fishing techniques, notably the *hukilau*, in which a large fishing party with nets encircled a school of fish in shallow water and dragged their catch to shore. Offshore fishing for pelagic fish, requiring special fishing equipment and large canoes, was also important. Along the shores and in the alluvial flats directly in back of the shore, fishponds were built in which small fry were raised especially for use by the chiefs (Kikuchi 1976). The technology of the ponds was simple, ranging from an enlarged taro pondfield to extensive areas enclosed by sea walls of rock and earth.

Other wild foods, although secondary, provided variety and additional protein. Shellfish and crabs were collected by women, seabirds were netted at offshore rookeries, feral chickens and pigs were hunted in the mountains, and many wild plant foods were collected. The interior of the islands, with little permanent habitation, were an important foraging zone. All in all, the diet of the Hawaiians, although heavily dependent on starchy staple crops, was good on the major counts of calories, protein, and variety.

The varied subsistence economy was of course a response to the environmental diversity of the high volcanic islands of Polynesia. There were three major zones in close proximity that permitted three very different types of exploitation: the alluvial bottomlands and gently sloping uplands for intensive agriculture; the shallow offshore bays and reefs for productive fishing; and the interior, "wild" forests for hunting and foraging. While Service (1962) has argued that chiefdoms frequently developed under such conditions to manage exchange among specialized communities, in fact, as we shall see, trade was remarkably limited and took place largely within community boundaries (Earle 1977).

Warfare would seem another likely outcome of the high population densities and the uneven distribution of productive resources from one locale to the next. Drawing attention to Carneiro's circumscription theory of warfare, Kirch (1988) notes that population growth in the naturally bounded island environment of Polynesia must pressure available resources and result in intergroup warfare. Warfare would then limit an individual's options, requiring membership in groups in order to guarantee access to the contested resources (Boone 1992). Although intergroup warfare over productive land characterizes smaller-scale chiefdoms such as the Maori (M. Allen 1996), in Hawaii warfare became primarily a political strategy designed to extend control.

As we will argue, most problems of production were handled at the family level or the local community level, although chiefs were undeniably important for managing risk and adjudicating intercommunity conflicts. More important, however, the particular form taken by intensification in Hawaii afforded opportunities for economic control that formed the basis for the development of social stratification.

Social Organization

Wittfogel (1957: 241) has argued that the development of irrigation systems in Hawaii required the development of a managerial system of chiefs and land managers that then formed the basis of Hawaiian political organization. Alternatively, Service (1962), discussing Polynesia in general, has argued that the environmental diversity of the islands required a centrally managed exchange system whose managers rose to power as chiefs. As we have argued elsewhere (Earle 1977, 1978), these theories are inadequate because neither irrigation nor exchange posed problems requiring a control system extending beyond the local community.

The independent nuclear family, organized along standard lines of division of labor by age and sex, could easily provide most of the labor needed in subsistence strategies (Earle 1978). Traditional sources often describe a rigid division of labor based on a cultural imperative to protect male mana, or sacred power (Handy and Pukui 1958: 176–78; Malo 1951: 27–30). Men and women ate separately, and a husband was responsible, at least in formal meals, for cooking taro in separate earth ovens for himself and his wife, as well as for pounding it separately into po'i. Women could not eat foods associated with the gods—such as pork—and the women could not enter the men's eating house, where offerings were made to household gods. Men were responsible for all work involved in the growing of the sacred taro, as women were responsible for the laborious pounding of tapa (bark cloth) used to dress both the family and the gods. A clear reciprocity existed in the culturally most important parts of domestic life. The husband gathered his close kin to collect the timbers and build the house frame, while women collected the thatching materials used by the men and wove the floor mats. While men worked in the taro fields and fished, women grew and collected other plants, such as the sweet potato, critical for the diversity of the family's meals and for its health. A sense of balance and appropriateness organized work within the family and across neighboring families.

The rigid division of labor described for the Hawaiian chiefdoms is most probably an exaggeration. The male-female division is largely a sacred-secular division that would most likely have affected chiefs, who were thought to be gods, and other men only when involved in sacred rituals. The archaeology of nonelite households does not display the division of space and specialized areas for cooking that the ethnohistory seems to indicate. We believe that the division of labor between men and women was probably flexible and complementary, except in public and sacred contexts associated with ceremonial occasions.

The most important food in the subsistence economy was taro, which was produced in irrigated gardens and upland fields. Irrigation systems were small and limited to a single local community; a system typically served only four or five farmers, and rarely more than twelve. Construction was apparently done by gradual extension; reconstruction—as today—was handled by small teams of workers. The historical records suggest that closely related families, brothers and brothers-in-law, lived together along a short ditch and cooperated in its maintenance. Although land managers certainly existed in Hawaii, they were not necessary for the irrigation systems.

As for exchange, the three major resource zones (inshore fishing, lowland farming, and upland foraging) were characteristically very close to each other; in many areas it is less than eight miles from the coast to the mountain peaks. A household located in the lower valley near the sea, as most households were, thus had access to all critical resources and was essentially self-sufficient. Where resource zones were more separated, as in some locales on the big island of Hawaii, households specialized to some degree in locally available resources. But because the land of a local community ran as a strip from the central mountains to the sea, exchange took place largely between households of the same community linked by close bonds of kinship (Handy and Pukui 1958). Exchange between households of different communities was not extensive and, where desirable, took place at small informal gatherings that functioned as simple markets (Ellis 1963 [1827]: 229–30). Individuals there exchanged ground stone adzes manufactured from local sources of basalt, and woven mats made of reeds available only in certain marshes. The system that the chief did manage, as we describe below, did not function as a commodity exchange system among specialized subsistence producers.

Chiefs and their land managers did, of course, have legitimate managerial functions, notably organizing the community's rebuilding efforts after periodic flooding and tidal wave damage, and controlling intraregional warfare by allocating use rights. We will return to the managerial roles of the chiefs after a discussion of the organization and finance of their domains.

Economic Control and Finance

The distinctive institution that developed in Hawaii was the generalized governing hierarchy of chiefs. Chiefs held positions at three levels according to their rank in the ruling line. At the apex of the sociopolitical hierarchy was the paramount chief. The owner of all lands, he allocated portions to his people in return for a share of the food, craft goods, and raw materials they produced and for their support in war. Competition for the paramountcy was intense, and at the death of a ruling chief the island characteristically split into warring regions supporting rival claimants. The victor in these wars of succession became the next ruler.

Second in the hierarchy were the district chiefs, high-ranking men of the ruling line with a strong private allegiance to the paramount. They were responsible for disseminating his orders and decisions to the community chiefs, and for mobilizing the goods and labor provided by the communities at his order. The district chief may have taken a share of the goods he mobilized for the paramount, but most of his income came directly from the individual communities allocated to him by the paramount.

Third were the many community chiefs (*ah'i 'ai ahupua'a*: "chiefs who eat the community"). A chief was usually a close relative of the paramount who had been his supporter; in return for his support he was awarded a community that provided his income. Each chief in the paramount's support group thus received what amounts to a land grant, but control over this land was dependent on the paramount and was typically reallocated by the paramount's successor. The chief in turn appointed a land manager who oversaw production in the community and performed a wide range of social, political, and religious duties. Land managers, like chiefs, were not people from the community; rather they were often chiefs' junior kinsmen. Land managers thus held the day-to-day responsibilities for community direction that are held by the local chief in simpler chiefdoms. They were specialists of a sort, but unlike the specialists we shall encounter in Chapter 12, they were not yet members of separate bureaucratic institutions. Their duty was directly to their chief, who was also usually a kinsman.

Warfare was an essential element of chiefly rule in Hawaii. Chiefs were warriors, and one of their functions was to maintain regional peace. Unlike the simple chiefdoms of the Maori, local communities in Hawaii were dispersed and unfortified. The regional peace of the island chiefdom allowed local communities to concentrate on production, as the chiefs guaranteed to local households their rights to subsistence plots. Boone (1992) emphasizes how competition for resources effectively limits the options available to a local household, making it dependent on the overarching chiefly polity. Warfare in Hawaii took on a strongly political dimension unrelated directly to competition for resources.

As in the Trobriand chiefdoms competition for high office was intense, among other things because income depended on position in the hierarchy. The warfare that followed the death of a paramount chief was not only for succession to the paramountcy but also for access to the full range of political offices and income estates. To obtain or retain an estate it was necessary to support a successful contender, and the land records accordingly show the wholesale replacement of chiefs with each succession.

In addition, there was a strong expansionist drive to acquire land by conquest from other island chiefdoms. These were granted as estates to the paramount's political supporters or provided added revenue for the paramount himself. Every paramount chief maintained a small cadre of highly trained military specialists for use in operations against neighboring chiefdoms.

Religious institutions helped to consolidate the chief's control. Throughout the chiefdom were shrines used to house the gods and to accommodate ceremonies conducted by priests drawn from the ruling elite. At large shrines dedicated to Ku, the god of war, ceremonies initiated and supervised by the paramount himself built a consensus for military action among his supporting chiefs. More common were small community altars used during the annual Makahiki ceremonies. For these ceremonies, Lono, the god of land and fertility, traveled around the island accompanied by the paramount chief. Acting for the god, the chief performed rites at community shrines designed to maintain the fertility of the community's land. In return he received food, craft goods, and raw materials. The ritual obligations and significance of the paramount were made explicit by these rites, which embedded the financing of the governing chief in a ceremony to guarantee the land's productivity.

The political economy, based on redistribution, financed the island chiefdoms. As we have seen, redistribution is tribute, and goods mobilized from subsistence producers are used to compensate warriors, religious functionaries, craft specialists, and other "nonproducers." In Hawaii the redistribution system was comparatively simple. For a specific operation, such as a large ceremony or military campaign, the paramount, in consultation with his immediate advisers, stipulated the goods and personnel needed and assigned quotas for each district. The district chief then allocated his quota among his communities, and the required goods and people were supplied by the households under the direction of their community's land manager.

By such means the Polynesian conical clan that originally organized small total populations by internal ranking was promoted and transformed into a generalized ruling institution, for which kinship and direct personal bonds remained the internal logic. The paramount could perhaps have known all chiefs, who probably numbered no more than a thousand in any chiefdom, but the commoners would have been largely faceless suppliers of the paramount's needs for goods and labor.

As the population of the chiefdom swelled from the low thousands to the tens of thousands, a new level of regional integration was required, one that would tie these faceless but indispensable commoners more securely into the system. A basis was found in the notion of restricted land tenure. Since all lands were owned by the paramount chief, the allocation of community lands to his supporters and the further allocation of small subsistence plots to commoners formed the basis for requiring payments in labor and goods. The chief's control of the basic productive resource of agricultural land was particularly clear when the chief's land manager organized the construction of capital improvements such as irrigation canals, terraces, or fish ponds. Subsistence plots in irrigated or terraced lands, with their high productivity, were allocated to commoners in exchange for a commitment to work on adjacent land owned by the chief. Each irrigation system was thus a mosaic of chiefly lands providing for political finance and commoner allotments providing for subsistence. An ideology of reciprocity between chief and commoner was thus established; commoners labored for the chief as a kind of "rent" for their subsistence plots.

This ideology of reciprocity can be extended more generally to a duality in the political economy. Subsistence producers, for their part, generated the wealth used by the chief to compensate nonproducing personnel, to invest in capital improvements, to make political payments that extended and consolidated his control, and to finance conquest warfare designed to enlarge his income. The chief's obligations to his subsistence producers were essentially reciprocal: to keep peace within the chiefdom and thus guarantee local communities access to productive resources; to make capital improvements designed to increase yields; to keep local families functioning as viable economic units; and to mediate as necessary between the local community and high-level religious and military institutions.

Hawaiian Prehistory: An Evolutionary Sequence

The evolutionary dynamics of the Hawaiian chiefdoms are best understood by examining their development over time. The history of this development, which can be reconstructed as a result of recent archaeological work, shows clearly the growth and elaboration of a chiefdom through three stages (Cordy 1974, 1981; Hommon 1976; Kirch 1982, 1984; Kolb 1994).

First was the stage of initial colonization and settlement, roughly A.D. 400 to 1200. The islands were apparently colonized before A.D. 500 by a small group (a boatload or two, perhaps fifty people) thought to have come from the Marquesas or perhaps the Society Islands (Kirch 1974). They were purposeful colonists, perhaps refugees, who carried with them what was needed to reproduce their society and economy. During the first eight centuries, when contact may have been maintained with their distant homeland, population expanded to fifty thousand by means of internal growth and new colonists. Early settlements were on the coast, occupying first the most desired locations where a mixed economy of fishing, simple horticulture, and irrigation could be practiced. Human-induced environmental changes included the extinction of many island birds (Kirch 1983), and over time domesticated foods such as pig increased in importance over fishing (Kirch and Kelly 1975). The archaeological evidence provides little evidence for social differentiation early on; the society was probably organized at the community level.

During the second stage, A.D. 1200 to 1500, the population grew rapidly to several hundred thousand (Dye and Komori 1992) and expanded into the interior, probably using shifting cultivation and small-scale irrigation. On the small island of Kaho'olawe, for example, nearly 50 percent of the population occupied the interior, but already by A.D. 1500, perhaps because of soil degradation, the interior was abandoned and populations moved back to the coast and likely to other islands (Hommon 1986). At this time in the Halawa Valley of Molokai, massive land slumps, changes in land snail populations associated with depleted forests, and an increased amount of carbon in the soil testify to expanding slash-and-burn horticulture, forest clearance, and heavy erosion (Kirch and Kelly 1975). Significantly, the upland erosion deposited alluvium that built the coastal plains, and on all major Hawaiian islands irrigation farming expanded (J. Allen 1992; compare Spriggs 1986).

The archaeological evidence indicates the formation of regional chiefdoms during this second stage (Kolb 1994). Social stratification is indicated by a differentiation in house sizes and forms, with the larger houses presumably those of the elite (cf. Cordy 1981). Religious shrines (*heiau*) appeared and grew in size; since these shrines were linked historically with ceremonies of chiefly legitimization and required a corporate effort to erect, they provide good evidence of chiefly organization. Chiefs were probably important in this period both as managers of intensified horticulture (as in the Trobriands) and as military leaders. Their control was enhanced by their circumscribed island environment, which severely limited the options of a dependent commoner.

During the third stage, from 1500 to 1778, the population may have initially continued to grow but later appears to have stabilized (Dye and Komori 1992; Kirch 1982). The major change was in agriculture (Kirch 1985). Shifting cultivation continued and was even expanded in areas of moderate slope, where erosion could be controlled by terracing (Ladefoged et al. 1996; Rosendahl 1972). At the same time that population growth stalled, there appears to have been a significant transformation in the Islands' agricultural capacity. Under chiefly supervision, communities built the highly productive irrigation systems that created an intensively farmed, entirely artificial environment producing diverse crops in addition to taro and fish. Each system was neatly divided into farming units that both provided subsistence for the working families and surplus for support of the chief. That is the basis for the staple finance economy that we have already described.

At this moment, the European explorers, traders, whalers, missionaries, and plantation farmers arrived. The external relationships quickly allowed the young paramount Kamehameha to conquer competing chiefdoms on Maui and Oahu and to institutionalize the new

Hawaiian state. The Western technologies of war, including large ships, cotton sails, and guns, bridged the isolation of the islands, and Western principles of law and government were studied by the rulers as models for their new state.

An age of opulent display followed, as the Hawaiian lords materialized their new institutions of statehood with the elaborate trappings of the European royalty whom they emulated. In what Sahlins (1992) called "the political economy of grandeur," Hawaiian chiefs adopted Western dress, housing, and military display. The lavishness of this new consumerism bankrupted the Hawaiian economy, and chiefs began selling their estates to American missionary families anxious to develop profitable plantations for sugar. The dynamics of the political economy that reached out to Western technologies and consumer goods created the conditions for rapid involvement with the world economy and colonial incorporation by the United States.

The evolution of the Hawaiian chiefdoms over fourteen centuries illustrates the close relationship between the subsistence and political economies. The push of a natural potential for growth found fertile ground in the alluvial soils of Hawaii. Chiefs managed the construction and maintenance of the irrigation systems that supported an expanding population, and the social economy then acted as a social cage that required commoners to surrender time to their chiefs in return for the use of that highly productive agricultural land. The surplus from the chiefs' lands financed the elaboration of the regional institutions of the chiefdoms with attached craft specialists, priests, managers, and warriors. The complex Hawaiian chiefdoms, with their tight mechanisms for control, were grounded in the fertile soil of irrigation where water, food, and power flowed through the hands of the ruling chiefs. Following "discovery," the islands became linked to the world economy, and the chiefs' control was quickly lost to the expanding ambitions of the West.

Case 14. The Basseri of Iran

The Basseri (Barth 1964) are organized as a regional chiefdom, with a number of local segments under a single paramount chief. The Basseri chiefdom is based on the management and control of subsistence trade between settled farmers and a pastoralist population using marginal lands at the outer limits of control exercised by an agrarian state. In fact, the efforts of a weak feudalistic state to extend its control over independent pastoralists helped create the Basseri chiefdom, both as a means to defend Basseri nomadism against outside interests and to gain resources and political advantages from the state (cf. Beck 1986: 9).

The Environment and the Economy

The Basseri number some sixteen thousand people living in three thousand tents along the arid steppes and mountains of Fars province in southern Iran. A well-defined political group under the authority of a paramount chief (khan), they move within a delimited corridor twenty to fifty miles wide and extending some three hundred miles from high mountains near Shiraz in the north to low deserts near Lar in the south. Basseri population density is about two persons per square mile. Both the higher elevations, up to thirteen thousand feet in the mountains near Kuh-i-Bul, and the lower ones, two to three thousand feet in the deserts near Lar, are unsuitable for agriculture. The sedentary farming populations, which outnumber the pastoralists by about three to one in the whole of Fars province, cluster in the middle altitudes, around five thousand feet. Small groups of Basseri follow carefully planned migration routes, which they must share with neighboring pastoralists such as the Qashqa'i (Beck 1986; 1991), around and through the farming regions to utilize the more extreme environmental zones.

Climate determines the broad outlines of Basseri migration. Although annual rainfall throughout the region averages only ten inches and agriculture is possible only with irrigation, precipitation is heavier in the higher elevations, where it is stored through the winter and spring in snow packs. In the winter, and in the spring as long as good pasture remains, Basseri camps are found in the low-elevation deserts to the south. As summer approaches and vegetation withers, the camps move northward, following the receding pastures toward ever higher mountains, where melting snows sustain late-season grazing. By autumn the mountain pastures have dried up or been grazed out, and herders must move into the agricultural zone, where they pasture their animals in recently harvested fields before returning south.

The economy centers on the production of meat and milk from mixed herds of sheep and goats. No cattle are raised; donkeys, horses, and camels are kept in small numbers for transport. Sheep and goats reproduce well in this environment, but early frosts and contagious diseases can kill as many as half of them in a bad year.

Milk is not consumed fresh but is immediately processed into sour milk or junket, then either eaten in that form or further processed into cheese. Sour milk may be pressed and sun dried in the spring, when milk production peaks, and stored for use during the following winter. The Basseri eat meat frequently, always fresh and never preserved by drying or salting. Animal hides and wool become tents, clothing, storage containers, ropes, and other products. Women spend a significant part of their time spinning and weaving.

For all the importance of meat and milk, the Basseri diet is actually dominated by agricultural products obtained through trade with farmers. Wheat is basic; an unleavened bread made from wheat flour is eaten with every meal and is the single most important foodstuff. Sugar, tea, dates, fruits and vegetables, utensils, and many other items are also obtained by trade in exchange for clarified butter, wool, and lambskins.

Some Basseri own plots of agricultural land on which wheat and other cereal crops are raised. A few Basseri actually farm these plots, but most disdain agricultural work and contract with sharecroppers from nearby agricultural villages. The Basseri view these plots as investments in security and economic well-being: a way of banking profits generated by successful herding, and a means of upward mobility for the elite.

Social Organization

Even more so than among subsistence pastoralists such as the Turkana (Case 8), the basic economic unit among the Basseri is the family, which alternates between the settlement patterns of tent (nuclear family household) and camp. The tent typically houses a nuclear family and an occasional added member; it is a self-contained production unit, particularly at that point in its developmental cycle when adolescent sons are available for herding. All the required productive property, including tent, rugs, utensils, sheep and goats, transport animals, and containers, is owned by the individual family, and little is shared with other households.

A tent household needs about a hundred goats and sheep for a satisfactory subsistence. These are not shared in reciprocal arrangements with relations or friends in other ecological zones but are concentrated in a single herd directly supervised by the household head and his sons. Men with unusually large herds will contract out a part of their herd to poor herdsmen, who then pay a share of meat, milk products, and newborn kids and lambs to their well-to-do patrons. Like peasant farmers (see Chapter 13), the Basseri use the market as a source of security instead of relying on extended social networks. In a good year they can sell surplus animals and buy land, which stores wealth securely and generates income that can be used to replenish herds after a bad year. Since they depend on the market for the agricultural foods that are the mainstay of their diet, what they need most in bad times is money and other secure property.

Soon after a couple are married, the groom's father releases his son's share of the anticipated inheritance from his herd. The newlyweds move into their own tent and strive to become economically autonomous. Since it is inefficient to use a vigorous adult male exclusively for herding a small flock, households commonly cluster in a hamlet-size group of two to five tents whose occupants travel together and share herding duties. In forming such groups, ties of friendship established over years of mutual aid are as important as kinship. Friendship also provides the basis for trading partnerships with agriculturalists. But the autonomy of the household is primary, and tent groups will disperse and reaggregate as conditions warrant.

In the winter, when tent groups are scattered throughout the sparse, low-elevation pastures in the south, large clusters of tents are rare. But at other times, when pastures are richer and more localized, tent groups form camps of from ten to forty tents. Camps travel together and, although they are liable to fission, are held together by cross-cutting ties of descent and marriage reinforced by endogamy.

Each camp has a recognized leader, but just as the camp has little formal structure, so its leader has little economic or political power. His primary role is to help smooth relations between households, to resolve disagreements over where to locate, and to control the constant pressure from independent-minded heads of households to break up the camp. Despite this pressure, camps are fairly stable and enduring units. Not only do ties of kinship and friendship help protect households against economic setbacks, but many families are reluctant to separate from the group out of fear of strangers, whom they distrust as thieves. Barth (1964: 47) describes the Basseri's view of their camp as "a small nucleus of human warmth surrounded by evil." Actual violence between camp groups is rare, and warfare is unknown. Indeed, despite the mutual suspicion between camps and the norm of endogamy, one-third of all marriages are between members of different camps; mobility between camps is not uncommon.

We thus have a picture of the Basseri as autonomous tent households or tent groups in self-centered pursuit of good pasture and largely unfettered by structural constraints on access to resources. Friendship is important in day-to-day economic cooperation, and leadership is based less on the control of wealth than on personal distinction and service as a negotiator and compromiser. Such a description could apply as readily to the pastoralists we have discussed in earlier chapters.

In this case, however, the political economy centers on the *oulad*, a larger group than we have encountered among our other pastoralists. *Oulads* are territorial units, averaging from forty to one hundred tents (that is, about the size of the local groups examined earlier), in which membership is rigorously determined by patrilineal descent, reckoned simply as direct descent from a distant ancestor and not involving a segmentary system of lineages and sublineages. Within an *oulad* relations remain informal, and economic life centers on tents and camps.

The *oulad* is easier to understand if we examine the economic role of the Basseri's paramount chief. He is simultaneously a Basseri chief and an elite member of the larger agrarian society. As a member of the elite he is much wealthier than other Basseri, owning thousands of animals, agricultural lands, and even whole villages. He and members of his family own houses in the city of Shiraz and move comfortably in elite urban circles.

One of the chief's functions is to allocate pasture rights to his subjects; the *oulad* is the corporate unit that receives these rights, in the form of an *il-rah*, or "tribal road." The *il-rah* specifies a definite route for the *oulad* through the Basseri region's various ecological zones and the precise pasture locations available to the *oulad* at each stage of the yearly cycle. Hence it is possible for more than one *oulad* to pasture its herds in the same location without causing conflict as long as each does so at a different time, according to its *il-rah*. The chief generally allots pasture to *oulads* according to their traditional *il-rahs*. But when demographic change causes one *oulad* to have an excess of pasture relative to the needs of another, the chief calls the heads of the two *oulads* together and works out new *il-rahs* to which the members of each *oulad* must adhere. Since all pastures in southern Iran are owned by somebody, individuals have no access to resources apart from the lands guaranteed to their *oulad* by the chief.

In the political economy of the Basseri, the *oulad's* territory is somewhat analogous to the village lands of the peasant community (Chapter 13). As in a peasant village, the households of an *oulad* are largely independent, self-contained domestic economies with less risk-sharing and kin-structuring between them than we find among the lineages and clans of the village-level and Big Man societies examined in Chapters 6 to 8. This is so largely because the superordinate state has taken over two functions that would otherwise be performed by kin groups: the defense of territory, now entrusted to a legal system that protects property rights; and risk-spreading, now entrusted to a market whose existence is protected by the state.

For these reasons the *oulad* is not the center of negotiation, network building, and conflict resolution that the local group is in less complex societies. It does not even have a leader, but only a spokesman who communicates messages from the chief in his absence. When the chief is present, individual heads of household address their concerns directly to him rather than to an intermediate official.

We view the Basseri chief as having two main functions in the political economy. First, he manages the use of pasture land in order to avert the "tragedy of the commons" (Hardin 1968), the degradation that occurs when family herders compete opportunistically for scarce pasture. He can impose restraints on pasture use that individual herders would not impose on themselves, since without group controls another herder would simply take the pasture for his own herd. He is empowered to impose his will by means of fines and beatings. He alternates his residence between town, where he cements his social relations with other elites, and country, where he travels with an entourage from camp to camp, holding "court" by handing down decisions, collecting tribute, and distributing wealth to especially deserving or needy followers.

The chief's second function is to represent the Basseri to other segments of Iranian society. As Barth points out, the Basseri are a distinct subunit of this society, set apart from its peasant and urban segments by their nomadic lifestyle and by deep ethnic divisions. When a Basseri comes into conflict with a farmer, for example, his mobility is a threat to the farmer, just as the farmer's ready access to the court system is a threat to the Basseri; direct negotiation between such different people is difficult. The chief, however, can take up the matter with the farmer's overlords, who are the chief's class equals; that is the way in which many such conflicts are resolved.

To summarize, the Basseri subsistence economy centers on the cyclical migration of tent households and camps in search of pasture for small, independently owned family herds. Separate camps, even when they are members of the same *oulad*, are in competition, distrusting and avoiding one another. This individualistic economy, however, is limited by a scarcity of pastureland and the necessity of coexisting with peasant farmers under state rule; careful regulation of access to land is necessary to avoid both interpersonal squabbles and overgrazing. A major share of total production is sold in the market, where staple foods and essential materials are obtained.

A paramount chief is needed to maintain order in the countryside, to protect the group from the destructive effects of unimpeded individual exploitation of the environment, and to act as a broker between his subjects and outsiders. In return the chief takes advantage of his central position to maintain exclusive paramountcy over the Basseri, and he uses his knowledge of the market system to garner exceptional wealth for himself and his family.

In the last half of the twentieth century the way of life of pastoralists like the Basseri has come under increasing threat (Beck 1991). The main changes have been:

1. Growing population density has increased pressure on all land resources in Iran.

2. The land, long dominated by human use, has come under increasing intensification as agriculture has spread to every available corner and the burden of animals on pasture has increased. Pastures today tend to be rocky, dry barrens:

[T]he vegetation upon which they relied took the form of scattered hardy ground plants and small shrubs. Reminiscing, men described lambs frolicking in new spring grass that was so tall and dense that one spotted only their ears occasionally poking from the lushness. Such memories were apparently not exaggerated: conditions for pastoralism had generally been much better before the 1950's. Since then, overgrazing and the destruction of trees and shrubs for fuel (which caused the loss of nearby ground vegetation) had created serious environmental degradation. (Beck 1991: 50)

3. As pasture becomes scarcer and more contested, households without strong local leaders are more vulnerable to losing their traditional grazing rights. This strengthens the authority of local leaders, increasing the importance of their role as broker between poor, uneducated herders and an increasingly complex landscape of urban capitalists, regional police, and governmental agencies.

4. Economic integration and political stratification strengthen as government and private business increase their control over land. Urban capitalists, with herds in excess of twenty-five thousand animals, now pay cash for grazing rights to land previously used by migrating pastoralists. They either try to prevent herders from using these pastures or require payment to compensate them for the lost pasture they now claim as their own (ibid.: 60).

5. In a manner similar to what happened in the developing economies of feudal France and Japan (Case 15), as the landscape fills in, property relations become more competitive and more tightly defined—registered in official documents and enforced by police and other governmental agents—a form of circumscription that reduces the range of choices available to the household and increases opportunities for elite control.

6. A developing capitalist economy, which is to say the growth of a centralized nation-state integrated by a market system, has increased governmental access to formerly distant areas by means of roads, military vehicles, and air travel. National and foreign interests have used this access to influence land use and political alliances among pastoralists, in-

troducing new economic interests (capitalist farming, ranching, and exploitation of oil and other resources). Even as groups like the Basseri take on more complex and orderly political hierarchies in response to these developments, their subsistence base is increasingly under siege and may eventually disappear. In the intensifying market economy, commercial ranchers are likely to replace nomadic pastoralists, just as millennia ago Neolithic pastoralists replaced the mobile hunter-gatherers who had preceded them (compare the Nganasan, Case 4).

Conclusions

Let us now examine chiefdoms and their evolution in terms of our three key evolutionary processes: intensification, integration, and stratification.

Intensification of the subsistence economy, although important as an underlying process, appears to be much the same in the chiefdom as in the Big Man societies described in Chapter 8. Population density is characteristically high (about twenty-five persons per square mile) but well within the range possible for Big Man societies and in some cases quite a bit lower. As in simpler societies, the forms of intensification vary with environmental conditions, ranging from the short-fallow, slash-and-burn cycle of the Trobrianders to the bottomland irrigation agriculture of the Hawaiians. Only the tightly regulated pasture use of the Basseri is not found in simpler societies.

It is interesting to note that the long-term trend toward a narrower, simplified, and thus potentially inferior diet that we observed in Chapters 6 through 9 is not evident in the chiefdoms we have examined. The Hawaiians enjoyed a remarkably varied diet, thanks to a diverse environment with many resource possibilities to which regional peace permitted them access. In the Basseri and Trobriand cases, external trade in subsistence products was important for dietary variety.

Integration is dramatically more in evidence in the chiefdom than in simpler societies. Leadership is institutionalized at both the local and regional levels, and chiefs at both levels are routinely relied upon to organize centralized exchange and storage, to construct facilities for the efficient production of staple products, to organize military operations, to guarantee land use rights, to mediate internal disputes, and to negotiate or manage external trade relationships.

We can identify the main causes of the evolution of centralized societies as being risk management (Athens 1977; Gall and Saxe 1977), warfare (cf. Boone 1992; Carneiro 1970b), technological complexity (Steward 1955; Wittfogel 1957), and trade (Sanders 1956; Service 1962).

Whether alone or in combination, it is argued, these prime movers, themselves an outcome of population growth and intensification, require central management and thus underlie the evolution of complex societies. This functionalist logic sees cultural evolution as adaptation, the solution of particular problems brought about by population growth under particular environmental conditions.

A similar logic is expressed by the nineteenth-century Hawaiian chief David Malo (1951 [1898]: 187): "The government was supposed to have one body (*kino*). As the body of a man is one, provided with a head, with hands, feet and numerous smaller members, so the government has many parts, but one organization. The corporate body of the government was the whole nation, including the common people and chiefs under the king. The king was the real head of the government; the chiefs below the king, the shoulders and chest." As Rathje and McGuire (1982: 705) point out, this biological analogy also underlies modern functionalism and its analysis of social systems. For Malo, a Hawaiian chief brought up before contact with Western missionaries, the ruling chief, as the body's head, provided the essential direction for society. To this Polynesian, a society without a ruling chief would be as unthinkable as a body without a head.

Are the functionalists correct? Can we explain the evolution of social complexity as a necessary correlate of intensification of the subsistence economy? Not quite, we think. Intensification is indeed necessary, but not sufficient; the crucial matter of control, as distinct from management, must also be considered. To put this another way, intensification of the subsistence economy necessitates centralized management, but some forms of management do not necessarily lead to the formation of chiefdoms. It is the particular forms of intensification favoring central control that result in chiefdoms and provide the opportunities for political growth.

Stratification involves the differential control of productive resources, and it is this control above all that distinguishes chiefdoms from simpler societies. Chiefdoms are based on generalized central leadership, as are Big Man societies; but a chief has sufficient institutionalized control over his society's political and economic organizations to be able to restrict leadership to an elite segment. Such control, based on restricted access to critical economic resources, may derive from any of four major conditions, which vary from place to place:

1. Central storage, instituted originally as a way of handling risk but providing control over capital for use in political affairs (Earle and D'Altroy 1982; D'Altroy and Earle 1985).

2. Large-scale technology, desirable to a local population for minimizing production costs but requiring a major capital investment that bonds subsistence producers to the chief (Gilman 1981; Earle 1978).

3. Warfare in naturally circumscribed regions, which requires leadership but allows the victorious chief to control a subjugated population (Carneiro 1970b; D. Webster 1975).

4. External trade, which may be necessary to a local population or attractive because of strong external demand but which is not available to most individuals because of the high costs of transport technology (Burton 1975) and the difficulties of intersocietal contracts.

Once regional control is established, the evolutionary development of chiefdoms toward greater centralization depends on investment opportunities and the costs of controlling or defending whatever investments are made. Some investments, such as irrigation agriculture and marine-based trade with foreign states, offer an exceptionally large potential for control and growth; these characteristically underlie the evolution of states, to which we turn in the next chapter.

TWELVE

The Archaic State

STATES ARE REGIONALLY organized societies whose populations number in the hundreds of thousands or millions and often are economically diverse. In contrast to chiefdoms, the populations of states are usually ethnically diverse as well, and state power depends on balancing and manipulating the divergent interests of these groups. Whereas chiefdoms vest leadership in generalized regional institutions, in states the increased scope of integration requires specialized regional institutions to perform the tasks of control and management. The military is responsible for conquest, defense, and often internal peace; the bureaucracy is responsible for mobilizing the state's income, meeting many local managerial responsibilities, and, more generally, for handling and monitoring information flow; the state religion serves both to organize production and to sanctify state rule. Along with this elaboration of the ruling apparatus comes increasing stratification. Elites are now unrelated by kinship to the populations they govern; their power, underwritten by economic control, is displayed in the conspicuous use of luxury goods and the construction of splendid buildings.

The ethnic, institutional, and class divisions in state societies create competing interests and divergent sources of power. Although the size of states implies a strong integration, the integrity of the polity is always elusive, appearing on the verge of dissolution into its constituent parts, which are often on the scale of chiefdoms (see Mann 1986).

State formation has been a central theoretical concern in anthropology, at least since the time of Lewis Henry Morgan (1877). Service (1977) distinguishes two anthropological perspectives on state origins: integration theories and conflict theories. Integration theories derive from cultural ecology (Binford 1964; Service 1962, 1975; Steward 1955) and systems theory more generally (Hill 1977; Flannery 1972; Wright 1977); they view the state as a new level of social integration necessi-

tated by new problems of risk (Gall and Saxe 1977), technological complexity (Wittfogel 1957), and trade (Rathje 1971). Conflict theories emphasize either conquest, whereby one ethnic group comes to dominate
others (Carneiro 1967; Ibn Khaldun 1956 [1377]), or class conflict (R.
Adams 1966; Engels 1972 [1884]; Fried 1967); they view the state as a
mechanism for maintaining the social, political, and economic domination by one segment over another.

These two theories are not mutually exclusive, and in fact they identify two interdependent processes. On the one hand, states are born out
of conflict and domination: one ethnic group becomes the ruling elite of
a huge empire, and imperial institutions operate to maintain and to
strengthen this domination. On the other hand, states develop and
function under certain basic conditions that both permit economic control and require central management; local populations are bound economically to the state through a carefully managed dependency that is
a consequence of long-term intensification in the subsistence economy.

A further division in theories of cultural development has arisen
between unilinear and multilinear evolutionists. Unilinear evolutionists have sought to identify a single line of development reflecting the
causal influence of one dominant variable or prime mover, notably
technological progress and increasing energy capture (Leslie White
1959) and the managerial requirements of irrigation (Wittfogel 1957).
By contrast, multilinear evolutionists (Steward 1955) have seen the development of new levels of complexity taking parallel but distinct lines
in accordance with local environmental conditions.

Capital-intensive technology is perhaps the most common basis for
the developing political economy of states. Increasing population density requires a level of agricultural intensification that ultimately can be
achieved only by large capital improvements such as irrigation systems. Although regional management of irrigation is necessary only for
those massive systems constructed well after state formation, irrigation
systems even on a fairly small scale permit economic control by elites,
who exchange access to irrigated areas for labor or shares of produce.
States based on the control of productive technology are typically financed through staples produced on state-controlled improved lands.
This form of staple finance, often associated with the "Asiatic mode of
production," formed the financial base of most primary states, including those of Mesopotamia and Egypt. The Inka state, discussed in this
chapter, is another good example.

Trade as a source of income for state finance is probably most important on the peripheries of agrarian states. In the eastern Mediterra-
nean, the rise of the Mycenean and Athenian states was based on mer-

cantile trade and the large-scale production of export goods by slave labor (Engels 1972 [1884]; Lee 1983; Renfrew 1972). The Aztec state, with a comparatively small bureaucracy in conquered areas, depended for its finance on tribute, often in wealth goods, and the expansion of both long-distance trade and local markets (Berdan 1975; Brumfiel 1980). In this chapter the evolution of medieval France and Japan from simple, staple-financed, chiefdomlike societies into well-financed states is attributed largely to the development of an integrated market system made possible by an increased exploitation of mercantilism and trade.

Although technology and trade are analytically separate sources of wealth, in practice they are usually interrelated. As might be expected, states typically seek out multiple sources of finance to maximize both the amount and the stability of their income. States that were initially dependent on staple finance, such as China, actively encouraged the development of currency, market exchange, and long-distance trade as new income sources. Indeed, there is a general tendency to replace staple finance with wealth finance because of its greater flexibility, storability, and, most important, mobility (D'Altroy and Earle 1985).

State development is closely linked to the development of broad-scale economies that, raising overall efficiency, create increased potential for surplus production. As a rule, states originally depend on the corporate control over land that forms the basis of staple finance. The high productivity of developed irrigation systems lays the economic foundation for all pristine state formations in coastal Peru, highland Mexico, Egypt, the Middle East, India, and perhaps China. The Inka empire illustrates how management of intensified agricultural production, in addition to handling risks of crop failure and warfare, provided the surplus to fund a strong state.

Wealth-finance states appear later, tied to the development of marketing and trading systems on the edges of primary states. These "secondary states" (Fried 1967: 240–42) derived wealth from managing trade. As we discuss in Chapter 14, the power and productivity of the market ultimately underlies the development of modern states, wherein the peasant is supplanted by the specialized farmer or agribusiness that produces for the increasingly urban and distant market.

Case 15. France and Japan in the Middle Ages

We now turn away briefly from our ethnographic and archaeological examples to examine some familiar historical materials. Our two examples, medieval France and Japan, are widely separated both spatially and culturally. Yet when the layers of aesthetic, technological, social, and philosophical differences are stripped away—when all that remains is the small set of variables that forms the core of our model of social evolution—we find astonishing similarities between the two societies. This is true even of their rates of change: although the specific complex of changes occurred at different points in the histories of the two countries, roughly the same time elapsed in each case between one stage of development and the next. Thus the first Middle Age occupied the tenth and eleventh centuries in France and the fifteenth and sixteenth centuries in Japan, whereas the second Middle Age occupied the twelfth and thirteenth centuries in France and the seventeenth and eighteenth centuries in Japan.

By referring to leaders of the Middle Ages as "kings" and "emperors," scholars have tended to exaggerate the extent and depth of centralized power available to those leaders. Applying the neutral standards of the previous chapter, we find medieval France and Japan to have been populated with communities ranging from simple to complex chiefdoms, with many areas not integrated beyond the family level or the local group. Under the relentless pressure of continuous population growth and its handservant, the intensification of production, the landscape filled in and the proportion of the countryside that was brought under chiefly control increased, as did the complexity of chiefdoms.

The term "feudalism" is also misleading for at least two reasons. First, we find that many "feudal" institutions, such as the establishment of personal bonds of fealty between lord and vassal, the obligation of military service to the lord, and the granting of estates in land to loyal vassals, are hallmarks of the economic organization of chiefdoms. That is, they are not uniquely "feudal" in and of themselves. Second, some of the uniqueness or idiosyncrasy of medieval society and economy in France and Japan comes from the strong cultural influence of imperial Rome and China, respectively. For example, whereas in chiefdoms the language of social relations, including hierarchical ties, remains rooted in kinship even when actual genealogical distance between individuals may be very great, medieval France and Japan used legalistic language to describe and enforce the various levels of the hierarchy. Yet beneath this largely formal difference the operation of the "feudal" economy, in such central matters as the control of land and capital improvements and the transfer of production to the elites, is essentially that of a chiefdom. A growing awareness of these similarities between medieval society and chiefdoms has led to some illuminating historical reconsiderations, notably of the Viking age in Denmark (Randsborg 1980).

Imperial Precursors

The Middle Ages of both France and Japan were influenced by contact with external empires. France had been under Roman control for centuries. Japanese rulers were fully aware of the politically developed Chinese state and, perhaps alert to the dangers of a powerful neighbor, had adopted a centralized legal system modeled on that of the Chinese. It was the "ghost" of these externally derived imperial political structures that gave their successors a degree of political structure uncommon in chiefdoms (Asakawa 1965: 196; Hall 1970: 77).

On paper, the Merovingian (400 to 687) and Carolingian (687 to 900) rulers of France, and the emperors of the Nara (646 to 794) and Heian (794 to 1185) periods of Japan, owned all the lands of their respective countries and ruled by decree. The subsequent growth of powerful regional lords who challenged the emperors' supremacy has been generally seen as a kind of "devolution" or "decay" of centralized power (e.g., Duus 1976: 61; Hall 1970: 75–134; Lewis 1974: 25–27), often explained as the inevitable consequence of the greed or inefficiency of the rulers. In this view the re-establishment of centralized rule at the end of the Middle Ages appears as a stage in a cyclical process of state formation, dissolution, and reformation.

Clearly, however, the centralized states of the late medieval eras in France and Japan were utterly different from the states that preceded them. In earlier times the territories claimed by the so-called emperors were settled by subsistence farming communities at the relatively low population densities characteristic of horticulturalists. Warfare was endemic, and political life centered around war chiefs allied in tenuous federations. In some places population densities were higher; for example, in the ninth century the region around contemporary Paris was settled by forty thousand peasants organized into eight political units (Duby 1968: 12). Such areas were characterized by significant intensification and local centralization, and they no doubt paid ample tribute to their rulers. But in both France and Japan these islands of control were surrounded by dangerous, unstable territories that were "owned" by the emperor in name only.

In France, slash-and-burn agriculture was practiced in sparsely settled areas, but intensive horticulture was already the more common pattern. The use of pigs, horses, cattle, sheep, and goats was widespread. Short fallows were common, and in some places even more intensive techniques were found: the plow (usually the light wooden *araire*), annual cropping, crop rotation (incorporating legumes), dikes, and manuring (Lynn White 1962: 40–77).

Japan was a hunter-gatherer economy until rice technology was adopted, perhaps around 250 B.C. Dry rice cultivation coexisted with foraging until about A.D. 300 to 600, when chiefdoms and archaic states arose in close association with irrigated wet rice cultivation. Taeuber (1958: 15) describes the feedback between population growth and technological change that accompanied the spread of wet rice agriculture:

That change took place very gradually in Japan, spreading from the southwest northward and eastward. At first it was a process of supplementation rather than substitution, but even in this early state the amount of food was increased. The demographic consequences involved both an increased rate of survival because of more regular and more adequate nutrition and a lessened incidence and severity of famine. Once people had increased in number, there was a strong compulsion to extend the cultivation of the soil and so secure the increased amount of subsistence essential to the survival of the greater number of people. The growing number of people whose survival was permitted by agriculture thus stimulated the further development of agriculture.

By imperial times, regions of population concentration showed such signs of intensification as irrigation, manuring, and transplanting, all of which increased rice yields per unit of land (Tsuchiya 1937: 60–78).

This basic pattern—localized population concentrations with intensive production surrounded by large regions of dispersed population and more extensive production—is reflected in other domains of the French and Japanese economies as well. In the central areas, economic specialization, markets, and money were of real, if limited, importance; but in peripheral regions roads were poor or nonexistent and subsistence production dominated. In the central areas, too, the new military technology of iron weapons, armor, and warhorses was beginning to create a specialized fighting force, in contrast to the lightly armed fighting forces to which nearly every able-bodied man of the peripheral areas belonged. The new equipment was expensive, and warriors so armed could be maintained only with the income of large estates granted by the emperor.

In short, the medieval eras of Japan and France began in times of authoritarian centralized control of smallish regions of intensifying production surrounded by larger regions not subject to central control and characterized by long fallows, some foraging, intercommunity warfare, and unpredictable political alliances. In each case the earlier extension of imperial control over the peripheral areas left its mark, but the economic base of these areas could not support a state. When the empires collapsed they were replaced by warring chiefdoms. The developments to which we now turn represent not so much the resurrection of formerly powerful states as the internal evolution of society resulting from the gradual filling in of the countryside and the accompanying socioeconomic changes.

The First Middle Age

A first Middle Age has been identified for France from 900 to 1100 (Bloch 1961: 59–71) and for Japan from 1334 to 1568 (Lewis 1974: 40–48). During this period we find a gradual, continuous unfolding of trends that were already visible in the premedieval era and that came into full bloom in the second Middle Age.

The contrast between "developed" and "undeveloped" areas remained marked in the first Middle Age, but the proportions slowly shifted in favor of developed areas. There was a steady growth of population and a dramatic change in food production (Taeuber 1958: 16). As population expanded, more and more land was brought under cultivation: in France there was an "incessant gnawing of the plough at forest" (Bloch 1961: 60) as the adoption of the heavy steel plow (*charrue*) made it possible to farm the dense, dark soils of river valleys like the Loire and the Seine. In both France and Japan regional lords intent on opening up their undeveloped lands offered farmers such incentives as private ownership of plots and low service obligations. In Japan the government and regional lords became active in undertaking major projects (such as swamp drainage and irrigation works) to create new areas of cultivable land. The resulting destruction of forest became so great that the Japanese state instituted forestry management programs (Nef 1977; Tsuchiya 1937: 126).

At the same time the use of existing lands was intensified to raise their productivity. In France a complex set of interrelated changes centered around the heavy steel plow. The plow opened up new lands to annual cropping but required a major investment in draft animals: first oxen, later the more expensive but more efficient workhorses. Draft animals were pastured on fallow fields, leaving their manure behind them; this change encouraged the aggregation of households into cooperative groups that rotated their fields together in order to pasture their animals in large fenced areas. A three-field system was devised whereby a household planted one field in winter wheat, another in summer crops (generally legumes), and left a third fallow, changing the use of each field every year. This system substantially increased productivity (Lynn White 1962: 40–77).

In Japan a similar intensification took place as irrigation was extended to increasingly marginal lands. Multiple cropping, draining of swamps, and the spread of new crop varieties made for a "great agricultural . . . revival" (Lewis 1974: 53). The threat of famine and intense land hunger are frequently mentioned in commentaries of this period. Population continued to grow, and average plot size per household began to decline. For efficiency in wet rice cultivation, households aggregated into self-sufficient cooperative groups that shared labor in periods of peak need (T. Smith 1959: 50–51).

At the beginning of the first Middle Age, settlement was still almost entirely in homesteads and hamlets spread across the countryside. Bush fallow and the foraging of secondary forest for wild foods were still common. There were few cities or towns, and trade was of minor importance to most people. But local lords were growing in power as their domains filled in with productive households, and their military power defeated imperial efforts to tax and regulate them. There ensued a time of intense warfare in which no large-scale, stable political centralization could take root.

Local lords had much in common with the more powerful chiefs described in Chapters 10 and 11. Kinship was sometimes still important in group formation, but truly tribal peoples disappeared as the warlords' power grew. A lord defended what he considered his territory by alliances if possible and by warfare if necessary. In order to maintain his private army, he allotted his dependents a share of the produce of a section of his territory in return for an oath of personal allegiance and service. Homage to a ruler was still viewed as an act of individual choice.

Population tended to cluster about the lord's residence. From early times it had been common for one house to exceed all others in size and complexity, a house in which the group's common property was stored and from which cooperative and defensive measures were organized (Mayhew 1973). As population grew, these nuclei gradually became manors surrounded by a peasantry dependent on the manor for protection and security. Beyond the orbit of the manor, however, large depopulated zones existed, sometimes inhabited by scattered hamlets of "free peasants."

A warrior aristocracy arose, characterized by military prowess and strong ties of loyalty to their lord. The values of this class later became rigidified into the high ideals of chivalry (asceticism, fearless defense of the lord and one's honor, strength and skill in battle) that characterized the knights and samurai of feudal France and Japan. But in this earlier stage the rights and duties of lords and dependents remained fluid, personal, and negotiable.

The community centering on the lord's manor was self-sufficient. Roads and waterways were only beginning to expand, and markets were just beginning to appear in areas of greater population density.

Hall (1970: 113) finds it paradoxical that so much agricultural progress could be made in Japan during a time of economic decentralization and political instability. But there is no paradox if we view the process at the local level rather than from the standpoint of the imperial government. In both countries population pressure was increasing hand in hand with the intensification of food production, and the social division of labor was becoming more complex. In Japan we find workshops of artisans long before towns and cities emerge (Tsuchiya 1937: 82), and in France we find the manor serving to some degree as a center for accumulation and distribution of wealth (Bloch 1961: 236). Hence what seemed to an emperor to be a dismaying loss of control must have seemed on the local level to be a gratifying increase in population, production, interdependence, and economic and political order.

The Second Middle Age

The second Middle Age, or "high feudalism," appears in France between about 1100 and 1300 and in Japan between 1568 and 1868, a period preceding and including the Tokugawa shogunate. By this time more powerful rulers were emerging, roads and waterways were being built, and towns and free markets were arising throughout the countryside. Local lords, formerly autonomous, were now compelled to swear fealty to regional overlords, who had superior might and wealth. The power of these regional overlords remained tenuous, however, and they had to shore it up by frequent tours with a retinue through their provinces, accepting food and lodging from local rulers in the so-called "moveable feast" (ibid. 1961: 62; for Japan, see Hall 1970: 111). Such tours are common in chiefdoms, as we noted for Hawaii and the Basseri. They are a sign of a leader's weakness when compared with fully developed state rulers, who for the most part confidently reside in palaces and require their subjects to come and pay court to them. The great seventeenth-century shogun Tokugawa Ieyasu was evidently the first to achieve this degree of centralized control in Japan (Perrin 1979: 60; Taeuber 1958: 18). Hence we see the second Middle Age as a period of transition from a society divided into competing chiefdoms to one united as a single state.

Throughout the early part of this period population continued to rise, perhaps at a more rapid rate than before; Japan's population increased by 50 percent (to about thirty million, or about 260 persons per square mile) in the seventeenth century alone, but then leveled off and grew very little thereafter (Hall 1970: 202). The second Middle Age in both France and Japan has been described as one of great agricultural innovation and progress (Duby 1968: 21–22; Duus 1976: 83; Hall 1970:

201–2). Thomas Smith (1959: 87) speaks of a "new attitude toward change, though the reason for it remains obscure." New technologies were perfected and old ones more widely adopted; iron tools were used increasingly, irrigation spread, and new seed varieties were developed and distributed. In Japan the expense of fertilizer became a major cost of production, and commercial fertilizers prepared from fish cakes, fish oil, and human night soil were widely available in marketplaces. Average field size continued to decline and labor input per field rose; a kind of "involution" of labor (Geertz 1963; see Chapter 13) took place, as ever greater care was devoted to spacing plants, selecting seedlings, conditioning the soil, and the like. The use of draft animals, double-cropping, and commercial cropping also increased. Cultivation was expanded into previously uncultivated marginal areas, and peasants began to complain of the resulting loss of firewood, manure, and fodder (T. Smith 1959: 95).

We recognize all these changes, of course, as integral to the systematic intensification of production in response to population growth, and this would explain the new attitude toward change. It is not the case that the changes inaugurated a period of abundance and ease. To the contrary:

This problem of the inadequacy of the rice lands for the maintenance of people and economy has been a recurring motif in the history of Japan. In the early centuries, as today, the difficulties were twofold: the paucity of land and the overproduction of people. Within the political and social structure of the ancient world, no culture could escape permanently from this problem of population pressure and food deficiency. Malnutrition and famine were the final results of political stability and economic advance.

... There is a monotonous regularity in the accounts of agricultural improvements, new lands, famine, epidemic and decline. (Taeuber 1958: 15)

The most dramatic changes during the second Middle Age, however, took place in the economic, social, and political integration of production and exchange. Lewis (1974: 66) refers to this period as an "age of elaboration and legalism." As items manufactured in towns and artisan guild-communities played a greater role in agriculture, and as it became necessary to put more and more land to its most profitable use by growing single crops for sale rather than multiple crops for subsistence, the market became increasingly important. The great lords (in Japan, *daimyo*) could guarantee the peace of the market and the highway, and could issue money and otherwise support trade.

The whole fabric of medieval society tightened in the second age. Ties of dependence were established through formal rituals, signed legal documents, stricter rules of inheritance, and military conscription. Villages became the key social units beyond the household, defining who could use village lands and also serving as convenient units for taxation. At this point fealty was no longer a matter of choice; nearly everyone was someone's vassal, and what had once been "free peasants" were now "outlaws." Rights to receive rent, taxes, titles, stipends, and shares from the land were elaborately and carefully defined, and the peasants' "fund of rent" (Wolf 1966a) appears to have become continuously more oppressive.

Successful warfare now required large, heavily equipped armies. As the landscape filled in, a kind of "social circumscription" (Carneiro 1970b) made it possible for one faction, by a mixture of threat and compromise, to establish a stable central government uniting all the separate lords. As this process was completed, cities and trade grew rapidly. Manufacture and trade became alternative routes of power and wealth, and even the medieval lords became increasingly profit-oriented. Landless laborers appeared and became migrant wage laborers or servants in the homes of land-owning peasants.

Land ownership hence became a matter of great concern. New land surveys were undertaken, legal deeds of ownership accompanied the increasing tendency to buy, sell, and rent land, and peasant uprisings and revolts occurred over issues of land ownership. Some of these issues were increases in taxes and tithes; the frequency of famine (perhaps indicating the inability of the land to sustain population increases); the replacement of ties of loyalty based on kinship and personal allegiance by legal, impersonal ties enforced by courts and police; and the creation of landless peasants as the feudal protection of land access gave way to an increasingly free market in land.

In the Tokugawa era, Japan had sought to keep the outside world away by restricting trade and cultural exchange, but the steady growth of commerce and markets was an irresistible consequence of the growing intensification of production. We can see how the second age spawned a new order. In the place of a "pure feudalism" of autonomous regional lords, a single, powerful unifying ruler emerged. The lord's exclusive position in control of land-based wealth began to fade as wealth was acquired by rising groups of merchants, craftsmen, industrialists, and bureaucrats, all managing their parts of an increasingly complex economy. Leadership came to depend more on control of "exchange" than on the means of production (see Chapter 13). Improvements in transportation, the peace of the internal market, and centralized political power capable of setting foreign policy all increased the importance of trade and commercial production at the expense of the subsistence sector.

In sum, France and Japan in the Middle Ages developed gradually into states, propelled by pressures and opportunities arising from population increase and the intensification of land use. The growth of a peasantry coincided with the expansion of state-level political structures into tribal areas. At what point does the tribesman paying tribute to a chief become a peasant paying rent to a lord (cf. Bloch 1961: 243)? Although no precise answer is possible, the intensification of labor on the land, and the increase in stratification and bureaucracy at the expense of kinship and personalism, are all clearly associated, and a peasantry is the inevitable result.

Case 16. The Inka: An Andean Empire

The Inka empire, Tawantinsuyu, was the largest and administratively most complex polity of the prehistoric New World. The empire, which extended from what is now Chile and Argentina through Peru and Bolivia to Ecuador and Colombia, incorporated about 350,000 square miles and perhaps eight to fourteen million persons. In contrast to the simpler societies discussed earlier, the scope of political and economic integration of the Inka empire is profound. It exercised power directly over more than one hundred ethnic groups, themselves originally fragmented into many autonomous polities (Rowe 1946: 186–98), and over many diverse environments with special crops and unusual resources.

The rise to power of the Inka was phenomenal. At the end of the Late Intermediate period (around A.D. 1400) the Andean highlands were divided among many warring chiefdoms (Rowe 1946: 274). In the Mantaro valley, north of Cuzco, archaeology documents conditions in the highlands prior to Inka expansion (Browman 1970; Hastorf 1993; Matos and Parsons 1979). The first sedentary villages date to perhaps 800 B.C., and new villages were founded throughout the region as population slowly grew. Villages remained small (five to six acres), probably with populations in the low hundreds, but their locations shifted through time to higher locations, probably for defense.

Midway through the Late Intermediate period (about 1350) there was a dramatic social change. As population continued to grow, settlements increased rapidly in size and many were now located on ridgetops and hills. For example, the settlement of Tunanmarca, a comparatively large center (of fifty-three acres), was located on a high limestone ridge overlooking the Yanamarca valley north of Jauja. In addition to its fortress location, the settlement was surrounded by two concentric fortification walls. The residential zone had an estimated four thousand house structures that would have housed nearly ten thousand people and a central public plaza with several special buildings. Three smaller contemporaneous settlements located within three miles of Tunanmarca appear to have been politically tied to this center. In all, the Tunanmarca chiefdom incorporated perhaps fifteen to twenty thousand people.

Prior to the Inka conquest, the Mantaro valley and apparently most of the Andean highlands were fragmented into chiefly polities that were more or less constantly at war with each other. The Inka were able to build their empire by systematically conquering these formerly independent polities and incorporating their populations and political systems within the empire. How did they do it?

Their unprecedented success is largely attributable to their innovative principles of institutional finance, bureaucratic control, and indirect rule. The problem was to unify warring chiefdoms by creating a new level of integration. Institutions such as the broad system of labor taxation, though based on existing precedents and ideologies, were transformed to suit the larger and more complex needs of an empire. Essentially, the empire was built on the structure and ideology of chiefdoms, but with new hierarchical relationships superimposed.

Prior to the Inka conquest, long-term population growth had caused an intensification of the subsistence economy, violent military conflict, and the initial growth of stratified societies in the Andean highlands. The constant state of war had high economic and psychological costs that made the regional organization and peace of the empire desirable. Warfare was over land; essentially, each community fought to protect the land necessary to its survival. The imperial superstructure imposed regional peace and a system of legal rights of land use in return for labor obligations. The cost of maintaining this system had been significantly lowered by the long-term growth in population density, which lowered administrative costs, and by the increased dependency of the population on intensive agricultural methods (such as irrigation and terracing) that were easily controlled. Another advantage was the prior evolution of chiefdoms, which permitted the Inka to rule indirectly through existing political systems. Although the Inka conquest must still stand as one of history's most remarkable events, the basic prerequisites for it were already in place.

To understand the operation of the Inka empire, we consider the dual economic bases of social and political integration: the subsistence economy, supporting the population of local communities; and the political economy, financing the state and its special interregional institutions. Much of what follows is drawn from the valuable summary descriptions by D'Altroy (1992), Moore (1958), Murra (1975, 1980 [1956]), Rowe (1946), Schaedel (1978), and Wachtel (1977: 60–84).

The Environment and the Subsistence Economy

The Andes, home to the Inka empire, are a jagged chain of high mountains a short distance inland from and parallel to the Pacific coast of South America. Three environmental zones can generally be recognized. Along the coast is a dry and barren desert punctuated by green valleys that are fed by streams from the high sierras. The streams were used to irrigate productive agricultural fields near the coast, and rich marine resources added important animal foods. Inland the mountains rise rapidly above the coastal desert, and a central sierran zone follows along the Andean range. This sierra contains towering snow-capped peaks, extensive rolling grasslands, and some broad intermontane valleys. The grasslands were used for extensive pasturage, and the rich intermontane valleys for agriculture. To the east the land descends rapidly and is dissected by many steep valleys and cascading streams. Within thirty miles elevations may drop nine thousand feet from the high alpine grasslands to a humid and lush tropical forest. Highland groups lived in the upper reaches of these streams, but the forest environment itself was occupied by tribal groups—such as the Machiguenga (Chapter 4), a mere one hundred miles from Cuzco—that were never incorporated into the empire.

In part because of these zonal contrasts, Andean society was quite variable in form. Populations on the coast were densely settled, dependent on large-scale irrigated agriculture and fishing, and characteristically organized as complex states: notably Chimu, with its urban capital of Chan Chan (Moseley and Day 1982). Populations in the sierra were less dense, dependent on mixed farming, and characteristically organized as local groups or competitive chiefdoms. Thus the Inka organized very different ethnicities, societies, and economies within a massive political superstructure; this economic and ethnic heterogeneity is a hallmark of states.

In the sierra communities, represented here by the Mantaro valley, archaeologists have documented a sustained and fairly dramatic population increase immediately prior to the Inka conquest (Hastorf 1993; LeBlanc 1981). Population density under the Inka was about thirty-seven per square mile overall in the highlands (LeVine 1985: 450) and locally much higher. Thanks to a mosaic of different soils, precipi-

tation rates, slopes, and elevations (Hastorf 1993), the typical sierra settlement was an island or pocket of very high population surrounded by
barren landscape.

The subsistence economy was a mixture of permanent and shifting
cultivation of crops and animal husbandry. The crops included maize,
potatoes, and quinoa; the animals were chiefly llamas (for meat and
transport) and alpacas (for wool). Maize was grown in irrigated fields
below eleven thousand feet; potatoes and other root crops were grown
with shifting cultivation in the uplands up to 13,000 feet; and the llamas
and alpacas were grazed on the higher-elevation grasslands.

The long-term growth in human population resulted in a selective
intensification of agriculture. Similar to the Trobriands (Case 12), the
shifting cultivation of the uplands is frequently described by early
sources as involving a community-regulated fallow cycle (Rowe 1946).
Where feasible, capital improvements for permanent cultivation included irrigation, terracing, and drained field systems (Donkin 1979;
Hastorf and Earle 1985). A side effect of this intensification was an increased risk of crop failure as production expanded into valley bottoms, which are susceptible to flooding, and into uplands, which are as-
sailed by hail and frost. In modern times such risks are in part anticipated, and Andean farmers prefer to plant in many diverse locations as
a hedge against disaster.

Ethnohistoric studies (D. LaLone 1982; Murra 1980 [1956]) emphasize that the Inka were largely a marketless society. In the Mantaro exchange was remarkably limited, especially in food (Earle 1985). As in
the Hawaiian case, the extreme environmental diversity in the Andes
made a variety of resources available to local populations, thus limiting
the need for exchange between communities.

Warfare, as we have seen, was endemic before the conquest. Local
leaders questioned by the Spanish about the pre-Inka period described
its nature: "Before the Inca, they engaged in wars with each other in order to acquire more lands, and they did not go outside this valley to
fight, but it was within the valley, with those from one side of the river
which passes through this valley fighting with the Indians from the
other side" (Vega 1965 [1582]: 169). Other informants, sounding almost
like modern-day anthropologists, interpreted this warfare as caused by
increasing population and competition between communities for lands,
herds, and women (Toledo 1940 [1570]: 28). The growing population in
the Andes created the now familiar problems of agricultural intensification, with its associated technology and risk and considerable warfare. These local circumstances prior to the Inka conquest produced the
necessary conditions for creating the Inka state.

Social Organization

Andean community organization had two significant levels: the individual household and the *ayllu*, a kinship and territorial group. The individual household was probably a nuclear or minimally extended family composed of a married pair and their children, sometimes joined by a widowed parent, an unmarried sibling, or some other close relative. In contemporary traditional Andean communities this nuclear family household forms the elemental economic unit (Lambert 1973: 3; Mayer 1977: 61). Although we cannot simply extend this pattern back to prehistoric times, highland sites dating to the Inka and immediate pre-Inka periods were typically subdivided into small "patio groups" of several structures opening onto an open work space (D'Altroy 1992; Hastorf 1993; Lavallée and Julien 1973). These groups of structures, with one or two buildings and rarely with more than four or five, appear to have been family compounds in which the family's subsistence labors were centered.

A division of labor by age and sex permitted the household to approximate a self-sufficient producing and consuming unit. Men were involved in especially heavy activities such as soil preparation, warfare, many crafts, and long-distance trading. Women were responsible for many agricultural tasks, food preparation, child rearing, water carrying, spinning, and weaving (Silverblatt 1978, 1987). But the division of these duties was not exclusive, and men and women could help each other out. The focus was on the complementarity of male and female tasks, each required for the support of the household. Within the household balanced contributions to everyday life were relatively equal and reciprocal. In agriculture, for example, a couple formed a working pair: while the man turned over the soil with a foot plow, the woman broke up the clods; while the man made a planting hole, the woman placed the seeds in the previous hole (Rowe 1946: 213). As long as pasturage was relatively close to the main settlement, the young of both sexes were responsible for tending the herd animals (Murra 1965: 188).

To judge from contemporary traditional Andean communities, a goal of household independence was probably cherished. Contemporary households resist entering into reciprocal relationships with other households lest they prove expensive in terms of future demands on household labor (Lambert 1973: 17). Politically or economically, of course, interhousehold relationships may be essential for household survival; such relationships are avoided, however, wherever possible.

The *ayllu*, a kin group descended from a single defining ancestor, was used first to prepare the community's fields required to produce staples for the state and for the community chief; then they together prepared the fields for the community's households. Similar community ceremonies involved annual clearing of the irrigation ditches that watered the community's most productive fields; women prepared the food that fed the men whose work freed the water. The ceremonial nature of the work team materially defined the hierarchy of the community and its corvée obligations to the state.

A single local community typically maintained a generalized subsistence economy that permitted it to be largely self-sufficient, thanks to a diversity of subsistence strategies reflecting the diversity of its geographical zones. In the Mantaro valley, for example (D'Altroy 1992; Hastorf 1993), late prehistoric settlements of the Inka and immediate pre-Inka periods were located on the upland slopes and low hills overlooking the river. The upland soils there are ideal for growing potatoes, which provided the starchy staple for the diet. Below the settlements are alluvial bottomlands suitable for intensive maize production, and above the settlements are rolling grasslands used for grazing. Within a few miles of a settlement a community's population had direct and immediate access to a diversity of lands.

During the pre-Inka period, community ownership was probably limited to nearby resources, as hostile neighboring communities would have opposed any attempt to maintain more distant control (LeBlanc 1981; Rowe 1946: 274). Even the restriction to nearby resources, however, would have permitted considerable community self-sufficiency. Communities in different zones would have had access to different resources, and some intercommunity exchange seems probable.

A second type of resource control was exercised by the archipelago community, in which the main community settlement was many days distant from key resource zones such as the tropical lowland agricultural areas. The *ayllu* in effect colonized these resource zones, establishing satellite settlements there and arranging for the long-distance transport of goods by porters or by llama caravans. For the Inka period, this type of extended community control has been documented for various locations through the empire (Murra 1972), among them the Mantaro valley communities of the sierra, whose land included lower-elevation zones to the east that produced crops such as coca and aji. Although thirty miles or more and high mountains separate this tropical agricultural zone from the valley, we know from historical documents (LeVine 1979; Vega 1965 [1582]: 168, 172–74) that highland communities controlled small villages there.

Can the archipelago community be documented from pre-Inka

times, or was it an outcome of the conquest? Although complete returns are not in from a number of archaeological projects that are addressing this problem (Hastings 1982; Lynch 1982), what evidence we now have for pre-Inka archipelago communities is at best thin. In times of inter-community hostility and warfare any such commitment of community resources would surely have been impractical because of the prohibi-tive costs of defense. It seems reasonable, then, that such communities first made their appearance after the conquest, when the Inka state was in a position to maintain peace and guarantee ownership of resources.

Organization above the level of the *ayllu* is little known and poorly studied. We know that some settlements in the pre-Inka period were quite large and thus probably composed of several *ayllu*; in the Mantaro valley these large communities were a response to warfare (LeBlanc 1981).

A broader regional formation of ethnic groups existed with closely related languages, customs, and cultural histories. In the upper Man-taro valley, for example, the local ethnic group was the Wanka, and modern communities in the area still identify themselves as Wanka. Prior to the Inka conquest, the Wanka did not form a united political group; local communities were politically autonomous and waged war with neighboring Wanka communities (Hastorf 1993). Although inter-community exchange and political alliance took place, a community was politically separate in most affairs.

Ethnicity, however, became very important under Inka domination. A hierarchy among a province's *ayllu*, reflecting differences in econom-ic wealth and political relationship to the Inka, was translated into con-trol of the administrative offices of the province's districts and subdis-tricts. The overall province, however, had no traditional basis beyond general ethnicity, and administrative control was vested in a nonlocal Inka official. The Inka then created an ethnic mosaic within a region by inserting internal colonists (*mitimas*) from different ethnic groups into a region where they held no traditional rights to land. These colonists were thus dependent on the state and could be counted on for state-directed craft production, for work on state farms, and, of course, for internal security.

Although the Andean *ayllu* has often been pictured as egalitarian and organized by principles of kinship and reciprocity, leadership and incipient social differentiation were important at least in some Andean areas. The *ayllu* leader (*curaca*) was an incipient aristocrat. The position descended in a local patriline, with some flexibility of choice among possible candidates (Rostworoski 1961). Certain specified lands were worked by *ayllu* members as part of a general obligation to provide for the *curaca* (Moore 1958: 527), and he apparently also had some rights to local labor and to special resources such as metals and coca (ibid.: 39).

In return for control over the community's agricultural and nonagricultural resources and its labor, the *curaca* was responsible for settling disputes, allocating agricultural lands, and organizing community activities, including local ceremonies and communal labor groups for work on state lands. As a member of the elite, a community leader, and a conductor of ceremonies, the *curaca* is similar to the community chief as discussed in Chapter 11; the main difference lay in his linkage to the state as a local bureaucrat.

The *ayllu* was organized primarily to solve problems of basic subsistence at both the household and local community levels. In the household, resources were pooled in generalized reciprocity; in the *ayllu* kinship ties were a basis for balanced reciprocal exchanges. On this system was imposed a social and economic differentiation, with leaders supported primarily by labor contributions from community members. In pre-Inka times the *curaca* apparently was needed largely for warfare and defense, but under the Inka the position was transformed.

Silverblatt (1987: 22) argues that the Andean bias toward masculinity in war became firmly established under Inka rule when war chiefs were appointed local administrators. The state instituted a male hierarchy for governance that heightened gender division within local communities, formalizing the distinctions between male (public) and female (private) spheres.

The Political Economy

The Inka empire was built economically and politically on a base of local communities. It made creative use of existing institutions of finance and control and developed new institutions. The empire arose out of a social milieu of chiefdoms—socially stratified societies engaged in intense competition for scarce land and other resources (Toledo 1940 [1570]: 169). The rapid transformation to an empire was made possible by a shift in goals away from the conquest of land and the expulsion of defeated populations to the conquest of populations and the incorporation of their productive capabilities into the financial base of the expanding political system (Rowe 1946: 203).

In many ways the Inka state was like a huge chiefdom. As in Hawaiian chiefdoms, political office was gained by competition among a group of hereditary elites, each seeking to marshal support among different factions. Office carried with it rights to income (Moore 1958: 32), and competition for the office of ruling Inka thus proliferated into a competition among elite factions for control of desirable political office. The government was manned by Inka elites in high position, and thus at least initially there was no separation between the social elite and the governing bureaucracy.

Nor was religion in any sense an independent institution. The state religion was represented at administrative settlements throughout the empire by temple mounds, or *ushnu*, that stood prominently in the main plaza and acted as a focus for ceremonial occasions, where they proclaimed the ruler's divinity and thus his legitimacy. The stability and fertility of the natural world, being dependent on the supernatural, were mediated by the ruling Inka. The Inka also tried explicitly to integrate local regions into the empire by moving their main idols to the capital of Cuzco, where they were placed in state shrines (Rowe 1946). In our discussion of chiefdoms, we emphasized the highly generalized nature of the chief as a representative of the social elite, a political leader, and a divine person; and so it continued to be in early empires such as the Inka, with religious institutions serving as an important agent of social and political integration (Conrad and Demarest 1984; cf. Kurtz 1978).

In sharp contrast to Hawaiian chiefdoms, however, the Inka empire incorporated a vast population of many ethnic groups, and that led to problems of integration and control that no chiefdom could solve. A bureaucracy was needed for the ongoing management of state affairs, and an army to maintain internal peace and repulse external threat: not a dozen kinsmen and their followers, as in the Hawaiian chiefdoms, but hundreds or even thousands of specialists linked together in large hierarchical institutions.

The way state societies develop specialized institutions from earlier precedents is seen clearly in the economic organization of finance and production under the Inka state as described by Murra (1980 [1956]; 1975). In the pre-Inka period, as we have seen, the *curaca* financed his position through staple goods grown on lands designated for his use and farmed by commoners as part of their community obligation. On a massive, empire-wide scale, this was the financial base for the Inka state.

After conquering a new region, the state asserted its ownership of all that region's lands. These lands were then divided into three sections whose produce went respectively to support the state bureaucracy and military, the state religion, and the local community. The community lands remained residually under state ownership, but the right to use them was granted to the community in exchange for its *mit'a*—obligatory labor on state and religious lands and on other state projects such as road maintenance, canal construction, and mining. An ideology of reciprocity was maintained: the use of land, the means of subsistence, was given in exchange for labor in state activities (Wachtel 1977: 66).

The Inka state economy was based on staple finance. Staple foods, including maize, potatoes, and quinoa, were grown on state lands by community labor. Following the harvest, the food products were stored in state granaries and used to feed administrators, military personnel, and others working for the state, including commoners working off their labor obligation. Commoner communities were also obligated to produce craft goods for state use. Women in each family were required to spin wool provided from state herds and to weave a certain amount of cloth, such as one blanket, each year (Costin 1993; Murra 1962). (This right to cloth goods may have originated with the community leader, who received products such as shirts and bags woven for him by his support group.) Cloth could then be used as a political currency (D'Altroy and Earle 1985). Thus the state's control over production gave it both products that could be used or consumed immediately by state personnel and convertible, storable wealth for use in later payments.

Although the system of finance through compulsory labor had precedents in the local pre-Inka economy, its scale in the Inka state led to a number of significant changes. One was the advent of record-keeping—not by the introduction of a writing system, as in other early states, but by *khipu*, mnemonic devices with rows of knotted strings used to record the transfer of goods. Local *khipu* specialists were employed by the state to record all goods going into and coming out of the state's many local storehouses.

Storage was also greatly elaborated under Inka domination. During the pre-Inka period the best evidence for centralized storage complexes is found in the coastal states such as Chimu (Day 1982); in the highlands, storage was mainly at the household level (Earle and D'Altroy 1982). The Inka empire, by contrast, needed massive storehouses to hold the staples and craft goods produced for the state. In the Mantaro valley, for example, over two thousand individual storage units, small silolike structures, were constructed in orderly rows placed throughout the valley (D'Altroy 1992). Many of these storage units were placed on the hills directly above the major Inka administrative center of Hatun Xauxa, but an equal number were distributed through the valley, some in close association with local community settlements. Those on the hills presumably provided for the support of state personnel at Hatun Xauxa, including administrators, state officials on local inspections, and the military. Those in the valley also supported state activities in the local communities, including agricultural work, public works projects, and such craft industries as pottery and metal production.

Additionally, these state stores would have provided the local resources necessary for supporting military operations, if necessary, and for maintaining local political stability. According to the chronicles, as summarized by Murra (1980 [1956]), they supplemented local shortfalls resulting from crop failure. Although reciprocal exchange relationships between families were the first and best way to get through a difficult period, the state provided stored goods as a last resort, thus performing a service that was formerly the *curaca*'s responsibility as both ritual leader and economic manager.

The Inka state also sponsored massive state farms with new irrigation and terracing projects, one of which, in the Cochabamba valley in Bolivia (M. LaLone 1985; Wachtel 1982), supported state institutions as far away as Cuzco. The storehouses were maintained by *mitmas*, and the land was farmed in rotation by various groups as part of their *mit'a* labor.

As a continuation of earlier economic arrangements with their *curacas*, local populations provided the state with craft goods such as cloth, sandals, valuables used as gifts and payments, and probably ceramics. Additionally, villages that could offer special crafts, such as metallurgy and stonemasonry, were required to provide specialists to work for the state. Removed like the *mitmas* from their native communities with their traditional system of rights and obligations, these individual specialists were attached to state institutions, laboring in workshops or work teams.

Among these specialist retainers were the *aclla*, or "chosen women," who were weavers attached to the state religious institution (Rowe 1946: 269). Recruited from communities throughout the empire, these women lived in administrative settlements, where they wove *cumbi*, a particularly fine grade of cloth, and made *chicha*, a kind of beer. *Cumbi* was a major wealth item in the empire, used especially for political gifts and ceremonial payments. The *aclla* represented a semi-industrialized form of production, organized for the large-scale manufacture of this highly specific product.

Another category of specialists, called *yana*, worked directly as agricultural laborers and domestic servants for elite patrons and shrines (Murra 1980 [1956]). Some researchers describe the *yana* as slaves because of their lifetime attachment to an "owner," but apparently they enjoyed many freedoms. Only one of a *yana* couple's children was required to remain with their father's employer.

The main importance of the *mitmas*, the *aclla*, and the *yana* is the change they represent in the relations of production. In the characteristic corvée or *mit'a* system, production is basically organized at the community and household levels, with the products of the labor provided as a rent. By contrast, these new groups were detached from the community and organized by governmental institutions and elites. As described by Murra (1980 [1956]) and Schaedel (1978), this restructuring of production transcends the limits imposed by community production and is a key organizational shift required by state societies to meet their expanded and increasingly specific needs.

Like the Chinese empire, which monopolized the production and sale of salt and iron, the Inka empire raised income by exercising a monopoly over certain important products that were in wide demand. Early chroniclers state that coca, the Andean equivalent of tobacco, was controlled by the state (see Moore 1958; Rowe 1946), which may even have attempted to expand the market demand for it by emphasizing its ceremonial importance in Inka rituals. All metal mines were owned by the state, being worked as part of a community's labor obligations under the direction of the *curaca* (Moore 1958: 39), and throughout the Inka empire, copper was alloyed with tin to create a bronze associated with imperial power (Lechtman 1977). The addition of the highly localized tin to the much more broadly available copper made metal production much easier for imperial administrators to control (Costin et al. 1989).

The *curaca* was a central figure in the operation and finance of the Inka empire. Important in pre-Inka times, at least in highland areas mainly for his leadership in warfare, in Inka times the *curaca* was selected and supported by the state on the basis of his economic efficacy. The *curaca* was in a pivotal position: his authority relied both on a local heritage of rights and obligations and on the state's guarantee of support. In the Mantaro valley (D'Altroy 1981) the status of the *curaca* and the strength of his control were greatly reinforced by imperial incorporation, and local elites accordingly remained strongly disposed to further the state's interests in the region.

Reasons for Inka Imperial Success

A state such as the Inka may be pictured by conflict theorists as operated by ruthless exploiters, or alternatively by functionalist consensus theorists as operated by beneficent managers. It was, and had to be, a little of both, depending as it did on a balance between exploitation and management. Inka rule is best described as rule by enlightened self-interest (Rowe 1946: 273). The empire was financed by mobilizing labor to produce staples and crafts, to construct public works projects, and to support the army; all households of the local community were required to provide corvée labor to these ends. In return the state provided resources and services to the local community that were essential to its subsistence economy, notably orderly access to agricultural land and pastures. Conquest thus established a new set of relations to the means of production that guaranteed the dependence of the local community.

An even greater service provided by the empire to its local communities was that of bringing intercommunity warfare to an end. Among the Wanka, for example, we can document a dramatic improvement in the diet and lifespan of both elite and commoner following the Inka conquest (Earle et al. 1986). The state as grantor of land in return for corvée labor also guaranteed a community's use rights, thus permitting some local communities to extend their resource control vertically and improve the stability and self-sufficiency of their subsistence economy. The state's monopoly over certain goods almost certainly made those goods available to distant communities, often for the first time. And finally, as we have seen, the state's storehouses, though constructed primarily to finance its own activities, provided a residual supply of food for the populace in times of need.

The enlightened self-interest of the Inka empire was characteristic of archaic states, in which the relationship between the subsistence and political economies is carefully balanced. The state continued to depend on the local community for labor and staple products. The community, in return, became dependent on the state. It was of course in the clear economic interest of the state to provide services and resources to strengthen the bond of dependency and to maintain the productive potential of the community, the state's financial base. The movement of people around the empire created a complex ethnic mosaic that was often accentuated by the state as a strategy to divide and rule. A group moved by the state into a new region had to be loyal to the state because its claim to land came only from state assignment and not from traditional rights.

Why were the Inka successful in the fifteenth century and not before? Earlier states had existed on the coast of the Central Andes region, notably the artistically renowned Moche state and the Chimu state (Lumbreras 1974); and in the highlands the imperial Wari state had long since established an extensive road system and administrative settlements (Isbell and Schreiber 1978). In part, therefore, the Inka empire can be seen as having been built on earlier precedent.

The real key to the Inka's success, however, was a series of developments in the subsistence economy. Long-term population growth through the central Andes had led to a marked escalation in intercommunity warfare and a major intensification of agriculture based on irrigation, terracing, and drained fields. A need for local leaders, mainly for warfare, led to the development of social stratification and chiefdoms throughout the highlands. In turn the high population density, the dependency on capital-intensive agriculture, and the existence of local elites created the ideal opportunity for incorporating these chiefdoms into an imperial state.

Above all, the Inka came along at a time when people were tired of war and ready to appreciate the advantages of peace. The imposition of peace on a region removed the tremendous costs of military preparedness, which included not only the direct costs of maintaining a fighting force and fortifications but also the indirect costs of inefficiencies and losses in subsistence production (Schaedel 1978). The restoration of peace and order released a tremendous surplus of potential energy that was channeled by the state into its own political and social purposes.

Conclusions

Intensification of the subsistence economy is a necessary but insufficient condition for state formation. The necessity of increasing food production, resulting from a consistent growth in population preceding state formation, leads to a filling in of the landscape, capital improvements, carefully managed rotation cycles, clearly demarcated land tenure, intense competition over productive lands, and ultimately a rural population dense enough to support market systems and a specialized urban sector. Without such conditions states cannot exist, except perhaps as satellites tied in through close economic relationships to a major state society. But even where all those conditions obtain, certain measures of economic control and political integration must be taken before a viable state can exist.

Integration on a massive regional or interregional scale is a defining characteristic of states. Minimally this integration involves a bureaucracy, a military establishment, and an institutionalized state religion. These institutions ensure the state adequate finance, capable economic management, stability, and legitimacy. Over and above these fundamentally political institutions, the establishment of regional peace by a powerful state permits a rapid increase in economic integration, either through the development of markets and trade, as in medieval France and Japan, or in the extension of community territories to incorporate diverse production systems, as in the case of the Inkas.

All states are stratified. They have to be, because the very institutions of state that are necessary to prevent economic chaos are based on a reliable income for finance. This income is possible only with economic control, and that control translates into rule by an elite, whether socially, politically, or religiously marked. At the state level, stratification appears to be inevitable. The socialistic and democratic alternatives seem only to decorate a fundamental stratification with an ideology of egalitarianism. As much as we may cringe from this conclusion, the only alternative would be a comprehensive simplification of world economic problems that is impossible with pressing populations.

Basic to both state finance and stratification is this element of control. As we have seen, two main kinds of control exist: control over production, made possible by such technological developments as irrigation or, more weakly, by short-fallow, carefully managed farm lands; and control over distribution (trade), made possible by market development and the generation of mercantile wealth. In the first instance, stratification is defined by the existence of two classes: a ruling and landowning elite class, and a producer class of commoners. In the second instance a third class is also present: a merchant class, often attached in one way or another to the ruling class.

As we have argued throughout the chapter, states can be formed only where two sets of conditions are present: high population density, with explicit needs for an overarching system of integration; and opportunities for sufficient economic control to permit the stable finance of regional institutions and to support a ruling class. Where these two sets of conditions occur together, we find the rapid expansion of the political economy and the beginning of the state.

THIRTEEN

The Peasant Economy in the Agrarian State

IN CHAPTER 12 we viewed the development of the state from the overall perspective of the larger political institution. Here we turn to a more ethnographic view of the state-level economy, focusing on the peasant household and the local community and describing the economy from the ground up. "Peasant society" is a label that applies to a wide range of social systems, each so complex and multitiered that we cannot hope to offer a complete explanation or even a complete typology of peasant economies. Belshaw (1965: 53–58), Halperin and Dow (1977), Potter et al. (1967), C. Smith (1976), and Wolf (1966a) provide admirable overviews and case studies.

Peasant economies are characterized by a relatively high population density and a relatively intensive production. But so are complex chiefdoms, and we have seen that in stratified societies, features of the production system alone no longer serve to distinguish evolutionary complexity; the local economy must increasingly be understood in the context of a regional economy integrated by market exchange.

In this chapter we review three cases, presented in ascending order of population density and degree of intensification of production. The most meaningful contrast is between the first, a Brazilian *fazenda* (plantation) on which a landlord and certain other local patrons stand as gatekeepers between peasant food producers and the market-dominated political economy, and the other two, villages in China and Java in which the peasant household directly sells its own labor and products on the open market. These three cases also represent different points along a continuum of "commercialization" (C. Smith 1976) that is a basic dimension distinguishing types of peasant economy.

In a way, the contrast between the Brazilian tenant farmers and the landowning peasants of China and Java recapitulates the contrast between feudalistic societies, such as chiefdoms and early states, and market-integrated agrarian states, such as China, and modern nation-states. Feudalistic societies tend to depend on staple finance more than wealth finance, to have limited market systems and unreliable currencies, and to be managed through chains of fictive-kin, patron-client relationships. By contrast, market-integrated states depend far more heavily on wealth finance than staple finance, have well-developed monetary, banking, and transportation systems, and are managed by bureaucrats whose loyalty to the state is stronger—at least in principle—than their personal ties to family, friends, and local elites. In the feudalistic state, power and wealth tend to be primarily determined by control over land; in the market-integrated state, power and wealth may include land, but they tend to be commercialized, depending more on success in the market than on simple ownership of land. As a rule, market-integrated states are more centralized and have stronger control over the hinterlands than the internally fractious feudalistic states.

In medieval France and Japan (see Chapter 12) the food-producing class had only a limited degree of market involvement, and the market itself was initially a localized exchange system controlled by the lord and limited to the area of his political influence. But as those systems evolved into nation-states, markets expanded rapidly. Some ruling elites benefited from the process, and others were reluctant to have their monopolistic powers shattered; there was, however, no halting the market's rapid expansion into the rural hinterlands (see, for example, C. Smith 1976: 356–60; Wolf 1969: 279–83).

We find, therefore, an evolutionary development from dependent peasants, bound to a lord who mediates their interaction with other peasants and elites, to independent or free peasants who compete directly in a marketplace for access to land, jobs, manufactures, and other essentials of life. In our view this freeing of the peasant is a continuation of the evolutionary expansion of the political economy. The economy is now so huge that any effort to move labor and goods through the system by the use of personal, hierarchical chains of command is necessarily less efficient than reliance on the impersonal free market. In essence the evolution from the complex chiefdom and the archaic state into a market-integrated nation-state is characterized by the increasing dominance of the economy by a competitive, price-fixing market, a dominance made possible by an institutional framework largely devoted to nurturing and protecting the market system (Chapter 14).

Peasants reluctantly enter the marketplace to obtain necessities for the domestic economy that they are unable to produce or obtain in their home communities. To be able to do so, they must produce crafts or foods to exchange for such things as metal tools, ceremonial paraphernalia, or the cash needed for tax payments. As we explore in Chapter 14, many of the solutions to the problems associated with population increase and technological change are now found in the impersonal operation of the self-regulating market, which both serves and threatens the household's economic interest.

In response to the vulnerability inherent in a market economy, households construct networks of personal ties that defy the impersonal efficiencies of the marketplace (Belshaw 1965: 78–81; Plattner 1989a). These "dyadic contracts" (Foster 1961) are balanced exchange relationships in which both parties seek personal advantage. In vertical ties, the commoner client seeks security while the elite patron seeks political standing. Systems such as *jajmani* in India (Dumont 1970) and *pratik* in Haiti (Mintz 1961) hark back to a premarket era, as peasants seek feudalistic ties of loyalty with well-to-do landowners, shopkeepers and vendors, government officials, physicians, and other local elites. These local elites in turn seek ties of dependence with still higher-ranking elites, so that everyone in the society is theoretically reachable through patron-client ties. If the formal structures of state societies integrate a mass of faceless strangers regulated by bureaucrats, the web of dyadic ties that each person constructs personalizes the system. Although often described by free market theorists as "imperfections," patron-client ties are essential: they allow the powerless commoners to gain access to goods and services that, in a large and impersonal market system, they would otherwise find beyond their reach.

In addition to the horizontal function of exchanging goods between specialized producers, markets have the vertical function of collecting goods that support urban populations distant from the farms and removed from subsistence production (Plattner 1989b). The urban settlement pattern, with its hierarchy of central places, creates concentrations of populations suitable for administration and control. Living in the urban centers are the personnel of the state—bureaucrats and record-keepers, warriors and planners, priests and clergy, craftsmen and merchants, and the ruling class itself. To support these essential functions, food must be mobilized from the rural base and made available to urban populations.

Markets characterize states because they make easier the settlement and finance of centralized, hierarchical institutions of regional governance. Provisioning large urban populations that do not produce the means of their own subsistence is potentially a logistical nightmare. The market, more or less free from state management, solves the problem. A functioning, integrating market system allows a state to adopt full-fledged wealth finance. For it to work, states use currencies as a means of payment to those working for the state. Currencies are concentrated, standardized objects of wealth that can be easily stored and moved. The state mints money in standard denominations, guaranteeing its value, and such wealth can be moved easily for central storage and distribution as part of state finance. The familiar act of salaried workers taking their currency to the marketplace to purchase the foods and other necessities they can no longer produce themselves constitutes the subsistence infrastructure sustaining the urban and specialist populations on which all states depend (Brumfiel 1980).

In evolutionary terms, the fund of rent is the final and most burdensome form of intrusion of the political economy into the household economy. It began as a reluctant "gift" from the producer to one or more current Big Men, hardened into the tribute demanded by a powerful chief, and eventually became the legally sanctioned right of landowners and bureaucrats to a share of peasant production. Only the subsistence fund represents income consumed by the peasant household. It is the small and often inadequate proportion of total production that remains after the ceremonial and rent funds have been paid out.

Our case studies will show state influences at work at all levels of the economy: the intensification of production through such methods as irrigation and use of manufactured tools and fertilizers; the regional integration of the economy through markets for labor and produce; and the stratification of the labor force into many varieties both of primary producers and of owners, managers, and bureaucrats.

Two of our cases also illustrate a phenomenon that is of great interest as an extension of processes we have examined: namely, the penetration of the world market into the local economy. In Brazil and Java a dual economy has been created by the intrusion of cash crops, primarily cane sugar, into prime agricultural lands that originally supported agrarian populations by the production of starchy staples. Although the switch to cash cropping denied local populations access to the best lands for food production, it stimulated the development of formerly marginal areas, in which state-supported technological investments underwrote huge increases in food production. It also increased the participation of subsistence farmers in a labor market and finally shattered whatever remained of the self-sufficiency of the farm household.

Case 17. The Brazilian Sharecroppers of Boa Ventura

Our first case illustrates the economy of "dependent" peasants who live under the direct control of landlords. The major production unit of this economy is the nuclear family household, which is individually linked to other households and to landlords and other elites through bonds of friendship maintained by frequent exchanges of gifts. Despite a semiarid climate and a terrain unsuited to irrigation, government water works and careful management of land use by landlords have made possible a comparatively dense population that produces staple crops for its own consumption while helping the landlord to raise cattle, cotton, and other products for sale. From our perspective, the landlord represents a kind of transitional middleman between the peasant and the political economy of the state. In more fully commercialized economies such paternalistic middlemen tend to decline in importance, a sign of the growing dominance of the market at all levels of the economy.

The Environment and the Economy

The peasants of Boa Ventura are tenants on a *fazenda* in Ceará, northeastern Brazil, a region distinguished by a rich, productive humid zone (*littoral*) along the coast and an impoverished, semiarid zone (*sertão*) in the interior (A. Johnson 1971a). Prior to the European conquest, the *littoral* was occupied by warlike horticultural villagers (Tupinamba) who raised root crops and maize in slash-and-burn gardens similar to those described for the Yanomamo in Chapter 6. The interior was sparsely inhabited by hunter-gatherers.

Shortly after the European conquest, the humid littoral was taken over for the production of export crops, particularly sugar. This land being now too valuable for food crops, the semiarid sertão was gradually populated by farmers who grew staple foods for sale and reared cattle to provide meat and draft animals to the coast. The labor for these interior *fazendas* was provided by subsistence-oriented peasant families who adopted the horticultural methods of their native American predecessors. In the ethnographic present of 1966–67 we find a basic subsistence economy in Ceará that is hardly distinguishable from preconquest horticulture, though it is now overlain by an export economy devoted to the production of cotton, sugar, cacao, cattle, and other commodities.

Over the past century, owing primarily to the construction of large reservoirs and irrigation networks, the population of the sertão has expanded to a density of about thirty persons per square mile. Whether on individual smallholdings or larger *fazendas*, people in the sertão prefer to live in nuclear family households with as much autonomy as possible in economic decisions. The vast majority are subsistence farmers practicing bush-fallow horticulture.

The intensification of the subsistence economy and the creation of a market-oriented production system have created a severe shortage of agricultural land. Land is owned largely by an elite class that manages it for profit. Landlords provide houses, water, and land to their tenants, requiring them in return to plant certain crops such as cotton, rice, or bananas and sell them at low prices to the landlord. Altogether, by paying shares or giving days of labor to the *fazenda*, a tenant pays out about 25 to 30 percent of his total production as rent.

Sharecroppers slash and burn their gardens from second growth that has lain fallow for about eight years. Because of the high risk of brush fires during the long dry season, workers carefully clear firebreaks at the borders of their gardens, sweeping them clean with brooms of brush. After the rains begin they plant gardens of intermixed crops such as maize, manioc, beans, squash, sesame, peanuts, and potatoes. In the second year the number of food crops is reduced to make way for tree cotton, which becomes the only crop by the third year and is cultivated for several more years before the field is returned to full fallow.

Sharecroppers obtain virtually all of their food from gardens and from backyard animals fed with garden produce. Pigs and goats, when slaughtered, provide occasions for meat-sharing in repayment of earlier gifts. But most protein comes from beans, the "strong food" (*comida forte*) of the region, without which no meal is considered nourishing. Occasionally a man hunts small birds or rodents with a rifle, but fishing areas are controlled by landlords and are fished by full-time specialists with exclusive contracts. In the broad scheme of things, wild foods are of little economic significance to the peasant household.

Tenant households each farm a clearly defined field and decide when, what, and how much to plant, when to weed, and so forth, with little outside influence. They also take most of the risks of production and thus are true peasants rather than farmworkers; but they can be forced off the land at the landlord's pleasure and thus are dependent peasants in contrast to independent, landowning peasants. In this dependency, and in their personal ties with landlords and other elites, they resemble the farmers found in chiefdoms.

Rainfall in the sertão is unpredictable, crop pests are an ever-present threat, and the land the peasant works belongs to someone else. These uncertainties generate economic and social strategies aimed at increasing security even at the expense of some "profit" (A. Johnson

1971b). For example, a sharecropper does not try to plant a single best crop in the best land to maximize production, but instead plants a wide mix of crops in as many microenvironments as possible: dry hillsides, fertile riverbanks, the riverbottom during the dry season, low-lying humid soils, and the margins of reservoirs (Johnson 1972). Whether the year is wet or dry, the risk-spreading farmer is assured of some food for his larder. This is risk management at the household level, of course, not involving group-level strategies organized by local leaders.

Another strategy is to store a year's supply of food at harvest time, and only then contemplate selling any surplus on the market. This household security strategy has two serious consequences. First, the amounts of food reaching the market fluctuate wildly from year to year, and the resulting insecurity of the food supply for the urban, nonagricultural population can lead to political disturbances. Second, surplus food tends to come on the market all at the same time, after the peasants see how their new crops are progressing and before prices fall with the new harvest. For that reason, the market value of staples like maize and beans begins to fall a month or two before the first harvests of the new year actually reach the marketplace, and peasants are paid less for their food than they might have been under other circumstances.

Perhaps unexpectedly, insecurity does not lead to the complete lack of innovation and experimentation that some observers have attributed to peasant agriculture (Schultz 1964; Wolf 1966a: 16). The sharecroppers are as interested in new crop varieties and techniques as farmers anywhere. Men constantly discuss new crops they have seen during their travels and try to obtain seeds of those crops for planting. They even perform controlled experiments in their gardens, planting two varieties of seed or using two planting techniques side by side to see which does best. They are not careless of the risk involved but rather minimize risk by restricting innovation to small experimental plots in which crop failure will have little effect on a household's overall production.

In fact, although there are many ideas, methods, and rules of thumb that most tenant farmers accept, the degree of individual variation in horticultural practices is remarkable. The reasons for this are various. For one thing, each household has a different composition of producers and consumers, and both of these affect the amount of land a household has under production. For another, people have rather firm opinions about how to farm, even when these opinions differ from those of their neighbors. This leads to no end of disagreement and even disparagement between otherwise friendly tenants. Finally, there are large differences in individual intelligence, skill, and motivation, and these are reflected in differences of wealth and prestige among households (cf. Cancian 1972).

Nonetheless the sharecroppers of the sertão live so close to the margin of survival that they visibly lose weight in the months before harvest. The poorest families may be unable to reach their goal of a full year's stored food supply, and may thus experience a shortage of food at a time when their work efforts reach a peak. Children are especially likely to receive less than their share of food (cf. Gross and Underwood 1971), and infant mortality and clinical malnutrition are high. In the frequent years of low rainfall, larger numbers of families suffer, and in the periodic droughts all peasant households face basic survival threats. In addition to their risk-spreading strategies in food production at the household level, therefore, they pursue various social means to greater security.

Social Organization

Household autonomy is a central goal of each married couple, which strives to become the *donos de casa* (masters of the house) of their own dwelling. A husband's labor is centered in the fields, tending crops and working to meet his labor obligations and to earn additional cash. The wife keeps house, prepares food, does laundry in the nearest reservoir, and rears children. Although a double sex standard characterizes the general culture of the region—supporting greater freedom of action for men in all areas of life—in fact the typical marriage is one of de facto equality between productive spouses, each of whom respects and values the contribution of the other. In common with many peasant societies, fathers are respected and obeyed, but the more accessible mothers gain a degree of emotional importance in the family that belies their culturally subordinate status.

Kinship is less important as a source of social security among Brazilian sharecroppers than among most groups discussed in earlier chapters. Indeed, to hear the sharecroppers tell it, kinsmen are unreliable and of little value. Yet groups of kinsmen do form residential clusters here and there on the *fazenda* (A. Johnson and Bond 1974). Even kinsmen who live some distance apart on the *fazenda* maintain close exchange ties, whereas non-kin form such ties only with near neighbors.

The emphasis of social relations between tenant households is on friendship. The importance of friendship in the social organization of peasant communities has been established by Foster (1961) and Wolf (1966b). Foster's model of the dyadic contract sets forth the essential features of friendship relations in a Mexican village as follows:

1. Relations are always dyadic. Although friendship between two people inevitably entails relations with the friend's friends, dyadic contracts are structured to minimize such extensions so that friends need not assume responsibility for each other's complete network of social and economic obligations.

2. Short-term exchanges are usually out of balance; that is, one friend owes the other. The debt, which shifts back and forth as gift repays gift, is a welcome sign of trust, and any effort to pay the debt off exactly is seen as an effort to end the friendship.

3. Over the long term, exchanges should strike a balance so that each friend finds the exchange fair (cf. Homans 1958).

4. Friendships are entered into and terminated freely. They are thus fundamentally different from kinship relations, debt-peonage relations, and other structural social relations that a person cannot avoid. The economic importance of friendship in peasant society derives especially from this characteristic: one chooses one's network of friends with one's own best interests in mind, and friends who fail to carry their weight can be dropped or avoided.

5. Since friendships are fragile, with weak structural underpinnings, frequent exchanges between friends are necessary to keep the relationship vital and reliable. Most gifts between friends are small, mere tokens of friendship. Overt displays of gratitude are avoided, since they may be interpreted as attempts to end the relationship by paying off the debt with gratitude.

For Brazilian sharecroppers, friends add much to the economic security and well-being of the household. Through their separate networks of friends, men and women obtain fresh meat, foods not grown in their own gardens, small temporary loans of cash, days of labor in times of critical labor need, the loan of tools they might not own, and other special favors. They work hard to establish and maintain these friendships, and when their efforts fail the disappointment may be bitter. Close kinsmen and many near neighbors maintain the frequent exchanges that mark friendship ties. But since too many ties can be cumbersome, close regular friendships are limited to two or three per person. Thus in the larger kin clusters not all members exchange equally with each other; some pairs of kin behave like friends, while others treat one another in economic terms more or less like non-kin.

Foster (1961) points out how different this casual, individual-centered relationship is from the rigidly structured, group-centered kinship groups of intensive horticultural societies. Yet friends make important contributions to the economic security and autonomy of

households everywhere: in fact, where kin groups control the individual economic lives of their members, friends tend to be chosen from
among non-kinsmen, to help one another and to serve as buffers
against the intrusions of the kin group (A. Johnson and Bond 1974).
Although Boa Ventura contains a village-level population of about
three hundred, it is a community only in the sense that it is subject to
the management policies of the landlord. The significant economic
groups in daily life tend to be much smaller than the *fazenda* community, being limited to hamlet-size clusters of kinsmen and friends in
small neighborhoods. This decomposition of the kin-based village
community during the evolution of the regional polity is one of the
most dramatic correlates of market integration and the growth of stratification.

Market Involvement

In addition to the social responses described above, the small landholdings and unpredictable yields of the sharecroppers necessitate
some degree of market involvement. The sharecropper often works
part-time in craft activities to augment his meager income and sells his
agricultural surplus in good years to provide a buffer against bad times
to come. Individual exchange ties integrate the *fazenda* community and
extend beyond the *fazenda*.

A *fazenda* usually contains an array of economic specialists. Most in
demand are blacksmiths for manufacturing and repairing tools, carpenters for making doors, windows, and furniture, and masons for
constructing buildings. These specialists are all sharecroppers whose
part-time specialties increase their income; they receive lower wages
for their work than do specialists who live in town, but they enjoy
greater security. Specialists who live in town have no gardens to fall
back on when customers fail to pay for their work, and they need powerful kinsmen or patrons in order to survive. One carpenter who left the
fazenda in 1966 to try his luck in town was back in 1967, his savings
wiped out in a financially disastrous half-year; having no patron, he
had no way to collect what his customers owed him (A. Johnson 1971a:
90–91).

Specialists on other *fazendas* are also available when needed, but
most tenant households obtain the things they do not produce from
shops on or off the *fazenda*. These shops are supplied from markets in
town, but peasants rarely go to those markets. Instead they do their
buying and selling of crops and commodities through the landlord and
shopkeepers, with whom they try to maintain close personal ties very
like the friendship ties they establish with one another.

Their rare attempts to raise cash crops or to use hired labor invariably fail, either because they cannot control some factor of production (e.g., obtaining transportation to market perishable goods) or because their profit margin is too low to sustain the risks of production over any length of time (e.g., losses due to bad weather in one year may more than overbalance the profits from a good year).

In such systems the market is in the control of the middlemen and elites. Landlords bulk produce from their own *fazendas* and ship to warehouses or other rural bulking centers, where goods are stored, partially processed or packaged, and shipped. Markets are primarily places where urban dwellers buy produce that has been bought wholesale from warehouses by middlemen who then break it down into small quantities for resale. Some farmers do sell directly on the market, but they tend to be independent cash-cropping truck farmers, not sharecroppers from outlying *fazendas.*

Marketing and the Political Economy

Every sharecropper on a *fazenda* has access to several shops, and since prices on individual items vary, it pays to shop around. The best prices are usually found in shops that accept only cash payments and never extend credit. Few sharecroppers, however, can afford to pay cash at all times; credit during scarce times is essential to their survival, and in order to obtain credit a man must become a "loyal customer" (*freguês*) of a single shopkeeper, whose prices are higher because by extending credit he runs a higher risk of nonpayment. Ironically, then, because the cost of credit is embedded in food prices, the poorest sharecroppers must pay higher prices for food than their economically more comfortable neighbors, in keeping with the universal principle that "the poor pay more" (Caplovitz 1963). Sharecroppers understand this very well but cannot forgo the security of being able to obtain beans, manioc flour, kerosene, and cooking oil on credit when there is no cash and the family is hungry.

A similar logic applies, in a more general way, to relations with the landlord. Dependent peasants do not see the landlord as "the greatest social enemy of the peasant" (Quijano 1967; cf. Feder 1971), but as a potential ally of fundamental importance to their well-being. They actively seek to transform him into a personal patron, since by calling on his personal resources and those of his network of powerful patrons and clients he can provide almost any service a tenant might need.

A change of ownership of a *fazenda* took place while one of the authors was doing fieldwork in the area. The original owner, known as "the General," had sold the *fazenda* to a wealthy merchant called Seu

Clovis. Although Seu Clovis espoused democratic ideals and reduced the tenants' obligations (fund of rent), they were dissatisfied with him and almost universally wished the General would return. Why?

One reason was that the General's family was old and prestigious, and he himself had held various high offices; Seu Clovis, although a wealthy man, was of lower-class origins. Not only did tenants share the values of the larger society, which places the old landed aristocracy above the new commercial class, but they also understood that the General's superior class status gave him potentially much greater political and economic influence for them.

The patron's access to resources, however important, counts less than his willingness to use that access for his clients' benefit. The General demanded higher shares from his sharecroppers than did Clovis, but they regarded him as the more generous patron. The General would buy and sell crops in his own "company store," making food and money available on credit to his tenants (albeit at high rates of interest). He provided milk from his cattle and fruits from his irrigated gardens to families with sick children. And he used his influence to intervene in state-level institutions in his tenants' behalf: for example, he had a tenant who had been arrested released from jail immediately, and he obtained free government hospitalization for a woman with cancer.

Clovis abolished the company store as exploitative, he sold his milk and fruit for a profit, and he lacked the political influence to intervene as the General had done. Although the General lost no profit by being generous, since his rent receipts were higher than Clovis's, he was viewed as a stronger and more protective patron. This view was no doubt reinforced by a certain air of class pride and bravado in the General, in contrast to Clovis's more unassuming, middle-class demeanor.

Agrarian states are often feudalistically organized in ascending chains of patronage (Silverman 1965). At the top, powerful patrons control major resources such as government money for irrigation, road building, farm machinery, and social services. This money they allocate to lower-level clients, who are in turn patrons to small landlords and local political leaders. Each lower-level patron distributes the money to his clients, receiving in return their political support for himself and his higher-level patron (Greenfield 1972). The General, for example, regularly told his tenants how to vote, and delivered them in trucks to the polls on voting day. Because Seu Clovis wished to remain apolitical, his manager took over this function (without which the tenants claimed they could not possibly know how to vote), increasing his own political power as a consequence.

The patron-client tie is so important to dependent peasants that it survives despite its numerous inherent contradictions. Patrons are idealized as parental figures, often called "father," who protect and care for their dependents; clients are called "my children" and are expected to be loyal and devoted. But both patron and client openly acknowledge that their tie is basically an instrumental one that works only when both partners strike a fair exchange. Sharecroppers on the *fazendas* of northeastern Brazil point out that they provide labor, votes, or some other item of value to the landlord, and they will move to a new patron if their old one fails to keep up his part of the exchange.

Patrons, like Big Men, must cultivate loyal followings by acts of generosity; yet the patron-client relation is also a power relation in a class-stratified society, and in this regard the patron is not like a Big Man. Behind the familistic phrases and the fair exchange expectations lies the ultimate police and military power of the state, a power that can and will be used to maintain differential access to wealth and resources. Dependent peasants do not negotiate whether or not to pay a fund of rent; the only issues are how large that fund will be and what fringe benefits the patron will offer.

In stable agrarian states most peasants see no alternative to this class structure. Thus their dominant worldview amounts to a sort of client consciousness that is a typological opposite of proletarian consciousness. The dependent peasant views his dependence as a source of security and strength (Hutchinson 1966). He feels isolated in a society in which democratic ideals and social security protections either do not exist or else do not reach the peasantry. He does not view other tenants as potential allies in a political movement to gain security through unionization and direct political influence over governmental programs. Rather he sees fellow tenants as being just as powerless and needy as himself, and as potential rivals for the benevolence of their common patron. Beyond his narrow circle of friends and kinsmen, he views members of his class with a competitor's wary regard.

Personalism and patronage are important in all peasant economies, but a single individual patron is more important in our present example than in many others. As we shall see, peasant villages often have political and ceremonial institutions that increase peasants' economic security and help to mediate their relations with the state. Alternatively, individual peasant households may seek a range of patrons, including physicians, pharmacists, notaries, shopkeepers, work-crew bosses, and even well-to-do peasants, spreading widely their efforts to seek security. But the basic goal always remains that of reducing the impersonal, distant, bureaucratic, and instrumental elements of the political economy of the state (markets, courts, police, tax offices, etc.) to personal, dependable ties with locally known and trusted patrons.

Recent Change

Subsequent field studies in Boa Ventura by Caroso Soares in 1981 (Caroso Soares 1982) and by Johnson and Caroso Soares in 1988 and 1989 (Johnson 1999) have documented significant changes. Although the general layout of the *fazenda* remains the same two decades later, and many of the same families can be found occupying the same houses, fundamental changes in the political economy have thrown the whole future of the peasant way of life into doubt.

In the early 1960's, the original study detected the beginning of these changes in the transfer of ownership of the *fazenda* from the General to Seu Clovis. The shift—from a prestige-oriented owner who took his traditional responsibilities toward his dependents seriously, to a profit-oriented businessman primarily motivated to increase his personal wealth—replicates in miniature the expansion of modern markets and the shift of rural largeholdings from feudalistic estates to capitalistic farms that are occurring in Brazil and in many developing regions of the world (Wolf 1969).

This shift is evident in a number of specific forms on Boa Ventura in the late 1980's:

1. The number of tenant families has declined by one-third, from forty-five to thirty.

2. Seu Clovis has substantially decreased the amount of hillside thorn-forest (*mata*) that he is willing to allow the tenants to clear for gardens. Opportunistically, he justifies this step by using the discourse of sustainable development and the threat of deforestation. But his more immediate motivation is to increase his cattle herd, which requires *mata* for forage. The tenants complain bitterly, since this change forces them to clear smaller plots in less fertile secondary forest, but to no avail. In fact, at every opportunity one of Seu Clovis's sons buys cattle to bring to Boa Ventura to augment his father's herd.

3. Simultaneously, Seu Clovis is removing river-margin land—a prime planting area used by tenants as a hedge against drought—from food production in order to plant sugar cane. Brazil's government-supported program of converting cane juice to alcohol for automobiles (gasohol) has created an economic situation in which this is a highly profitable endeavor. Again, the tenants protest in vain.

4. As indicated by the decline in the number of tenants, Seu Clovis does not value tenant labor as much as was done before. He even hired

temporary crews from the coast to cut cane until his tenants pleaded for the opportunity to earn additional cash by doing such work themselves. But the landlord's sons have said that once they own the *fazenda* they will expel all tenant farmers and rely entirely on wage labor to meet their needs. They see this as a key step in modernizing the whole *fazenda*, following models of nearby *fazendas* that have already modernized.

5. Not coincidentally, the number of independent homesteads in pockets of private land between the large *fazendas* has grown rapidly. In part this represents a new generation of tenants, who are buying small house plots on which to build when the funds are available, as a first step in "escaping" (*escapar*) the *fazenda*: if they are good workers, the landlord allows them to continue to farm his land under a sharecropping contract even after they move into their own house off the *fazenda*. When the day comes that the tenants are asked to leave Boa Ventura, some will have their house plots and may succeed in finding other land to sharecrop. Others—perhaps the majority—will be landless and with few options.

6. Of great importance also is a new governmental social security program that allows even nonliterate tenants to file for retirement benefits (*aposentadoria*) at the age of sixty-six, and thereafter go each month to a nearby municipal center to receive their retirement pension payment at a bank. Everyone among the rural poor and middle class is entirely pleased by this development, which they regard as virtually lifesaving.

7. Potentially as significant to the tenants is the establishment of a public health post in the nearby town of Madalena. Although in 1989 it stocked no medicines but birth-control pills, and its consulting hours were severely restricted because of a lack of personnel, the eventual availability of greater services would fill a huge gap in the security net that tenants used to find in patrons.

8. Following a rural electrification project, the landlord brought an old black-and-white television set from town to be kept in his mansion and brought onto the verandah each evening, so that interested people could congregate and watch the popular *telenovelas* (soap operas) on *Rede Globo*, the leading Brazilian network. The *telenovelas* are preceded by national news programs that cover events from politics to natural catastrophes all over the country. Then a series of *telenovelas* present dramas of love, power, and wealth among largely white and affluent protagonists that draw a picture of modern life, with consumer goods and urban occupations. Among the messages being conveyed are mid-

dle-class values and aspirations, along with information on the work-ings of the Brazilian polity and the legal rights of the people.

9. Tenants also point to an increasing availability of consumer goods, of which bicycles and aluminum furniture have become most pervasive. Bicycles, which have largely replaced donkeys as a means of transport, are widely cited by tenants as indicators of progress.

10. The new Brazilian constitution offers rural workers many un-precedented rights, including land reform provisions. Radio programs, television news, and local religious and secular activists teach them about these rights and encourage tenants to take action. Although they remain largely powerless and therefore timid, tenants discuss these new rights among themselves and seek ways to implement them. On Boa Ventura, for example, there is a sizable section of land to which the landlord's title is not fully recorded in his deed. A group of families there has begun to claim that land as their own, leading to a tense stand-off with Seu Clovis.

The net effect of these changes is that a peasantry of dependent ten-ant farmers is transforming—partly by choice and partly by necessity—into a more independent and self-sufficient working class of share-croppers, wage laborers, and smallholders. The way tenants speak about the landlord in 1989 is sharply different from what was heard in 1967, and it could be summed up in the mildly approving formula, of-ten repeated, that "Seu Clovis does very little for us, but he does not interfere in our lives, either." Although some people will still hold out their hand with tightly clenched fingers to illustrate Seu Clovis's stingi-ness, they are inclined to say of the need for a patron, "*A gente arranja o patrão quando precisa*" ("You can find a patron when you need one"). Younger householders especially reflect a new attitude of confidence that owes much to the increasing availability of government services. They explicitly comment that the landlord is a less important figure in their lives than in the past.

Case 18. The Chinese Villagers of Taitou

Prior to the revolution of 1949, Taitou was an agricultural village of about seven hundred members in Shantung province in northeastern China (Yang 1945). Although a peasant economy, it was very different from the Brazilian *fazenda*. Two differences are especially worth em-phasizing. First, the population density of the Taitou region ranged from three to five hundred persons per square mile, more than ten

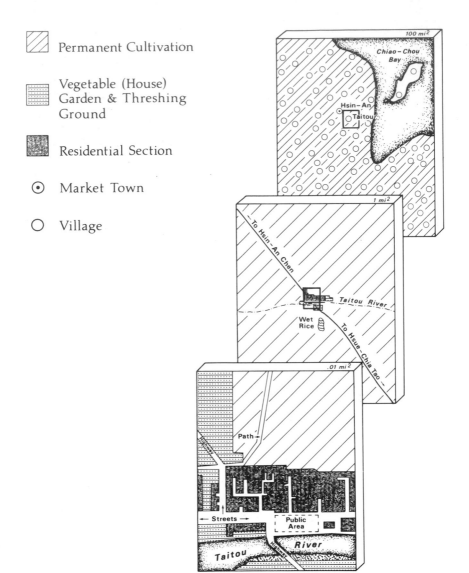

Permanent Cultivation

Vegetable (House)
Garden & Threshing
Ground

Residential Section

⊙ Market Town

○ Village

100 mi²

Chiao-Chou
Bay

Hsin-An
Taitou

1 mi²

To Hsin-An Chen

Taitou River

To Hsue-Chia Tao

Wet
Rice

.01 mi²

Path

← Streets →

Public
Area

Taitou River

Fig. 13. Settlement Pattern of Rural China. The landscape is crowded with villages, each linked to a standard market town. Every inch of land has been used for terraced gardens, rice paddies, paths and roads, and settlements. Each settlement has its blocks of private houses and central public park.

times the density of the Brazilian sertão. Figure 13 shows the Chinese landscape densely packed with villages. Second, the peasants of Taitou, as was common but not universal in China prior to 1949, were independent, landowning peasants who rarely lived as tenants on the property of others (cf. J. Buck 1937: 9). In fact, for a millennium China had been a market-integrated society, with a wealth-finance government based on a system of paper money, tax collection, and banking. The family economy of the Chinese peasant was centered on the need to acquire and manage land carefully, and to buy and sell products in the market, under conditions of extreme land scarcity.

The Subsistence Economy

The Taitou region is one of the oldest agricultural areas of China. Virtually all of its land had been put to human use. Microenvironmental differences are of great importance, and most families had small holdings scattered among the different zones: sandy hillsides where sweet potatoes and peanuts were grown on agricultural terraces, flatland fields of heavier soils where millet and wheat were grown, and tiny and expensive plots of wet rice. According to Yang (1945: 14):

Even within the environs of a single village there is a wide range in the value of soil. The extreme fragmentation prevents ownership of all the land of a given quality by one or a few families and thereby reduces the possibility of complete crop failure for any one family. Since different land is more or less suited to different crops, a family which has land in several places can grow various kinds of food, will always get some return from its land, and, being, therefore, self-sufficient, has less need to trade.

The main staples of the diet were millet, sweet potatoes, wheat, peanuts, and soybeans. To round out the diet, barley, maize, and rice were grown in the fields, and cabbage, turnips, onion, garlic, radishes, cucumbers, spinach, string beans, squashes, peas, and melons were grown in small vegetable gardens.

The peasants of Taitou practiced intensive multiple cropping with some seasonal fallowing. The common crop rotation was between winter crops, such as wheat and barley, and spring crops such as sweet potatoes, peanuts, and millet. Every phase of production was accompanied by intensive applications of labor to tease extra produce from the soil. Fertilizer was required for virtually all crops. A family carefully gathered all its animal and human wastes into a compost pit located in the family compound. When the pit was full, the contents were removed, covered with mud, and allowed to ferment. Then the compost was sun-dried and ground into fine powder. Ashes from household fires were carefully swept up and added to the compost; even the soot and oxidized bricks from the oven and chimney were periodically ground up and added. Green manure was rarely used, since twigs, brush, and plant stalks were needed as fodder or fuel, but even those materials eventually made their way into the compost heap as dung or ashes. When a field was planted, seeds and fertilizer were carefully mixed by hand to get the proportions right (soybean residue was also added), and the mixture was then spread by hand on the tilled soil. It was exacting, tedious work, but the people realized that, in Yang's words (ibid.: 17), "Human labor is cheap and fertilizer and seeds are scarce."

Sweet potatoes, which were a staple of particular importance in poorer families, required heavy inputs of labor in all phases of growth. The seedlings were first sprouted in carefully constructed warm, moist beds of sand and then transplanted in heavily fertilized nursery beds that had to be kept wet. Following the harvest of winter wheat or barley, the field was plowed and carefully ridged. Vines were selected from the nursery beds and transplanted a second time in the ridges, where they were individually hand watered. They had to be continuously weeded thereafter, and after every rain each plant had to be hand turned to prevent new roots from growing off the vines into the soil. Ridges required constant repair. Even when the harvest had been completed, the sweet potatoes had to be sliced and sun dried for storage. Yang (ibid.: 21) comments on the fatigue and muscle pain that accompanied the cultivation of sweet potatoes.

Peasant families generally owned one or two draft animals (mules or oxen) and a number of farm implements: a plow, a harrow, a weeding hoe, a wooden rake, an iron rake, a sickle, a pitchfork, a wheelbarrow. Poorer families did not own all the animals or tools they needed and had to find patrons among the wealthier peasants to loan them what they needed to complete their tool kit. Although many families raised pigs, they rarely ate pork because they needed the money they earned from selling pigs to make purchases essential to the household economy.

Wealth differences between families were substantial, although the villagers themselves tended to de-emphasize the extent of stratification in their village. All families had a similar diet, centering on staples such as millet and sweet potatoes; but some families were limited to these staples for most of the year, whereas others regularly enjoyed wheat bread, fish, and other prized foods. The basic wealth difference was in the amount of land owned. A few successful families owned twenty or more acres of land; many families owned about ten acres, but the poorest families owned less than two acres. Since the wealthier families tended to be larger, they did not own ten times as much land per capita as poor families; nonetheless, these figures show a significant degree of stratification in a village of only seven hundred inhabitants, and inter-family competition was a basic feature of the economy.

Social Organization

The village of Taitou was a compact residential area surrounded by an intensively developed and used landscape (Fig. 13). Its households formed nearly continuous streets of houses, tiny yards, and alleys. At the social center, an attractive open area along the Taitou River, people gathered to pass the time in small tasks of repair or manufacture, in order to hear and repeat the latest news. Surrounding this public area were the houses of the well-to-do, while the poorer neighborhoods tended to be on the village periphery.

The average household contained between five and six members. Most village households were landholding "middle peasants." Only a few were rich enough to rent out their land to others, and only a few were poor enough to be considered hired labor. Wealthy families tended to be larger and lived in large compounds of many rooms. Families were eager to be admired by other villagers for their economic success, and a display of large, sturdy buildings, fine clothing, or fat oxen tied in front of a house evoked neighbors' envy. A wealthy family allowed itself a more varied diet, conducted more elaborate ceremonials, and enjoyed a distinctly superior standard of living.

However, a wealthy family that was consuming its wealth rather than saving and investing it was liable to decline. The villagers believed that no family could stay wealthy for as long as four generations; they said of the houses of formerly prestigious families, "Aren't they now only piles of broken bricks and fallen walls?" (ibid.: 53). To understand the rise and fall of a peasant family's fortunes, however, we need to examine the social organization of the economy in Taitou.

Although the large family was an ideal, the typical household comprised a single nuclear family or, less commonly, a family extended to include one married son (the "stem family"). We find the expected division of labor by sex into a domestic sphere dominated by women and an external sphere (fields, commerce, politics) dominated by men. The economic complementarity of husband and wife gave the subsistence-oriented household a large measure of economic self-sufficiency, at least in comparison to nonfarming families.

Yet no Taitou household was completely self-sufficient; all had to produce commodities for the market, chiefly peanuts, soybeans, and pigs. The cash obtained for these commodities was needed to pay taxes and to buy food, tools, and other essential goods and services. For farming families, life in Taitou involved considerable give and take. They neither made nor repaired their own tools; they also had to pay day laborers during certain phases of the agricultural cycle. Women bought raw cotton in the market and spun it into thread; but they had to pay specialists to dye this thread and weave it into cloth, which they then cut and sewed into clothing for their families. Other specialists in the village included one carpenter, three soy oil pressers, five or six masons, a schoolteacher, and various public officials.

A far more complex division of labor was found in the larger system of villages of which Taitou was a part. In China, a unit of major social and economic significance beyond the village was the "standard market area" (Skinner 1964). Taitou and some twenty other villages all did business in one standard market town (Hsinanchen), located about two-thirds of a mile from the village along a dusty road. Hsinanchen was much larger than any of these peasant villages and had large buildings and broad avenues lined with shops and restaurants. There were drugstores, blacksmiths, silversmiths, bakeries, hardware stores, wine-makers, carpenter shops, a bookstore, and many inns and restaurants. On regular market days a large market opened and villagers poured into town. These market days were coordinated with market days in other standard markets in the region, so that itinerant tinkers and peddlers could move from one market to the next in succession without missing a market day (Yang 1945: 90–202; cf. Skinner 1964). A network of paths joined the region as an economic entity.

Villagers from Taitou and other villages visited the market town regularly. In addition to buying and selling, villagers established important economic ties. Men obtained credit from shopkeepers and tradesmen that was essential for maintaining their economic production. While drinking in tea shops or wine shops, they learned how the regional economy was doing and considered how to gear their own efforts accordingly. Even men who had nothing to buy or sell at the market still traveled there every few days, carrying empty baskets, just to be seen and to keep their lines of credit and communication open.

The regional elites made the standard market town their center of operations. Whereas peasants seldom traveled beyond the borders of their standard market area, elites maintained economic and social ties with elites in other market towns. Higher-level markets and administrative centers were further concentrations of more powerful elites. This central-place hierarchy was almost exclusively economic rather than political; no chain of patronage was associated with it. "In the contract-oriented and highly commercialized traditional Chinese society, 'patron-client' relationships were almost insignificant" (Myron Cohen 1984).

Although peasant farm families predominated in Taitou, many opportunities for income existed in part-time or full-time specialty occupations off the farm. It was the ability of a large, united family to tap these additional sources of wealth and convert them into holdings of farmland that laid the basis for economic stratification in Taitou. Not only was this economic truth plain to all, but powerful ideals, deeply ingrained in childhood and reinforced through ceremonies, religious teachings, mottoes, and folktales, supported family loyalty and unity. Yet most married sons asked for their share of the family estate soon after marriage and set up independent households of their own.

Even though this is a general characteristic of peasant social organization (Myron Cohen 1970: xx–xxiv), it is not always easy to explain why some families remain united and flourish while the majority do not. It is instructive, however, to examine how the decision to set up an independent household was typically arrived at in Taitou. Before marriage a young man worked exclusively for the household, turning all his earnings over to his father and receiving a small allowance at his father's discretion. His parents selected his wife for him; indeed, he and his wife might meet face to face for the first time at their wedding. A room was provided for them in the parents' house, where his new wife came under the economic direction of her mother-in-law. The son continued to turn all his income over to his father and to follow his father's wishes in his choice of career and in any business dealings.

The parents welcomed the daughter-in-law as a source of labor that would increase the wealth and prestige of the household, but they also said, "A son is lost when he is married" (Yang 1945: 58). The son's loyalty to his natal family eroded as he became increasingly devoted to his wife and their children. The daughter-in-law encouraged this change. As an outsider, she felt no great loyalty to her husband's family; indeed, she might pointedly wonder whether her husband's economic contribution to the family exceeded that of his brothers, and whether, when the family estate was finally divided, her husband would receive a fair share of the wealth he had helped to generate. Yang (ibid.: 80) speaks of her attitude as "menacing" the communal spirit. Furthermore, daughters and daughters-in-law did not come under the same communal financial control as did sons. Daughters were entitled to work at odd jobs to earn money for themselves, and a diligent daughter might accumulate thirty to fifty dollars by the time she was married. After marriage she was entitled to invest this money in chickens, loans, or other enterprises and to keep the profits for herself. Out of these funds she might buy special foods and other gifts for her husband and children, and her savings became a financial base for establishing a separate household when the family estate was divided among the sons (Myron Cohen 1968).

A daughter-in-law was typically treated as a drudge by her mother-in-law, and she suffered along with everyone else in the family from her father-in-law's authoritarianism and stinginess. Small wonder that she was always after her husband to leave his parents' household and set up his own. In most families the pressure built to the breaking point, and the sons demanded their share of the family estate. This destroyed the basis of the father's absolute economic authority, although some forms of aid and strategic cooperation might continue among family members.

There are two main reasons why large families could gain more wealth than small families. One was the frugality imposed on all members by strict parents. Families seeking to better their lot grimly refused to spend even small sums. Yang (1945: 130) recalls a father lecturing his family in these terms: "Listen, children, there is nothing in this world that can be won easily. A piece of bread must be earned by one day's sweat. You cannot buy any piece of land unless you save all that you can spare through two or three years. The desire for better food, better dress, a good time, or the easy way will lead but to the ruin of our family."

The other advantage of a large family lay in its division of labor. Unless a family already had a great deal of land, it did not need all its sons' labor to run the farm. One son might be enough, freeing other sons to become merchants, tradesmen, artisans, petty officials, or farmworkers. Supporting his extended family as far as possible from farm income, the father could invest the additional income earned by his sons in new pieces of land. As the family's landholdings increased, it rose to prominence in the village.

A large family, then, was often one whose members were sufficiently motivated by pride and ambition to undertake great individual sacrifice, both in material terms and in lost autonomy to the nuclear family. Although for a time the successful family's wealth would help it to remain intact, in due course there would be strong pressures to spend the money on a higher standard of living rather than more land, or to divide the family property among the sons and let them decide how to spend their share. Few families could hold up under these pressures. Only occasionally did one hear of middle-aged sons, themselves fathers of large families, still living in their aged father's house, turning their earnings over to him and accepting his direction in economic matters.

The common pattern was for large families to dissolve into separate nuclear units, which remained tied together by strong loyalties and typically cooperated and lived together in neighborhoods. Owing to patrilocal residence, these hamlet-size groups of families had the same surname and formed "clans" that had certain functions vis-à-vis social security. In strong clans, well-to-do families helped their less fortunate clansmen; widows, orphans, the elderly, and the sick were given money and food if they had been moral people and loyal members of the clan. In addition, unrelated neighbors formed dyadic contracts that made everyday life more convenient and enjoyable, joining in one another's ceremonies and doing favors such as loaning small sums of money without interest.

The village as a whole was united in common cause for limited purposes. At the time of Yang's study, the main such purpose was defense against outlaws, who were prevalent because the central government was weak. Villagers built and manned barricades, organized armed night patrols, and provided armed battalions that joined similar battalions from neighboring villages in fighting off bandit attacks. Villagers also pooled resources to hire a full-time "crop watcher," who guarded the fields against animal pests and thieves.

Public standards were enforced mainly by gossip, threats of "loss of face" (shame), and ostracism. Villagers rarely instituted legal proceedings against one another and did not report one another to governmental officials. The posture of the village toward the outside was in this sense defensive. As far as possible, disputes were resolved by village leaders, men who commanded respect by virtue of their economic success and "proper" behavior. Government officeholders in the village, by contrast, tended to have low status; to obtain the cooperation of villagers in such government projects as road-building and canal repair, they first had to win the support of village leaders.

These leaders appear also to have provided minor forms of patronage. Not only did wealthy clan members help their poorer kin, as we have seen, but in addition wealthy families hired workers, loaned money, rented land, and in other ways provided resources that poor families needed whether they were kin or not. Poor families had to be respectful, honest, and hardworking in order to obtain such resources, but they expected to be treated respectfully and generously in return. For example, unless a family that hired farmworkers on a regular basis provided them with good meals and other favors, it might have trouble hiring workers the next time they were needed.

Recent Change

In 1949, Taitou was "liberated" by the People's Liberation Army and brought under socialist management. For a few years little changed, but during the 1950's its economy underwent a substantial transformation (Diamond 1983; 1985). Decisions on what to plant were made at the level of the commune, an administrative unit composed of many villages, now called brigades (Taitou became a "grain brigade"). Produce was turned over to the commune and ultimately to the state, which in turn distributed necessities to the people. In Polanyi's terms, an economy that had been based on reciprocity at the village level and market exchange at the regional level was restructured into an economy based largely on redistribution, with the Communist party-state being the center to and from which all resources flowed. Neither individuals nor their brigades could defy or circumvent the decisions of the commune management, the "cadres" who with impunity could fine, beat, or imprison opponents of their policies (cf. Yan 1995).

These changes had a mixed impact. At first, beneficial public works and access to new chemical fertilizers and pesticides raised the villagers' standard of living. But then, an intrusive national policy of self-sufficiency in the production of grains forced the farmers of Taitou to limit their production to wheat, maize, and sweet potatoes. With minor exceptions, they were forbidden to grow the other crops—millet, barley, peanuts, soybeans, cotton, fruits, and vegetables—that had formerly diversified their economy. Householders were forbidden to invest privately in pigs, chickens, and small subsistence plots.

As a result of their inability to grow the appropriate crops, their small industries of oil-pressing and bean curd–processing were forced to close, the skilled labor from these shops being diverted to grain production. A similar fate befell the carpentry shop during the tumultuous Cultural Revolution of the late 1960's, when virtually all entrepreneurs were labeled "capitalist roaders" and punished. By 1980, Taitou's income from grain production was average for its region, and the brigade was playing its part in achieving China's goal of self-sufficiency. But it was also economically stagnant. Only a government project to build a new city nearby provided additional wages (but no investment in technology), giving villagers a brief period of comparative affluence.

Yet, during the 1970's, a nearby brigade, Gangtouzangjia, was identified as eligible for governmental development into a "model village." It received the technology to improve irrigation, permission to diversify crops in a manner similar to Taitou's prior to 1949, and such other technological improvements as a generator, mechanical seeder, and additional tractors. In 1978 its per capita gross value of production, 257 yuan, was 37 percent greater than Taitou's, which was 188 yuan. The reason for this government help was that Gangtouzangjia, with a greater population density, was deemed more deserving of help than Taitou, owing to its lower amount of land per person. This decision appears to have reflected the centralized government's political preference for allowing formerly impoverished villages—"the ones to which no one wished to send brides in the past"—to progress faster than their neighbors, as demonstrations of the advantages of "taking the socialist road" (Diamond 1983: 170; 177).

The Chinese economic liberalization of the 1980's helped lift some of the restrictions on Taitou's economy, allowing for greater diversification. In a visit to Taitou in 1986, Diamond (1998) found a significant expansion of household-based petty capitalism, in China called "sidelines." With the restoration of household private plots, small household economic ventures, and specialization in livestock or poultry, the peasant family's income has been rising (Diamond 1983: 179–80). Small shops offering daily necessities have appeared in the village, and many men now work full-time in construction projects outside the village. It appears that, as in comparable rural villages in China (Yan 1992; 1995; 1996), the consequences of the economic liberalization are having a profound impact:

1. Householders feel more in control. Although the party-state was famous for providing security in the form of the "iron rice bowl," peasants now say, "With a piece of land, you have a rice bowl of your own" (Yan 1995: 220).

2. Women have achieved more independence and respect through their elaboration of household economic ventures allowed under liberalization.

3. The power of cadres has been greatly diminished, as their central role in redistribution has been replaced by household economic autonomy. Under collectivization the popular saying had been "It's better to have a good team leader than to have a good father." Now, the popular saying is "A fish has its way, and a shrimp has its way, too," meaning that each individual is free to pursue his own talents, networks, and prospects (ibid.: 232–33). The political economy of redistribution appears to be giving way to the older patterns of reciprocity and exchange.

4. An explosion in access to television has exposed peasant households to new social and political possibilities as government propaganda has given way to entertainment from worldwide sources that

contains alternative political messages emphasizing individual rights and democratic forms of government. These reinforce the probably irreversible individualizing effects of the economic liberalization.

For decades, the vast Chinese experiment with collectivization denied household decision-making. That may have benefited the entire nation by slowing population growth and, except for a tragic relapse in 1959–61, averting famine. But the primacy of the household in all subsistence economies is undeniable. It cannot be wished away by any amount of central planning, as the new economic policies in China appear to be recognizing.

Case 19. The Javanese Villagers of Kali Loro

Our final case study is of the village of Kali Loro in central Java (B. White 1976). It is a fitting last case for our book, since the economy of Kali Loro reflects extremes of population density and intensification of production that are rarely exceeded in nonindustrial economies. Since the degree of intensification, as we shall see, is due partly to the encroachment of a world industrial market in Java over the past century or more, this case also illustrates the changes that take place in an agrarian economy as it becomes incorporated in the world market.

The Subsistence Economy

Kali Loro is a "village complex" located twenty miles northwest of the coastal city of Yogyakarta on a narrow plain between the Progo River and the Menorah Mountains. Although the dense planting of house gardens with fruit trees and a diversity of crops gives the countryside the appearance of a jungle, the landscape here has been radically transformed over hundreds of years of dense human settlement, and there remain virtually no wild or natural habitats in the region. Since the early nineteenth century, the population of Java has grown at a steady rate of between 1 and 2 percent a year. Low as that rate seems by modern standards (it is roughly the current rate of growth in the United States), Java's population increased from five million in 1815 to about eighty million in 1975, and many areas now have population densities well over one thousand persons per square mile. As may be imagined, rural Javanese today experience great pressure on land resources, and most achieve only a marginal subsistence.

Under the circumstances, why has Java's population continued to grow? One reason has been its great potential for intensification by means of new crops, expanded irrigation and (recently) green revolution technology (Guest 1989). Another reason is that the Javanese value large families: White found that the women of Kali Loro want on the average to rear five children to maturity. Because of the frequency of infant and child mortality, many poor women fail to achieve this number and are disappointed, but large families are common. To heighten the paradox, the people of Kali Loro frequently complain about the growth of population and the resulting extreme scarcity of land—yet they continue to desire and produce large families.

In the Yogyakarta region, population appeared to have reached some sort of maximum by the 1970's: the region was a net importer of rice and a net exporter of people (McDonald and Sontosudarmo 1976). Population in Kali Loro is so dense (about 1,850 persons per square mile) that the village areas—consisting of houses with small gardens— occupy nearly as much land as the wet-rice fields. Wet-rice land is so scarce that there is only enough to provide the average adult with about forty days of work a year. This has led some economists to postulate a "hidden unemployment" among rural workers. White shows, however, that there is no hidden unemployment in Kali Loro, where even children's labor is a valued and necessary part of the peasant household's adaptation to extreme land scarcity.

Hence the paradox shifts focus. Instead of wondering why parents continue to have large families where population is overabundant, we now wonder why, in an economy seemingly oversupplied with people, labor is so scarce that households strive to increase their labor supply by having many children.

To resolve this paradox we must first understand that although opportunities for work in rice cultivation are scarce, there are many other ways of earning income. Most of these are less profitable than agriculture and by themselves do not generate even a marginal subsistence income. But in the peasant household, short of land and without alternatives, even starvation wages are preferable to no wages at all. Hence "we should speak not of unemployment ('no work to do'), nor of underemployment ('not enough work to do'), but of low labor-productivity or labor-efficiency, which for a landless or near-landless household means 'a lot of work to do, with very low returns'" (B. White 1976a: 91; 1976b: 272–76).

Everybody wants land for wet rice cultivation, and most people manage to own some. But in order to reach the "poverty line" of bare subsistence a household must farm at least 0.2 hectare of wet rice, and most families in Kali Loro fall below this minimum. In order to bring their household income up to a more comfortable level (*cukupan*, or "enough"), families employ a variety of strategies.

Foremost among these is, and has been for generations, labor-intensive gardening on small plots. Geertz (1963) describes the Javanese as applying "hair-splitting techniques" to extract ever larger quantities of rice from the same land, a process he calls "agricultural involution." By careful and frequent weeding, the application of manure by hand, the laborious preparation of seedbeds, the careful transplanting of seedlings, the grading of plots to equalize the distribution of water in a field, and other techniques, the diligent farmer can get the most out of his small plot. By expanding Java's irrigation networks the government has greatly increased the amount of land available for this kind of cultivation.

Another strategy for dealing with the scarcity of land for wet rice is to plant a garden on the family's home site. Such gardens typically produce as much *food per hour of labor* as rice fields. They are used to grow as many as fifty distinct cultigens, including root crops, tree crops, and items of utilitarian value such as firewood and wrapping leaves. They add diversity to the diet and increase household security. But they are unirrigated and cannot be intensified to yield as much *food per hectare* as wet rice yields.

Wet rice and garden activities together account for only a small proportion of an adult's time (about 2.5 hours per day for men, and 0.5 hour per day for women). The average adult's workday in Kali Loro is filled up by a wide variety of additional activities:

1. Livestock are kept in a stable next to the house. Because very little pasture land is available, grazing animals like sheep or cattle require heavy labor inputs in raising fodder. Fodder must also be raised or bought for draft animals. It is in such demand, and therefore so expensive, that some families in Kali Loro cannot afford to maintain a draft team and have been forced to operate their plows with human labor.

2. Various opportunities for wage labor in and out of agriculture are exploited seasonally.

3. Many handicrafts and foods are produced in the home for sale in the marketplace.

As Table 9 shows, none of these activities is dominant. Rather, the average household is characterized by an "occupational multiplicity" that allows its members to keep working and earning additional income even when, for seasonal or other reasons, any single source of employment fails. Considering that the averages in Table 9 take into account all days including holidays and periods of illness, it is striking that the average workday, including necessary home-centered activi-

TABLE 9

Kali Loro Time Allocation

(Hours per day)[a]

Activity	Men		Women	
Food production				
Hunting	0.0		0.0	
Fishing	0.0		0.0	
Collecting	0.0		0.0	
Agriculture	2.6		0.5	
Livestock	1.3		0.1	
		3.9		0.6
Food preparation	0.1		2.7	
Food consumption[b]	—		—	
Commercial activities				
Collecting natural products	0.3		0.4	
Cash cropping	0.4		2.3	
Manufacturing	1.4		1.0	
Wage labor	0.7		1.7	
Marketing	1.1		0.2	
		3.9		5.6
Housework				
Housekeeping	0.1		1.0	
Water and fuel	0.2		0.1	
		0.3		1.1
Manufacture	0.0		0.0	
Social				
Socializing, visiting[b]	—		—	
Child care	0.4		1.0	
Public events[b]	—		—	
		0.4		1.0
Individual	—		—	
TOTAL	8.6		11.0	

SOURCE: B. White 1976: 209

[a]Workdays, including weekends and holidays.

[b]Social and recreational activities not reported.

ties such as child care and food preparation, is 8.6 hours for adult men and 11.0 hours for adult women.

Peasant communities in Java and other parts of Southeast Asia are unusual among the world's peasantry for their egalitarian gender roles and relatively high status of women (Michaelson and Goldschmidt 1971). In Kali Loro, as in most peasant societies, the men tend the livestock, raise food crops, and do family marketing, whereas women do the bulk of the housekeeping and child care. But women are also heavily engaged in raising cash crops, making and selling handicrafts, and working for wages, important contributions to the household economy that give them an unusual degree of respect and influence (Stoler 1977). This is especially true of the land-poor households in this stratified agrarian community: lacking land, both husband and wife seek wagework with landed families, participating in all phases of farm production. Furthermore, 40 percent of the adult women are engaged in some form of trade (ibid.: 83), and women are the main economic actors in interhousehold exchanges, or *slametan* (see below). The comparatively high status of women in this community, therefore, reflects a form of intensification—wet rice, household-based commercial crops, handicrafts, and local wage labor—that offers as many economic opportunities to women as it does to men.

Tasks are not all valued equally, however. Some pay much better than others (agricultural labor pays several times better than other kinds of work), whereas some pay so little that they barely cover the worker's subsistence needs and add little to the family's cash supply. But low-paying tasks have the advantage of being available when agricultural employment is scarce and alternatives for labor are few, and many can be performed by people with few skills, including children. From age eight on, in fact, both boys and girls perform productive tasks for several hours per day and make highly valued contributions to the household economy (B. White 1976b: 285).

Social Organization

As in other peasant societies, households tend to be self-contained nuclear families. In Kali Loro, households average 4.6 members and are clustered together in twenty-six villages of approximately three hundred members each. Most social contacts between households take place within the village or between members of immediately neighboring villages. Villagers who live more than two miles apart are generally strangers.

"Essential to household survival is . . . a highly flexible division of labour among most household members. Since the returns to labour in most occupations can barely support an adult let alone a whole household, the burden of subsistence is shared by men, women and children together" (ibid.: 280). Changes in the domestic cycle over time greatly influence the economic status of the family. Newly married couples strive to set up independent housekeeping as soon as possible, although that is made difficult by the scarcity of land. As they begin to have children, they enter what White calls the "early expansion" phase, when large amounts of parental time, including fathers' time, is devoted to child care. With hungry mouths to feed, mere subsistence is a struggle, and accumulating capital is nearly impossible.

As children grow up, the family moves into a "late expansion" phase. Older siblings take over the care of children, freeing the parents for directly productive labor: food- or income-producing work increases by more than 25 percent above levels in early expansion households. With children helping to feed themselves and with older members free to seek productive work, late expansion families are able to save money and invest in land, houses, and capital goods.

As in other peasant societies where land is owned and inherited, however, a struggle arises when children prepare to marry. Children demand a share of the household's wealth in order to establish their independent households, but parents are reluctant to give up their control of their children's income and fear that children who have established separate households will not support them in their old age. Parents seek to retain a secure hold on their children's production by holding on to their land and having their married children work for them as sharecroppers.

Even parents of large families fear that they do not have enough children to look after them when they are too old to work. Their fear reflects the tenuousness of kinship ties in peasant society, where security depends as much on friendship as on kinship.

Still another security mechanism is found in Kali Loro: the *slametan*, a series of exchanges of gifts and services organized by the ceremonial system. Although larger families have larger networks and participate more fully in the *slametan*, even small families with marginal incomes spend remarkably large sums in these exchanges, which account for an average of 15 percent of total household expenses for the village as a whole. Here the women's hands-on management of the gift exchanges makes a major contribution to the household economy:

Focusing our attention on the distribution of food, rather than the symbolic aspects of ritual, it becomes clear that the real mediators of interhousehold relationships in the *slametan* are the women and not the men. The women buy, cook, and make the decisions as to how the food will be distributed. (Stoler 1977: 86)

In return, villagers become part of a security network on which disadvantaged families can call, sustaining an ethic of "shared poverty" (Boeke 1953) in which ceremonial exchanges act to some extent as a leveling mechanism (Wolf 1957), equalizing life chances for all community members.

The pressure to equalize life chances intensifies with population density; those villages with the greatest abundance of land per capita are those with the most unequal distribution of land. In the more densely settled communities, practices such as sharecropping, sharing harvests, and cooperative labor exchanges help equalize household incomes.

Nonetheless, economic stratification within villages persists. Some families are landless; others have exceptionally large holdings. The ownership of prized wet rice land is particularly skewed: 37 percent of the villagers own none, whereas the wealthiest 6 percent own more than 50 percent of wet rice acreage. Many landless households have access to wet rice land by renting or sharecropping, and 90 percent of the villagers own at least some garden land. But unequal access to resources is the rule.

As a result, we find patron-client ties between wealthy and poor families. Clients work their patron's lands or care for his animals at lower than average wages in exchange for an acknowledged status as a quasi-member of the patron's family, a status that entitles them to protection and aid. Wage labor for patrons, whether agricultural or not, is a highly desired source of income, even in families with wet rice plots of their own.

When colonial enterprises converted much of Java's best land from rice to sugarcane and other export crops, peasants were forced to intensify their production of rice on inferior lands, including new lands made available for cultivation by government irrigation projects. At the same time, colonialism opened up opportunities for wage labor and craft manufactures destined for the world market. It is not clear exactly how these developments affected population growth, but this much seems certain: the proportion of peasant family income derived from subsistence farming has declined as population and occupational multiplicity have risen.

To return by way of summary to White's main argument, we can see that it is rational for a husband and wife in Kali Loro to want many children. Although young children are a hardship, older children make a major labor contribution to all areas of household production. Households with older children are more efficient to the degree that older children produce more income than they consume, and larger families produce a greater surplus above subsistence needs, which can be invested to increase income and security. Where land is extremely scarce and alternatives to agriculture yield even smaller returns than the overworked fields themselves, every effort is made to increase family income by the exploitation of family labor.

The extraordinarily long working day of the Javanese adult is an index of the scarcity of opportunities for productive work. The people of Kali Loro correctly attribute this scarcity to population growth, yet they are victims of their own tragedy of the commons. Any household that strives to serve the common good by limiting its births achieves nothing but the disadvantage of being short of labor in a highly competitive economy in which more labor means better living for the family.

Given a nonindustrial technology, peasant economies generally make maximum use of the land, with little or no fallowing and virtually no dependence on wild foods. But, more important, peasants are integrated into large, hierarchically structured economic systems, and in this sense, despite a significant measure of household subsistence autonomy in comparison to modern families, they are the least self-sufficient of all the peoples examined in this book.

Even Boa Ventura, at much lower population densities than Taitou and Kali Loro, represents a high degree of intensification of agriculture: many hours of labor and much husbandry of resources are needed to keep the household going. But Taitou and Kali Loro are our most dramatic and poignant examples of intensification: the "involuted" application of family labor to tiny plots of sweet potatoes and wet rice, with each plant hand-tended through every demanding step of production; the expropriation of all available land to human purposes; the need to use all resources, even human feces and the soot of a brick oven, to replenish the land and coax any small additional measure of food from it; and the scattering of efforts among several very small plots, each in a different microecological zone, to minimize risks of crop failure and maximize the diversity of foods in the diet.

Yet, for all this hard work and careful management, peasant economies provide a less satisfactory subsistence than others we have examined. Although many economic systems may be exposed to sudden, unpredictable disasters that result in famine and death, only among peasants do we find a substantial portion of the population persistently fluctuating, not between feast and famine, but between barely adequate diets and serious undernourishment. The larger economy may provide them with opportunities to bolster their economic security, but competition is intense and the net gain in security is meager and costly.

The peasant household is in one sense self-sufficient: the needs of the political economy have grown beyond the limits of effectiveness of extended corporate kin groups. These large but comparatively intimate social units, such as the clans of the Central Enga and the Trobriand Islands, have fallen away as their risk-spreading, technological, defensive, and trade functions have passed on to still larger, more distant institutions such as armies, markets, and bureaucratic agencies.

What is left for the peasant family are dyadic friendship ties designed to ensure that short-term scarcities will be made up by gifts and other aid from friends. That very poor families, such as those in Kali Loro, will spend up to 15 percent of their household budget on gifts, feasts, and other social expenses is not a sign of economic foolishness but a measure of the importance of exchange ties to neighbors and of full membership in the village community.

Despite its village ties, however, the peasant family is quite alone and exposed in relation to the larger society. As the state expands toward bureaucracy and market-integration, elites are less willing to maintain a rural power base through paternalism and noblesse oblige. Market efficiencies are acquired at the expense of traditional social arrangements that once served household security. Peasants find themselves in an insecure world full of powerful and indifferent interests.

They respond by adopting economic strategies that increase their security in small ways that count. They tend to diversify crops—an age-old strategy—to reduce risks of massive crop loss; to build friendship ties through acts of generosity; and to build patron-client ties with local elites as hedges against disaster. They seek employment opportunities in the labor market to increase household income but are reluctant to abandon even small farm plots that give them at least partial control over their food supply. They know that the market is beyond their control and that it is sometimes manipulated by aggrandizers, so they minimize their dependence on it by storing food for home consumption, converting cash into livestock and other material items that can always be converted into staples in an emergency, and avoiding banks, courts, and other agencies of elite power.

They seek, therefore, relations to known local elites who through god-parenthood or other ritual relationships show a willingness to contribute to the peasant family's well-being. They view personal dependence on a patron as a source of strength and thus, paradoxically, of freedom. This "client consciousness" puzzles observers from more fully commercialized economies, who equate freedom with a free market and see any patron-client relationship as smacking of exploitation. Historically, however, class consciousness—a political viewpoint that sees group activities such as unions, strikes, and rebellions as means to control exploitation in the marketplace—takes root among the rural poor only after the traditional paternalistic systems of protection have been broken down by commercialization (Johnson 1999). A patron-client relationship, despite its class inequality, is still an effort to build trust and loyalty into vertical economic relations, whereas the market, which takes over management of the vertical flows of labor, crops, handicrafts, raw materials, and money, is, at its most efficient, an impersonal "invisible hand" that knows no loyalty and is unmoved by human suffering.

Overall, we find the peasant family to be highly vulnerable in a land-scarce, competitive, densely populated economy. Although the family carries most of the risks of production, it enjoys little profit. Why? Primarily because such labor-intensive methods of production as we have encountered in this chapter produce low returns to labor; secondarily because elites and governmental agencies are too powerful, and too removed from local control, to feel any pressure to return much of the wealth they extract from the agrarian sector. The capacity for intensification depends to a considerable extent on services provided by the state, but these merely serve to keep production levels up and avoid mass starvation, not to relieve individual families of the burden of scarcity. Significantly, a married couple's greatest fear is that they will be abandoned in their old age by offspring whose own battle with scarcity is too all-consuming to leave them the time and energy to care for their aged parents.

FOURTEEN

The Evolution of Global Society

COMMERCE DEFIES EVERY WIND
OUTRIDES EVERY TEMPEST AND INVADES
EVERY ZONE—BANCROFT
(Inscription on the U.S. Department of
Commerce Building, Washington D.C.)

THE INDUSTRIAL REVOLUTION has been the fourth great techno-logical leap for humankind, after the Urban Revolution; the Neolithic domestication of plants, animals and humans; and, of course, the origin of culture itself at the dawn of prehistory. In a widely accepted view, the Industrial Revolution was the prime example of mastery over na-ture brought on by technological progress (Beard 1927: 1). New means of harnessing power (water, steam, petroleum), along with the applica-tion of scientific method to technological development, allowed in-creased production of goods that raised living standards and encour-aged population growth. But the revolution was more than the inven-tion of industrial technology. It was above all "commercialization" (Bodley 1996: 3), the spread of a capitalist system of market exchange instituted (embedded) in a "liberal state," and it wrought such dra-matic and far-reaching changes to the whole of society that Polanyi (1944) called it *The Great Transformation*. It moved like a tidal wave out of England, across Europe and North America, and in the twentieth century it has reached into every last corner of the planet. All of the so-cieties that make up our case studies have been touched by it. Some, with varying success, have adapted, while others have been virtually destroyed. Is our understanding of the process of social evolution in previous chapters—up to and including the rise of agrarian states—robust enough to explain these changes, or are we facing something utterly new for which new theoretical tools are needed?

A vast literature on the subject has provided new tools for understanding modern change. Our purpose in this chapter will be to review the most powerful of those tools and make explicit how they relate to our theoretical argument. As we have seen, in chiefdoms and agrarian states most people still lived their lives in the countryside, producing their own food and manufactures in the home, even as they paid rent to a landlord and purchased specialized products in local markets. Power was distributed in hierarchies of political patronage and military command. Although places on earth still fit this description today, the clear trend of history is to supplant them with increasingly urban populations; production there takes place outside the home, and a minority of the population produces food for a majority who do not. Political power is increasingly vested in politicians and bureaucrats with access to some form of electoral process and to the wealth needed to influence it. To what degree is this pattern of change a continuation of the process of social evolution that preceded it?

At the very least, we may say that the technodemographic engine we identified in Figure 3 has been more prominent than ever. The twin processes of population growth and technological development have accelerated in mutual feedback at unprecedented rates—it was at the beginning of the "modern period" that the sharp J-curve of human population growth took its definitive turn upward (Fig. 1b). Can it also be said, as our model implies, that this accelerated development was a form of intensification that generated new problems whose solutions would take familiar forms: risk management, warfare, capital investment, and trade? The answer is not simple. The course of recent change in many of our cases raises theoretical challenges for the model we have been working with. Specifically, building causal arguments outward from the subsistence base to the larger structures of society becomes ever more complicated and tenuous as the political economy feeds back upon and shapes the subsistence economy:

In an industrial world, capital and credit arrangements, trade systems and the like are crucial. Socially-derived needs—special tastes in foods, more ample housing and clothing, and a great variety of appurtenances to living—become increasingly important in the productive arrangement as culture develops; and yet these originally were probably more often effects of basic adaptations than causes. (Steward 1955: 40)

In short, the political economy has become so distant from—so seemingly independent from—subsistence that many powerful influences on the economy, like currency exchanges or fashion, seem hardly connected to subsistence matters at all.

Recent Change in Nonindustrial Societies

To a degree, the engine of population growth and technological change can be found at work in modern change among our cases. In her review of Japanese feudal history (Case 15), Taeuber (1958: 15) had noted a correlation between population growth and "a monotonous regularity in the accounts of agricultural improvements, new lands, famine, epidemic and decline." In many of our cases we see an association between population growth, technological change, and an overexploitation of resources that puts households at risk. The Machiguenga (Case 3)—already liable to deplete resources locally under traditional population densities—have faced a surge of immigration from the overpopulated highlands (altiplano), restricting them to less land per household, degrading fish and game resources across whole regions. The Basseri (Case 14) have experienced a huge loss of pasture due to overgrazing in the last half of the twentieth century, a period of rapid population growth in Iran.

Yet in most of our cases, even among the Machiguenga and Basseri, the most visible and direct influences on modern change come from an expanding central government, an expanding market, or both. Let us recall a few examples:

1. Among the Nganasan (Case 4), the first circumstances pushing them out of their family-level subsistence economy was the growing market demand for animal products among expanding populations to the south. In response, the Nganasan became reindeer pastoralists emphasizing private herds, larger kin groups, and patron-client relationships.

The next circumstance for change was the effort by the Soviet government to bring these independent people under state control. Nganasan resistance to control was gradually overwhelmed by immigration of soviet miners, imposition of schools with state-sponsored curricula, organization of herders into soviet-style management groups, and the growing availability of consumption goods.

In a turnabout, the latest circumstance for change is the inability of the overextended post-Soviet government to maintain its efforts at control, leading to a shrinking flow of cash, fewer market opportunities, and more incentive for Nganasan pastoralists to revert to their former independence and self-reliance.

2. For the Eskimo of the North Slope of Alaska, change came primarily as the U.S. Congress imposed free market legislation on the development of the oil fields that lay under Eskimo lands. Although long integrated into the market to the degree of hunting from snowmobiles

and heating their houses with fuel oil, the Eskimos had remained largely subsistence-oriented even after oil was discovered at Prudhoe Bay. But they surprised many people by understanding what Congress was up to, taking full advantage of their legal rights as Alaska Natives, and taking a degree of control of the development process. Still, Congress wrote a law that strongly imposed free enterprise legalities on the oil business, so that community efforts to eliminate poverty through public spending have to be vigorously defended against the tendency for new wealth to become individually concentrated, splitting their community into a small wealthy class and a large impoverished one.

3. The Kirghiz pastoralists (Case 11) first experienced drastic change when surrounding nation-states (China and the Soviet Union) closed their borders and in so doing prevented their seasonal migration through diverse ecological zones. This created a political circumscription that forced them greatly to intensify production in the remaining region open to them, the Pamir. There followed an expansion of risk-management and trade, both of which favored a stronger khan and a more kin-based ownership of intensified pastures. Increased danger from Russian military incursions, however, related to the growing conflict with Afghanistan, put the Kirghiz in the middle of tragic violence from which they finally escaped by appealing to their ethnic/linguistic affiliation with Turkey. They were accepted there as refugees and offered an opportunity to re-establish themselves as mixed farmers and herders.

4. Change came to the Basseri (Case 14) most broadly as a steady reduction in the amount of resources available to them and in their freedom to exploit them opportunistically. With the Iranian population explosion, pastures were extended into more distant arid zones as the government dug wells and farmers transformed former pastures. What pastures remained were sought by multitudes of herders, including urban capitalists seeking to raise hardy animals for market, employing professional herders (who did not travel with their families but simply tended herds). The national government—concerned to protect pastures endangered by overuse and to extend control into marginal regions where the state had formerly been weak—often developed policies contrary to the wishes of the Basseri, enforcing them by police and military power where necessary.

5. The tenant farmers of Boa Ventura (Case 17) actually saw their population decline by one-third over a twenty-year period, even as the overall population of Brazil doubled. The change came primarily from the landlord's perception of changing market realities, where raising sugar cane and cattle for a growing market made more economic sense

than trying to profit from shares of his tenants' production of grains and cotton. The landlord's family also feared the impact of the new Brazilian constitution, which gave tenants expanded rights via land reform, and saw a solution in letting the population of tenants shrink through attrition, relying more instead on hired farm labor. Expanding government social security programs also increased the confidence of some tenants that they could survive without a landlord's patronage, breaking down the old paternalism still further.

6. For the Chinese peasants of Taitou (Case 18), modern change came drastically when their region was conquered by the People's Liberation Army. A rural economy that had largely been managed by individualistic small farm families integrated into regional marketing systems was gradually transformed into a centralized redistributive economy under the control of the Communist Party and administered locally by party cadres. The goals of the party were to redistribute wealth and resources from the rich to the poor and to distribute food and other products fairly to avoid the extremes of wealth and poverty that had been associated many times in the past with famine. The creation of an "iron rice bowl" of security for every family was achieved to a considerable degree, except for a devastating famine from 1959–61. But the intrusive redistributive economy stifled local decision-making and destroyed many income-producing opportunities. Hence the reforms of the 1990's, allowing individual land-ownership and decision-making responsibility, have had the effect of partly restoring the rural economy to a form it had prior to the revolution.

In most of these cases, we can see some evidence that the growth of population has hemmed people in, limiting their choices. Yet the intrusions of central government, and the penetration of the market, seem equally decisive in directing change, if not more so. In order to see how expanding government and commercialization—preeminent features of the political economy—fit into our model of the evolution of human societies, we need to examine three main lines of theoretical argument and debate, and to translate their key ideas into terms consistent with our approach.

Theorizing Contemporary Change

For Polanyi (1944), the real drama in the Industrial Revolution was not the proliferation of amazing new technologies but the complete social transformation it wrought via the self-regulating ("free") market and the liberal state:

The fount and matrix of the system was the self-regulating market. It was this innovation which gave rise to a specific civilization. . . . The liberal state was itself a creation of the self-regulating market. The key to the institutional system of the nineteenth century lay in the laws governing market economy. (ibid.: 3)

Polanyi believed that the hegemony of the self-regulating market was but a phase in modern change that had spent its force by World War I. What would he have said today, when many observers celebrate the triumph of the same self-regulating market for transforming the world into one global economic system in its inexorable progress?

Before we dismiss Polanyi as hopelessly outdated, we should keep in mind that projecting the future belongs to the present, and that we are so immersed in our moment of time that we most likely do not see the larger historical processes that will determine the ultimate fate of the free market. Had we, for example, lived in the desperate times of the Black Death, we might have foreseen a future in which humankind was to disappear from the face of the earth in an apocalyptic demise engineered by divine wrath. Yet the huge population losses suffered in those years were quickly restored by rapid reproduction in the next few generations, so that the upward curve of human population growth predicted by the Doomsday Equation shows barely a dip when viewed over the long term (Fig. 1b; Ehrlich and Ehrlich 1970: 12–13). Whether or not the self-regulating market is the wave of the long-term future is not a question we can answer here. But we can try to explain why it has played such a dominant role in economy and society from the Industrial Revolution until now.

The self-regulating market and the liberal state are, as Polanyi said, closely linked, if not indeed part and parcel of the same process. The U.S. Constitution is a prototypical document creating a liberal state largely structured to nurture a free market (e.g., Beard 1935). In order to see the continuity between the emergence of the instituted free market and the processes of social evolution we have analyzed throughout this book, we will examine two major theoretical lines (the second having two subtypes):

1. Liberal economics, a theory that identifies the strengths of the free market and spells out the political-institutional requirements that must be met if these strengths are to be allowed their fullest development.

2. The antimarket critique, taking two forms that are related in theory but propounded by distinct groups of scholars:

  2.1. Substantive economics, an antimarket critique based on the recognition that the free market dissolves social bonds, atomizing individuals to stand alone against an overwhelming array of power-centers that seek to exploit market opportunities to their own benefit. In addition to substantivist economic anthropology, this critique includes political economy (encompassing varieties of Marxism and institutional economics).

2.2. Political ecology, another antimarket critique based on the potential damage that market behavior does to ecology and the environment. This set of critiques points to the role of markets in environmentally destructive activities such as deforestation, fisheries depletion, pollution, global warming, and many tragedies of the commons that increasingly result from unfettered individualism and competition in free market economies (Bodley 1996). It also debates the complex relationship between market penetration and population growth (e.g., Durham 1979; Goodland 1992).

As anthropologists, we need to be aware that, just as much as these theoretical lines are carefully reasoned scholarly arguments backed by evidence, each is also a moral position, a political philosophy to which its adherents are deeply committed. This helps to explain a certain inability among enthusiasts to step back from the debates, to acknowledge that each theoretical approach identifies and analyzes only a piece of the whole evolutionary process as it is occurring. Yet it is in the complementarity of these theories that we will find the links between modern change and the general theory of human social evolution.

The Theory of the Free Market

The free market in theory is a complex system with no one in charge. It requires a liberal state (civil society) to provide the institutional matrix needed if capitalism is to be successful: standard money, property rights, enforcement of contracts voluntarily entered into, rules against fraud and in favor of open access, the peace of the market, and so forth. Beyond that, however, the state is to step aside. Any effort of government to decide what people do with the market—how they make decisions, what they should or should not do with their resources, how much commodities should cost, who should deal with whom—is seen as an unwelcome intrusion or imperfection in the market. The impersonal operation of the market, wherein prices are set by the law of supply and demand—Adam Smith's "invisible hand" (1993)—guarantees its efficiency. Governmental controls, or efforts by powerful individuals to use wealth and force to exclude others from market opportunities, reduce the efficiency of the market and cause unnecessary suffering to the marketing populace.

In the political sphere, the emergence of the self-regulating market makes possible the triumph of wealth finance over staple finance. In staple finance, the appropriation of surplus foodstuffs, their transport, storage, and allocation, all required central management by state functionaries. In a smoothly functioning market system, all accumulation, transport, storage, and distribution are managed by self-interested parties (truckers, wholesalers, warehousers, bankers, retailers, consumers), with money as the measure of value.

The adaptiveness of the basic principle of the self-regulating market long precedes the Industrial Revolution. This "market principle" (Bohannan and Dalton 1965)—referring to transactions where the value of the goods and services exchanged is set by supply and demand—is found in marketplaces in nonindustrial societies where no liberal state exists, and it characterizes some exchanges we associate with societies on the family and local group level. Indeed, if human populations had to live exclusively from resources found only in their home ranges, then many small but crucial shortages—say for obsidian or salt—would be enough to prevent them from surviving there, and humankind would never have spread into the variety of habitats it has. Some form of trade between groups at a distance (i.e., strangers) may well go back hundreds of thousands of years, to the beginning of humankind (Hayek 1988: 40–41). Certainly, the "trading depots" where inland and coastal Eskimos (Case 6) exchange their specialized production, the bazaars where Middle Eastern pastoralists and farmers trade (Cases 11 and 14), even the gifts between peasants known as "dyadic contracts" (Cases 17, 18, and 19) all exhibit an opportunistic effort to maximize personal benefit in light of local supply and demand, even where the institutional framework of a liberal state is lacking. As Sahlins (1972: 280–301) has shown for Melanesia, supply and demand affects the prices of bartered goods such as axes, spears, pigs, and coconuts, even in the absence of a liberal state—that is, in the absence of a legal and cultural framework institutionalizing competition and profit-seeking.

The market principle, found wherever bargaining takes place (Cancian 1968), solves many problems in the subsistence economy without control or direction by elites. Individuals approach transactions as opportunities to obtain what they lack by offering what they can afford to give up. Each individual is empowered to make the best deal he or she can, given the realities of the situation. The accumulation of individual choices—to trade with this person or that, to offer this item or withhold it, to invest labor and resources in preparing an item for trade—amounts to a kind of "unconscious collaboration of individuals . . . [that] leads to the solution of problems" (Hayek 1939: 14). Even as some transactions are heavily determined by social rules and ritual formulas—such as how much to offer in bride price, or to whom valuable arm bracelets or necklaces may be given—many other transactions quietly and without fanfare allow goods and services to move effectively between households according to supply and demand (e.g., the Trobriand *kula* ring, Case 12).

When the market principle is given expression as political philosophy, the underlying moral imperative is individual freedom and responsibility (M. Friedman 1962; Murray 1997). The freedom-with-responsibility evoked by the philosophy is one we are amply familiar with from our case studies. In much of the world throughout history, individuals and their families have confronted a world of risks and opportunities requiring them to evaluate their options in terms of their perceived self-interest. Should I burn my field today or risk rain by waiting for a few more days of dry weather? Should I weave or go in search of food? To which Big Man should I contribute my gifts? How much grain should I store at home and how much sell in the market? These choices are rarely compelled by force of arms: they are the business of the individuals or families involved. They may involve rational cost-benefit calculations, or may simply involve imitation of respected members of their communities (Hayek 1988: 24; Henrich 1998). In either case, the decision is theirs, and they must accept responsibility for their choices (although it is only human to shift the blame to agencies such as witches and demons when outcomes prove disappointing). Occasionally, bad choices can be fatal, but more often than not some of the individual's choices have included acts of generosity in building social ties that may be called upon when his or her resources are exhausted. Still, it is a hard world, and poor management is seldom rewarded. The implied morality behind the theory of the free market is Darwinian, a kind of Puritan ethic whereby individuals are blessed for cleverness, self-sacrifice, and diligence, and cursed for indolence and poor judgment (Tawney 1926).

Antimarket Critique I: Substantive Economics

Even free market theorists acknowledge that "there are unquestionably fields . . . where the price mechanism is not applicable, either because some services cannot be priced, or because a clear object desired by an overwhelming majority can only be achieved if a small dissenting minority is coerced" (Hayek 1939: 13). Although these theorists, perhaps understandably, pay little attention to exceptional cases where some process other than the market (say, public education) must be entrusted with meeting economic needs, they do acknowledge that government has a part to play in controlling such threats as monopolism, pollution, and contagious disease. Furthermore, in accepting that the self-regulating market flourishes only when a strong infrastructure of government exists, market theorists allow room for a significant institutional setting in which the free market is embedded. Indeed, much of the bureaucracy that free market theorists criticize for inhibiting the market actually sustains it, through regulation of property rights, standard weights and measures, truth in advertising, and a host of services that allow the market to function smoothly. This is as true today as it was a thousand years ago, when China first attempted to bolster its market economy with a bureaucracy that would be as free as possible from local corruption while intruding as little as possible into the local political economy.

The antimarket critique arising from Marxism, institutional economics, and substantivist economic anthropology, however, goes beyond even the most generous concessions from free market theorists. It has a general and a specific form. The general critique is that the free market promotes an egocentric individualism that dissolves the integument of society (Wolf 1969: 283), placing competition above cooperation and selfish motives above community. The specific form of the critique is that free market competition results in the accumulation of wealth in the hands of a few, leaving the rest in poverty and vulnerable to exploitation. In this view, "the capitalist state exists to ensure the domination of one class over another" (Wolf 1982: 308), whereas the proper role of government would be to place restraints on aggrandizers in the market in order to enhance values other than greed and bring about a fair distribution of wealth (distributive justice; see Plattner 1989c: 380).

As moral philosophy, this critique, which Cook (1968: 212) once called "romantic," challenges the hard-nosed individualism of the market principle. Specifically, it draws attention to the way the market creates and sustains class inequalities that increase suffering for the great majority of workers while opening the door to grotesque excesses of consumption for an exclusive few. More generally, it sees the power of the market as a solvent of traditional social ties, a shortsighted way of managing economic problems through efficiency while sacrificing tested, security-oriented social relations and the communal spirit with which to tackle injustice and threats to the common good.

Antimarket Critique II: Political Ecology

The logic of the second antimarket critique is akin to that of the substantivist, but its focus is less on the breakdown of human community than on the destruction of the health and sustainability of the natural world on which we depend. In this view, until the free market became dominant, human communities lived more or less in balance with nature, having developed traditional mechanisms—both ecological and political—for containing damage to the environment and ensuring the sustainability of production systems over the long term (Balée 1989). The free market, by contrast, dissolves a sense of interconnection with the natural world just as it dissolves the social integument. Ferreting out profits tends to be a short-term goal: extract the resource, market it, pocket the income, and move on when the resource is exhausted (Bodley 1996: 74–75). Strip mining, clear-cut forestry, and fisheries depletion all stand as dramatic contemporary examples of this tendency. To a degree, the original model of the tragedy of the commons (Chap. 1) fits these cases: it is more profitable to exploit the resource to exhaustion than to protect it for some future-oriented abstraction like "the whole earth," or "our grandchildren."

The approach of political ecology is still emerging. As a combination of approaches from the well-developed fields of political economy and human ecology, it requires a balance of sometimes contradictory positions. For example, many political economists believe that the world's capacity to produce food is far greater than the existing population, and that poverty and starvation are the results of an unequal distribution of wealth and political power: "It is commonly accepted that humanity could easily be fed if available resources were put into production using existing technology" (De Janvry 1981: 144). A redistribution of resources—a political goal—would therefore eliminate world hunger. Yet others, more ecologically oriented, believe that the world has already reached or exceeded carrying capacity and that redistributing resources from rich to poor, while it would ease some hunger, would not eliminate it (Ehrlich and Ehrlich 1990: 66–69). One study of possible redistribution of the world's available food found that the only way to bring the food consumption of the poorest populations up to a minimum level of adequacy would be to lower the food consumption of affluent populations to the same nutritional minimum—any strategy less drastic, such as reducing the consumption of meat by 25 percent in affluent nations, would reduce food deficits in poor populations but would still leave hundreds of millions of people short of reaching recommended levels of food intake (Heady et al. 1978). Those who see hunger as a problem of distribution emphasize the "political" aspect of political ecology, whereas those who see it as a problem of limited carrying capacity emphasize the "ecological" aspect. The truth no doubt lies somewhere in the contested middle ground between the two.

As in the substantivist critique, the political ecological critique argues that community controls, whether local or at the highest levels of political integration, are required to prevent individuals from unleashing on the environment the full destructive potential of capitalist exploitation. As moral philosophy, the political ecological position places a premium on reaching a sustainable accommodation with the natural world. We owe it to ourselves and to future generations to consume only what we can replace, and to clean up what we despoil. In this view, the well-being of the earth's ecosystem is of concern to everyone. In an ideal world, individuals would perceive their interconnection with each other and the intricate web of life and voluntarily restrain themselves, as is implied by some religious belief systems that promote an environmental ethics based on human reciprocity with nature (Tucker and Williams 1997). In a real world of diverse perspectives and values, entities (individuals, corporations, governments) that destroy the natural resource base must be restrained by political means, a contradiction of the free market ideal.

The Market and the State as Problem-Solvers

The promarket vs. antimarket debate is fundamentally a debate about the relative importance of the free market versus government in solving problems basic to the well-being of families and communities, replicating a common theme in political debates everywhere. Market theorists sometimes seem to imagine the liberal state as mere background, a functional setting in which to place the jewel of the free market. Yet the achievement of the liberal state came as late as it did in the evolution of human societies because it represents a monumental, difficult, and often fragile triumph over the self- and family-centered practices—corruption, gangsterism, oligarchy, and fraud, as well as various forms of local protest against incorporation into the larger political economy—that would destroy it. For example, recent efforts to create democratic capitalism in Russia without the infrastructure of laws and institutions to contain it illustrate how potentially disastrous untrammeled economic individualism can be, and how difficult the establishment of a rule of law (Alexiev 1998). The self-regulating market cannot thrive without a powerful, centralized state to tame its most destructive extremes.

On the other hand, critics of the free market seem to underestimate the vast number of economic problems the market solves daily for households that participate in it. Critics of the free market have focused on the role of greed in motivating market participation. They see the proper role of the state as restraining greed and encouraging a sustaining mutuality between people and their human and natural communities. An integrative approach to the evolution of human societies, however, must go beyond greed as the dominant explanation for the expansion of commercialization (cf. Harvey 1989: 103) and acknowledge its power to solve problems of real significance to households and communities.

In our model of social evolution, we have identified four problem areas that require new solutions at each new level of intensification: production risks, raiding and warfare, inefficient resource use, and resource deficiencies. A brief look at how these problems are being addressed in the transforming economies of the cases we reviewed earlier in this chapter illustrates how an integrative theory of social evolution applies to the emerging global system. Again, as elsewhere, we stress that the direction of change toward greater scale and complexity does not imply progress, and that the "solutions" to the four problem areas offered by an integrated market system do not mean that life is getting better for ordinary people, who in many cases appear to be worse off for the change.

Production Risks. The market offers various instruments for averting risk at competitive prices (bank savings, insurance policies, commodity options). Many of these take advantage of the role of money as a storage device, on the principle that money can be exchanged for necessities, as was previously true for primitive valuables and wealth finance. Farmers engaged in a secure market system can store value in money with confidence that in times of need their money can be converted into food and other necessities. Many peasant farmers, who with good reason distrust markets and money in societies where corruption debilitates the market system, continue to seek security directly by storing food in storage bins or invested in livestock (which can be sold for staples when needed). Storing staples at home, however, is a comparatively wasteful form of economic security that tends to disappear when market systems become strong and reliable.

The market also moves commodities quickly from seller to buyer—reducing risk of loss due to glut or spoilage—and allows purchases of life-sustaining supplies by buyers whose own supplies have been destroyed in calamities. Most contemporary peasants (e.g., Cases 17, 18, and 19) store less food in their homes and buy more on the market than was true in the past, a strategy that, to be successful, depends on the farmers' confidence that they will have money on hand when their larders are empty.

From the substantivist perspective (antimarket critique I), however, the market intensifies risk for working families by severing their ancient ties to primary resources (land and fisheries, etc.). Instead, re-sources become commodities that can be alienated through sale. Fur-thermore, by turning labor itself into a commodity that is only as valu-able as the prevailing wage rate, free laborers become "free to contract with an employer on an individual basis. They are also 'free' to go hun-gry, wear cheap clothing, and become homeless if they have no in-come" (Plattner 1989c: 382).

This process is underway on Boa Ventura (Case 17), as the landlord's family increasingly seeks to do away with the old system of embedded patron-client ties, to deal instead with free labor to be hired and fired at will. The national government has stepped in with retirement benefits and health services that help replace the lost security net once provided by patrons. The family- and community-centered Basseri are also finding their ancient ties to pastures severed by modern market ar-rangements favoring salaried herders in the employ of urban capital-ists. What will become of both the Brazilian tenant farmers and the Basseri herders when the market transformation is complete and they are left landless? The efforts of the Eskimo (Case 6) and the Machi-guenga (Case 3) to fend off commercialization and establish commu-nity-based control over resources are aimed at preventing the market from dissolving their traditional ties to their land. And the Chinese government pursued a Marxist antimarket policy by redistributing wealth from better-off villages like Taitou (Case 18) to poorer ones like Gangtouzangjia, and by providing an iron rice bowl of security for every household.

With respect to production risks, the political ecological view (anti-market critique II) points to the risk-spreading techniques of traditional farmers, in contrast to capital-intensive, high-yield food production strategies that are vulnerable to massive threats from pests, disease, or drought (e.g., Boa Ventura farmers [Case 17]; cf. Bodley 1996: 89; John-son 1972). The market also encourages overconsumption and degra-dation of resources like that described for twentieth-century Iran (Case 14), which could take generations to restore, lowering the earth's carry-ing capacity at a time when populations are growing (Bodley 1996: 26).

In sum, an integrated, self-regulating market system solves certain risk problems efficiently, allowing food surpluses to move to meet de-mand before they spoil, developing insurance policies and other in-struments for spreading risk at the lowest possible cost, and so on. But these efficiencies of risk management are achieved impersonally. The market has no compassion for individual families that have been placed at risk from landlessness and unemployment as a consequence of market efficiencies. The free market in effect assumes a Darwinian "survival of the fit" stance toward families living in poverty. Furthermore, being blind to many long-term effects of resource degradation (e.g., soils and fisheries) and pollution (e.g., water), the market's very efficiency at mobilizing masses of capital to extract resources increases the risks of future catastrophe. If the food supply should start to fall while population continues to rise, a condition that appears already to be happening in some locales (Ehrlich and Ehrlich 1990: 69), a market system that favors short-term gain over long-term management of food-production resources would share the blame for the crisis.

From the standpoint of social evolution, by managing some kinds of risk—such as reducing the loss due to spoilage of staples stored by individual households for security purposes—the market allows greater intensification (that is, a greater population can live on the same resources because the resources are being distributed more efficiently). At the same time, the increased integration of household producers into the de facto community formed by market participation means a loss of family-based security. The system works well much of the time, but when the market is disrupted for some reason—say, due to regional drought or political instability—the households have no fall-back position and are extremely exposed. They depend on a state system of redistribution (based on taxation) to help them through the crisis, a politically charged moment in time when their subjection to the highly stratified police power of the state is reinforced by the clear realization that they can put food on the table only through loyalty to the elites who control the emergency food supplies.

Raiding and Warfare. Population increase and technological improvements raise the value of land and other natural resources, making them ever more worth fighting over. The market, as a powerful integrative force, may discourage warfare, to the extent that it increases the benefits of peaceful relations between trading partners. This continues the pattern in smaller scale societies where trade establishes intergroup trust and (sometimes) prevents war (Cases 9 and 12).

True, the market, as a bastion of self-interest, in and of itself does nothing to prevent profit-seekers from turning to negative reciprocities such as organized crime and the military seizure of rich resource zones. Yet it is the value of the market in solving real economic problems that sustains the political will to institute a civil society capable of guaranteeing the peace of the market. By defining and guaranteeing property rights, the free market/liberal state channels disputes over resources toward peaceful resolution. The allocation of mineral rights to Eskimos (Case 6), for example, gave them real bargaining power in peacefully negotiating with capitalists bent on exploiting their resources. It is the liberal state that wields the heavy hand of police and judicial power to preserve the peace of the market.

To an extent, the free market also offers aggrandizers pathways to wealth and power that do not require military dominance and tributary wealth flows. The imposition of market peace allowed (and required) the Indians of the Northwest Coast (Case 9) to "fight with property" instead of weapons. In France and Japan (Case 15), growth of the integrative market accompanied a shift in the centers of power from landed property (control over the means of production) to commercial wealth (control over the means of exchange) that marked the end of warlord-based feudalism.

On the other hand, the free market has often motivated warfare. Capital's restless search for resources and consumers becomes a motivation for wars of conquest, as when Europeans fought the Opium War to open China to Western markets, or the United States seized its southwestern territory from Mexico. The border hostilities between Afghanistan, China, and the Soviet Union that victimized the Kirghiz (Case 11) were partly about establishing national control over distant resource zones and trade routes, as is the contemporary internal expansion of Iranian government control over the Basseri.

Local communities often want to have nothing to do with the market, or at least to set the terms of their market involvement to protect their own interests. Capitalists, with vast wealth and a willingness to buy votes or other government access through prestations, mobilize state force when they wish to overcome resistance from populations that withhold their resources from market exploitation. Many, perhaps most, parts of the world, therefore, were originally brought into the expanding world market over the last several centuries by force of arms, by means of conquest, colonialism, and imperialism. Forcing communities to open to the market against their will generally entails undermining local cultural integrity and self-determination in forging a global integration of producers and consumers.

The market, therefore, does not inherently reduce the role of violence in human affairs any more than have preceding developments in social evolution. As we have come to expect, the ability to regulate violence within ever-larger groups contributes to increasing intensification, stabilizing economic integration, and extending the reach of stratified authority—all within the regulated group. At the same time, these very accomplishments mean that violence on an ever-larger scale becomes available as a tool for elites to use to achieve their goal of growth in the political economy on terms most favorable to themselves, both in overcoming opposition within their market arena and in conquering new zones to be absorbed into it.

Inefficient Resource Use. The market offers opportunities to accumulate capital at unprecedented levels, allowing for the construction of artifacts and facilities (such as ships, bridges, and factories) that increase economies of scale, the rate at which resources can be captured, and the flow of commodities to consumers. Capital opened up the Prudhoe Bay oil fields, the Siberian mines, and the arid backlands of Brazil in ways that Eskimo hunters, Nganasan herders, and subsistence tenant farmers could never have done.

This capital, which is no more than the coordinated—or, as Marxists would say, expropriated—wealth of multitudes, can reach a vastness to inspire awe in many. Money itself has an abstract and magical quality that Marx recognized in the process he called the "fetishism of commodities" (Harvey 1989: 100). Money in great quantities, and anyone who possesses it, acquires an aura of sanctity—of unquestioned authority—not unrelated to the awesomeness of the rulers of ancient agrarian states. The sanctity of capital, partly a consequence of its power to produce works of great scale and complexity, and partly owing to its intimate link to oppressive police power (Rappaport 1994: 160–61), adds to its legitimacy in further transforming the landscape, especially in overcoming local political opposition.

To a degree, the market also opens production systems to competition, allowing certain efficiencies. The introduction of modern ranching methods, with "superior" varieties of sheep and professional herders displacing the Basseri (Case 14), is a typical example. The introduction of coffee, cacao, and cattle to the rain forest surrounding the Machiguenga (Case 3) is an as-yet unproven effort to achieve the same kind of efficiency—that is, to earn more wealth or profit from a fixed amount of land, a form of intensification. In both cases, expanding outside populations encroaching on the territories of these small communities have increased market demand, exposing them to competition and ultimately threatening to eliminate them as identifiable economic communities.

Capital is not merely a passive capability, mobilized as needed when problems arise. It constantly seeks new opportunities for investment, driven by huge accumulations in commercial centers. Prior to market expansion, local economic needs were usually being met by an adequately capitalized subsistence economy, such as that of the Indian fishermen of the Northwest Coast (Case 9). The expanding market system, however, opens localized resources such as salmon to international demand, raising their value and attracting capital in the form of new equipment for harvesting, preserving, and transporting resources. That in turn greatly increases the rate of harvest, leading ultimately to depletion. And the access to a worldwide market may price such resources out of the range of the indigenous communities that used to live off them.

In such cases, the local population (which is already well adapted) tends to resist the encroachment, but it is powerless against sanctified capital backed by the military might of the liberal state, which, in this light is not benevolently lubricating the market machinery but imperialistically seizing resources and labor from smaller, weaker communities (Wolf 1982: 299–302). In a quieter but equally significant form, the changing market realities on Boa Ventura mean that capitalist farming with hired farm workers makes more profitable use of land resources than do subsistence tenant farmers: in the process, a community of farmers with traditional ties to the land is replaced by rootless wage laborers with no ties to the land.

As noted, the expanding market enables capital-intensive solutions to production problems that increase the rate at which ecosystems are destroyed: capitalist ranching denudes millions of acres of forest, industrial mining pollutes whole river systems, and so on. The worldwide decline of fisheries in recent decades, as factory-ship fishing depletes once abundant sea life, is the ominous fruit of aggressive capitalization that Ehrlich and Ehrlich (1990: 85) refer to as "vacuuming the sea."

In many such cases, market-based technological solutions to increasing the food supply are only apparently efficient. When the costs of nonreplaceable inputs are added into the equation—especially in the form of energy used in machinery, fertilizer, transportation, refrigeration, and packaging—the actual cost of additional foods can be far higher than in traditional food-producing technologies (Pimentel and Pimentel 1979). In addition, under capital-intensive technology, yields often decline over time even as capital inputs increase (Ehrlich and Ehrlich 1990: 92–93).

The free market, not being a person or any kind of living being, cannot conceptualize (let alone cherish) a healthy ecosystem. It typically rewards capitalist firms for extracting the value from nature without considering the cost of restoring that value. If polluters had to include the cost of cleaning up pollution as a business expense, their profit line would be very different and they would be motivated to protect the environment. If loggers had to include the cost of restoring forest, their calculations of profit would motivate them toward more sustainable logging (Hecht 1992). Under many current systems of market-based resource use, while the profits go to private investors, these long-term costs of business—toxic cleanup, reforestation, restoring waterways—are borne, tragedy-of-the-commons style, by the general public (Bodley 1996: 74–77).

The market brings undeniable efficiencies to the task of procuring resources to meet human needs, and this certainly helps explain its continuing spread into remote areas (Harvey 1989: 103). The market does not care that local populations lose control of their own resource base, because market economics define such traditional systems as inefficient, underproductive, and wasteful. But the short-term focus of market behavior—motivated by the imperative that capital earn a profit relatively quickly (within months, or a few years at most)—may actually encourage highly inefficient behavior in the long term. In this regard, market-based resource management is something like a family going into debt to support a lavish lifestyle—in the long run, the debt will come due, but, in the famous words of one market theorist, "In the long run we are all dead."

The main significance of more efficient resource use for social evolution is that the market brings an ever greater proportion of the world's useful resources within the orbit of supply and demand. Canadian wheat feeds not only Canadians but also Russians; fish from the Atlantic Ocean feed populations thousands of miles away, in every direction; so do Central American cattle. By ferrying demand to remote places, it becomes economically worthwhile to intensify production via capital investments. The market brings about the intensification of production throughout the whole world ecosystem, increasingly through industrial-based inputs such as fertilizers, pesticides, and factory-in-the-field and factory-at-sea technologies. The result is economic integration on an unprecedented scale, and increasingly stratified decision-making control over production at distant locales.

Resource Deficiencies. The market expands trade between ever more distant traders, extending the sources of demand and of supply (a producer in Kenya can supply an item desired by a complete stranger in Indonesia) while requiring very little actual management beyond the innumerable self-interested decisions of traders, money-changers, shippers, and retailers along the way. It was market access to the demand for meat among populations to the south that encouraged the Nganasan (Case 4) to increase their production of meat in order to obtain goods they wanted (tea, sugar, and metal) through trade.

In fact, trade via markets *is* demand at a distance. As population grows, demand grows accordingly: what the free market does is to transmit that demand impersonally to wherever supplies can be found to satisfy it. The Shoshone (Case 1), for example, lived traditionally in a region rich in iron ore, but that resource was of no use to them or anyone else until the capital to exploit it and the demand for iron arrived, both transmitted by the market. The Machiguenga (Case 3), expanding their use of the land to raise coffee and other crops for market, may also be thought of as the market seeking out resources—in this case, land that would have lain fallow or as unfarmed forest—that are in demand elsewhere.

The capacity of the market to address resource deficiencies also has the consequence, as we discovered in the case of inefficient resource use, that resources that might have been more than sufficient to sustain a local subsistence economy become increasingly expensive for locals as the market opens up worldwide demand. That is how the demand for lobster in affluent northern countries drew local Miskito fishermen of Honduras to work for wages as lobster divers collecting a resource that was abundant in 1970 but nearly depleted by 1990 (Dodds 1994: 178–89).

From the social evolutionary perspective, the implications of how the market meets resource deficiencies are virtually identical with those of solving inefficient resource use. This is the pervasive two-edged sword of world trade: it increases the efficiency with which goods are moved to where demand (the price they can command) is highest, playing an important role in sustaining global population growth. But opening a conduit for worldwide demand increases the effective population pressure on resources at any particular location, even in areas of low local population density where people once lived in a sustainable balance with nature. In those cases, the market is not solving a problem that matters much to the local community. Before the arrival of the market, for example, the Miskito of Honduras had an abundant subsistence base. Intensification in the use of their resources has integrated them into a world economic community, but both the intensification and the integration are ultimately manifestations of a stratified world system managed by elites who live far from local communities and resources, and who use capital and the political/military resources at their command to ensure that their interests remain paramount.

Social Evolution and the Free Market

Debates between the free marketers and the anti-market critics are endemic wherever economy, population, and the environment are discussed. They tend often to be reduced to the simple dichotomy between proponents of the free market who are against government interventions, and antimarket proponents who are in favor of government interventions. In these debates, promarket arguments tend to minimize the social and environmental costs of the free market, whereas progovernment arguments minimize the role of the market in solving the massive economic problems brought on by population growth and technological change.

The theory of social evolution not only allows but also requires that these approaches be integrated and kept in some degree of balance. Many of the difficult situations blamed by antimarket theorists on the instituting of greed in the free market really arise in evolutionary conditions to which the market is simply a response, not a cause. Population growth in agrarian regions will increase the need to intensify food production, usually by reducing the size of farms and increasing capital inputs such as labor, improved seed, fertilizer, and pesticides. Without intensification, population growth cannot take place, and the market becomes a way (one among several, but an increasingly important one) to make intensification happen.

Similarly, population growth among unskilled workers will inevitably drive down wages unless there is a compensating rise in the demand for unskilled labor. That is true even though it is also true that elites will use political force to keep wages low whenever they can, independent of whether or not population is growing. People will leave their kin-based natal communities to achieve a higher level of consumption elsewhere, and they will even resist sharing their new wealth with demanding relatives back home. To say that the shrinking size of farm plots, low wages, or community breakdown are caused by the market does not shed much light on the conditions that make these market responses likely for so many households.

At the same time, we have demonstrated throughout this book that a basic rule of social evolution is that every expansion of the political economy, while solving problems in the subsistence economy, comes with an associated opportunity for control, enabling leadership, and ultimately, self-aggrandizing elites. Liberal economics recognizes this in an abstract way and calls for legal restrictions on monopoly. But it does not adequately admit to the close feedback between wealth and political power that limits the access of the poor to the political process, facilitates the concentration of wealth, and promotes the development of class differences that are inherited from parent to child, creating de facto aristocracies. The lesson of social evolution is that increased intensification of production and integration of economic communities inevitably leads to increased stratification. Elites, as aggrandizers, can always be expected to use their control over the means of production to "skim all the cream off production at home and abroad" (Engels 1972: 225). Only by introducing political controls on market behavior—by such means as minimum wages, progressive taxes, antitrust and anti-corruption laws, and inheritance taxes—can the aggrandizing tendencies of elites be contained.

Similarly, we have seen ample evidence that the evolution of human society, as an evolution of the political economy, requires political solutions to prevent environmental destruction resulting from population increase. Even in the smallest societies occasions arise, such as the Shoshone antelope shaman (Case 1), in which restrictions have to be placed on the freedom of individuals to exploit common resources. The government reforestation projects of feudal Japan (Case 15) and the chief's management of migratory herding routes among the Basseri (Case 14) illustrate the need for communitywide restrictions on individual behavior even before the free market revolution.

The Emerging World Order

The number of independent polities in the world stopped declining after World War II. The colonial approach to economic expansion via conquest proved unnecessarily costly compared with the advantages of economic integration by means of the self-regulating market. In the current political climate, at least, nations can retain some political independence of the major world powers yet be highly interdependent with the world economy.

The emerging world order reminds us politically of the Big Man systems that integrate the most complex of the local group societies. No single power is able to claim ownership of all the resources of the region, but wealthier local groups have more powerful leaders and more bargaining power in their relations with their less wealthy neighbors. Groups and their leaders struggle with balancing their short-term self-interest (such as hoarding wealth and resolving disputes through war) with their long-term interest (such as building ties of trust and using resources nondestructively). They use a good deal of bluff, pomp, and self-promotion in their public negotiating and continue at times to resort, for the most part unwisely, to war to achieve their goals. Yet they also recognize that it is in their own groups' interest to establish regions of peace and cooperation, a political strategy that seems especially to characterize the foreign policies of democratic nations (Ember et al. 1992; Rummel 1997).

The compromise between short-term and long-term self-interest recapitulates the dialectic between freedom and responsibility that is already basic at the family level. Individuals want the freedom to use resources as they see fit to meet the needs of their own families, but they recognize that fighting with others over resources is dangerous and that trying to stand completely alone would abandon one of humankind's greatest tools of survival, cooperative group activity.

In some very fundamental sense, as population grows, freedom declines. The world does not grow any bigger, so with more people there is less of a share of the world for each. True, technology increases the availability of resources to serve human purposes, but to the degree that the law of diminishing returns applies to technology, people must work harder to meet their needs as the environment becomes more crowded. In Chapter 1 we learned that time allocation data show a general rise in the length of the workday as economic systems evolve from hunting-gathering to extensive agriculture to intensive agriculture and industrialism.

As implied in our discussion of the domestication of humankind in Chapter 5, the evolution of human society involves a loss of freedom and the acceptance of greater responsibility. This may run counter to the impression that the fortunate residents of affluent modern democracies enjoy the greatest degree of personal freedom in history. But the constraints on time and space experienced in largely urban societies, and the pervasiveness of laws governing a wide latitude of individual behaviors in gaining access to resources and determining how they may be used, are much greater now than in less populous, less centralized societies. As we have learned, people have not welcomed the progressive erosion of familistic autonomy, but over time they have been overwhelmed by increasing circumscription and opportunities for control.

The problems posed by population growth and technological change have always required some compromise between free individual problem-solving and community-based political controls. The world today is changing much as it has in the past. The emerging world order of global economic integration, which liberal economists hope will encourage the democratic, middle-class structures of the liberal state, is in reality a further development of the intensification, integration, and stratification that have always characterized social evolution. Now the intensification is heavily influenced by markets for technology, labor, and commodities; the integration is largely in the form of expanding market involvement; and stratification increasingly finds the elites in positions of great commercial wealth and deeply engaged in funding elections to defend their special interests. So-called imperfections in the market persist, both because the market itself exacerbates problems such as pollution that must be controlled by government intervention, and because the expanding market creates opportunities for control that lead to monopolies, corruption, wars over resources, and other self-serving activities that the emerging world order strives—with heroic, if often unsuccessful, efforts—to overcome.

Bibliography

Bibliography

Adams, J. 1973. The Gitksan potlatch. Toronto: Holt, Rinehart & Winston.

Adams, R. 1966. The evolution of urban society. Chicago: University of Chicago Press.

Alexiev, A. 1998. A march toward the abyss. *Los Angeles Times*, September 6, p. M1.

Allen, J. 1992. Farming in Hawai'i from colonisation to contact: radiocarbon chronology and implications for cultural change. *New Zealand Journal of Archaeology* 14: 45–66.

Allen, M. 1996. Pathways to economic power in Maori chiefdoms. *Research in Economic Anthropology* 17: 171–225.

AMRF. 1979. Studies on the epidemiology and treatment of hydatid disease in the Turkana District of Kenya. Third annual report. Nairobi: African Medical and Research Foundation.

Anduze, P. 1960. Shailili-Ko: descubrimiento de las fuentes del Orinoco. Caracas: Talleres Graficos Ilustraciones.

Appadurai, A. 1986. The social life of things: commodities in cultural perspective. Cambridge: Cambridge University Press.

Arnold, J. 1996a. Organizational transformations: power and labor among complex hunter-gatherers and other intermediate societies. *In* Emergent complexity: the evolution of intermediate societies, ed. J. Arnold, pp. 59–73. Ann Arbor, Mich.: International.

———. 1996b. The archaeology of complex hunter-gatherers. *Journal of Archaeological Method and Theory* 3: 77–126.

Arvelo-Jimenez, N. 1984. The political feasibility of tribal autonomy in Amazonia. Manuscript. Instituto Venezolano de Investigaciones Cientificas, Caracas.

Asakawa, K. 1965. Land and society in medieval Japan. Tokyo: Japan Society for the Promotion of Science.

Athens, J. 1977. Theory building and the study of evolutionary process. *In* For theory building in archaeology, ed. L. Binford, pp. 353–84. New York: Academic Press.

————. 1984. Prehistoric taro pondfield agriculture in Hawaii: modeling constraints for its development. Unpublished manuscript.

Atlas. 1979. Atlas de Venezuela. 2d ed. Caracas: Ministerio del Ambiente y de los Recursos Naturales Renovables.

Austen, L. 1945. Cultural changes in Kiriwina. *Oceania* 16: 15–60.

Baksh, M. 1984. Cultural ecology and change of the Machiguenga Indians of the Peruvian Amazon. Unpublished Ph.D. dissertation. Department of Anthropology, University of California, Los Angeles.

Balée, W. 1989. The culture of Amazonian forests. *In* Resource management in Amazonia: indigenous and folk strategies, ed. D. A. Posey and W. Balée (*Advances in Economic Botany* 7), pp. 1–21. New York: New York Botanical Garden.

Barnett, H. 1968. The nature and function of the potlatch. Eugene: Department of Anthropology, University of Oregon.

Barth, F. 1956. Ecological relationships of ethnic groups in Swat, North Pakistan. *American Anthropologist* 58: 1079–89.

————. 1964. Nomads of south Persia. London: Allen & Unwin.

Bartholomew, G., and J. Birdsell. 1953. Ecology and the protohominids. *American Anthropologist* 55: 481–98.

Beard, C. 1927. The industrial revolution. Westport, Conn.: Greenwood Press.

————. 1935. An economic interpretation of the Constitution of the United States. New York: Free Press [1986 ed.].

Beck, Lois. 1986. The Qashqa'i of Iran. New Haven: Yale University Press.

————. 1991. Nomad: a year in the life of a Qashqa'i tribesman in Iran. Berkeley: University of California Press.

Beckerman, S. 1979. The abundance of protein in Amazonia: a reply to Gross. *American Anthropologist* 81: 533–60.

————. 1980. Fishing and hunting by the Bari of Columbia. *In* Studies in hunting and fishing in the neotropics, ed. R. Hames, pp. 67–109. Bennington, Vt.: Working Papers on South American Indians 2.

————. 1983. Does the swidden ape the jungle? *Human Ecology* 11: 1–12.

Bell, D. 1998a. The social relations of property and efficiency. *In* Property in economic context, ed. R. Hunt and A. Gilman, pp. 29–45. Lanham, Md.: University Press of America.

————. 1998b. Power and survival within groups. Manuscript. Irvine: University of California. http://orion.oac.uci.edu/~dbell/

Belshaw, C. 1955. In search of wealth. American Anthropological Association Memoir 80.

————. 1965. Traditional exchange and modern markets. Englewood Cliffs, N.J.: Prentice-Hall.

Benedict, R. 1934. Patterns of culture. Boston: Houghton Mifflin.

Bennett, V. 1997. Reindeer herders of Russia hunt for a future. *Los Angeles Times*, October 3, pp. A1 and A16.

Berdan, F. 1975. Trade, tribute and market in the Aztec Empire. Unpublished Ph.D. dissertation. Department of Anthropology, University of Texas, Austin.

Bergman, R. 1974. Shipibo subsistence in the Upper Amazon rainforest. Unpublished Ph.D. dissertation. Department of Geography, University of Wisconsin, Madison.

Berlin, E., and E. Markell. 1977. An assessment of the nutritional and health status of an Aguaruna Jivaro community, Amazonas, Peru. *Ecology of Food and Nutrition* 6: 69–81.

Bernal, I. 1969. The Olmec world, tr. D. Heyden and F. Horcasitas. Berkeley: University of California Press.

Bernard, A. 1992. Hunters and herders of southern Africa: a comparative ethnography of the Khoisan people. Cambridge: Cambridge University Press.

Best, E. 1924. The Maori. Polynesian Society Memoir.

———. 1925. Maori culture. Bulletin 9. Wellington, N.Z.: Dominion Museum.

Bettinger, R. 1978. Alternative adaptive strategies in the prehistoric Great Basin. *Journal of Anthropological Research* 34: 27–46.

———. 1982. Aboriginal exchange and territoriality in Owens Valley, California. *In* Contexts for prehistoric exchange, ed. J. Ericson and T. Earle, pp. 103–27. New York: Academic Press.

Binford, L. 1964. A consideration of archaeological research design. *American Antiquity* 29: 425–41.

———. 1968. Post-Pleistocene adaptations. *In* New perspectives in archaeology, ed. S. Binford and L. Binford, pp. 313–41. Chicago: Aldine.

———. 1980. Willow smoke and dogs' tails: hunter-gatherer settlement systems and archaeological site formation. *American Antiquity* 45: 4–20.

Binford, L., and S. Binford. 1966. A preliminary analysis of functional variability in the Mousterian of Levallois facies. *American Anthropologist* 68: 238–95.

Binford, S. 1968. Early Upper Pleistocene adaptations in the Levant. *American Anthropologist* 70: 707–17.

Biocca, E. 1971. Yanoama: the narrative of a white girl kidnapped by Amazon Indians. New York: Dutton.

Birdsell, J. 1953. Some environmental and cultural factors influencing the structure of Australian aboriginal populations. *American Naturalist* 87: 171–207.

———. 1968a. Comment on infanticide. *In* Man the hunter, ed. R. Lee and I. DeVore, p. 243. Chicago: Aldine.

———. 1968b. Some predictions for the Pleistocene based on equilibrium systems among recent hunter-gatherers. *In* Man the hunter, ed. R. Lee and I. DeVore, pp. 229–40. Chicago: Aldine.

Blanton, R., G. Feinman, S. Kowalewski, and P. Peregrine. 1996. A dual-processual theory for the evolution of Mesoamerican civilization. *Current Anthropology* 37: 1–14.

Blaut, J. M. 1993. The colonizer's model of the world. New York: Gilford Press.

Bloch, M. 1961. Feudal society. Chicago: University of Chicago Press.

Blumenschine, R. J. 1995. Percussion marks, tooth marks, and experimental determinations of the timing of hominid and carnivore access to long bones at FLK Zinjanthropus, Olduvai Gorge, Tanzania. *Journal of Human Evolution* 29: 21–51.

Blurton Jones, N., and R. M. Sibly. 1978. Testing adaptiveness of culturally determined behaviour: do Bushman women maximize their reproductive success by spacing births widely and foraging seldom? *Society for the Study of
Human Biology Symposium* 18: 135–57. London: Taylor and Francis.

Boas, F. 1898. Final report on the northwestern tribes of Canada. B.A.A.S. Report, pp. 628–88.

———. 1910. Kwakiutl tales. New York: Columbia University Press.

———. 1921. Ethnology of the Kwakiutl. 35th annual report of the Bureau of
American Ethnology to the Secretary of the Smithsonian Institution. Washington, D.C.: U.S. Government Printing Office.

———. 1949 [1896]. The limitations of the comparative method of anthropology. *In* Race, language, and culture, pp. 270–80. New York: Macmillan.

———. 1949 [1920]. Methods of ethnology: Race, language, and culture, pp.
281–89. New York: Macmillan.

———. 1966. Kwakiutl ethnography, ed. Helen Codere. Chicago: University of
Chicago Press.

Bodley, J. H. 1996. Anthropology and contemporary human problems. 3d ed.
Mountain View, Calif.: Mayfield.

Boeke, J. 1953. Economics and economic policy of dual societies, as exemplified
by Indonesia. New York: Institute of Pacific Relations.

Bohannan, P. 1955. Some principles of exchange and investment among the
Tiv. *American Anthropologist* 57: 60–69.

Bohannan, P., and G. Dalton. 1965. Introduction. *In* Markets in Africa: eight
subsistence economies in transition, ed. P. Bohannan and G. Dalton, pp. 1–
32. Garden City, N.Y.: Doubleday.

Boone, J. 1992. Competition, conflict, and the development of social hierarchies. *In* Evolutionary ecology and human behavior, ed. E. Smith and B.
Winterhalder, pp. 301–37. New York: Aldine.

Boserup, E. 1965. The conditions of agricultural growth. Chicago: Aldine.

Boyd, R., and P. J. Richerson. 1985. Culture and the evolutionary process. Chicago: University of Chicago Press.

Briggs, J. 1970. Never in anger: portrait of an Eskimo family. Cambridge: Harvard University Press.

Browman, D. 1970. Early Peruvian peasants: culture history of a central highlands valley. Unpublished Ph.D. dissertation. Department of Anthropology,
Harvard University.

Brown, P. 1972. The Chimbu: a study of change in the New Guinea highlands.
Cambridge, Mass.: Schenkman.

Brown, P., and A. Podolefsky. 1976. Population density, agricultural intensity,
land tenure and group size in the New Guinea highlands. *Ethnology* 15: 211–
38.

Brumfiel, E. 1980. Specialization, market exchange, and the Aztec state. *Current
Anthropology* 21: 459–78.

Brumfiel, E., and T. Earle. 1987. Specialization, exchange, and complex societies. Cambridge: Cambridge University Press.

Brush, S. 1976. Man's use of an Andean ecosystem. *Human Ecology* 4: 147–66.

Buchbinder, G. 1973. Maring microadaptation: a study of demographic, nutritional, genetic and phenotypic variation in a highland New Guinea population. Unpublished Ph.D. dissertation. Department of Anthropology, Columbia University.

Buck, J. 1937. Land utilization in China. Shanghai: Commercial Press.

Buck, P. (Te Rangi Hiroa). 1932. Ethnology of Tongareva. Honolulu: Bernice P. Bishop Museum Bulletin 92.

————. 1934. Mangaian society. Honolulu: Bernice P. Bishop Museum Bulletin 122.

————. 1938. Ethnology of Mangareva. Honolulu: Bernice P. Bishop Museum Bulletin 157.

Burling, R. 1962. Maximization theories and the study of economic anthropology. *American Anthropologist* 64: 802–21.

Burrows, E. 1936. The ethnology of Futuna. Honolulu: Bernice P. Bishop Museum Bulletin 138.

————. 1937. The ethnology of Uvea. Honolulu: Bernice P. Bishop Museum Bulletin 145.

Burton, R. 1975. Why do the Trobriands have chiefs? *Man* 10: 544–58.

Bye, B. A., F. H. Brown, T. E. Cerling, and I. McDougall. 1987. Increased age estimate for the Lower Paleolithic hominid site at Olorgesaile, Kenya. *Nature* 329: 237–39.

Byers, D. 1967. The prehistory of the Tehuacan Valley: environment and subsistence. Austin: University of Texas Press.

Camisea 1998. The Camisea natural resource project in the jungle of Peru. http://www.camisea.com

Campbell, B. 1966. Human evolution. Chicago: Aldine.

Cancian, F. 1965. Economics and prestige in a Maya community. Stanford, Calif.: Stanford University Press.

————. 1968. Maximization as norm, strategy and theory: a comment on programmatic statements in economic anthropology. *In* Economic anthropology: readings in theory and analysis, ed. E. E. LeClair and H. K. Schneider, pp. 228–33. New York: Holt, Rinehart, Winston.

————. 1972. Change and uncertainty in a peasant economy. Stanford, Calif.: Stanford University Press.

Caplovitz, D. 1963. The poor pay more. Glencoe, Ill.: Free Press.

Carneiro, R. 1960. Slash-and-burn agriculture: a closer look at its implications for settlement patterns. *In* Men and culture, ed. A. Wallace, pp. 229–34. Philadelphia: University of Pennsylvania Press.

————. 1967. The evolution of society: selections from Herbert Spencer's *Principles of Sociology*. Chicago: University of Chicago Press.

————. 1970a. Scale analysis, evolutionary sequences, and the rating of cultures. *In* A handbook of method in cultural anthropology, ed. R. Naroll and R. Cohen, pp. 834–71. New York: Columbia University Press.

————. 1970b. A theory of the origin of the state. *Science* 169: 733–38.

———. 1977. Political expansion as an expression of the principle of competitive exclusion. *In* Origins of the state: the anthropology of political evolution, ed. G. Jones and E. Service, pp. 205–23. Philadelphia: ISNI.

———. 1981. The chiefdom as precursor to the state. *In* The transition to statehood in the New World, ed. G. Jones and R. Kautz, pp. 37–79. Cambridge: Cambridge University Press.

———.1982. Comment on A. Johnson, Reductionism in cultural ecology: the Amazon case. *Current Anthropology* 23: 413–28.

Caroso Soares, C. 1982. Sharecroppers of the Sertão: Boa Ventura revisited. Unpublished research report. Department of Anthropology, University of California, Los Angeles.

Cashdan, E. 1983. Territoriality among human foragers: ecological models and application to four Bushman groups. *Current Anthropology* 24: 443–63.

Chagnon, N. 1968a. Yanomamo: the fierce people. New York: Holt, Rinehart & Winston.

———. 1968b. Yanomamo social organization and warfare. *In* War: the anthropology of armed conflicts and aggression, ed. M. Fried, M. Harris, and R. Murphy, pp. 109–59. New York: Natural History Press.

———. 1980. Highland New Guinea models in the South American lowlands. *In* Studies in hunting and fishing in the neotropics, ed. R. Hames. Bennington, Vt.: Working Papers on South American Indians 2: 111–30.

———. 1983. Yanomamo: the fierce people. 3d ed. New York: Holt, Rinehart & Winston.

———. 1992. Yanomamo. Fort Worth: Harcourt Brace Jovanovich. 4th ed.

Chagnon, N., and R. Hames. 1979. Protein deficiency and tribal warfare in Amazonia: new data. *Science* 203: 910–13.

Chance, N. 1966. The Eskimo of north Alaska. New York: Holt, Rinehart & Winston.

———. 1990. The Iñupiat and Arctic Alaska: an ethnography of development. Fort Worth, Tex.: Holt, Rinehart and Winston.

———. 1996. The Iñupiat Eskimo and Arctic Alaska: a cultural update. *General Anthropology* 2: 1–5.

Chayanov, A. 1966 [1925]. The theory of peasant economy. Homewood, Ill.: Irwin.

Chibnik, M. 1981. The evolution of cultural rules. *Journal of Anthropological Research* 37: 256–68.

Childe, V. 1936. Man makes himself. London: Watts.

———. 1942. What happened in history? Baltimore: Penguin.

———. 1951. Social evolution. London: Watts.

Christenson, A. 1980. Change in the human niche in response to population growth. *In* Modeling change in prehistoric subsistence economies, ed. T. Earle and A. Christenson, pp. 31–72. New York: Academic Press.

Claessen, H. 1978 . The early state: a structural approach. *In* The early state, ed. H. Claessen and P. Skalnik, pp. 533–96. The Hague: Mouton.

Clarke, W. 1966. From extensive to intensive shifting cultivation: a succession from New Guinea. *Ethnology* 5: 347–59.

———. 1971. Place and people: an ecology of a New Guinean community. Berkeley: University of California Press.

———. 1982. Comment: individual or group advantage, ed. J. Peoples. *Current Anthropology* 23: 301.

Coale, A. 1974. The history of the human population. *Science* 231 (3): 40–51.

Codere, H. 1950. Fighting with property. Seattle: University of Washington Press.

Cohen, Mark. 1977. The food crisis in prehistory. New Haven: Yale University Press.

———. 1994. Demographic expansion: causes and consequences. *In* Companion encyclopedia of anthropology, ed. T. Ingold, pp. 265–96. London: Routledge.

Cohen, Myron. 1968. A case study of Chinese family economy and development. *Journal of Asian Studies* 3: 161–80.

———. 1970. Introduction. A. Smith, Village life in China, pp. ix–xxvi. Boston: Little, Brown.

———. 1984. Personal communication.

Cole, S. 1959. The neolithic revolution. London: British Museum.

Conkey, M. 1978. Style and information in cultural evolution: toward a predictive model for the Paleolithic. *In* Social archaeology: beyond subsistence and dating, ed. C. Redman et al., pp. 61–85. New York: Academic Press.

Conrad, G., and A. Demarest. 1984. Religion and empire: the dynamics of Aztec and Inca expansion. Cambridge: Cambridge University Press.

Cook, S. 1968. The obsolete "anti-market" mentality: a critique of the substantive approach to economic anthropology. *In* Economic anthropology: readings in theory and analysis, ed. E. E. LeClair and H. K. Schneider, pp. 208–27. New York: Holt, Rinehart and Winston.

Cordy, R. 1974. Cultural adaptation and evolution in Hawaii: a suggested new sequence. *Journal of Polynesian Society* 83: 180–91.

———. 1981. A study of prehistoric social change: the development of complex societies in the Hawaiian islands. New York: Academic Press.

Costin, C. 1993. Textiles, women, and political economy in late prehispanic Peru. *Research in Economic Anthropology* 18: 3–26.

Costin, C., T. Earle, B. Owen, and G. Russell. 1989. Impact of Inka conquest on local technology in the upper Mantaro Valley, Peru. *In* What's new?: a closer look at the process of innovation, ed. S. van de Leeuw and R. Torrence, pp. 107–39. London: Allen and Unwin.

Cowgill, G. 1980. On causes and consequences of ancient and modern population changes. *American Anthropologist* 77: 505–25.

Dalton, G. 1961. Economic theory and primitive society. *American Anthropologist* 63: 1–25.

———. 1977. Aboriginal economies in stateless societies. *In* Exchange systems in prehistory, ed. T. Earle and J. Ericson, pp. 191–212. New York: Academic Press.

D'Altroy, T. 1981. Empire growth and consolidation: the Xanxa region of Peru under the Incas. Unpublished Ph.D. dissertation. Department of Anthropology, University of California, Los Angeles.

————. 1984. Personal correspondence.

————. 1992. Provincial power in the Inka empire. Washington, D.C.: Smithsonian Institution.

D'Altroy, T., and T. Earle. 1985. Staple finance, wealth finance, and storage in the Inca political economy. *Current Anthropology* 26: 187–206.

D'Aquili, E. 1972. The biopsychological determinants of culture. Module in Anthropology 13. Reading, Mass.: Addison-Wesley.

Day, K. 1982. Storage and labor service: a production and management design for the Andean area. *In* Chanchan: Andean desert city, ed. M. Moseley and K. Day, pp. 333–49. Albuquerque: University of New Mexico Press.

De Janvry, A. 1981. The agrarian question and reformism in Latin America. Baltimore: Johns Hopkins University Press.

De Laguna, F. 1983. Aboriginal Tlingit sociopolitical organization. *In* The development of political organization in native North America, ed. E. Tooker, pp. 71–85. *Proceedings* 1979. Washington, D.C.: American Ethnological Society.

DeMarrais, E., L. J. Castillo, and T. Earle. 1996. Ideology, materialization and power strategies. *Current Anthropology* 37: 15–31.

Denbow, J. R., and E. N. Wilmsen. 1986. Advent and the course of pastoralism in the Kalahari. *Science* 234: 1509–15.

De Sapio, R. 1978. Calculus for the life sciences. San Francisco: W. H. Freeman.

DeVore, I., and K. Hall. 1965. Baboon ecology. *In* Primate behavior, ed. I. DeVore, pp. 20–52. New York: Holt, Rinehart & Winston.

Diamond, N. 1983. Model villages and village realities. *Modern China* 9: 163–81.

————.1985. Taitou revisited: state policies and social change. *In* Chinese rural development: the great transformation, ed. W. L. Parish, pp. 246–69. Armonk, N.Y.: M. E. Sharpe.

————. 1998. Personal communication.

Dodds, D. 1994. The ecological and social sustainability of Miskito subsistence in the Rio Platano biosphere reserve, Honduras: the cultural ecology of swidden horticulturalists in a protected area. Ph.D. dissertation. University of California, Los Angeles.

Donald, L. 1984. The slave trade on the Northwest Coast of North America. *Research in Economic Anthropology* 6: 121–58.

Donald, L., and D. H. Mitchell. 1975. Some correlates of local group rank among the Southern Kwakiutl. *Ethnology* 14: 325–46.

————. 1994. Nature and culture on the Northwest Coast of North America: the case of Wakashan salmon resources. *In* Key issues in hunter-gatherer research, ed. E. S. Burch, Jr., and L. J. Ellanna, pp. 95–117. Oxford: Berg.

Donkin, R. 1979. Agricultural terracing in the aboriginal New World. New York: Viking Fund Publication in Anthropology 56.

Driver, H. 1969. Indians of North America, 2d ed. Chicago: University of Chicago Press.

Drucker, P. 1955. Indians of the northwest coast. Anthropological Handbook No. 10. New York: American Museum of Natural History.

———. 1965. Cultures of the north Pacific coast. San Francisco: Chandler.

Drucker, P., and R. Heizer. 1967. To make my name good: a reexamination of the Southern Kwakiutl potlatch. Berkeley: University of California Press.

Duby, G. 1968. Rural economy and country life in the medieval west. Columbia: University of South Carolina Press.

Dumont, L. 1970. Homo hierarchicus. Chicago: University of Chicago Press.

Dunbar, R. 1996. Grooming, gossip, and the evolution of language. Cambridge: Harvard University Press.

Durham, W. H. 1979. Scarcity and survival in Central America: ecological origins of the Soccer War. Stanford, Calif.: Stanford University Press.

———. 1982. Interaction of genetic and cultural evolution: models and examples. *Human Ecology* 10: 289–323.

Durkheim, E. 1947 [1912]. The elementary forms of the religious life. Glencoe, Ill.: Free Press.

Duus, P. 1976. Feudalism in Japan. New York: Knopf.

Dye, T., and E. Komori. 1992. A pre-censal population history of Hawai'i. *New Zealand Journal of Archaeology* 14: 113–28.

Dyson-Hudson, R. 1989. Ecological influences on systems of food production and social organization of South Turkana pastoralists. *In* Comparative socioecology: the behavioural ecology of humans and other mammals, ed. V. Standen and R. A. Foley, pp. 165–93. Oxford: Blackwell Scientific Publications.

Dyson-Hudson, R., and J. McCabe. 1985. South Turkana nomadism: coping with an unpredictably varying environment. New Haven: HRAFLEX.

Earle, T. 1976. A nearest-neighbor analysis of two formative settlement systems. *In* The early Mesoamerican village, ed. K. Flannery, pp. 196–223. New York: Academic Press.

———. 1977. A reappraisal of redistribution: complex Hawaiian chiefdoms. *In* Exchange systems in prehistory, ed. T. Earle and J. Ericson, pp. 213–29. New York: Academic Press.

———. 1978. Economic and social organization of a complex chiefdom: the Halelea district, Kauai, Hawaii. Anthropological Paper 63. Ann Arbor: Museum of Anthropology, University of Michigan.

———. 1980a. A model of subsistence change. *In* Modeling change in prehistoric subsistence economies, ed. T. Earle and A. Christenson, pp. 1–29. New York: Academic Press.

———. 1980b. Prehistoric irrigation in the Hawaiian islands: an evaluation of evolutionary significance. *Archaeology and Physical Anthropology in Oceania* 15: 1–28.

————. 1982. The ecology and politics of primitive valuables. *In* Culture and ecology: eclectic perspectives, ed. J. Kennedy and R. Edgerton, pp. 65–83. Washington, D.C.: American Anthropological Association Special Publication 15.

————. 1985. Commodity exchange and markets in the Inka state: recent archaeological evidence. *In* Markets and marketing, ed. S. Plattner, pp. 369–97. Monographs in Economic Anthropology 4.

————. 1987. Chiefdoms in archaeological and ethnohistorical perspectives. *Annual Review of Anthropology* 16: 279–308.

————. 1997. How chiefs come to power: The political economy in prehistory. Stanford, Calif.: Stanford University Press.

Earle, T., and T. D'Altroy. 1982. Storage facilities and state finance in the upper Mantaro valley, Peru. *In* Contexts for prehistoric exchange, ed. J. Ericson and T. Earle, pp. 265–90. New York: Academic Press.

————. 1989. The political economy of the Inka empire: the archaeology of power and finance. *In* Archaeological thought in the Americas, ed. C. C. Lamberg-Karlovsky, pp. 183–204. Cambridge: Cambridge University Press.

Earle, T., T. D'Altroy, C. LeBlanc, C. Hastorf, and T. Levine. 1980. Changing settlement patterns in the upper Mantaro valley, Peru. *Journal of New World Archaeology* 4(1).

Earle, T., T. D'Altroy, C. Hastorf, C. Scott, C. Costin, G. Russell, and E. Sandefur. 1986. The impact of Inka conquest on the Wanka domestic economy. Institute of Archaeology Monograph. Los Angeles: University of California.

Ehrenreich, R., C. Crumley, and J. E. Levy. 1995. Heterarchy and the analysis of complex societies. Archeological Papers 6. Washington, D.C.: American Anthropological Association.

Ehrlich, P. R. 1968. The population bomb. New York: Ballantine.

Ehrlich, P. R. , G. C. Daily, and L. H. Goulder. 1992. Population growth, economic growth, and market economies. *Contention* 2: 17–33.

Ehrlich, P. R., and A. H. Ehrlich. 1970. Population, resources, environment: issues in human ecology. San Francisco: W. H. Freeman.

————. 1990. The population explosion. New York: Simon and Schuster.

————. 1997. The population explosion: why we should care and what we should do about it. *Environmental Law* 27: 1187–1208.

Ellanna, L. J. 1988. Demography and social organization as factors in subsistence production in four Eskimo communities. *Research in Economic Anthropology* 10: 73–87.

Ellis, W. 1853. Polynesian researches during a residence of nearly eight years in the Society and Sandwich Islands. London: H. G. Bohn.

————. 1963 [1827]. Journal of William Ellis. Honolulu: Advertiser Publishing.

Ember, C., M. Ember, and B. Russett. 1992. Peace between participatory polities: a cross-cultural test of the "democracies rarely fight each other" hypothesis. *World Politics* 44: 573–99.

Emerson, A. 1960. The evolution of adaptation in population systems. *In* The evolution of life. Vol. 1 of Evolution after Darwin, ed. Sol Tax, pp. 307–48. Chicago: University of Chicago Press.

Emmonds, G. T. 1991. The Tlingit Indians. Seattle: University of Washington Press.

Engels, F. 1972 [1884]. The origin of the family, private property, and the state. New York: International Publishers.

Ericson, J. 1977. Egalitarian exchange systems in California: a preliminary view. *In* Exchange systems in prehistory, ed. T. Earle and J. Ericson, pp. 109–26. New York: Academic Press.

Evans-Pritchard, E. 1940. The Nuer. Oxford: Oxford University Press.

Feder, E. 1971. The rape of the peasantry. New York: Doubleday.

Feil, D. K. 1978. Women and men in the Enga tee. *American Ethnologist* 5: 263–79.

———. 1984. Ways of exchange: the Enga tee of Papua New Guinea. St. Lucia, Australia: University of Queensland Press.

———. 1987. The evolution of highland Papua New Guinea societies. Cambridge: Cambridge University Press.

Feinman, G., and J. Neitzel. 1984. Too many types: an overview of prestate sedentary societies in the Americas. *In* Advances in archaeological method and theory 7, ed. M. Schiffer, pp. 39–102. New York: Academic Press.

Fergusen, R. B. 1997. Violence and war in prehistory. *In* Troubled times: violence and warfare in the past, ed. D. L. Martin and D. W. Frayer, pp. 321–55. Amsterdam: Gordon and Breach.

Firth, R. 1929. Primitive economics of the New Zealand Maori. London: Routledge.

Flannery, K. 1969. Origins and ecological effects of early domestication in Iran and the Near East. *In* The domestication and exploitation of plants and animals, ed. P. Ucko and G. Dimbleby, pp. 73–100. Chicago: Aldine.

———. 1972. The cultural evolution of civilizations. *Annual Review of Ecology and Systematics* 3: 399–426.

Foerster, H. von, P. M. Mora, and L. W. Amiot. 1960. Doomsday: Friday, 13 November, AD. 2026. *Science* 132: 1291–95.

Forsyth, J. 1989. The indigenous peoples of Siberia in the twentieth century. *In* The development of Siberia: people and resources, ed. A. Wood and R. French, pp. 72–95. London: Macmillan.

———. 1992. A history of the peoples of Siberia: Russia's north Asian colony, 1581–1990. Cambridge: Cambridge University Press.

Fortes, M. 1949. The web of kinship among the Tallensi. London: Oxford University Press.

Foster, G. 1961. The dyadic contract: a model for the social structure of a Mexican peasant village. *American Anthropologist* 63: 1173–92.

Fowler, D. 1966. Great Basin social organization. *In* The current status of anthropological research in the Great Basin: 1964, ed. W. D'Azevedo et al., pp. 57–74. Reno: Desert Research Institute.

Fried, M. 1967. The evolution of political society. New York: Random House.

Friedman, J. 1974. Marxism, structuralism and vulgar materialism. *Man* 9: 444–69.

Friedman, M. 1962. Capitalism and freedom. Chicago: University of Chicago Press.

Frisch, R. 1978. Population, food intake and fertility. *Science* 199: 22–30.

Frisch, R., G. Wyshak, and L. Vincent. 1980. Delayed menarche and amenorrhea in ballet dancers. *New England Journal of Medicine* 303: 17–19.

Gall, P., and A. Saxe. 1977. Ecological evolution of culture: the state as predator in succession theory. *In* Exchange systems in prehistory, ed. T. Earle and J. Ericson, pp. 255–68. New York: Academic Press.

Geertz, C. 1963. Agricultural involution. Berkeley: University of California Press.

———. 1980. Negara: the theater-state in nineteenth-century Bali. Princeton: Princeton University Press.

Gibson, J. L. 1994. Before their time?: early mounds in the Lower Mississippi Valley. *Southeastern Archaeology* 13: 162–81.

Gilman, A. 1976. Bronze Age dynamics in southeast Spain. *Dialectical Anthropology* 1: 307–19.

———. 1981. The development of stratification in Bronze Age Europe. *Current Anthropology* 22: 1–23.

———. 1984. Explaining the Upper Paleolithic revolution. *In* Marxist perspectives in archaeology, ed. M. Spriggs, pp. 115–26. Cambridge: Cambridge University Press.

Godelier, M. 1977. Perspectives in Marxist anthropology. Cambridge: Cambridge University Press.

Goldman, I. 1970. Ancient Polynesian society. Chicago: University of Chicago Press.

Goldschmidt, W. 1959. Man's way: a preface to the understanding of human society. New York: Holt, Rinehart & Winston.

Goodfellow, D. 1968. The applicability of economic theory to so-called primitive communities. *In* Economic anthropology, ed. E. LeClair and H. Schneider, pp. 55–65. New York: Holt, Rinehart & Winston.

Goodland, R. J. A. 1992. Neotropical moist forests: priorities for the next two decades. *In* Conservation of neotropical forests: working from traditional resource use, ed. K. H. Redford and C. Padoch, pp. 416–27. New York: Columbia University Press.

Goody, J. 1971. Technology, tradition and the state in Africa. Cambridge: Cambridge University Press.

Greenfield, S. 1972. Charwomen, cesspools, and road building: an examination of patronage, clientage, and political power in southeastern Minas Gerais. *In* Structure and process in Latin America: patronage, clientage, and power systems, ed. A. Strickon and S. Greenfield, pp. 71–100. Albuquerque: University of New Mexico Press.

Gross, D. 1975. Protein capture and cultural development in the Amazon basin. *American Anthropologist* 77: 526–49.

Gross, D., and B. Underwood. 1971. Technological change and caloric costs: sisal agriculture in northeastern Brazil. *American Anthropologist* 73: 725–40.

Grossman, L. 1984. Peasants, subsistence ecology, and development in the highlands of Papua New Guinea. Princeton: Princeton University Press.

Gubser, N. 1965. The Nunamiut Eskimos. New Haven: Yale University Press.

Guest, P. 1989. Labor allocation and rural development: migration in four Javanese villages. Boulder, Colo.: Westview.

Gulliver, P. 1951. A preliminary survey of the Turkana. Cape Town, South Africa: Colonial Social Science Research Council.

———. 1955. The family herds. London: Routledge & Kegan Paul.

———. 1975. Nomadic movements: causes and implications. *In* Pastoralism in tropical Africa, ed. T. Monod, pp. 369–84. London: Oxford University Press.

Gunther, E. 1972. Indian life on the northwest coast of North America. Chicago: University of Chicago Press.

Haas, J. 1982. The evolution of the prehistoric state. New York: Columbia University Press.

———. 1996. War. *Encyclopedia of cultural anthropology* 4: 1357–61. New York: Henry Holt.

Hall, J. 1970. Japan: from prehistory to modern times. New York: Dell.

Halperin, R. 1994. Cultural economies past and present. Austin: University of Texas Press.

Halperin, R., and J. Dow, eds. 1977. Peasant livelihood: studies in economic anthropology and cultural ecology. New York: St. Martin's.

Hames, R. 1982. Comment on A. Johnson, "Reductionism in cultural ecology: the Amazon case." *Current Anthropology* 23: 421–22.

———. 1983. The settlement pattern of a Yanomamo population bloc: a behavioral ecological interpretation. *In* Adaptive responses of native Amazonians, ed. R. B. Hames and W. T. Vickers, pp. 393–427. New York: Academic Press.

———. 1996. Costs and benefits of monogamy and polygyny for Yanomamö women. *Ethology and Sociobiology* 17: 181–99.

———. 1997a. Trekking variation among the Yanomamo. Manuscript. University of Nebraska.

———. 1997b. Personal communication.

Hamilton, W. 1963. The evolution of altruistic behavior. *American Naturalist* 97: 354–56.

Handy, E. 1923. The native cultures in the Marquesas. Honolulu: Bernice P. Bishop Museum Bulletin 9.

Handy, E., and E. Pukui. 1958. The Polynesian family system in Ka'u, Hawaii. Rutland, Vt.: Tuttle.

Hardesty, D. L. 1977. Ecological anthropology. New York: John Wiley and Sons.

Hardin, G. 1968. The tragedy of the commons. *Science* 162: 1243–48.

Harris, M. 1959. The economy has no surplus? *American Anthropologist* 51: 185–99.

———. 1974. Cows, pigs, wars, and witches: the riddles of culture. New York: Random House.

————. 1977. Cannibals and kings: the origins of cultures. New York: Random House.

————. 1979. Cultural materialism. New York: Random House.

Harris, M., and O. Johnson. 2000. Cultural anthropology. 5th ed. Boston: Allyn and Bacon.

Harvey, D. 1989. The condition of postmodernity: an inquiry into the origins of cultural change. Oxford: Basil Blackwell.

Hastings, C. 1982. Implications of Andean verticality in the evolution of political complexity: a view from the margins. Unpublished paper presented at the 81st annual meeting of the American Anthropological Association, December 4–7, Washington, D.C.

Hastorf, C. 1983. Prehistoric agricultural intensification and political development in the Jauja region of central Peru. Unpublished Ph.D. dissertation. Department of Anthropology, University of California, Los Angeles.

————. 1993. Agriculture and the onset of political inequality before the Inka. Cambridge: Cambridge University Press.

Hastorf, C., and T. Earle. 1985. Intensive agriculture and the geography of political change in the upper Mantaro region of central Peru. *In* Prehistoric intensive agriculture in the tropics, ed. I. Farrington, pp. 569–95. Oxford: British Archaeological Reports, International Series 232.

Hawkes, K., and J. O'Connell. 1981. Affluent hunters? Some comments in light of the Alyawara case. *American Anthropologist* 83: 622–26.

Hayden, B. 1981a. Subsistence and ecological adaptations of modem hunter/gatherers. *In* Omnivorous primates, ed. R. Harding and G. Teleki, pp. 344–421. New York: Columbia University Press.

————. 1981b. Research and development in the stone age: technological transitions among hunter-gatherers. *Current Anthropology* 22: 529–48.

————. 1995. Pathways to power: principles for creating socioeconomic inequalities. *In* Foundations of social inequality, ed. T. D. Price and G. M. Feinman, pp. 15–86. New York: Plenum.

Hayek, F. A. 1939. Freedom and the economic system. Chicago: University of Chicago Press.

————. 1988. The fatal conceit: the errors of socialism. London: Routledge.

Heady, E. O., D. C. Faber, and S. C. Griffin. 1978. "Some potentials for lessening world food deficits." *Ecology of Food and Nutrition* 7: 181–85.

Hecht, S. 1992. Valuing land uses in Amazonia: colonist agriculture, cattle, and petty extraction in comparative perspective. *In* Conservation of neotropical forests: working from traditional resource use, ed. K. H. Redford and C. Padoch, pp. 379–99. New York: Columbia University Press.

Heider, K. 1970. The Dugum Dani. New York: Viking Fund Publication in Anthropology 49.

Henrich, J. 1997. Market incorporation, agricultural change, and sustainability among the Machiguenga Indians of the Peruvian Amazon. *Human Ecology* 25: 319–51.

————. 1998. Ultimatum game bargaining among the Machiguenga: why culture matters in economic behavior. Unpublished manuscript, Department of Anthropology, University of California, Los Angeles.

Herdt, G. H., and R. J. Stoller. 1990. Intimate communications: erotics and the study of culture. New York: Columbia University Press.

Herskovits, M. 1952. Economic anthropology. New York: Knopf.

Hill, J. 1977. Systems theory and the explanation of change. *In* Explanation of prehistoric change, ed. J. Hill, pp. 59–103. Albuquerque: University of New Mexico Press.

Hipsley, E., and N. Kirk. 1965. Studies of dietary intake and the expenditure of energy by New Guineans. Noumea, New Caledonia: South Pacific Commission Technical Paper 147.

Hitchcock, R. 1978. The traditional response to drought in Botswana. *In* Proceedings of the symposium on drought in Botswana, ed. M. Hinchey, pp. 91–97. Gaborone: Botswana Society.

Holmberg, A. 1969. Nomads of the longbow. Garden City, N.Y.: Natural History Press.

Homans, G. 1958. Social behavior as exchange. *American Journal of Sociology* 62: 597–606.

————. 1967. The nature of social science. New York: Harcourt, Brace.

Hommon, R. 1976. The formation of primitive states in pre-contact Hawaii. Unpublished Ph.D. dissertation. Department of Anthropology, University of Arizona.

————. 1981. A model of the pre-contact history of the island of Kaho'olawe. Paper delivered at the 46th annual meeting of the Society for American Archaeology, San Diego.

————. 1986. Social evolution in ancient Hawaii. *In* Island societies: archaeological approaches to evolution and transformation, ed. P. Kirch, pp. 55–68. Cambridge: Cambridge University Press.

Howell, N. 1979. Demography of the Dobe !Kung. New York: Academic Press.

Hutchinson, B. 1966. The patron-dependent relationship in Brazil. *Sociologia Ruralis* 6(1): 3–30.

Ibn Khaldun. 1956 [1377]. The mugaddimah: an introduction to history. New York: Pantheon.

Ingold, T. 1980. Hunters, pastoralists and ranchers: Reindeer economies and their transformations. Cambridge: Cambridge University Press.

Irons, W. 1979. Political stratification among pastoral nomads. *In* Pastoral production and society. Cambridge University Press.

Irwin, G. 1983. Chieftainship, kula, and trade in Massin prehistory. *In* The Kula, ed. J. Leach and E. Leach, pp. 29–72. Cambridge: Cambridge University Press.

Isaac, G. 1978. The food-sharing behavior of protohuman hominids. *Scientific American* 238: 90–108.

Isbell, W., and K. Schreiber. 1978. Was Hurai a state? *American Antiquity* 43: 372–89.

Jackson, J. 1975. Recent ethnography of indigenous northern lowland South America. *Annual Review of Anthropology* 4: 307–40.

Jochim, M. 1984. Paleolithic complexity and salmon productivity. Paper presented at the 49th annual meeting of the Society of American Archaeology, Portland, Oregon.

Johnson, A. 1971a. Sharecroppers of the Sertão. Stanford: Stanford University Press.

———. 1971b. Security and risk-taking among poor peasants: a Brazilian case. *In* Studies in economic anthropology, ed. G. Dalton, pp. 143–78. Washington, D.C.: American Anthropological Association.

———. 1972. Individuality and experimentation in traditional agriculture. *Human Ecology* 1: 149–59.

———. 1975a. Time allocation in a Machiguenga community. *Ethnology* 14: 301–10.

———. 1975b. Landlords, patrons, and "proletarian consciousness" in rural Latin America. *In* Ideology and social change in Latin America, ed. J. Nash and J. Corradi, pp. 78–96. New York: City University of New York.

———. 1978. Quantification in cultural anthropology. Stanford, Calif.: Stanford University Press.

———. 1980. The limits of formalism in agricultural decision research. *In* Agricultural decision making, ed. P. Bartlett, pp. 19–43. New York: Academic Press.

———. 1982. Reductionism in cultural ecology: the Amazon case. *Current Anthropology* 23: 413–28.

———. 1983. Machiguenga gardens. In Adaptive responses of native Amazonians, ed. R. Hames and W. Vickers, pp. 29–63. New York: Academic Press.

———. 1989. Horticulturalists: economic behavior in tribes. *In* Economic anthropology, ed. S. Plattner, pp. 49–77. Stanford, Calif.: Stanford University Press.

———.1999. Political consciousness on Boa Ventura: 1967 and 1989 compared. *In* Critical comparisons in politics and culture, ed. J. Bowen and R. Petersen, pp. 173–99. New York: Cambridge University Press.

———. 2000. Families of the forest. Manuscript.

Johnson, A., and C. Behrens. 1982. Nutritional criteria in Machiguenga food production decisions: a linear programming analysis. *Human Ecology* 10: 167–89.

Johnson, O. 1978. Domestic organization and interpersonal relations among the Machiguenga Indians of the Peruvian Amazon. Unpublished Ph.D. dissertation. Department of Anthropology, Columbia University.

Jones, W. 1959. Manioc in Africa. Stanford, Calif.: Stanford University Press.

Jorgensen, J. 1990. Oil age Eskimos. Berkeley: University of California Press.

Kan, Sergei. 1989. Symbolic immortality: the Tlingit potlatch of the nineteenth century. Washington, D.C.: Smithsonian Institution Press.

Keeley, L. 1988. Hunter-gatherer economic complexity and "population pressure": a cross-cultural analysis. *Journal of Anthropological Archaeology* 7: 373–411.

———. 1996. War before civilization. New York: Oxford University Press.

Keesing, R. 1975. Kin groups and social structure. New York: Holt, Rinehart & Winston.

———. 1983. 'Elota's story: the life and times of a Solomon Islands Big Man. New York: Holt, Rinehart & Winston.

Kelly, R. 1977. Etero social structure. Ann Arbor: University of Michigan Press.

———. 1995. The forager spectrum. Washington, D.C.: Smithsonian Press.

Khalid, Z. 1987. Pakistan in the Pamir Knot: geostrategic imperatives. Lahore, Pakistan: Vanguard.

Kikuchi, W. 1976. Prehistoric Hawaiian fishponds. *Science* 193: 295–99.

Kirch, P. 1974. The chronology of early Hawaiian settlement. *Archaeology and Physical Anthropology in Oceania* 9: 110–19.

———. 1977. Valley agricultural systems in prehistoric Hawaii: an archaeological consideration. *Asian Perspectives* 20: 246–80.

———. 1980. Polynesian prehistory: cultural adaptation in island ecosystems. *American Scientist* 68: 39–48.

———. 1982. Advances in Polynesian prehistory: three decades in review. *In* Advances in world archaeology, vol. 1, pp. 51–97. New York: Academic Press.

———. 1983. Man's role in modifying tropical and subtropical Polynesian ecosystems. *Archaeology and Physical Anthropology in Oceania* 18: 26–31.

———. 1984. The evolution of Polynesian chiefdoms. Cambridge: Cambridge University Press.

———. 1985. Intensive agriculture in prehistoric Hawaii: the wet and the dry. *In* Prehistoric intensive agriculture in the tropics, ed. I. Farrington, pp. 435–54. Oxford: British Archaeological Reports, International Series 232.

———. 1988. Circumscription theory and sociological evolution in Polynesia. *American Behavioral Scientist* 31: 416–27.

Kirch, P., and M. Kelley. 1975. Prehistory and ecology in a windward Hawaiian valley: Halawa Valley, Molokai. Honolulu: Pacific Anthropological Records 24.

Kirchhoff, P. 1955. The principles of clanship in human society. *Davidson Anthropological Society Journal* 1: 1–11.

Kolb, M. 1994. Monumental grandeur and the rise of religious authority in precontact Hawaii. *Current Anthropology* 34: 1–38.

Konner, M. 1982. The tangled wing: biological constraints on the human spirit. New York: Harper & Row.

Konner, M., and C. Worthman. 1980. Nursing frequency, gonadal function and birth spacing among !Kung hunter-gatherers. *Science* 207: 788–91.

Kroeber, A. L. 1939. Cultural and natural areas of native North America. Berkeley: University of California Publications in American Archaeology and Ethnology 38.

———. 1948. Anthropology: culture patterns and processes. New York: Harcourt, Brace and World.

Kurtz, D. 1978. The legitimation of the Aztec state. *In* The early state, ed. H. Claessen and P. Skalnik, pp. 169–89. The Hague: Mouton.

Ladefoged, T., M. Graves, B. O'Connor, and R. Jennings. 1996. Dryland agricultural expansion and intensification in Kohala, Hawai'i Island. *Antiquity* 70: 861–80.

LaLone, D. 1982. The Inca as a nonmarket economy: supply on command versus supply and demand. *In* Contexts for prehistoric exchange, ed. J. Ericson and T. Earle, pp. 292–316. New York: Academic Press.

LaLone, M. 1985. Indian land tenure in southern Cuzco, Peru: from Inca to colonial patterns. Unpublished Ph.D. dissertation. Department of Anthropology, University of California, Los Angeles.

Lambert, B. 1973. Bilaterality in the Andes. *In* Andean kinship and marriage, ed. R. Bolton and E. Mayer, pp. 1–27. Washington, D.C.: American Anthropological Association.

Langness, L. 1977. Ritual, power, and male dominance in the New Guinea highlands. *In* The anthropology of power, ed. R. Fogelson and R. Adams, pp. 3–22. New York: Academic Press.

Lathrap, D. 1970. The upper Amazon. New York: Praeger.

Lavallée, D., and M. Julien. 1973. Les établissements Asto à l'époque préhispanique. Lima: Travaux de l'Institut Francais d'Etudes Andiens 15.

Leach, J., and E. Leach, eds. 1983. The Kula: new perspectives on Massim exchange. Cambridge: Cambridge University Press.

Leacock, E., and R. Lee. 1982. Politics and history in band society. Cambridge: Cambridge University Press.

LeBlanc, C. 1981. Late prehispanic Huanca settlement patterns in the Yanamarca Valley, Peru. Unpublished Ph.D. dissertation. Department of Anthropology, University of California, Los Angeles.

Lechtman, H. 1977. Style and technology—some thoughts. *In* Material culture: styles, organization and dynamics of technology, ed. H. Lechtman and R. Merrick, pp. 3–20. New York: West.

LeClair, E. 1962. Economic theory and economic anthropology. *American Anthropologist* 64: 1179–1203.

Lee, R. 1976. !Kung spatial organization. *In* Kalahari hunter-gatherers, ed. R. Lee and I. DeVore, pp. 73–97. Cambridge: Harvard University Press.

———. 1979. The !Kung San. Cambridge: Cambridge University Press.

———. 1983. Greeks and Victorians: a re-examination of Engels' theory of the Athenian polis. Unpublished manuscript.

———. 1984. The Dobe !Kung. New York: Holt, Rinehart & Winston.

Lee, R., and I. DeVore. 1968. Man the hunter. Chicago: Aldine.

———, eds. 1976. Kalahari hunter-gatherers. Cambridge: Harvard University Press.

Lee, R., and M. Guenther. 1991. Oxen or onions? The search for trade (and truth) in the Kalahari. *Current Anthropology* 32: 592–601.

———. 1995. Errors corrected or compounded. *Current Anthropology* 36: 298–305.

Legros, D. 1977. Chance, necessity, and mode of production: a Marxist critique of cultural evolutionism. *American Anthropologist* 79: 26–41.

LeVine, T. 1979. Prehispanic political and economic change in highland Peru: an ethnohistorical study of the Mantaro Valley. Unpublished master's thesis. Department of Archaeology, University of California, Los Angeles.

———. 1985. Inka administration in the Central Highlands: a comparative study. Unpublished Ph.D. dissertation. Department of Archaeology, University of California, Los Angeles.

Lewis, A. 1974. Knights and samurai: feudalism in northern France and Japan. London: Temple Smith.

Linder, S. B. 1970. The harried leisure class. New York: Columbia University Press.

Lizot, J. 1989. Sobre la guerra: una respuesta a N. A. Chagnon (Science, 1988). *La Iglesia en Amazonas* 44: 23–34.

Lowman, C. 1980. Environment, society and health: ecological bases of community growth and decline in the Maring region of Papua New Guinea. Unpublished Ph.D. dissertation. Department of Anthropology, Columbia University.

———. 1984. Personal correspondence.

Lumbreras, L. 1974. The people and cultures of ancient Peru. Washington, D.C.: Smithsonian.

Luttwak. E. 1976. The grand strategy of the Roman empire from the first century A.D. to the third. Baltimore: Johns Hopkins University Press.

Lynch, T. 1982. Personal correspondence.

MacNeish, R. 1964. Ancient Mesoamerican civilization. *Science* 143: 531–37.

———. 1970. Social implications of changes in population and settlement pattern of the 12,000 years of prehistory in the Tehuacan Valley of Mexico. *In* Population and economics, ed. P. Deprez, pp. 215–50. Winnipeg: University of Manitoba Press.

Maine, H. 1870. Ancient law. London: John Murray.

Malinowski, B. 1922. Argonauts of the western Pacific. New York: Dutton.

———. 1929. The sexual life of savages in northwestern Melanesia. London: Routledge.

———. 1935. Coral gardens and their magic. London: Allen & Unwin.

———. 1944. A scientific theory of culture and other essays. Chapel Hill: University of North Carolina Press.

Malo, D. 1951 [1898]. Hawaiian antiquities. 2d ed. Honolulu: Bernice P. Bishop Museum Special Publication 2.

Malthus, T. 1798. An essay on the principle of population. London: Johnson.

Mann, M. 1986. The sources of social power. Cambridge: Cambridge University Press.

Manson, J. H., and R. W. Wrangham. 1991. Intergroup aggression in chimpanzees and humans. *Current Anthropology* 32: 369–90.

Marquardt, W. H., ed. 1992. Culture and environment in the domain of the

Colusa. Monograph 1, Institute of Archaeology and Paleoenvironmental Studies. Gainesville: University of Florida Press.

Marshall, J. 1957. Ecology of the !Kung bushmen of the Kalahari. Unpublished senior honors thesis. Department of Anthropology, Harvard University.

Marshall, L. 1976. Sharing, talking, and giving. *In* Kalahari hunter-gatherers, ed. R. Lee and I. DeVore, pp. 349–71. Cambridge: Harvard University Press.

Maryanski, A., and J. Turner. 1992. The social cage: human nature and the evolution of society. Stanford, Calif.: Stanford University Press.

Matos, M. R., and J. Parsons. 1979. Poblamiento prehispanico en la cuenca del Mantaro. *In* Arqueologia peruana, ed. R. Matos M., pp. 157–71. Lima: Centro de Proyeccion Cristiana.

Mauss, M. 1967 [1925]. The gift: forms and functions of exchange in archaic societies. New York: Norton.

Mayer, E. 1977. Beyond the nuclear family. *In* Andean kinship and marriage, ed. R. Bolton and E. Mayer, pp. 60–80. Washington, D.C.: American Anthropological Association.

Mayhew, A. 1973. Rural settlement and farming in Germany. New York: Harper & Row.

McDonald, P. F., and A. Sontosudarmo. 1976. Response to population pressure: the case of the special region of Yogyakarta. Population Institute, Monograph Series No. 3. Yogyakarta, Indonesia: Gadja Mada University.

McIntosh, S. 1999. Beyond chiefdoms: pathways to complexity in Africa. Cambridge: Cambridge University Press.

Mead, M. 1930. Social organization of Manu'a. Honolulu: Bernice P. Bishop Museum Bulletin 76.

Meggers, B. 1954. Environmental limitation on the development of culture. *American Anthropologist* 56: 801–24.

Meggitt, M. 1964. Male-female relations in the highlands of New Guinea. *American Anthropologist* 66: 202–24.

———. 1965. The lineage system of the Mae Enga of New Guinea. New York: Barnes & Noble.

———. 1967. The pattern of leadership among the Mae Enga. *Anthropological Forum* 2: 20–35.

———. 1972. System and subsystem: the Te exchange cycle among the Mae Enga. *Human Ecology* 1: 111–23.

———. 1974. Pigs are our hearts!: the Te exchange cycle among the Mae Enga of New Guinea. *Oceania* 44: 165–203.

———. 1977. Blood is their argument: warfare among the Mae Enga tribesmen of the New Guinea highlands. Palo Alto, Calif.: Mayfield.

———. 1984. Personal correspondence.

Meillassoux, C. 1972. From reproduction to production. *Economy and Society* 1: 93–105.

Michaelson, E. J., and W. Goldschmidt. 1971. Female roles and male dominance among peasants. *Southwestern Journal of Anthropology* 27: 330–52.

Migliazza, E. 1972. Yanomama grammar and intelligibility. Unpublished Ph.D. dissertation. Indiana University.

Minge-Klevana, W. 1980. Does labor time decrease with industrialization?: a survey of time-allocation studies. *Current Anthropology* 21: 279–98.

Mintz, S. 1961. Pratik: Haitian personal economic relations. *In* Proceedings of the 1961 annual spring meeting of the American Ethnological Society.

Mitchell, D. 1984. Predatory warfare, social status, and the north Pacific slave trade. *Ethnology* 23: 39–48.

Moffat, A. S. 1996. Ecologists look at the big picture. *Science* 273: 1490.

Moore, S. 1958. Power and property in Inca Peru. New York: Columbia University Press.

Moran, E. 1979. Human adaptability. North Scituate, Mass.: Duxbury.

———. 1993. Through Amazonian eyes: the human ecology of Amazonian populations. Iowa City: University of Iowa Press.

Morgan, D. 1986. The Mongols. Oxford: Basil Blackwell.

Morgan, L. H. 1877. Ancient society. Chicago: Kerr.

Morrell, M. 1985. The Gitksan-Wet'suwet'en fishery in the Skeena river system. Hazelton, B.C.: Gitksan-Wet'suwet'en Tribal Council.

Moseley, M. 1975. The maritime foundations of Andean civilization. Menlo Park, Calif.: Cummings.

Moseley, M., and K. Day. 1982. Chan Chan: Andean desert city. Albuquerque: University of New Mexico Press.

Murphy, R. 1971. The dialectics of social life. New York: Basic Books.

———. 1979. Lineage and lineality in lowland South America. *In* Brazil: anthropological perspectives, ed. M. Margolis and W. Carter, pp. 217–24. New York: Columbia University Press.

Murra, J. 1962. Cloth and its functions in the Inca state. *American Anthropologist* 64: 710–28.

———. 1965. Herds and herders in the Inca state. *In* Man, culture, and animals, ed. A. Leeds and A. Vayda, pp. 185–215. Washington, D.C.: American Association for the Advancement of Science.

———. 1972. El "control vertical" de un máximo de piso ecológicos en la economia de las sociedades andinas. *In* Visita de la provincia de León de Huánuco en 1562, ed. J. Murra, 2: 429–76. Huánuco, Peru: Universidad Nacional Hermilio Valdizán.

———. 1975. Formaciones económicas y politicas del mundo andino. Lima: Instituto de Estudios Peruanos.

———. 1980 [1956]. The economic organization of the Inka state. Greenwich, Conn.: JAI Press.

Murray, C. 1997. What it means to be a Libertarian: a personal interpretation. New York: Broadway Books.

Nef, J. U. 1977. An early energy crisis and its consequences. *Scientific American* 237: 140–51.

Nelson, E. 1899. The Eskimo about Bering Strait. Bureau of American Ethnology Annual Report 18. Washington, D.C.: U.S. Government Printing Office.

Netting, R. 1968. Hill farmers of Nigeria: cultural ecology of the Kofyar of the Jos Plateau. Seattle: University of Washington Press.

———. 1977. Cultural ecology. Menlo Park, Calif.: Cummings.

Newman, P. 1957. An intergroup collectivity among the Nootka. Masters thesis. Department of Anthropology, University of Washington.

Nordyke, E. 1989. Comment. *In* Before the horror: the Polynesian population of Hawai'i on the eve of western contact, by D. Stannard, pp. 105–13. Honolulu: University of Hawaii Press.

Nyrop, R. F., and D. M. Seekins. 1986. Afghanistan: a country study. Washington, D.C.: U.S. Government Printing Office.

Oberg, K. 1973. The social economy of the Tlingit Indians. Seattle: University of Washington Press.

Odum, E. 1971. Fundamentals of ecology. 3d ed. Philadelphia: Saunders.

Oliver, D. 1974. Ancient Tahitian society. Honolulu: University of Hawaii Press.

Oswalt, W. 1976. An anthropological analysis of food-getting technologies. New York: John Wiley and Sons.

———. 1979. Eskimos and explorers. Novato, Calif.: Chandler & Sharp.

Paksoy, H. B. 1984. Observations among Kirghiz refugees from the Pamirs of Afghanistan settled in the Turkish Republic. *Anthropological Society of Oxford Journal* 16: 53–61.

Patton, M. 1981. The ecology of hydatid disease in Turkana District, Kenya. Masters thesis. Department of Geography, University of Minnesota.

———. 1982. *Idia* to *ekile nawi*: career development of the Turkana pastoralist. Unpublished manuscript. Department of Geography, University of California, Los Angeles.

Pearl, R. 1925. The biology of population growth. New York: Alfred A. Knopf.

Pearson, H. 1957. The economy has no surplus. *In* Trade and markets in the early empires, ed. K. Polanyi, C. Arensberg, and H. Pearson, pp. 320–41. Glencoe, Ill.: Free Press.

People of Ksan. 1980. Gathering what the Great Nature provided: food traditions of the Gitksan. Seattle: University of Washington Press.

Peoples, J. 1982. Individual or group advantage? A reinterpretation of the Maring ritual cycle. *Current Anthropology* 23: 291–310.

Perrin, Noel. 1979. Giving up the gun: Japan's reversion to the sword, 1543–1879. Boston: G. K. Hall & Co.

Pianka, E. 1974. Evolutionary biology. New York: Harper & Row.

Pimentel, D., and M. Pimentel. 1979. Food, energy and society. New York: Wiley.

Pinkerton, E. 1985. Personal communication.

Plattner, S. 1989a. Economic behavior in markets. *In* Economic anthropology, ed. S. Plattner, pp. 209–21. Stanford, Calif.: Stanford University Press.

———. 1989b. Markets and marketplaces. *In* Economic anthropology, ed. S. Plattner, pp. 171–208. Stanford, Calif.: Stanford University Press.

———. 1989c. Marxism. *In* Economic anthropology, ed. S. Plattner, pp. 379–96. Stanford, Calif.: Stanford University Press.

Polanyi, K. 1944. The great transformation. Boston: Beacon Press.
———. 1957. The economy as instituted process. *In* Trade and market in the early empires, ed. K. Polanyi, C. Arensberg, and H. Pearson, pp. 243–70. New York: Free Press.
Popov, A. 1964. The Nganasans. *In* The peoples of Siberia, ed. M. Levin and L. Potapov, pp. 571–81. Chicago: University of Chicago Press.
———. 1966. The Nganasan. Bloomington: Indiana University Publications.
Population Reference Bureau. 1995. Speaking graphically. *Population Today,* December, p. 6.
Potter, J., M. Diaz, and G. Foster, eds. 1967. Peasant society: a reader. Boston: Little, Brown.
Potts, R. 1984. Home bases and early hominids. *American Scientist* 72: 338–47.
Powell, H. 1960. Competitive leadership in Trobriand political organization. *Journal of the Royal Anthropological Institute* 90: 118–45.
———. 1969. Territoriality, hierarchy and kinship in Kiriwina. *Man* 4: 580–604.
Price, D., and J. Brown. 1985. Prehistoric hunter-gatherers: the emergence of complexity. New York: Academic Press.
Quijano, A. 1967. Contemporary peasant movements. *In* Elites in Latin America, ed. S. Lipset and A. Solari. New York: Oxford University Press.
Quilter, J., B. Ojeda, D. Pearsall, D. Sandweiss, J. Jones, and E. Wing. 1991. The subsistence economy of El Paraíso, an early Peruvian site. *Science* 251: 277–83.
Ramos, A. 1972. The social system of the Sanuma of northern Brazil. Ph.D. dissertation. University of Wisconsin, Madison.
Randsborg, K. 1980. The Viking age in Denmark. London: Duckworth.
Rappaport, R. A. 1967. Pigs for the ancestors. New Haven: Yale University Press.
———. 1971. Nature, culture, and ecological anthropology. *In* Man, culture, and society, ed. L. Shapiro, pp. 237–67. New York: Oxford University Press.
———. 1979. Ecology, meaning, and religion. Richmond, Calif.: North Atlantic Books.
———. 1994. Humanity's evolution and anthropology's future. *In* Assessing cultural anthropology, ed. R. Borofsky, 153–66. New York: McGraw-Hill.
Rathje, W. 1971. The origin and development of lowland Classic Maya civilization. *American Antiquity* 36: 275–85.
Rathje, W., and R. McGuire. 1982. Rich man . . . poor man. *American Behavioral Scientist* 25: 705–15.
Read, D. 1986. Mathematical schemata and archaeological phenomena: substantive representations or trivial formalism? *Science and Archaeology* 38: 16–23.
———. 1998. Kinship based demographic simulation of societal processes. *Journal of Artificial Societies and Social Simulation.* http://www.soc.surrey.ac.uk/JASSS/1/1/1.html
Reidhead, V. 1980. The economics of subsistence change: a test of an optimization model. *In* Modeling change in prehistoric subsistence economies, ed. T. Earle and A. Christenson, pp. 141–86. New York: Academic Press.

Renfrew, C. 1972. The emergence of civilization: the Cyclades and the Aegean in the third millennium B.C. London: Methuen.

———. 1973. Monuments, mobilization, and social organization in neolithic Wessex. *In* The explanation of culture change, ed. C. Renfrew, pp. 539–58. London: Duckworth.

Rick, J. 1978. Prehistoric hunters of the high Andes. New York: Academic Press.

———. 1984. Structure and style at an early base camp in Junín, Peru. Paper presented at the 49th annual meeting of the Society for American Archaeology, Portland, Oregon.

Ridley, Matt. 1997. A new synthesis of Middle Paleolithic variability. *American Antiquity* 55: 480–99.

Rolland, N., and H. L. Dibble. 1990. The origins of virtue: human instincts and the evolution of cooperation. New York: Penguin.

Rosendahl, P. 1972. Aboriginal agriculture and residence patterns in upland Lapakahi, island of Hawaii. Unpublished Ph.D. dissertation. Department of Anthropology, University of Hawaii, Honolulu.

Rosman, A., and P. Rubel. 1971. Feasting with mine enemy: rank and exchange among Northwest Coast societies. New York: Columbia University Press.

Rostworoski de Diez Canseco, M. 1961. Curacas y sucesiones (Costa Norte). Lima: Imprenta Minerva.

Rowe, J. 1946. Inca culture at the time of the Spanish Conquest. *In* Handbook of South American Indians, ed. J. Steward, 2: 183–300. Bureau of American Ethnology Bulletin 143. Washington, D.C.: U.S. Government Printing Office.

Rummel, R. J. 1997. Power kills: democracy as a method of nonviolence. New Brunswick: Transaction.

Ruyle, E. E. 1973. Slavery, surplus, and stratification on the Northwest Coast: the ethnoenergetics of an incipient stratification system. *Current Anthropology* 14: 603–31.

Sackett, J. 1984. Personal communication.

Sackett, R. D. 1996. Time, energy, and the indolent savage: a quantitative cross-cultural test of the primitive affluence hypothesis. Ph.D. dissertation. Department of Anthropology, University of California, Los Angeles.

Sackschewsky, M. 1970. The clan meeting in Enga society. *In* Exploring Enga culture, ed. P. Brennan, pp. 51–101. Wapenamanda, New Guinea: Kristen Press.

Sadr, K. 1997. Kalahari archaeology and the Bushman debate. *Current Anthropology* 38: 104–12.

Sahlins, M. 1958. Social stratification in Polynesia. Seattle: University of Washington Press.

———. 1961. The segmentary lineage system: an organization of predatory expansion. *American Anthropologist* 63: 322–45.

———. 1963. Poor man, rich man, big man, chief: political types in Melanesia and Polynesia. *Comparative Studies in Society and History* 5: 285–303.

———. 1968a. Notes on the original affluent society. *In* Man the hunter, ed. R. Lee and I. DeVore, pp. 85–89. Chicago: Aldine.

———. 1968b. Tribesmen. Englewood Cliffs, N.J.: Prentice-Hall.

———. 1972. Stone age economics. Chicago: Aldine.

———. 1976. The use and abuse of biology. Ann Arbor: University of Michigan Press.

———. 1992. Anahulu: the anthropology of history in the kingdom of Hawaii. Vol. 1. Chicago: University of Chicago Press.

Sanchez, P. 1976. Properties and management of soils in the tropics. New York: Wiley-Interscience.

Sanday, P. R. 1973. Toward a theory of the status of women. *American Anthropologist* 75: 1682–1701.

Sanders, W. 1956. The central Mexican symbiotic region. *In* Prehistoric settlement patterns in the New World, ed. G. Willey, pp. 115–27. New York: Viking Fund Publication in Anthropology 23.

Sanders, W., J. Parsons, and R. Santley. 1979. The basin of Mexico: ecological processes in the evolution of a civilization. New York: Academic Press.

Sauer, C. 1948. Geography of South America. *In* Handbook of South American Indians, ed. J. Steward, 6: 319–44. Washington, D.C.: Bureau of American Ethnology.

Savoskul, S. 1989. Urbanisation and the minority peoples of the Soviet north. *In* The development of Siberia: people and resources, ed. A. Wood and R. French, pp. 96–123. London: Macmillan.

Schaedel, R. 1978. Early state of the Inkas. *In* The early state, ed. H. Claessen and P. Skalnik, pp. 289–320. The Hague: Mouton.

Schmeck, H. M., Jr. 1960. Physicist offers a Doomsday date. *New York Times*, November 4, 1960, p. 10.

Schmitt, R. 1971. New estimates of the pre-censal population of Hawai'i. *Journal of the Polynesian Society* 80: 241–42.

Schultz, T. 1964. Transforming traditional agriculture. New Haven: Yale University Press.

Scitovsky, T. 1976. The joyless economy. New York: Oxford University Press.

Scott, C., and T. Earle. n.d. The development of chiefdoms among the Wanka ethnic group in the central highlands of Peru. Unpublished manuscript.

Scott, J. 1976. The moral economy of the peasant: rebellion and subsistence in Southeast Asia. New Haven: Yale University Press.

Sergeyev, M. 1956. The building of socialism among the peoples of northern Siberia and the Soviet far east. *In* The peoples of Siberia, ed. M. Levin and L. Potapov, pp. 487–510. Chicago: University of Chicago Press.

Service, E. 1962. Primitive social organization. New York: Random House.

———. 1975. Origins of the state and civilization. New York: Norton.

———. 1977. Classical and modern theories of the origins of government. *In* Origins of the state, ed. R. Cohen and E. Service, pp. 21–34. Philadelphia: ISHI.

Shahrani, M. N. 1979. The Kirghiz and Wakhi of Afghanistan: adaptation to closed frontiers. Seattle: University of Washington Press.

———. 1984. Afghanistan's Kirghiz in Turkey. *Cultural Survival* 8: 31–34.

Sherratt, A. 1981. Plough and pastoralism: aspects of the secondary products revolution. *In* Pattern of the past, ed. I. Hodder, G. Isaac, and N. Hammond, pp. 261–305. Cambridge: Cambridge University Press.

Silberbauer, G. 1981. Hunter and habitat in the central Kalahari desert. Cambridge: Cambridge University Press.

Silverblatt, I. 1978. Andean women in the Inca empire. *Feminist Studies* 4: 37–61.

———. 1987. Moon, sun, and witches. Princeton: Princeton University Press.

Silverman, S. 1965. Patronage and community-national relationships in central Italy. *Ethnology* 4: 172–89.

Skinner, G. 1964. Marketing and social structure in rural China. Part 1. *Journal of Asian Studies* 24: 3–43.

Smith, A. 1993 [1776]. An inquiry into the nature and causes of the wealth of nations. New York: Modern Library.

Smith, B. 1978. Mississippian settlement patterns. New York: Academic Press.

Smith, C. 1976. Exchange systems and the spatial distribution of elites: the organization of stratification in agrarian societies. *In* Regional analysis, ed. C. Smith, Vol. 2, Social systems, pp. 309–74. New York: Academic Press.

Smith, M. E. 1985. An aspectual analysis of political formations. *In* Development and decline: the evolution of sociopolitical organization, ed. H. Claessen, P. van de Velde, and M. E. Smith, pp. 97–126. South Hadley, Mass.: Bergin and Garvey.

Smith, T. 1959. The agrarian origins of modern Japan. Stanford, Calif.: Stanford University Press.

Smole, W. 1976. The Yanoama Indians: a cultural geography. Austin: University of Texas Press.

Solway, J., and R. Lee. 1990. Foragers, genuine or spurious? Situating the Kalahari San. *Current Anthropology* 31: 109–46.

Sponsel, L. E. 1996. The natural history of peace: a positive view of human nature and its potential. *In* A natural history of peace, ed. T. Gregor, pp. 95–125. Nashville, Tenn.: Vanderbilt University Press.

Spriggs, M. 1986. Landscape, land use and political transformation in southern Melanesia. *In* Island societies: archaeological approaches to evolution and transformation, ed. P. Kirch, pp. 174–89. Cambridge: Cambridge University Press.

Steinvorth-Goetz, I. 1969. Uriji jami! Life and belief of the forest Waika in the Upper Orinoco. Caracas: Asociacion Cultural Humboldt.

Steward, J. 1930. Irrigation without agriculture. Ann Arbor: Papers of the Michigan Society of Science, Arts, and Letters 12: 144–56.

———. 1933. Ethnography of the Owens Valley Paiute. University of California Publications in American Anthropology and Ethnology 33: 233–335.

———. 1936. The economic and social basis of primitive bands. *In* Essays on anthropology in honor of Alfred Louis Kroeber, ed. R. Lowie, pp. 311–50. Berkeley: University of California Press.

———. 1938. Basin-Plateau aboriginal sociopolitical groups. Washington, D.C.: Bureau of American Ethnology.

———. 1955. Theory of culture change. Urbana: University of Illinois Press.

———. 1977. The foundations of Basin-Plateau Shoshonean society. *In* Evolution and ecology, ed. J. Steward and R. Murphy, pp. 366–406. Urbana: University of Illinois Press.

Steward, J., and L. Faron. 1959. Native peoples of South America. New York: McGraw Hill.

Stewart, H. 1977. Indian fishing: early methods on the Northwest Coast. Vancouver: J. J. Douglas.

Stoler, A. 1977. Class structure and female autonomy in rural Java. *Signs* 3: 74–89.

Strathern, A. M. 1972. Women in between. New York: Seminar Press.

Suttles, W. 1968. Coping with abundance: subsistence on the Northwest Coast. *In* Man the hunter, ed. R. Lee and I. DeVore, pp. 56–68. Chicago: Aldine.

Taagapera, R. 1981. Super-cancer of the biosphere: a world population growth model. Paper delivered to the Jacob Marschak Interdisciplinary Colloquium on Mathematics in the Behavioral Sciences, University of California, Los Angeles, April 10, 1981.

Taeuber, Irene B. 1958. The population of Japan. Princeton: Princeton University Press.

Taguchi, M. 1981. Swidden agriculture in Japan. Unpublished manuscript. Department of Anthropology, University of California, Los Angeles.

Tanaka, J. 1976. Subsistence ecology of central Kalahari San. *In* Kalahari hunter-gatherers, ed. R. Lee and I. DeVore, pp. 98–119. Cambridge: Harvard University Press.

Tawney, R. H. 1926. Religion and the rise of capitalism. New York: Harcourt, Brace.

Tax, S. 1953. Penny capitalism. Institute of Social Anthropology Publication 16. Washington, D.C.: Smithsonian Institution.

Taylor, K. 1974. Sanuma fauna: prohibitions and classifications. Instituto Caribe de Antropologia y Sociologia, Monografia 18. Caracas: Fundacion La Salle de Ciencias Naturales.

Thomas, D. H. 1972. Western Shoshone ecology: settlement patterns and beyond. *In* Great Basin cultural ecology: a symposium, ed. D. Fowler, pp. 135–53. Reno: Desert Research Institute Publication in the Social Sciences 8.

———. 1973. An empirical test for Steward's model of Great Basin settlement patterns. *American Antiquity* 38: 155–76.

———. 1983a. The archaeology of Monitor Valley: 1. Epistemology. Anthropological Papers 58(1). New York: American Museum of Natural History.

———. 1983b. On Steward's models of Shoshonean sociopolitical organization: a great bias in the Basin. *In* The development of political organization in North America, ed. E. Tooker, pp. 59–68. Washington, D.C.: American Ethnological Society.

Thomas, E. M. 1959. The harmless people. New York: Knopf.

Thompson, R. 1983. Modern vegetation and climate. *In* The archaeology of Monitor Valley, ed. D. Thomas, pp. 99–106. New York: American Museum of Natural History.

Time. 1960. Doomsday in 2026 A.D. *Time* 76 (November 14): 89–90.

Toledo. 1940 [1570]. Informacion hecha pororden de Don Francisco de Toledo. . . . *In* Don Francisco de Toledo, supremo organizador del Peru, su vida, su obra, ed. R. Levillier, 2: 14–37. Buenos Aires: Espasa-Calpe.

Tooby, J., and L. Cosmides. 1992. The psychological foundations of culture. *In* The adapted mind, ed. J. H. Barkow, L. Cosmides, and J. Tooby, pp. 19–136. New York: Oxford University Press.

Truswell, S., and J. Hansen. 1976. Medical research among the !Kung. *In* Kalahari hunter-gatherers, ed. R. Lee and I. DeVore, pp. 166–94. Cambridge: Harvard University Press.

Tsuchiya, T. 1937. An economic history of Japan. Tokyo: Asiatic Society of Japan Transactions 15.

Tucker, M. E., and D. R. Williams, eds. 1997. Buddhism and ecology: the interconnection of dharma and deeds. Cambridge: Harvard University Press.

Tylor, E. 1913 [1871]. Primitive culture. London: John Murray.

Uberoi, J. 1962. Politics of the Kula ring. Manchester: Manchester University Press.

Umpleby, S. A. 1987. World population: still ahead of schedule. *Science* 237: 1555–56.

United Nations. 1996. World population growth slowing, but United Nations still estimates total of 9.4 billion by year 2050. News Release, Population Division, Department for Economic and Social Information and Policy Analysis. New York: United Nations. (Cited in Ehrlich and Ehrlich 1997: 1193.)

Vayda, A. 1961. A reexamination of Northwest Coast economic systems. New York: New York Academy of Sciences Transactions 23: 618–24.

———. 1967. Pomo trade feasts. *In* Tribal and peasant economies, ed. G. Dalton, pp. 494–500. Garden City, N.Y.: Natural History Press.

Vayda, A., A. Leeds, and D. Smith. 1961. The place of pigs in Melanesian subsistence. *In* Proceedings of the American Ethnological Society, ed. V. Garfield, pp. 69–77. Seattle: University of Washington Press.

Vega, A. 1965 [1582]. La descripción que se hizo en la provincia de Xauxa. . . . Relaciones Geográficas de Indias, Biblioteca de Autores Españoles 183: 166–75. Madrid: Ediciones Atlas.

Veja. 1982. O país afinal comprou o sonho do jari. *Veja* (Rio de Janeiro), 13 de Janeiro, pp. 68–73.

Waal, Frans B. M. de. 1996. The biological basis of peaceful coexistence: a review of reconciliation research on monkeys and apes. *In* A natural history of peace, ed. T. Gregor, pp. 37–69. Nashville, Tenn.: Vanderbilt University Press.

Wachtel, N. 1977. The vision of the vanquished, tr. B. and S. Reynolds. Hassocks, Sussex: Harvester Press.

———. 1982. The *mitimas* of the Cochabamba Valley: the colonization policy of Huayna Capac. *In* The Inca and Aztec states, 1400–1800, ed. G. Collier, R. Rosaldo, and J. Wirth. New York: Academic Press.

Waddell, E. 1972. The mound builders. Seattle: University of Washington Press.

Wagley, C. 1976. Amazon town: a study of man in the tropics. New York: Oxford University Press.

Weber, M. 1947. The theory of social and economic organization. New York: Free Press.

Webster, C., and P. Wilson. 1966. Agriculture in the tropics. London: Longmans.

Webster, D. 1975. Warfare and the evolution of the state. *American Antiquity* 40: 464–70.

Webster, S. 1971. An indigenous Quechua community in exploitation of multiple ecological zones. *In* Actas y Memorias del XXXIX Congreso Internacional de America, 3: 174–83.

Weiner, A. 1976. Women of value, men of renown. Austin: University of Texas Press.

———. 1983. "A world of made is not a world of born": doing Kula in Kiriwina. *In* The Kula: new perspectives on Massim exchange, ed. J. and E. Leach, pp. 147–70. Cambridge: Cambridge University Press.

———. 1992. Inalienable possessions: the paradox of keeping-while-giving. Berkeley: University of California Press.

Wenke, R. 1980. Patterns in prehistory. Oxford: Oxford University Press.

White, B. 1976a. Production and reproduction in a Javanese village. Bogor, Indonesia: Agricultural Development Council.

———. 1976b. Population, involution and employment in rural Java. *Development and Change* 7: 267–90.

White, Leslie. 1959. The evolution of culture. New York: McGraw-Hill.

White, Lynn, Jr. 1962. Medieval technology and social change. Oxford: Oxford University Press.

Widmer, R. 1988. The evolution of the Calusa: a nonagricultural chiefdom on the southwest Florida coast. Tuscaloosa: University of Alabama Press.

Wiessner, P. 1977. Hxaro: a regional system of reciprocity for reducing risk among the !Kung San. Unpublished Ph.D. dissertation. Department of Anthropology, University of Michigan, Ann Arbor.

———. 1982. Beyond willow smoke and dogs' tails: a comment on Binford's analysis of hunter-gatherer settlement systems. *American Antiquity* 47: 171–78.

Wilbert, J. 1966. Indios de la region Orinoco-Ventuari. Caracas: Fundacion La Salle de Ciencias Naturales.

———. 1972. Survivors of El Dorado. New York: Praeger.

Wilkinson, R. 1973. Poverty and progress: an ecological perspective on economic development. New York: Praeger.

Willey, G. 1953. Prehistoric settlement patterns in the Virú Valley. Washington, D.C.: Bureau of American Ethnology Bulletin.

Williams, B. 1974. A model of band society. Washington, D.C.: Memoir of the Society for American Archaeology 29.

———. 1981. A critical review of models in sociobiology. *Annual Review of Anthropology* 10: 163–92.

Wilmsen, E. 1978. Seasonal effects on dietary intake in Kalahari San. *Federation of American Societies for Experimental Biology Proceedings* 37: 65–71.

———. 1989. Land filled with flies: a political economy of the Kalahari. Chicago: University of Chicago Press.

Wilmsen, E., and J. R. Denbow. 1990. Paradigmatic history of San-speaking peoples and attempts at revision. *Current Anthropology* 31: 489–524.

Wilson, P. J. 1988. The domestication of the human species. New Haven: Yale University Press.

Winterhalder, B., and E. A. Smith, eds. 1981. Hunter-gatherer foraging strategies. Chicago: University of Chicago Press.

Wittfogel, K. 1957. Oriental despotism. New Haven: Yale University Press.

Wobst, M. 1976. Locational relationships in Paleolithic society. *Journal of Human Evolution* 5: 49–58.

Wolf, E. 1957. Closed-corporate peasant communities in Meso-America and central Java. *Southwestern Journal of Anthropology* 13: 1–13.

———. 1966a. Peasants. Englewood Cliffs, N.J.: Prentice-Hall.

———. 1966b. Kinship, friendship, and patron-client relations in complex societies. *In* The social anthropology of complex societies, ed. M. Banton. London: Tavistock.

———. 1969. Peasant wars of the twentieth century. New York: Harper and Row.

———. 1982. Europe and the people without history. Berkeley: University of California Press.

Wright, H. 1977. Toward an explanation of the origin of the state. *In* Explanation of prehistoric change, ed. J. Hill, pp. 215–30. Albuquerque: University of New Mexico Press.

———. 1984. Prestate political formations. *In* On the evolution of complex societies, ed. T. Earle, pp. 41–77. Malibu, Calif.: Undena Publications.

Wright, R. 1994. The moral animal: evolutionary psychology and everyday life. New York: Random House.

Yan, Y. 1992. The impact of rural reform on economic and social stratification in a Chinese village. *Australian Journal of Chinese Affairs* 27: 1–23.

———. 1995. Everyday power relations: changes in a North China village. *In* The waning of the communist state: economic origins of political decline in China and Hungary, ed. A. G. Walder, pp. 215–41. Berkeley: University of California Press.

———. 1996. The flow of gifts: reciprocity and social networks in a Chinese village. Stanford, Calif.: Stanford University Press.

Yang, M. 1945. A Chinese village: Taitou, Shantung province. New York: Columbia University Press.

Yellen, J. 1976. Settlement pattern of the !Kung: an archaeological perspective. *In* Kalahari hunter-gatherers, ed. R. Lee and I. DeVore, pp. 47–72. Cambridge: Harvard University Press.

———. 1977 Archaeological approaches to the present. New York: Academic Press.

Yellen, J., and H. Harpending. 1972. Hunter-gatherer populations and archaeological inference. *World Archaeology* 4: 244–53.

Yellen, J., and R. Lee. 1976. The Dobe-/Du/da environment: background to a hunting and gathering way of life. *In* Kalahari hunter-gatherers, ed. R. Lee and I. DeVore, pp. 27–46. Cambridge: Harvard University Press.

Yengoyan, A. 1972. Ritual and exchange in aboriginal Australia: an adaptive interpretation of male initiation rites. *In* Social exchange and interaction, ed. E. Wilmsen, pp. 5–9. Ann Arbor: Museum of Anthropology, University of Michigan, Anthropological Papers 46.

Zerries, O., and M. Schuster. 1974. Mahekodotedi. Munich: Klaus Renner Verlag.

Index

In this index an "f" after a number indicates a separate reference on the next page, and an "ff" indicates separate references on the next two pages. A continuous discussion over two or more pages is indicated by a span of page numbers, e.g., "57–59." *Passim* is used for a cluster of references in close but not consecutive sequence.